**Institute for
Research on
Public Policy**

**Institut de
recherche
en politiques
publiques**

Founded in 1972, the Institute for Research on Public Policy is an independent, national, nonprofit organization.

IRPP seeks to improve public policy in Canada by generating research, providing insight and sparking debate that will contribute to the public policy decision-making process and strengthen the quality of the public policy decisions made by Canadian governments, citizens, institutions and organizations.

IRPP's independence is assured by an endowment fund, to which federal and provincial governments and the private sector have contributed.

*Centre for the
Study of Living Standards
Centre d'étude des
niveaux de vie*

The Centre for the Study of Living Standards (CSLS) is a national, independent, not-for-profit research organization which began operations in August 1995. Its objectives are twofold. First, to contribute to a better understanding of trends and determinants of living standards in Canada through research. Second, to contribute to public debate on living standards by developing and advocating specific policies based on expert consensus.

Fondé en 1972, l'Institut de recherche en politiques publiques (IRPP) est un organisme canadien, indépendant et sans but lucratif.

L'IRPP cherche à améliorer les politiques publiques canadiennes en encourageant la recherche, en mettant de l'avant de nouvelles perspectives et en suscitant des débats qui contribueront au processus décisionnel en matière de politiques publiques et qui rehausseront la qualité des décisions que prennent les gouvernements, les citoyens, les institutions et les organismes canadiens.

L'indépendance de l'IRPP est assurée par un fonds de dotation, auquel ont souscrit le gouvernement fédéral, les gouvernements provinciaux et le secteur privé.

Institute for Research on Public Policy

Institut de recherche en politiques publiques

Le Centre d'étude des niveaux de vie est un organisme de recherche national, indépendant et sans but lucratif qui a été mis sur pied en août 1995. Il a deux objectifs : d'abord, améliorer par la recherche, la compréhension des tendances et des facteurs déterminants du niveau de vie au Canada. Ensuite, contribuer aux échanges publics sur le niveau de vie par l'élaboration et le soutien de politiques précises basées sur le consensus de spécialistes.

Centre for the Study of Living Standards
Centre d'étude des niveaux de vie

The Review of Economic Performance and Social Progress 2002

Towards a Social Understanding of Productivity

Edited by
Andrew Sharpe
France St-Hilaire
Keith Banting

National Library of Canada
Bibliothèque nationale du Québec

Canadian Cataloguing in Publication Data

The review of economic performance and social progress 2002:
towards a social understanding of productivity
edited by Andrew Sharpe, France St-Hilaire and Keith Banting

(Nexus)
Co-published by: Centre for the Study of Living Standards
Includes bibliographical references.
ISBN 0-88645-198-1

1. Canada—Economic conditions—1991-.
2. Canada—Social conditions—1991-.
I. Sharpe, Andrew II. St-Hilaire, France
III. Banting, Keith G., 1947-
IV. Institute for Research on Public Policy
V. Centre for the Study of Living Standards
VI. Series: Nexus (Montréal, Quebec)

HC115.R523 2002   330.971'0648   C2002-905567-9

Suzanne Ostiguy McIntyre
Vice-President, Operations

Copy Editor
Jane Broderick

Concept & Design
Groupe Gignac communication marketing

Production
Chantal Létourneau
Isabelle Veronneau

Published by
The Institute for Research on Public Policy (IRPP)
l'Institut de recherche en politiques publiques
1470 Peel Street, Suite 200
Montreal, Quebec H3A 1T1
irpp@irpp.org / www.irpp.org

Centre for the Study of Living Standards
111 Sparks Street, Suite 500
Ottawa, Ontario K1P 5B5
csls@csls.ca / www.csls.ca

Contents

Preface

This book represents the second issue of the *Review of Economic Performance and Social Progress*, a continuing collaboration of the Institute for Research on Public Policy and the Centre for the Study of Living Standards. This series is founded on two fundamental beliefs: that the integration of economic and social objectives lies at the heart of the policy agenda, and that the quality of life that Canadians will enjoy for decades to come depends in important ways on how well we meet this challenge.

Many people have contributed to this second issue. We thank Hugh Segal for his continued support of the series. We also thank our contributors, who met our impossible deadlines with grace. In addition, a distinguished group of discussants at the authors' workshop also improved the volume immeasurably, and we gratefully acknowledge the contributions of Miles Corak, Pierre Fortin, Peter Hicks, Brian MacLean, Marcel Mérette, Someshwar Rao, Elizabeth Ruddick, Tom Rymes and Ian Stewart.

Finally, we record our appreciation of the skills and professionalism of the IRPP team who oversaw the production of the volume. Thanks are due to Isabelle Veronneau of Groupe Gignac for concept and design, Jane Broderick for copy editing, Brian Fitzgerald for proofreading, Maxime Legault for research assistance, and Chantal Létourneau for the coordination and execution of the many stages of the production process. Their patience in the face of the endless foibles of researchers deserves far more recognition than we can hope to convey.

Keith Banting
Andrew Sharpe
France St-Hilaire

Towards a Social Understanding of Productivity: An Introduction and Overview

Keith Banting
Andrew Sharpe
France St-Hilaire

Following intense debates over free trade in the 1980s and the fiscal crisis in the 1990s, the focus of concern in the policy world has shifted in recent years to the widening productivity gap between Canada and the United States. Business leaders, government officials and media commentators have sounded alarms about the productivity gap and have engaged in vigorous debates about the causes of the problem and the best policy responses. Advocates have advanced their favourite culprits, with regulatory inefficiencies, innovation lags, relative tax burden and weak entrepreneurialism often cited, usually without much evidence. The wider Canadian public seems to regard the debate with a large dose of scepticism and perhaps concern about the implications of the productivity agenda for labour market prospects and potential trade-offs between social and economic objectives.

Part of the difficulty, in our view, is that the productivity debate in Canada has traditionally focused on narrow economic issues. It has given inadequate attention to the broader ramifications of productivity, not just for our material standard of living but also for the choices we make collectively to enhance our social well-being. The debate has also paid too little attention to the social determinants of productivity — that is, to the feedback mechanisms running from social conditions and factors to productivity growth.

The objective of this second issue of *The Review of Economic Performance and Social Progress* is to fill, at least in part, the parallel lacuna in the research literature in Canada. As in the public debates, most research focuses on one side of the duality, emphasizing the impact of productivity growth on the standard of living of citizens. Much less attention is paid to the impact of social conditions on productivity. However, economic factors alone cannot explain differences in the growth rates and productivity levels of countries around the world, and a comprehensive understanding needs to incorporate institutional and social factors. A country's basic human and social resources are important to its economy. The levels of education and health of its citizens, the demographic profile of its population, the strength of the social networks that link people, the level of inequality among individuals and families, and the effectiveness of its institutions may all have important implications for a country's economic performance. In short, people and society matter.

The papers in this volume address the two-way nature of the linkages between productivity and social progress. They are organized into five sections. The three papers in the first section discuss productivity concepts and trends in Canada and OECD countries. The two papers in the second section examine the impact of productivity on government balances and natural resources and environmental sustainability. In the third section, four papers explore the implications of population aging, education, health and social diversity for productivity. In the fourth section, the focus shifts to the normative dimension of the issue, with three papers that ask whether productivity should be a social priority, including one that surveys the attitudes of Canadians on the question. In the fifth and final section, two papers examine the relationship among social policy, inequality and productivity.

The purpose of this introduction is twofold. First, it provides a detailed overview of the main findings of all chapters in the volume. Second, it provides a synthesis of the main themes that emerge from the different chapters and their implications for public policy.

THE TOOLS OF ANALYSIS: CONCEPTS AND LINKAGES

Before plunging into complex issues surrounding the linkages between productivity and social progress, it is important to establish as much clarity as possible about the concepts at the heart of the study, and the linkages among them.

Defining the term "productivity" poses little problem, certainly much less than the concept of "economic performance," which was the focus of last year's volume. As used in this volume, productivity is defined as the relationship between output and inputs. The level of labour productivity is the ratio of real output at the level of the firm, industry or the economy as a whole (measured in physical units or constant price terms) to the amount of labour input used to produce the output (measured in terms of hours or number of workers). Labour productivity growth is the change in this ratio over time. Total factor or multifactor productivity is the ratio of real output to an index of inputs, which normally includes labour and capital and may also include raw materials, purchased services and energy. Total factor productivity growth is the change in this ratio over time. While the definition of productivity is straightforward, it should be noted that the measurement of productivity, particularly in the service sector, is notoriously tricky. Technical measurement issues, however, are not addressed in any detail in the volume.

In contrast with the clarity of the meaning of productivity, "social progress" is a much broader idea. As was noted in the introduction to last year's volume, social progress can be manifested by improvements in a wide range of measures, including the incomes of families and individuals, the sense of economic security enjoyed by workers, the levels of poverty and social exclusion, the extent of inequality in life chances, the vibrancy of our distinctive communities, the strength of social cohesion and the sustainability of our environmental heritage. Such a complex and multifaceted phenomenon is thus best thought of as an overarching societal goal rather than as an analytical concept, and the contributors to this volume tend to focus on specific dimensions of our collective social experience.

Any assessment of social progress is also complex because it must move beyond aggregate measures. Overall indicators of the average level of social well-being always mask important variations in the experiences of different individuals and groups. Economic and social change on a major scale always produces winners and losers, groups who benefit from the new order and others whose economic and social prospects are eroded by the same forces. The history of wars, it is often observed, is written by the winning side. The history of social progress needs to be more balanced.

As well as being complex, social progress is inevitably a contested idea, because different people have very different conceptions of what constitutes the "good" society. Even if members of society agree on whether specific indicators tap dimensions of social progress, they will differ on the relative importance to be attached to the various indicators and hence on whether social progress, in the aggregate, is advancing or declining. For certain indicators, there may even be disagreement about which direction of change represents social progress, reflecting the ideological or world view of the observer. For example, some may see a rising proportion of students in private schools as a negative indicator because they believe such a trend threatens the development of an inclusive society. Others may see such a trend as positive since it means individuals have more choice in the educational options for their children. In the end, therefore, there can be no single measure of social progress or well-being. Exploring the relationships between productivity and social progress remains a compelling task, but the judgements rendered in this volume are best

seen as contributions to an open and pluralistic debate on the topic.

Not surprisingly, perhaps, the linkages between productivity and social progress are many and varied. In some cases the links are direct and immediate; changes in the average incomes of Canadians are tightly tied to productivity trends. In other cases the links are much more indirect and conditioned by other factors. For example, there may be a significant lag between productivity improvement and increased incomes on the one hand, and Canadians' own sense of economic security, as measured by opinion polls, on the other. In yet other areas, the link between changes in productivity and important dimensions of social well-being may be especially weak. For example, productivity may have little impact on indicators of social capital such as membership in associations and groups; cultural or social factors are probably much more decisive in shaping this aspect of our collective experience. Finally, in some cases the link between productivity and social progress may be negative. For example, the economic growth made possible by productivity gains may have a negative effect on certain environmental indicators such as greenhouse gas emissions, or on quality-of-life indicators such as time spent commuting.

It is also important to note that the relationship between productivity and social progress may not be constant over time. For example, the impact of higher aggregate real incomes arising from productivity growth on the rate of poverty may be strong in certain periods and weak in others, because of changes in the nature of growth or the influence of other factors on poverty.

The importance of the indirect linkages between productivity and the social lives of citizens is evident in its implications for public policy. In part, the impact of productivity on social well-being flows through public policy. To take the most obvious example, the post-1973 productivity slowdown that took place in all OECD countries reduced government revenues and increased deficits, and the growth of social programs in OECD countries, including Canada, was much less rapid after 1973. Of course, governments did have options, and fundamentally political judgements inevitably had to be made about how to proceed. But the erosion of the fiscal dividend enjoyed during capitalism's golden era from 1945 to 1973 because of slower productivity growth left governments with fewer fiscal resources and hence less room to manoeuvre. Thus productivity performance is a powerful factor influencing public policies, even if its impact is indirect and mediated by political and social pressures.

Finally, in comparison with the links running from productivity to social progress, those running from social well-being to productivity performance are less obvious and less well documented. Nevertheless, these links are likely to be significant. To take the most obvious example, in a knowledge-based economy, social and cultural factors that influence the desire and capacity of families to invest in their children's education and development have potentially powerful long-term consequences for productivity growth. Changes in family structures and other social patterns that influence the capacity of families and communities to make such investments matter. For these and other reasons, some analysts have argued that social inequality can have negative implications for the accumulation of human capital, and that greater equality can boost long-term productivity growth. Similarly, many analysts have argued that the strength of social networks and the levels of social and political trust represent a form of social capital with important implications for economic activity.

The links between productivity and social progress are thus multiple and complex and tracking the relationships in a comprehensive manner is a challenging analytical task. Nevertheless, it is possible to make at least provisional judgements about the core dynamics at work. The contributors to this year's volume provide significant insight into some of the key issues, and point to areas worthy of further investigation.

PRODUCTIVITY CONCEPTS AND TRENDS

The three papers in this section discuss productivity concepts and trends in Canada and in OECD countries. In the first chapter, Andrew Sharpe provides a comprehensive non-technical introduction to the productivity issue, including discussion of the concept of productivity, measurement issues, trends and prospects. He begins by noting that productivity is the relationship between the output of goods and services and the input of resources, both human and non-human, used in their production. In terms of productivity concepts, the most important are:

> The distinction between productivity *growth rates* and productivity *levels*. The term "good productivity performance" is ambiguous. It can refer to a situation in which a worker produces a large quantity of output — that is, a high level of labour productivity — or to a situation in which the output a worker produces increases rapidly over time —

that is, rapid labour productivity growth. These concepts are often confused in public debates on productivity.

> The distinction between output *per worker* and output *per hour*. With the long-term decline in the length of the workweek during the first three-quarters of the 20th century, growth in output per hour significantly exceeded growth in output per worker. For international productivity level comparisons, countries with fewer average annual hours worked per employed person will fare relatively better in terms of output per hour than in terms of output per worker.

> The distinction between *labour* productivity and *total factor* productivity. The former is a partial productivity measure relating labour input to output, while the latter relates a combination of inputs, or the growth of these inputs, to output or output growth. Sharpe argues that for discussion of living standard issues, labour productivity is the more appropriate concept as it is the ultimate determinant of real income growth. For discussion of efficiency in the use of existing resources, total factor productivity is the more appropriate concept.

The measurement of productivity is fraught with conceptual and empirical issues, and there can be a significant margin of error associated with productivity growth rates, even at the aggregate level. Sharpe identifies two particularly important measurement problems, namely the estimation of real output in the non-market sector (i.e., public and non-profit sectors) and the estimation of price indices (which are needed to calculate real output) for products where quality has improved significantly or for new products (e.g., computers).

According to Sharpe, the most important productivity trends that the general public should be aware of are:

> *The post-1973 productivity slowdown*, which has affected all industrial countries. Business-sector output per hour growth fell in Canada from an average annual growth rate of 4.0 percent in the 1946-73 period to 1.4 percent in the 1973-2001 period, increasing the time required for living standards to double, from 18 years to 50 years.

> *The post-war convergence in OECD productivity levels towards the US level.* At the end of the Second World War, labour productivity levels in all OECD countries were well below those in the United States, the technological leader. Through the importation of US technology, these countries were able to catch up to, and in certain cases exceed, US productivity levels.

> *The post-1995 acceleration in labour productivity growth in the United States.* The revolution in information technology, which originated and is strongest in the United States, appears to have produced a one-percentage-point upward shift in trend labour productivity growth since 1995 in that country, a development that has not occurred in other industrialized countries. Despite the sharp downturn in the high-tech sector, and even greater declines in the stock-market valuations of high-tech companies, the productivity gains of the second half of the 1990s appear to be have been sustained in the early years of the current decade.

> *The decline in Canada's relative international productivity ranking.* In 1950, Canada

ranked second out of 21 industrialized countries in terms of the level of output per hour, behind the United States only. With productivity convergence, a number of countries have enjoyed very rapid productivity growth in the post-war period. By 1973, Canada had fallen to fourth place, by 1985 to 12th place and by 2001 to 13th place. Canada's level of output per hour fell from 94.7 percent of the US level in 1950 to 91.2 percent in 1973, 89.0 percent in 1995 and 83.3 percent in 2001.

> *The widening of the Canada-US manufacturing productivity gap.* Canada has always had a lower level of labour productivity in manufacturing than the United States. Since the mid-1990s, this gap has widened significantly, growing 20 percentage points: the Canadian level was 87 percent of the US level in 1994 and 67 percent in 2001.

Labour Productivity and Canadian Living Standards

In the second chapter in this section, Tony Fisher and Doug Hostland examine, from an historical perspective, the relationship among labour productivity, labour income and living standards in Canada. The authors focus in particular on the recent divergence between labour productivity growth and real wage gains and its implications for Canadian living standards. They find that, once the appropriate adjustments are made, the labour share and the non-labour share (composed of profits, interest and investment income, and incorporated business income) in national income tend to revert to their historical means over the 1926-2001 period, although divergences may last for several years. They note, for example, that the decline in the labour share in Canada since 1994 is due not to any increase in profit share, but to an increase in the share of depreciation or capital consumption allowances associated with the short service lives of high-tech investment goods.

Traditionally, productivity trends have been related to trends in real wages, with the latter serving as a proxy for trends in living standards. The authors argue that this approach is too narrow, as non-labour sources of income also affect living standards. Shifts in labour and non-labour shares have little effect on aggregate household wealth and income, as households receive income from all components of national income. For example, labour productivity growth in excess of real wage growth does not mean that total income will lag behind productivity growth. The relatively slower rate of growth of wages will be offset by faster growth in other components of national income such as investment income or unincorporated business income.

Fisher and Hostland also point out that the national income accounts are not the appropriate framework for addressing the important issue of income distribution (e.g., extravagant CEO compensation represents a transfer from capital's income share of national income to labour's income share!). Rather, discussion of income distribution is more fruitfully based on personal income distribution measures such as the Gini coefficient and the ratio of incomes between the top and bottom quintiles.

Like other contributors to the volume, Fisher and Hostland stress that labour productivity was the chief source of advances in living standards in Canada throughout the 20th century. More importantly, however, they note that the other factors that contributed to growth in living standards in the past, including increases in the working-age component of the population and increased female labour force participation, are unlikely to play as much of a role in the future. Consequently, productivity will become even more important as a source of increase in living standards.

The authors conclude by emphasizing the limitations of GDP per capita and productivity as measures of economic progress. They strongly support work on broader measures of economic well-being that incorporate stocks of wealth and income distribution, which they believe will provide a more meaningful basis for policy decisions than the basic indicators presented in the national income accounts.

Productivity and Income Performance in OECD Countries

In the third and final chapter in this section, Bart van Ark develops a framework for understanding the significant differences in productivity and income growth rates among OECD countries. The framework breaks GDP per capita into two basic drivers: labour supply and labour productivity. Labour supply is in turn determined by the hours worked per person employed, the share of employment in the working-age population, and the share of the working-age population in the total population. Within-industry productivity growth rates and inter-sectoral shifts in employment shares determine labour productivity. The former is affected by the efficiency in factor use (i.e., total factor productivity), investment in physical capital and investment in intangible capital.

Van Ark's useful decomposition of GDP per capita into its components for OECD countries in 2001 leads to a number of key findings:

> The United States, not surprisingly, had by far the highest GDP per capita, 17 percentage points higher than second-place Norway.

> The United States, however, did not have the highest level of labour productivity (output per hour), ranking fifth behind Belgium, Norway, France and the Netherlands.

> The key reason for the large gap in GDP per capita between the United States and other OECD countries was the much shorter working time in these countries. Relative to the average worker in the United States, the average worker in Norway put in 29 percent fewer hours per year in 2001. The corresponding figures were 28 percent in the Netherlands, 19 percent in Belgium, 18 percent in Austria and France, 17 percent in Germany and 16 percent in Denmark.

> In certain countries, lower rates of labour force participation were also important in accounting for lower GDP per capita relative to the United States. Lower participation rates reduced GDP per capita relative to that in the United States by 15 percent in Belgium, 12 percent in Spain, and 10 percent in Ireland and France.

> Higher unemployment was also a factor in accounting for lower GDP per capita relative to that in the United States in certain countries, including Spain (7 percent), France and Italy (4 percent), and Germany and Finland (3 percent). Differences in the size of the working-age population relative to the total population was a much less important factor in accounting for the differences in GDP per capita across countries.

Van Ark points out that, while from 1950 to 1990 most OECD countries saw a narrowing of their income gap with the United States, this has not been the case since

7

1990. In the first half of the 1990s the under-performance of the labour market in many OECD countries accounted for this failure to close the income gap with the United States. In the second half of the 1990s, it was the acceleration of productivity growth in the United States. Van Ark observes that information and communication technologies (ICTs) have been the main source of the productivity revival in the United States, and the smaller size of the sector in other OECD countries explains their more sluggish productivity growth.

Van Ark argues that the development of intangible capital has been a necessary condition for exploiting the productivity advantages of ICT investment, although the linkages between intangible capital and productivity growth are still poorly understood. He defines intangible capital to include human capital, knowledge capital, organizational capital, marketing of new products and social capital. In particular, van Ark notes that the relationship between organizational capital and productivity growth may be particularly strong and in need of additional research.

THE IMPACT OF PRODUCTIVITY ON SOCIAL WELL-BEING: THE CASES OF GOVERNMENT FISCAL BALANCES AND ENVIRONMENTAL SUSTAINABILITY

The theme of the second section is the positive impact that productivity can have on different aspects of social progress or well-being. The two chapters in this section examine the impact of productivity on government balances and natural resource and environmental sustainability.

In examining the linkages between productivity and social progress, one of the first considerations is the potential impact of changes in productivity growth on governments' fiscal balances, which in turn affects their ability to contribute to social progress. Of course, larger fiscal balances do not necessarily translate into enhanced social measures, as governments may have other competing objectives. But, clearly, determining the sensitivity of fiscal balances to alternative productivity growth rates is an initial step in determining how productivity growth can affect the ability of governments to pursue social objectives.

In the first chapter in this section, Peter Dungan investigates the sensitivity of Canadian government fiscal balances to alternative long-run productivity growth rates using elements of the FOCUS macroeconometric model to conduct simulations to the year 2030. The simulation strategy employed here in part parallels the technique used by the Department of Finance in recent budgets and fiscal statements to estimate the implicit size of the "fiscal dividend." A total of five alternative growth paths and sensitivity tests are presented.

Overall, the simulations indicate that even relatively small changes in productivity growth rates can cumulate over several decades to produce large changes in GDP and living standards, and this can alter significantly the fiscal "room to manoeuvre" of the federal and provincial governments and of public pension plans. This is true whether we are contemplating higher or lower productivity growth rates. For instance, a relatively modest addition of 0.3 percent to annual productivity growth from 2004 to 2030 increases real GDP by 8 percent, or $171 billion ($2000), over the base-case scenario by the end of the period.

This translates into an increase of $71 billion in aggregate government revenues. As Dungan demonstrates, however, an important factor in determining more precisely the size of the fiscal impact is the response of government-sector wages to the changes in private-sector real wages that would likely occur under alternative productivity growth rates. His sensitivity results show that if there is a pass-through of higher productivity growth into higher public-sector wages (as would seem most likely), then the fiscal impact of higher productivity growth is muted. Since approximately 75 percent of government spending on goods and services is wage-based, this effect is quite substantial. Under higher productivity growth, some of the enhanced government revenues ($29 of the $71 billion) simply go to pay higher government-sector wages, leaving $42 billion, equivalent to roughly 6 percent of government (base-case) expenditures, available for expenditure enhancement, tax cuts or debt reduction.

If, on the other hand, projected productivity growth is reduced by 0.3 percent, then the negative impact on government revenues ($66 billion by 2030) is partly offset by a reduction in government wages from what they would otherwise have been, leaving a fiscal-impact shortfall of $39 billion. This offsetting effect is more important for provincial governments than for the federal government. Of course, the size of the fiscal impact would also depend on whether real interest rates are affected by higher or lower productivity growth rates, in which case the fiscal impact is on average very small. This would likely be the case if the change in productivity growth did not occur only in Canada but rather was a worldwide phenomenon.

As Dungan points out, this study is only the beginning of a full inquiry into the inter-connections between productivity growth and fiscal policy. The results focus on the effect of productivity growth on government fiscal room to manoeuvre, but there are undoubtedly important feedback effects from fiscal policy onto productivity growth. How the fiscal room to manoeuvre is used could have important effects on productivity growth itself: some tax cuts or expenditure increases could in turn raise productivity growth, through either improved technology or capital accumulation, while some poorly designed new social programs could reduce incentives and lower productivity growth. This feedback from fiscal policy to productivity becomes more important the further we go into the future. Finally, the issue of whether productivity change is confined to Canada or is part of a broader trend would also raise competitiveness issues that would affect domestic policy choices.

As the intense debate on Canada's ratification of the Kyoto Accord indicates, the issue of sustainability of natural capital and its implications for economic growth ranks high in the interests of both policy-makers and the general public. In the second chapter in this section, Nancy Olewiler makes an important contribution to the debate on natural resource sustainability by exploring the crucial, but often ignored, linkages among natural capital, sustainability and productivity.

Olewiler defines sustainability as the ability of the economy to maintain the flow of production necessary to prevent a decline in per capita consumption so that future generations can have a standard of living equal to or better than that of the present generation. In looking at natural capital as an input into production, Olewiler draws a clear distinction between those forms of natural capital, such as water and our atmosphere, that are essential to human existence, and other resources for which there are substitutes. This distinction between essential and non-essential inputs in turn leads to the concepts of weak and strong sustainability. Weak sustainability assumes that all the forms of capital involved are perfectly substitutable for each other, and that sustainability requires only that an aggregate stock of capital be maintained at a level necessary to ensure indefinite production. Strong sustainability on the other hand recognizes that specific forms of natural capital are essential — that is, they have no substitutes — and that stocks of these resources must be kept intact to ensure continued production. The challenge is to determine what forms of natural capital are essential and how to sustain the necessary stocks.

In her chapter, Olewiler examines productivity in natural resource industries in Canada and the United States to determine whether depletion in natural resource capital has affected productivity growth. Based on her detailed analysis of labour and total factor productivity growth rates, the author observes that:

> For Canadian non-renewable resource industries, changes in the stock of natural capital have not led to a sustained decrease in labour or total factor productivity. Indeed technological change, whether induced by environmental regulation or stock depletion, appears to be contributing to continued productivity growth in these industries.

> For Canadian renewable resource industries, such as logging and fishing, productivity has been declining due to poor resource-management practices. While these industries are certainly not essential for the overall sustainability of production in the Canadian economy, their loss does affect the viability of many communities.

> Ignorance of the state of our environmental capital and its relationship to productivity and sustainability is particularly apparent in our lack of knowledge about *threshold effects*. Once a threshold is exceeded, damage to production and productivity from environmental degradation may be severe and irreversible. This uncertainty regarding thresholds has led many researchers to advocate a precautionary approach to environmental policy.

Olewiler concludes that the development of reliable productivity estimates for natural capital sectors is important for monitoring the sustainability of the Canadian economy. Reductions in productivity may be seen as a warning that production and consumption are moving into a path of non-sustainability. Falling productivity in sectors that rely on natural capital may signal three possibilities: (1) technological change is not keeping up with depletion, (2) substitute inputs are not readily available, or (3) regulation is not addressing, in an appropriate manner, the market failures associated with the use of particular resources.

SOCIAL DETERMINANTS OF PRODUCTIVITY: DEMOGRAPHICS, HUMAN CAPITAL AND SOCIAL DIVERSITY

As noted earlier, most research on the drivers of productivity growth has focused on economic factors, such as investment, new technology and innovation, market structures and openness to trade. The chapter by Richard Harris, however, makes clear that economic variables alone do not fully explain differences in the levels of productivity and economic growth of countries around the world. This is especially the case when attention is focused on the growth experience of countries at all levels of development, from the richest to the poorest. The differences in productivity from the most to the least developed countries are enormous, and Harris concludes that coherent explanations must go beyond standard economic variables to incorporate a wider range of institutional and social factors. When attention narrows to the experience of industrialized or OECD countries, economic factors do a better job of explaining differences in their productivity. Nevertheless, even here a significant portion of productivity growth is unexplained by models built on purely economic factors, leaving open the question of the role of the institutional and social characteristics of different countries.

The chapters in this section analyze the implications for productivity of three dimensions of the social structure of countries: their demographic profile; the nature of their human capital — defined broadly to include the skills, education and health of their citizens; and the level of social diversity of the population.

Aging and Population Growth

As the retirement of the baby boom cohorts inexorably approaches, the implications of the aging of the population and the consequent fall in the ratio of consumers to producers receive growing attention from policy-makers and the general public. Many believe that the aging of the population will have negative effects on productivity and economic growth, with dire implications for the sustainability of social programs. In the first chapter in this section, William Scarth examines the relationship among population aging, productivity and

growth in living standards, and reaches a more optimistic conclusion. Indeed, he contends that aging may in fact lead to increases in productivity, even if no policy initiative is taken. He argues that our economy possesses at least three adjustment mechanisms that insulate living standards from the adverse effects of an aging population.

The first adjustment mechanism is changes in relative factor prices. Scarth constructs a closed-economy model based on overlapping generations that shows that when the baby boomers constitute the old generation, capital becomes the relatively abundant factor of production. Interest rates fall and wages rise, decreasing living standards for the old and raising them for the young. The change in relative factor prices leads to greater substitution of capital for labour, which increases labour productivity. However, Scarth expresses caution regarding the extent to which such closed-economy effects apply to a small, open economy like Canada where the return on capital and the wage level are largely determined outside the country. It is thus primarily population aging in the rest of the world, not in Canada, that will affect relative factor prices in this country, and the rest of the world is not facing as intense demographic pressures as Canada faces.

A second mechanism insulating living standards from an aging population is changes in saving behaviour motivated by fear of falling living standards in old age. This increased savings means that foreign debt is paid off. Future interest payments to foreigners are thus lower, leading to higher levels of domestic consumption. Finally, a third mechanism is the increasing returns to human capital arising from the increased relative scarcity of labour. This leads to greater human capital investment, which in turn raises productivity growth and living standards. Scarth concludes that, because of the adjustment mechanisms inherent in a market economy, the implications of the retirement of the baby boom cohorts for productivity and living standards in Canada may be significantly less than many observers currently believe.

The Role of Human Capital

The increased focus and attention of researchers and policy-makers, in recent years, on the potential determinants of productivity growth has generated considerable interest in human capital as a key contributing factor. Skills, innovation and human capital feature prominently on the policy agenda of industrialized countries concerned with productivity and competitiveness issues. Not surprisingly, formal education is the preferred and most conventional policy instrument of governments in pursuing these objectives. Indeed, "more is better" is often the guiding principle here. The actual linkages, however, are not as straightforward as they may appear. Certainly, there are gains to be achieved through a better understanding of the relationship between the skills developed through formal education and their causal impact on productivity, as well as a more nuanced approach to policy in this area. The former is the task Arthur Sweetman sets for himself in the second chapter in this section on social determinants. As he points out, "the issue is not whether education has benefits but, rather, the magnitude of its 'true' benefits, the benefits relative to costs, and the distribution of costs and benefits."

Sweetman examines three different sets of evidence, focusing on the impact of education on earnings at the individual level and on productivity at the macroeconomic level, and on issues related to the operation of the Canadian educational system. He begins with a review of recent challenges to the idea that more education is always better. For instance, an important issue is the extent to which the higher earnings attributed to higher education are in fact a function of higher innate ability which causes individuals to both acquire more education and achieve higher wages. As Sweetman argues, this would certainly have a bearing on the effectiveness of additional investment in education as a policy lever to aid disadvantaged groups. Another concern in recent years is whether Canada, which ranks among the top countries in terms of public spending on education and levels of educational attainment, has reached a point where its population is overeducated and underemployed. Survey results indicating that many people feel they are overqualified for their job or their skills are under-utilized have helped fuel this debate. Finally at a macroeconomic level, a significant number of studies looking at the relationship between country-level measures of educational attainment or inputs and per capita economic growth have failed to establish a positive link.

The chapter provides a detailed review of the literature on the impact of education on the earnings of individuals. Sweetman makes a clear distinction between studies that simply measure the correlation between an additional year of schooling and earnings outcomes and research on the causal impact of education, where the methodology explicitly discounts the effects of unobserved ability. While the former type of analysis suggests that the return on a year's education (in terms of employment earnings) is in the range of 7 to 15 percent (with most estimates clustering around

10 percent), one might expect the rate of return to be somewhat lower when only the causal effect is measured. Yet Sweetman finds little evidence that this is the case, and he concludes that the causal private rate of return for individuals is substantial.

Sweetman's examination of the relationship between education and economic growth highlights several key findings. Having pointed to the mixed macroeconomic evidence on the central role of human capital for economic growth, the author concludes that the problem is basically one of measurement. The studies that failed to find a correlation tend to use educational attainment, enrolment rates or educational spending as measures of a country's human capital. However, recent studies that use more direct measures of labour force skills based on the quality of education (e.g., standardized test results or literacy scores) have found a "substantial, and remarkably precise, correlation between human capital and growth." Based on his review of endogenous growth literature, Sweetman concludes that both the quality and content of education have a sizeable impact on overall productivity and economic growth. He cites as an example the results of a study by Barro (2001) which suggest that an additional year of education of "average" quality is associated with an annual increase of 0.44 percent in GDP. This implies a real social rate of return on education of about 7 percent. Educational quality is thus clearly more important for national economic outcomes than credentials or inputs. Indeed, on the latter Sweetman finds that there is "little evidence at the international level that school resources are highly correlated with the quality, or skill level, of the labour force."

Sweetman's chapter also addresses several issues related to the functioning of the Canadian education system. Canadian data not only show the expected positive relationship between levels of education and labour market outcomes such as hourly wages and the likelihood of employment, but also reveal remarkably good educational outcomes. In addition to the consequent increases in the national standard of living, his analysis suggests that the large-scale increases in Canadian educational enrolment in previous decades may have prevented increases in inequality due to the rapid growth in the supply of skilled labour. Sweetman's conclusion is that there has been and clearly will continue to be a key role for education policy in improving Canada's productivity and standard of living. An important question for policy-makers, however, is whether the education system is achieving its full potential. The main challenge is one of resource allocation in a context in which there seems to be on the one hand little correlation between the magnitude and the allocation of resources and educational outcomes and on the other hand insufficient information to channel these resources wisely.

While human capital is commonly associated with education and skills, health also has potential links to productivity. In the third chapter in this section, Emile Tompa provides a comprehensive review of the theoretical underpinnings and empirical evidence of the health productivity relationship with an emphasis on the implications for public policy. As the author demonstrates, this relationship goes well beyond the obvious effect of health on capacity to work in terms of both energy level and working time. Tompa describes three additional pathways through which health can affect productivity at an aggregate level. For instance, individuals with a longer life expectancy may choose to invest more in education as they

13

receive greater returns from their investment. They may also be motivated to save more for retirement, which would lead to greater accumulation of physical capital. Finally, improvement in the survival and health of young children may provide incentives for reduced fertility and may result in increased labour force participation.

Tompa's review of historical economic trends reveals "substantive evidence concerning the productivity impact of increased life expectancy and reduced morbidity over the last few centuries in Europe and the United States." He cites estimates indicating that substantial improvements in health and nutrition explain as much as 30 percent of growth in per capita income in the United Kingdom since 1790. Similar estimates of the impacts of health are also found in cross-country studies based on data for the last 50 years, which would suggest that these historical trends have not fully run their course.

As expected, Tompa finds considerable emphasis on human capital in recent macroeconomic research on productivity, but much less attention to human capital in the form of health. Nevertheless in those studies that did include a measure of health, the association with productivity was significant and positive. The author reports results from a range of studies indicating that between 21 and 47 percent of GDP growth per worker over the last 25 to 30 years can be linked to improvements in the health of populations. As Tompa points out, however, most of the research in this area has focused on life expectancy as a measure of health, which, given significant convergence among developed countries, has become a less salient indicator in explaining productivity differences among these countries. In his view this clearly underscores the need for more refined and relevant indicators (e.g., morbidity, vitality, mental health and acuity) if we are to fully comprehend the contemporary role of health as a productivity driver in developed economies.

Looking at the health-productivity relationship from a microeconomic perspective, Tompa highlights the extensive costs attributable to work-related injuries and illnesses. For instance, in Canada the direct costs (i.e., indemnity payments, insurance and medical expenses) were estimated on the order of $5.7 billion in 2000. The indirect costs, in terms of lost earnings and employer adjustment costs, were more than twice that amount. While there was a 40-percent reduction in injury claims in Canada between 1990 and 1998, it is not clear to what extent this can be attributed to the effectiveness of insurance and regulatory mechanisms, the main policy levers in this area, or some broader economic trends. Another concern is the fact that occupational health and safety regulation and workers' compensation programs are still focused on the types of injuries and exposure that are characteristic of manufacturing and resource-based industries. There are indications that policy has not kept pace with the changing needs brought on by the dramatic changes in the labour market and the workplace as a result of the shift from manufacturing to services, technological change, and new management and organizational practices.

In the final section of his chapter, Tompa reviews the evidence on the causes and the costs of absences from work due to sickness. Canadian absence rates due to illness and disability have increased substantially since the mid-1990s. Surprisingly, he finds that most of the research on potential causes of sickness tends to focus on potential contributing factors that are perceived as amenable to change and therefore pays relatively little attention to health status as an explanatory factor. The work that does examine this link indicates that chronic and acute physical and mental conditions, along with health-related behaviour, do account for a significant portion of sickness absence. However, the evidence on workplace health-promotion initiatives shows only modest results in terms of reduction in sickness absence. According to Tompa, such initiatives are often too narrowly focused on behavioural and lifestyle factors and need to be broadened to include organizational factors. Moreover, the more limited and short-term objectives of firm-level initiatives in this area underscore the important role that governments can play in improving the health of the labour force and the population as a whole and in turn overall productivity.

Given the multifaceted nature of the factors that influence health and, by extension, productivity, a more holistic approach to population health, including initiatives in areas traditionally considered outside the purview of health policy, may prove useful. Indeed Tompa's review of the health-productivity relationship from a human capital perspective suggests that education policy, child-care and family policy, and labour market policy are all important avenues through which the public sector can have an impact on population health.

Social Diversity

In the final chapter in this section, Quentin Grafton, Stephen Knowles and Dorian Owen examine the implications for productivity arising from the level of social diversity along a variety of dimensions, including ethnic, linguistic and religious differences, and inequalities between rich and poor. Their basic intuition is that human beings tend to associate and communicate most readily with people similar to themselves, and their hypothesis is therefore that "social divergence" generates social barriers to communication among groups, inhibiting the diffusion of knowledge and lowering the level of productivity in the economy. As a consequence, the more diverse the society and the greater the number of distinct social groups, the higher the communication costs and the greater the barriers to the exchange of ideas and innovation.

Grafton and his colleagues compare their concept of social distance to related concepts such as social capital, trust and social networks. They also survey the existing research on the economic consequences of different indicators of social divergence. The impact of the polarization of societies along ethnic lines has received considerable attention in the literature on economic development. A variety of analysts have concluded that ethnic diversity tends to generate high levels of rent-seeking among competing ethnic groups, at the expense of general economic policies that promote growth. Ethnolinguistic and religious diversity is also a predictor of conflict, political instability and weak institutional frameworks, all of which can retard growth. Similar findings emerge in terms of income inequality and inequalities in levels of educational attainment, a theme to which we return below in our discussion of the chapter by Richard Harris.

The chapter by Grafton, Knowles and Owen also summarizes the result of research conducted by the authors themselves, in which they analyze the impact on total factor productivity of a set of measures of social divergence, using data from a cross-section of 31 developing countries. Their findings

15

also support the proposition that social diversity and economic inequality weaken economic performance.

These research findings are clearly preliminary, and are subject to important limitations, as the authors indicate. For example, indicators of social divergence do not directly measure the extent and quality of communication among individuals and across social groups in a society. More direct measures of the links and exchanges among individuals would allow a clearer test of the proposition that social diversity inhibits the diffusion of knowledge and innovation. In addition, most of the literature on the economic consequences of social fragmentation uses data sets that are dominated by the experience of developing countries, and the authors own analysis is limited to third world nations. The applicability of such findings to high-income countries that are socially diverse, including Canada, is an open question. Such countries tend to have much stronger institutional frameworks and richer communications networks that may well reduce the barriers to exchange across groups.

Finally, Grafton and his colleagues stress that their analysis does not imply that social homogeneity is to be preferred. Social diversity can also have important economic benefits, as suggested by J.S. Mill in a passage quoted by the authors: "It is hardly possible to overrate the value…of placing human beings in contact with persons dissimilar to themselves, and with modes of thought and action unlike those with which they are familiar." The danger, the authors argue, is that barriers to communication across groups can prevent the benefits of diversity from being realized. The challenge for multicultural countries like Canada is therefore to develop institutions and

policies that facilitate communication among groups. From this perspective, initiatives such as bilingualism, multiculturalism and services for recently arrived immigrants are not simply instruments of cultural integration; they are also instruments of productivity enhancement.

Social factors such as demography, educational levels, health care and social diversity may not be standard features of the debate about the determinants of productivity growth. But the chapters in this section illustrate the importance of understanding the potential linkages that run from social dynamics to economic performance in advanced economies.

SHOULD PRODUCTIVITY GROWTH BE A SOCIAL PRIORITY?

Although the debate over productivity turns in part on empirical evidence of the relationships at work, it also touches on fundamental normative questions about values, the nature of the good society and the purposes of public action. In the most general sense, it is difficult to challenge a commitment to productivity or efficiency, understood as the best possible use of scarce resources to achieve a valued end. Who could be opposed to achieving greater human welfare — to meeting our economic, social and psychological needs more fully — with the resources at our disposal? In most policy debates, however, the concept of productivity tends to take on a narrow economic focus, one concerned with maximizing economic output. The social priority of this conception of productivity is certainly open to challenge, both in theory and in active politics, and the challenge emerges strongly in the three contributions in this section. The first questions the benefits that productivity growth has brought society in the last quarter century. The second analyzes survey results of the attitudes of Canadians towards the productivity issue. The third discusses productivity and accountability across the private, public and voluntary sectors.

In a provocative contribution, Joseph Heath argues that we tend to overestimate the contribution that further productivity growth will make to the welfare of Canadians. Traditionally, productivity growth was thought to contribute to increased leisure time, greater consumer satisfaction, the elimination of poverty and greater public support for redistributive efforts to narrow social inequality. While accepting that such benefits have flowed in the past, Heath argues that in the last 25 years productivity growth has contributed less and less to the well-being of Canadians. He points to the following indicators:

> After a long period of growth in leisure time, average working hours per week have begun to edge up again in North America over the last two decades. Moreover, a dramatic increase in two-income families — reflecting in part the widespread perception that it is impossible to maintain a middle-class lifestyle on the basis of one salary — has made the juggling of work and family increasingly difficult for many Canadians.

> While productivity growth has led to higher consumption, there is no evidence that it has produced greater overall consumer satisfaction or happiness. Heath draws on a number of surveys that show that whereas economic growth is strongly associated with increased happiness in poor countries, there is no correlation between higher consumption and increased happiness in richer countries. Certainly, there is little evidence

that people in rich countries have become happier in the last 25 years.

> Economic growth alone no longer seems to be reducing poverty. Important gains were made in the post-war decades as a result of the expansion of redistributive government programs, but Heath points to studies finding no reduction in the level of "basic needs" poverty since the late 1970s.

> Economic growth during the last 25 years has not increased people's willingness to share through redistributive programs. Heath argues that there seems to be growing middle-class resistance to redistribution and the taxation needed to support it.

The key puzzle for Heath is why further economic growth does not lead to greater happiness. In attempting to solve this puzzle, he canvasses three currents of thought in the literature. One possible explanation is that increased consumption does not generate lasting increments in welfare, because the process of satisfying our desires generates new desires, an interpretation that Heath traces from classical Greek philosophers to modern analysts such as John Kenneth Galbraith. A second explanation, which Heath describes as neo-Veblenian, contends that consumption not only satisfies needs but also communicates status, class, upbringing and tastes. The difficulty with this element of consumption is that such status hierarchies have a zero-sum structure. If a spurt of economic growth suddenly allowed everyone to purchase an exotic car, the process would cancel out the status inherent in driving one. A third possible explanation draws on the work of Fred Hirsch, who argues that the supply of some goods, which he labels positional goods, is fixed. Waterfront property is a classic example. For these goods, the process of economic growth does not increase their quantity; it increases only their relative prices. As people become richer, therefore, some goods may become easier to acquire but positional goods continue to recede over the horizon.

Heath argues that if these three forms of consumption absorb a significant portion of the benefits of economic growth, there will be little increase in satisfaction, at either the individual or the aggregate level. For Heath, this argues against making productivity growth a social priority. For this reason, he is sceptical about investing scarce public dollars in a productivity agenda, and believes that other forms of investment will be more effective in enhancing the welfare of Canadians. He suggests a number of possibilities, including dealing seriously with the externalities generated by economic growth for the environment, reducing crowding in urban areas, increasing the supply of public goods, promoting leisure and increasing individuals' sense of security. However, his key point is that since productivity growth does not generate the benefits we expect, it should not be treated as an unchallenged priority, and we should not worry about our relative productivity compared to other countries, such as the United States. There is no reason why a decline in our relative "standard of living" should necessarily mean a decline in our quality of life.

Canadian Attitudes Towards Productivity Issues

These philosophical debates are echoed in the attitudes of the Canadian public, which are explored in the chapter by Frank Graves and Richard Jenkins. The distinction between our standard of living and our quality of life is a powerful one for Canadians.

The economic citizen who emerges from Graves and Jenkins's data is relatively aware of the terms of the productivity debate. Canadians appear to have a broadly optimistic view of the economy, but give the country only a lukewarm overall rating of its productivity. They are certainly aware of the divergent trends in Canada and the United States. Moreover, although improved productivity does not rank as high as health care, education, the environment and crime prevention, the public does see it as an important goal. Admittedly, this broadly positive orientation is qualified by some scepticism. A slim majority of Canadians believe that recent concern about productivity has been manufactured by large corporations and wealthy Canadians, and a minority see talk about productivity as ideological code for job losses and lower pay. Nevertheless, a strong majority believes that improved productivity will create more jobs and especially more high-skill jobs. Overall, Graves and Jenkins conclude, the public leans towards a positive view of a productivity agenda.

Nevertheless, the Canadian public's attitude towards productivity is qualified by a commitment to a broader sense of quality of life. Graves and Jenkins report that Canadians place considerably greater emphasis on quality of life as a goal as compared with a high standard of living when these are traded off. While Canadians are keenly aware that incomes are higher in the United States, the public overwhelmingly believes that the quality of life in Canada is superior to that enjoyed south of the border.

This attitude also influences the public's reaction to the policy debate about how to improve Canada's productivity. Graves and Jenkins find a strong preference among Canadians for human and social investment priorities (e.g., improving health care, enhancing workers' skills and supporting early childhood development) in contrast to prescriptions such as tax cuts or R&D investments often advocated by key voices in the debate. This dichotomy is particularly apparent when the general public and members of various elite groups are asked to choose among three government strategies to improve productivity: (a) a national learning strategy to invest in the education and training of Canadian workers, (b) corporate and income tax cuts to reduce costs and stimulate growth, and (c) a national technology strategy to help business and citizens access the latest high-tech processes and equipment. According to Graves and Jenkins, "there is clearly a significant gap in the understanding of how productivity should be dealt with between the residents of Canada's family rooms and the residents of its boardrooms." A majority of opinion leaders (57 percent) support a strategy of cutting corporate and income taxes, and this preference is almost unanimous among private-sector elites (86 percent). However, for Canadians generally the preferred option is a national learning strategy (40 percent), with tax cuts clearly in second place (33 percent).

The public also overwhelmingly rejects the idea that the current level of social spending is an impediment to improving Canadian productivity. Rather, they see social programs as a form of investment that increases productivity by ensuring a healthy, educated and secure population. How Canadians would measure a successful innovation agenda is also consistent with this view. Having more skilled workers electing to stay in Canada and achieving a higher quality of life are considered the best indicators.

Thus in both philosophical debates and public opinion, support for productivity as a social priority is conditioned by an insistence that the larger goal is quality of life rather than a narrow conception of our standard of living defined in purely economic terms, and that a policy agenda focusing on increasing productivity should not come at the expense of other priorities.

Implications for the Public and Voluntary Sectors

The chapter by Janice Gross Stein also cautions against the dangers of adopting a narrow conception of productivity and efficiency. Building on her analysis in *The Cult of Efficiency* (2001), she argues that the language of efficiency, understood narrowly as cost-effectiveness, confronts distinctive problems when transferred from the private sector to the public and voluntary sectors. The efficiency or productivity of a public service is determined by measuring the value or utility that it creates. However, such measurements are much more difficult than those carried out in the private sector, where the feedback provided by the market provides a continuous measure of value. As a result, demands for efficiency or productivity in public services have tended to be translated into simple exercises in cost-containment and a determination to deliver public services at the lowest possible cost.

Stein contends that the collapse of the language of efficiency into mere cost-containment has actually undermined the effectiveness and productivity of the public and voluntary sectors. She illustrates the perverse results along three dimensions: the inability to provide for unexpected contingencies, cuts in investment in research and development, and the problems in maintaining full accountability.

The private sector, Stein insists, understands that redundant capacity is essential in an uncertain world. She observes that on 11 September 2001 most of the firms housed in the World Trade Center were operational again within a few hours because they had built redundancy into their operations, not only backing up their data systems but also providing for alternative command-and-control capacities. Such redundancy is normally understood as excess or unproductive capacity, but firms in the private sector have been willing to back up their essential systems to cope with emergencies, breakdowns and unanticipated needs. The public sector, she argues, is not allowed this luxury. With the exception of security and defence, redundant capacity is seen as "inefficient," leaving our emergency services, health systems, environmental protection programs and other essential services ill-equipped to respond effectively to the unexpected.

A similar pattern appears in research and development. The private sector invests in research and development and does not insist that R&D divisions be productive within short time horizons. The drive for "efficiency," however, leaves little tolerance for similar investments in the public and voluntary sectors. During the cost-containment drives in the public sector during the 1980s and 1990s, research advisory bodies were closed, and policy units within departments shrank in size. Many leaders within the public service at the federal and provincial levels worry about the policy capacity of the organizations they lead. Stein sees even stronger constraints in the voluntary sector. In the era of downsizing and alternative service delivery, the voluntary sector is expected to deliver a wider range of important public services with limited resources. But the voluntary sector is not financed to conduct the serious research and evaluation required to constantly refine and improve the services it provides.

Finally, Stein argues that the concepts of efficiency and productivity, as they have been applied to the public and voluntary sectors, do not give sufficient scope to the multiple forms of accountability expected of those sectors. In addition to accountability "upward" to elected representatives in the case of the public sector and to funding agencies in the case of the voluntary sector, Stein argues that public and voluntary organizations also have accountabilities "outward" to clients, stakeholders and the wider community. Pressures for greater accountability in the name of efficiency and cost-containment have tightened accountability upward, reducing the operating flexibility needed for accountability outward in daily program activities. As a result, it has compromised this wider social responsibility of public and voluntary organizations, weakening their roots in the community and eroding the public's trust in them.

SOCIAL POLICY, INEQUALITY AND PRODUCTIVITY

The question of whether productivity growth is a social priority raises the related question of whether there is an implicit trade-off between economic growth and social well-being. Establishing the relative priority of different goals is especially important if the tradeoffs are harsh, if more of one requires deep sacrifices of another valued goal. But is this the situation we face? Is there a sharp tradeoff between productivity growth and social policy objectives? Or could there actually be a positive relationship between these two agendas? The two chapters in this section tackle these questions from different perspectives.

In the first chapter in this section, Richard Harris surveys recent challenges to the traditional view that there is an inherent conflict between economic efficiency and social equality, a view neatly summarized in the title of Okun's famous book, *Equality and Efficiency: The Big Tradeoff* (1975). This view gained renewed currency in the policy debates of the 1990s, as commentators contrasted the economic performance of Europe and the United States in that decade. The European record was one of slow economic growth, particularly of employment, a pattern many commentators dubbed "Eurosclerosis" and blamed on the welfare state. In contrast, the United States was recording a major surge in employment and strong productivity growth, which was widely heralded as the advent of a new economy — indeed a third industrial revolution — rooted in innovation in the information, communications and telecommunications fields. This growth was preceded by a significant rise in inequality in the United States, leading many to infer that higher levels of inequality seemed to contribute to growth.

More recently, however, this traditional view has been challenged both by cross-national empirical studies and by theoretical advances. This recent research seems to suggest that there is no efficiency-equity tradeoff and that social policy and greater equality may actually contribute to higher productivity growth. Richard Harris surveys two streams of recent research that point in this direction. In the early 1990s a number of researchers analyzed cross-sectional and time-series data for both developing and developed countries, and identified a robust negative correlation between measures of income inequality and economic growth. This evidence would seem to suggest that greater equality can actually contribute to stronger economic growth. However, the majority of these studies involved samples dominated by devel-

oping countries. When attention is focused on OECD countries alone, the evidence is far from conclusive. Indeed, Harris concludes that the empirical case for a link running from greater income equality to higher economic growth for high-income countries is "at best statistically fragile and at worst insignificant." But he also cautions that there is no significant evidence for the traditional idea of a tradeoff between equality and growth.

The chapter also examines new theoretical literature, especially the new endogenous growth theory, which suggests that increases in inequality can hurt growth. However, Harris concludes that the theoretical literature is too diverse and too susceptible to changes in assumptions and parameters to form the basis for reliable policy formulation without empirical validation. And that validation, as we have seen, is not available, at least not yet.

Harris then narrows his focus to the direct relationship between social policy and growth, without reference to an intervening effect on social inequality. After all, many social programs are not designed primarily to alter the level of inequality in a society, but nonetheless may have an impact on productivity. Here the evidence seems more persuasive. While there is some evidence that high overall levels of government spending on social programs may reduce growth, much stronger results are found when social spending is disaggregated into different functions. Initial findings suggest that passive social spending, such as traditional income-support programs, is prejudicial to growth but that active social spending, such as expenditures on training and labour market adjustment, promote growth. Moreover, education stands in a class by itself. As Sweetman does in his chapter on human capital, Harris points to considerable evidence that increasing education has a substantial effect on productivity and that much of Canada's economic growth can be attributed to Canadians' high levels of educational attainment. While the evidence for health expenditures is less strong, Harris concludes that the productivity case for improving human capital is compelling.

At the broadest level, then, Harris concludes that the general case for linking social policy and inequality to productivity remains unproven. The productivity case for active social spending and for improving human capital is clear, but more research is needed before a wider claim can be established.

The second chapter in this section, that by William Watson, also engages these themes. Watson challenges Joseph Heath's interpretation of the benefits of productivity growth, but agrees with Richard Harris's views on the state of our knowledge about the potential contribution of social programs to productivity growth.

Watson tackles Heath's assessment of the social benefits of productivity growth directly, starting with the issues of social inequality and poverty. He argues that there has been no flagging in redistributive effort in Canada. Although market incomes have become more unequal, the tax-and-transfer system has continued to offset the impact, with the result that the post-tax/transfer distribution of income has, in his words, "remained almost eerily constant," at least through 1997. In the case of poverty, Watson counters Heath's focus on the last 25 years with an appeal to the long view of human history, which demonstrates that productivity increases have dramatically reduced poverty in Canada and throughout the Western world. Watson is less direct in his critique of Heath's focus on consumer satisfaction or happi-

ness, but argues that citizen choice may reveal an underlying preference for income over leisure. Moreover, he challenges what he sees as Heath's preference for enhancing public expenditures, emphasizing the scope for government failures and the possibility that higher tax rates in the contemporary period have increased the marginal cost of public funds.

Even if one were able to resolve the question of the appropriate balance between the public and private sectors, Watson believes that the case for higher productivity would remain compelling. In his words, it is "hard to understand how getting more 'stuff' for a given effort would be wasteful." He therefore turns to the issue of the determinants of productivity growth and the role that social programs might play in enhancing it. Here, Watson remains a sceptic. Drawing on Hayek, he argues that societies are extremely complex phenomena, and that we simply do not know enough to advance confident policy prescriptions about the role of social policy in enhancing productivity. Even if we did succeed in analyzing the relationships between social policy and growth in the past, we cannot be sure that the drivers in the past will be the drivers in the future. In addition, Watson remains concerned about the problems he sees as inherent in public action: the possibility of government failure, the possibility of duplicating private action and the marginal cost of public funds.

In the absence of powerful analytical guidance, Watson concludes, reform of social policy will inevitably be guided primarily by intuition, politics and hunches. In these circumstances, he counsels modesty in aspirations. Social policy changes should be made at the margin, in small steps, program by program.

Within that overall approach, Watson's personal intuitions and hunches call for more competition in health care and education, more support for women who wish to take time off to raise their young children, and continued awareness that — whatever the broad relationship between social policy and growth — poor design in individual welfare programs can have harmful effects on productivity.

The broad conclusions emerging from the papers in this section actually increase the challenges facing policy-makers. The old mythology that there is an inevitable tradeoff between efficiency and equality must be set aside. But new ideas suggesting that inequality is harmful for economic growth as yet lack compelling empirical support. As a result, the policy-maker must make do without convenient intellectual crutches, and the implications of social programs for productivity must be assessed on a case-by-case basis. As often is the case, research has increased, rather than decreased, the analytical complexity facing governments.

THE RELATIONSHIP BETWEEN PRODUCTIVITY AND SOCIAL PROGRESS: KEY THEMES

Standing back from the detailed analyses presented in the various chapters brings into focus a number of larger themes that run through the volume as a whole. Three major implications leap out from the pages: the two-way nature of the relationship between productivity and social progress, the long-term and largely indirect nature of the role of public policy in enhancing productivity, and need to broaden the debate over productivity in Canada.

A Two-Way Relationship

The two-way or reciprocal relationship between productivity and social progress is the central theme of the volume. Both sides of this relationship are relevant to social progress. Looking at the first linkage, productivity increases the amount of material wealth that a given hour of labour can produce. However, too often advocates of a productivity agenda highlight only its importance for our material standard of living, giving such an agenda an unnecessarily narrow political appeal. The additional wealth created by productivity growth can be taken in different forms: private consumption, enhanced social programs, lower taxes, more leisure time, or some combination of all four of these. In effect, productivity growth provides more opportunity for society.

Greater productivity is not a necessary condition for social progress; indeed, we could choose to devote a larger proportion of our existing income to social purposes if we wished; and certainly greater productivity does not guarantee greater social well-being, as Joseph Heath correctly emphasizes. What paths are taken depend on social and political choices. In the real world of politics, however, productivity growth does expand the choices open to society, and reduces the apparently zero-sum nature of choices inherent in a weak economy. It is no accident that the welfare state expanded greatly during the golden years of capitalism following the Second World War. There is a social as well as an economic case to be made for productivity growth, and it is unfortunate that the advocates of a productivity agenda tend to cast it in such narrow terms.

These realities should inform assessments of the performance of different countries around the world. Much has been made of the contrast

Keith Banting, Andrew Sharpe
and France St-Hilaire

between the economic performance of the United States and that of Europe in the last decade. Clearly, the link between productivity and living standards, in terms of both levels and growth rates, is crucial. Countries with high levels of output per hour tend to have high levels of income, as measured by GDP per capita, and countries with rapid labour productivity growth tend to have fast GDP per capita growth. But as the data presented in the van Ark paper show, certain European countries have very high levels of output per hour but relatively low levels of income. This is because average annual hours worked and/or labour force participation are low. The working-age population in these countries thus enjoys greater leisure but less income than would be the case if they worked longer and had higher labour force participation. It is misleading to characterize these countries as having a lower standard of living than countries with comparable productivity levels and higher income levels, when a conscious choice is made to use productivity gains for additional leisure instead of income. Indeed, a broadly defined measure of living standards or economic well-being would include leisure as well as income. This inclusion of leisure, as well as income, in the measurement of living standards thus more fully defines and tightens the link between productivity and living standards. Productivity growth increases the production possibility frontier of society, allowing both greater income and greater leisure. Societies make different choices about which combination of these two variables they prefer.

Gaining a socially aware understanding of the role of productivity growth will be especially important in the years to come. While labour productivity was the main source of advances in living standards in Canada through the 20th century, other factors were also important, including increases in the relative size of the working-age component of the population and increased female labour force participation. These trends have by now largely run their course. As noted by a number of contributors, with the retirements of the baby boom cohorts and the attainment of high levels of female labour force participation, the contribution of these factors to further increases in living standards will be considerably smaller in the future. Consequently, productivity growth will become even more important, in a relative sense, for the advancement of living standards.

Productivity advance is also an essential element of any strategy to ensure the sustainability of natural resources and the environment. While environmental sustainability is high on the public agenda, there appears to be limited public awareness of the positive role that productivity can play. The paper by Nancy Olewiler in this volume sheds new light on the contribution that productivity growth and technical progress — the two go hand in hand — can make to sustainability. Technological progress can help improve the functioning of eco-systems through the production of more energy-efficient producer and consumer goods and the development of products that do less damage to the environment.

A socially aware understanding of productivity must also incorporate the reciprocal nature of the relationship. Productivity growth is influenced by social factors that are the manifestations of the social progress of a society. Higher levels of educational attainment of the workforce enhance productivity growth. Better health makes workers more productive. Stronger communications flows across diverse groups in modern multicultural societies promote learning from others and lead to improved productivity. The role of education is fundamental here. Indeed, several chapters in the volume highlight the essential role that education has played and will continue to play in productivity and real income growth. At the level of both the individual and society, high levels of educational attainment are associated with high productivity and high incomes, while low levels have the opposite effect. Indeed, it is impossible to imagine a productive 21st-century economy and society that does not have a highly literate and numerate workforce. Because of the externalities associated with education and training, public policy has an important role to play in fostering human capital development. This perspective also applies to health. It is a well-known fact that improvements in population health have also contributed significantly to increased productivity and living standards over time. However, the productivity effects of health go well beyond those associated with increased life expectancy. We are only now beginning to understand the multifaceted nature of the factors that influence the health of the labour force and of the population as a whole.

In addition to highlighting the positive role of human capital, it is important to clear away traditional mythologies that do not stand up to close scrutiny. The belief that there is an inevitable tradeoff between efficiency and equality has long been an influential assumption underlying policy debates in Canada and many other Western nations. This hardy perennial has been seriously undermined by new research. To be sure, the more recent argument that greater equality and social spending actually contribute to productivity growth also seems to lack convincing support, at least in the case of advanced economies. But in the real world of

public policy, debunking the assumption of an implicit tradeoff represents a significant corrective to the intuitions and hunches that shape choices. The need to assess social programs on a case-by-case basis, without the aid of such default positions, may raise the complexities confronting policy-makers. But clearing away unsupported intuitions is a healthy contribution to the policy process.

It is time to end the political posturing between the advocates of productivity growth and the defenders of social well-being. Doing so requires accommodations on both sides. Advocates of the productivity agenda need to broaden their focus by highlighting the ways in which productivity can enhance social Canada and recognizing the contribution of social well-being to future productivity. But defenders of social Canada need to incorporate productivity into the causes they hold dear. Productivity growth does not automatically fulfil collective aspirations, but it increases the choices available to society and reduces the zero-sum nature of alternatives facing government decision-makers.

The Long-Term and Indirect Role of Public Policy

The primary drivers of labour productivity growth are to be found in the accumulation of physical and human capital and technological progress, and both of these drivers have their own dynamic that is affected by public policy only in the long term. Appropriate government framework policies such as the rule of law are a prerequisite for economic and productivity growth. Long-term investments in human capital, as represented by education and health care, are important. In the short term, specific economic policies such as corporate tax rates and R&D subsidies can affect productivity growth, and poor macroeconomic policies can have detrimental effects.

But government seems to have much less power on the upside to increase long-run productivity growth beyond the trend productivity determined by the underlying technological progress. For example, a recent study by David Card and Richard Freeman (2002) of the impact of the Thatcher reforms on British productivity growth illustrates this point. They found that the overall impact on aggregate labour productivity growth of these sweeping economic reforms (including laws that weakened the coverage and power of trade unions, privatized nationalized industries, and created incentives for self-employment and share ownership) was 0.35 percentage points per year. While the cumulative effects of 0.35 percentage points per year should not be dismissed, the economic legacy of the Thatcher era is a lesson in humility for ambitious political reformers.

Another example of the overselling of the positive productivity effects of public policy is the structural reforms instituted by the Canadian government in the second half of the 1980s and the early 1990s. A key rationale for the implementation of the Canada-US Free Trade Agreement, the introduction of the GST, the privatization of Crown corporations, deregulation, tax reform and other structural measures was that these policies would foster productivity growth. While certain of these policies may have had some positive impact, the overall effect seems not particularly large. Productivity growth in the Canadian economy did not pick up after these reforms were implemented.

Trend output per-hour growth in Canada is projected to be around 2 percent per year over the next decade based on technological advances.

It is doubtful that government policies aimed at increasing productivity growth could improve productivity growth dramatically above this trend line. Trend productivity growth is still largely determined by technological change, which takes place outside Canada, and by the investment behaviour of Canadian business.

Finally, determining which public policies and programs should be defined as productivity-related can be difficult. Indeed, many government policies and programs that are not motivated by productivity concerns can have positive (and negative) effects on productivity. A good example is the NASA program in the United States, which was initially set up to put a man on the moon by 1970, an initiative motivated by the Cold War and the desire of the Americans to beat the Russians in the space race. This program led to massive R&D, and much of this public research effort produced important technological spinoffs that improved productivity in the private sector, an unintended consequence. Another example is the construction of divided highways motivated by public concerns over road safety. The construction of these new highways in turn fosters productivity growth by reducing transportation costs and stimulating economic development in general.

All of this suggests that the role of public policy is long-term and indirect, more akin to the patient investor than the day trader.

Broadening the Productivity Debate: From Standard of Living to Quality of Life

The attitudes of Canadians towards productivity appear to be surprisingly positive, an elemental reality that should not be ignored. According to survey results reported by Frank Graves and Richard Jenkins,

Canadians recognize the importance of productivity but prefer to link productivity to quality-of-life issues than to narrower economic concerns. Thus support for productivity as a societal priority is conditioned by an insistence that the larger goal is a better quality of life rather than simply a raised economic standard of living, and that a policy agenda focused on increasing the productivity of the Canadian economy should not come at the expense of other priorities. Governments would be well advised to take this observation into account in developing policies that relate to productivity growth and in promoting any productivity or innovation agenda.

Despite the importance of productivity growth for improvements in economic well-being, productivity is not a panacea for society's problems, and should not be oversold. Productivity gains and the resulting higher incomes alone will not solve social problems such as poverty, pollution and crime. But they do widen the choices open to Canadians, by increasing the public and private resources that can be allocated to address these issues.

CONCLUSION

In the end, our plea is for a social understanding of productivity. Productivity does not simply enhance our material standard of living; it also expands the range of choices available to Canadians. Enhanced productivity will not automatically increase the social well-being of Canadians, but it will reduce the apparently zero-sum nature of many of the decisions that we face today, and make it easier to achieve the economic and social goals that have defined Canada as a distinctive society on the northern half of the North American continent.

REFERENCES

Barro, R.J. 2001. "Human Capital and Growth." *American Economic Review* 91(2):12-17.

Card, D., and R. Freeman. 2002. "What Have Two Decades of British Economic Reform Delivered in Terms of Productivity Growth?" *International Productivity Monitor*, 5(Fall). Posted at www.csls.ca

Okun, A. 1975. *Equality and Efficiency: The Big Tradeoff.* Washington: Brookings Institution.

Sharpe, A. 2002. "Raising Canadian Living Standards: A Framework for Analysis." *International Productivity Monitor*, 5(Fall). Posted at www.csls.ca

Stein, J.G. 2001. *The Cult of Efficiency.* Toronto: Anansi.

Productivity Concepts and Trends

Productivity Concepts, Trends and Prospects: An Overview

Andrew Sharpe

INTRODUCTION

The issue of productivity and the related issue of innovation continue to be high on the public policy agenda. There is especially strong interest among policy-makers in the social aspects of productivity. The objective of this second issue of *The Review of Economic Performance and Social Progress* is to examine the two-way linkages between productivity and various measures of social progress in Canada. The purpose of this paper is to provide a succinct, non-technical overview of the productivity issue, including discussion of productivity concepts, measurement issues, trends and prospects. Such information may serve as useful background for the papers in this volume.

The paper is divided into six parts. The first part looks at the reasons why productivity is important. The second discusses key productivity concepts, including the link between productivity and welfare. The third provides some theoretical perspectives on productivity growth. The fourth part briefly examines productivity measurement issues and their relevance for the productivity debate. The fifth part presents the key productivity trends and developments that have taken place in Canada and other developed countries. Finally, the sixth part briefly discusses the prospects for productivity growth.

WHY IS PRODUCTIVITY IMPORTANT?

Productivity is the relationship between the output of goods and services and the inputs of resources, human and non-human, used in the production process, with the relationship usually expressed in ratio form. Both outputs and inputs are measured in physical volumes and thus are unaffected by price changes. Multiplying quantities of the various outputs and inputs by the price each has commanded in a base year yields the comparable or constant price values that can be added up to provide measures of aggregate output and input.[1] The ratios may relate to the national economy, to an industry, or to a firm or even a plant. Output growth that exceeds growth in measured inputs — that is to say, an increase in the ratio of output to inputs — is what analysts mean when they say productivity is increasing.

Productivity growth is the most important source of long-term economic growth. From 1946 to 2001, real GDP per hour growth — the productivity of labour — accounted for 66 percent of real GDP output growth in the business sector in Canada, the remaining 34 percent being growth in total hours worked — an input that itself was growing rapidly (Table 1).

Over the long term, increasing productivity is the only way to increase the standard of living, defined as real GDP per capita. Growth in per capita income can result from: increases in the employment-total population ratio, reflecting increased labour force participation, lower unemployment or a larger share of working-age population; or improved terms of trade. But these sources of income growth are unsustainable in the long run, as they have upper bounds (except possibly for the terms of trade). Productivity growth, on the other hand, is not constrained by the size of the population or other factors, and its growth is, at least in principle, sustainable through technological advances.

Thus, trends in productivity are the key determinant of long-run trends in both absolute and relative living standards. The fall-off in real income growth in Canada and other developed economies since 1973 is a direct result of slower productivity growth. The decline in Canada's living standards in the 1990s relative to those in the United States is largely attributable to our weaker labour-productivity growth (Sharpe 2001). Slower increases in the amount of output each worker produces mean that there is slower growth in the output or income that can be shared among the total population.

The magnitude of the productivity growth estimates that economists debate — almost always below 1 percent for the aggregate economy — may seem small or even trivial to non-economists. But small differences matter, and the implications for society of a

TABLE 1

Productivity Trends in the Business Sector, 1961-2001

	Average annual rates of change									
	Real GDP	Number of Jobs	Average Hours	Hours Worked	Real GDP per Hour	Hourly Labour Compensation	Total Labour Compensation	Unit Labour Cost	Real Consumer Wage	Real Producer Wage
1946-1973	5.05	1.72	-0.73	0.98	4.03	7.51	8.54	3.38	3.90	3.42
1973-1981	3.52	2.71	-0.65	2.04	1.43	11.09	13.34	10.61	1.28	1.13
1981-1989	3.18	1.97	0.05	2.02	1.13	5.52	7.65	4.28	0.22	0.88
1989-2001	2.83	1.34	-0.07	1.26	1.56	3.14	4.42	0.80	0.85	1.34
1989-1995	1.39	0.19	-0.25	-0.06	1.47	2.70	2.65	0.26	0.04	0.65
1995-2001	4.29	2.49	0.10	2.59	1.65	3.57	6.23	1.34	1.67	2.04
1946-2001	4.07	1.82	-0.46	1.35	2.68	6.76	8.18	3.96	2.31	2.26
1973-2001	3.13	1.91	-0.20	1.70	1.40	6.04	7.83	4.52	0.79	1.15

Notes: The growth rate of the Number of Jobs plus the growth rate of Average Hours gives the growth rate of Hours Worked. The growth rate of Hours Worked plus the growth rate of Hourly Compensation gives the growth rate of Total Compensation. The growth rate of Real GDP subtract the growth rate of Hours Worked gives the growth rate of Real GDP per Hour. The growth rate of Total Compensation subtract the growth rate of Real GDP gives the growth rate of Unit Labour Cost. Real Consumer Wage is defined as Hourly Compensation deflated by CPI and Real Producer Wage is defined as Hourly Compensation deflated by the GDP deflator.
Source: Aggregate Productivity Measures, Statistics Canada, August 2002.

1-percent, as opposed to a 3-percent, trend productivity growth rate are huge. Based on the mathematical rule of 72, a 1-percent productivity growth scenario means that it will take 72 years, or three generations, for real output — and hence income — per worker to double. In contrast, under a 3-percent productivity scenario it would take only 24 years, or one generation, for real income to double. Even moving from a 1-percent to a 2-percent trend productivity growth world — a distinct possibility, as discussed later in the paper — cuts in half (to 36 years) the time needed to double living standards.

There is, of course, much more to life than productivity and the real income growth it generates, as even economists realize. The economic well-being and quality of life of the population — much broader concepts than GDP per capita — are determined by many factors, of which productivity is only one. A focus on productivity does not mean that economists consider these other determinants of well-being and quality of life unimportant. Economists study productivity because it is crucial for real income growth and important for improving economic well-being and quality of life, or at least its material aspects. They also believe that a better understanding of productivity trends and determinants can lead to the development of public policies and private-sector actions that will serve to improve productivity performance.

CONCEPTUAL ISSUES RELATED TO PRODUCTIVITY

This section reviews a number of productivity concepts essential to an understanding of the productivity debate.

Partial Versus Total Factor Productivity

A fundamental distinction is made between *partial* and *total* productivity measures. The former relate output to only one input, most often labour or capital, although intermediate goods or raw materials also regularly figure in some compilations of inputs, even though it is recognized that other inputs have contributed to output. Labour productivity is the best-known partial productivity measure. The latter relates output to a *combination* of inputs, such as capital and labour. They are known as total-factor or multifactor productivity measures and represent the growth in output not accounted for by input growth.

The most readily available and widely used measure of productivity is labour productivity, the ratio of output to some measure of labour input (employment or hours). This term sometimes creates confusion, as it can be seen to imply that the level of labour productivity or the rate of growth of labour productivity is attributable solely to the effects of labour. In fact, labour productivity reflects the influence of all factors that affect productivity, including capital accumulation, technical change and the organization of production. While the intensity of labour effort obviously does affect labour productivity, it is generally significantly less important than the amount of capital a worker has to work with or the level of production technology.

The concept of total or multifactor productivity has been developed to measure the contribution of all factors of production to productivity growth. The rates of growth of all inputs are weighted to yield one growth rate for the combined inputs. Total factor productivity (TFP) growth is defined as the growth

33

rate of output minus the growth rate of the combined inputs (just as labour-productivity growth equals output growth minus labour input growth). As the growth rate of the capital stock is generally greater than that of employment (and hence the capital-labour ratio is rising), the growth rate of TFP (using labour and capital as inputs) is generally less than the growth rate of labour productivity. This situation arises from the fact that the growth rate of the combined inputs of capital and labour exceeds that of labour alone.

A key issue in TFP measurement is the weighting of these inputs. Under competitive conditions, the current dollar-income share of the factor of production — labour income for hours worked and interest, gross capital income (profits and depreciation) for the capital stock — is normally considered the relative contribution of the factor to output and consequently used to weight the factor to produce an index of total input, or the growth rate of the index. When markets are not competitive, as in the case of monopolies, the weighting issue is much more complex.

The meaning of TFP is also controversial. Some economists interpret it as a measure of overall technical change, others as a measure of disembodied technological change — that is, technical change that is not embodied in new machinery and equipment — while still others argue that TFP is in no way a measure of technological change (Lipsey and Carlaw 2000).

It is incorrect to say that TFP is a superior or preferred measure of productivity compared to labour productivity, as the two concepts serve different purposes. For those interested in how efficiently all factors of production are used in the production process, TFP is the relevant productivity measure since it takes into account the productivity of factors of production other than labour, such as capital, intermediate goods and energy. For those interested in the potential of the economy to raise the standard of living, labour productivity is the relevant productivity measure: it tells us how much output or income is produced by each worker and, when combined with the total number of workers, how much total income there is to be distributed among the population.

Output Per Worker Versus Output Per Hour

Labour input can be measured either in terms of the average annual number of workers or in terms of the total number of hours worked in a year. The latter is the more appropriate for labour productivity since it represents a more precise measure of labour input than persons employed. One should always specify which concept of labour productivity is being used. The growth rates of output per worker and output per hour may differ when there is a change in the hours worked over time. Indeed, historically the large fall in average working time has meant that output per hour has grown significantly faster than output per worker.

International productivity comparisons can also differ greatly when annual hours per worker vary across countries. American workers put in more hours annually than workers in many European countries. Therefore, productivity measures based on output per worker portray US productivity levels in a much more favourable light than measures based on the more relevant output per hour. For example, in 2001 Norway's GDP per person employed was 81.5 percent of that in the United States on the basis of output per person employed, but 110.6 percent on the basis of output per hour — a difference of 29.1 percentage points. The Netherlands also shows a large difference (28.4 points) between the two productivity measures, from 73.4 percent of the US level for output per person employed to 101.8 percent for output per hour worked (see Tables 3 and 5 below).

Productivity Levels Versus Growth Rates

A second important distinction is that between productivity levels and growth rates. The former refers to the output per unit of input at a given point. For example, in the year 2001 the level or value of output per hour in the business sector in Canada was $30.06, expressed in constant 1992 prices. The latter refers to the percentage change in levels of output per hour, expressed in constant prices, between two points in time. An example would be the 20.4-percent increase in labour productivity between 1989 and 2001, when output per hour was $24.97. One often hears the complaint that Canada's productivity is poor. This could be in reference to a low aggregate productivity level, to a low productivity growth rate, or both. Commentators should always specify whether they are referring to levels or growth rates, as the implications can differ significantly.

International comparison of productivity levels requires that levels expressed in a domestic currency be converted into a common currency. This conversion can be done using either market exchange rates or exchange rates based on purchasing power parities (PPPs) — that is, the exchange rate that equalizes the price of a basket of goods and services between two countries. For accurate comparison, it is imperative that PPPs be used, although the development of reli-able PPPs is a complex matter, particularly at the industry level.[2] A range of PPPs, produced by different agencies and researchers, has resulted in a wide range of estimates for levels of relative international productivity.

The Cyclical Behaviour of Productivity

The short- to medium-term movement of productivity is determined by two influences — an underlying productivity trend and a cyclical component. Over the long term, the cyclical component is offsetting, with cyclical upturns cancelling out cyclical downturns so that actual productivity growth tends to converge on trend growth. Actual productivity growth between cyclical output peaks provides an approximation of trend productivity, although the trend may also be influenced by average capacity utilization over the cycle and differences in capacity utilization at the peaks.

The short-term behaviour of labour productivity is explained by lags in the adjustment of labour input to changes in output. If labour input adjusted simultaneously with changes in output, productivity growth would always be at trend. Lags in the adjustment of labour input, both employment and total hours worked, are caused by a number of factors, including firms' unfulfilled expectations concerning demand conditions, the existence of overhead labour that is relatively invariant to output levels, and a tendency for firms to hoard skilled labour in downturns so as not to lose their investment.

For the reasons outlined above, the rate of change in output per worker tends to move in a procyclical pattern, declining below trend in downturns and rising above trend in recoveries. The rate of change in output per hour shows a slightly more dampened procyclical movement, as it is easier to adjust average weekly hours through short-time or overtime than to adjust employment levels. Total factor productivity, which includes the capital stock as well as labour as an input, exhibits even greater procyclical variation in movement than output per worker because of the fixity of the capital input.

The cyclical behaviour of productivity has two implications. First, one should not extrapolate long-term productivity trends from short-term developments. For example, with the Canadian economy entering a period of weak growth in 2001, due to falling aggregate demand, slower productivity growth can be expected for cyclical reasons. This does not mean that long-term productivity growth has necessarily deteriorated, as any productivity shortfall now can be recovered later in the cycle. Second, to minimize the impact of cyclical influences on productivity, growth rates should be calculated at comparable points in the cycle, preferably on a peak-to-peak basis.

THEORETICAL PERSPECTIVES ON PRODUCTIVITY GROWTH

Economic theory advances in stages. First, a simple framework based on highly restrictive and often unrealistic assumptions is developed. Then, these assumptions are gradually eliminated as the model attempts to incorporate more elements of reality. The development of the theory of economic and productivity growth from the 1950s to the 1990s has conformed to this pattern.

The modern study of economic growth and long-run productivity growth dates from the 1950s when Robert Solow, Moses Abramovitz and Dale Jorgenson identified the basic inputs of a growing economy as labour, capital and technology. Solow (1957), in a widely cited article, concluded that technological change, not labour and capital, was responsible for most economic growth. However, he did not measure the contribution of technological change to economic growth directly, but rather measured it as a residual after the contribution of labour and capital had been calculated. Solow characterized this residual as "a measure of our ignorance." In the Solow model, technological change was exogenous, or "manna from heaven," although this treatment of technology was not meant to be taken literally but rather was intended as an abstraction, to simplify and facilitate the model's focus on long-term growth.

Solow's theoretical framework for the analysis of economic growth served as the basis for the development, by Edward Denison (1962), of a growth-accounting framework that attributed economic growth to a number of sources, including increases in the education of the labour force, the contribution of capital, the shift of resources from low-productivity endeavours to the mainstream of the modern economy, gains from knowledge and economies of scale.

The limitations of both the neoclassical, or Solow, growth model and growth-accounting methodology in explaining the growth process — in particular their inability to account for the post-1973 productivity slowdown — have in recent years led to the development of more sophisticated models of economic growth by such economists as Paul Romer. A key feature of many of these models is their emphasis on knowledge as the driving force of productivity growth.

Romer (1990) points out that "the neoclassical assumptions of diminishing returns to increasing investment and perfect competition placed the accumulation of new technologies at the centre of the growth process and simultaneously denied the possibility that economic analysis could have anything to say about this process." In other words, while early versions of growth theory convincingly demonstrated the importance of studying technology, the aggregate macroeconomic models used left little room for the analysis of the sources of invention or innovation, new and improved products or processes, or organizational or structural change (Landau et al. 1996).

In recent years, the basic neoclassical model has been enhanced and expanded upon in at least five broad areas (Landau et al. 1996). These developments reflect the elimination of many of the model's restrictive and unrealistic assumptions.

> Neoclassical growth theory assumed that all firms behaved in the same manner in their effort to maximize profits. It is now widely recognized that while the profit motive is still important, behaviour can differ greatly among firms. Economists interested in economic growth are now exploring such issues as how firms learn from experience, how good management differs from bad management, how firms differ in their means of gathering and transmitting information internally, and how firms compete in international markets.

> The neoclassical model also assumed perfect competition. This is a particularly unrealistic assumption for a growth model, because in a world characterized by perfect competition firms have no incentive to undertake research and development, since they can sell at the market price all they can produce. Such a model

also assumes away the important real-world issue of the appropriability of the gains from technical progress. Many models of economic growth now assume monopolistic competition and give explicit treatment to patents as a mechanism for influencing the appropriability of the gains from technical progress.

> The neoclassical model assumes that the secrets of technical progress are available to all. The implication is that productivity levels in all countries will converge on that of the technological leader, as each country avails itself of the technological knowledge. This assumption ignores the obvious point that the social ability to gain technological advantage varies greatly among nations, which is why productivity levels have not converged. Putnam (2001) has developed the concept of "social capital" as a factor of production to explain international variation in growth rates and productivity levels.

> The neoclassical model assumes that all industries are equally important. But some economists now argue that certain industries may be more important to long-run productivity growth than others because they yield a greater rate of social return through externalities (e.g., the information technology sector) or may exhibit increasing returns to scale.

> An implication of the early growth theory is that the long-term steady-state rate of growth is determined by the rate of technical progress and population growth and is independent of the rate of saving and investment. But recent research suggests that higher rates of accumulation and investment

can increase productivity growth, that there is no steady-state rate of growth and that the inputs in the growth process act independently. For example, Boskin and Lau (1992) find that the higher the capital stock, the greater the ability of technology to increase productivity, because most technology is embodied in capital goods.

Multi-faceted Determinants or Sources of Productivity

Building on the recent theoretical developments reviewed above, a large literature has developed aimed at deriving their implications for public policy. In Canada, recent contributions in this area include Harris (1999) and Sharpe (1998).

Based on a review of the cross-country growth literature, Harris (1999) identifies three proximate drivers (the Big Three) of productivity growth: investment in machinery and equipment; education, training and human capital; and openness to trade and investment. In addition, he notes that once one moves from the proximate determinants to the indirect linkages, productivity growth can be influenced by a large number of factors. His compendium of potential indirect productivity determinants includes innovation (both product and process), diffusion of technology (national and international), spatial agglomeration (e.g., Silicon Valley), external economies of scale at the industry level, government consumption (negative), management practices, public infrastructure (positive), income inequality (negative), high taxes (negative), small firms (negative), labour market flexibility (positive), exchange rate stability (positive) and low inflation (positive).

Sharpe (1998) identifies the following seven determinants of productivity growth:

> *The rate of technical progress*, determined by the rate of developing new product and process innovations and the pace of diffusing those innovations.

> *Investment in physical capital* such as machinery and equipment and structures. The more capital a worker has to work with, the greater the output he can produce. It is estimated that 80 percent of technical change is embodied in new capital equipment, particularly machinery. Without gross investment, technical progress would be all but impossible. Hence, physical investment is essential for productivity growth.

> *The quality of the workforce*, including average educational, training and experience levels. Literacy and numeracy skills as well as technical skills are essential if an industry is to benefit from technical advances and make effective use of machinery.

> *The size and quality of the natural resource base*. For example, the high level of output per hour in Alberta reflects the concentration of the oil and gas industry in this province and the high value added (which includes economic rent) per worker generated by the industry.

> *Industrial structure and intersectoral shifts*, since the aggregate level of labour productivity is a weighted average of industry labour productivity levels, where the weights are the labour input shares.

> *The macroeconomic environment* or aggregate demand conditions defined by the size of the output gap and the relationship between actual and potential output growth. Prolonged periods of insufficient demand can have a negative long-term effect on productivity growth.

> *The microeconomic policy environment*, broadly defined as the policies that affect behaviour at the firm level, including trade policy, tax policy, industrial policy, competition policy, and policies on privatization, intellectual property, regulation and foreign ownership.

There is still considerable uncertainty about the drivers of productivity. The relative and absolute contributions made by the different determinants may vary over time and across space. Many of the factors in productivity growth are interrelated and may act in synergy.

Productivity and Unemployment

Labour productivity is technically defined as the relationship between output and the employed labour force. It ignores the unemployed and others outside the labour force who would like to have a job but do not. From this perspective, conventional productivity measures do not represent an appropriate indicator of the efficient allocation or uses of labour from a societal perspective. Rising productivity can and sometimes does coexist with high or even rising unemployment, although one could argue that in such a situation societal productivity is not rising. It is very unproductive or inefficient to have a large number of workers producing zero output.

One way to deal with this issue is to develop a productivity measure that defines labour input as inclusive of the employed and unemployed. Such a measure expresses the social relationship between the labour resources that society has available for production and actual output, in contrast to the economic relationship between the labour resources actually used in production and output. Chart 1 shows trends in Canada from 1976 to 2001 for economic productivity, defined as output per person employed, and social productivity, defined as output per labour force participant. Not surprisingly, the level of social productivity is about 7-10 percent below that of economic productivity over the period, reflecting the addition of the unemployed to the denominator and no change in the numerator. The recessions of the early 1980s and early 1990s produced much larger declines in social productivity than in economic productivity. From a societal productivity perspective, economic downturns have a very negative effect on overall productivity of the labour force.

Productivity, Economic Well-Being and Happiness

Productivity growth can contribute to greater economic well-being. One approach

CHART 1

Economic Productivity (Output Per Person Employed) vs. Social Productivity (Output Per Person in the Labour Force) in Canada

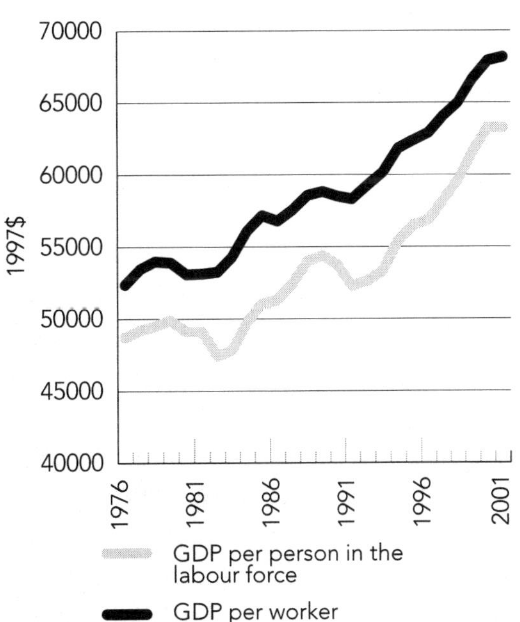

Source: Labour Force Historical Review 2001(R) CD-ROM, Statistics Canada Cat. No. 71F0004XCB; and GDP data from CANSIM II v3860085, June 3, 2002.

39

to the measurement of economic well-being is the Index of Economic Well-being developed by the Centre for the Study of Living Standards (Osberg and Sharpe 1998, 2002*a*, 2002*b*) based on Osberg (1985). This index is based on four components of economic well-being: consumption flows; non-financial stocks of wealth; equality; and economic security in terms of low risk of unemployment, financial distress due to illness, single-parent poverty and poverty in old age. Sharpe (2002*b*) demonstrates how real income growth arising from productivity gains can lead to increased private and public consumption, higher stocks of capital, lower poverty and greater economic security.

Despite the importance of productivity for real income growth, one should retain a sense of perspective on the productivity issue. Just because productivity can contribute to higher levels of economic well-being, it does not necessarily follow that it should be the top social priority.

Two points are relevant in this regard. First, in poor countries productivity growth is absolutely crucial to raise the material standard of living to an acceptable level and reduce absolute poverty. In contrast, Canada is already a rich country with high living standards for the vast majority of the population. Increased productivity leads to higher consumption levels and greater economic well-being, but it may do little for subjective well-being or happiness. Studies have found that after a certain income level has been achieved in rich countries, further real income growth can have little if any additional impact on happiness for the overall population (Easterlin 1974, 1995). Money cannot buy happiness, at least not in the long run. Since the goal of public policy is to increase the overall well-being, not just the economic well-being, of the population, productivity should not be sold as a panacea for society's ills.

Second, productivity can provide the basis for potential increases in a number of the components of economic well-being, such as equality and economic security. But there is no mechanism whereby higher productivity growth automatically translates into less income inequality or lower poverty, as in the case of higher real wages leading to greater private consumption. For example, growing wage inequality may prevent low-skilled workers from benefiting from productivity growth. Government action may be needed to eliminate poverty and decrease social inequality.

MEASUREMENT ISSUES

Statistical agencies do not gather productivity statistics directly from economic agents. Rather, they construct productivity measures from data on inputs and outputs. Indeed, almost the entire body of economic statistics collected by statistical agencies — data on output, employment, prices, investment, raw materials, inventories — is used in the compilation of productivity statistics. An examination of the reliability of productivity statistics thus becomes, in effect, an examination of the reliability of much of the system of economic statistics.

Figure 1 is a schematic representation of the basic data requirements of productivity statistics, or the building blocks of productivity measurement. At the extreme left is the productivity ratio, defined as the ratio of real output to input. This ratio may be a partial productivity measure, such as labour

FIGURE 1
The Building Blocks of Productivity Measurement

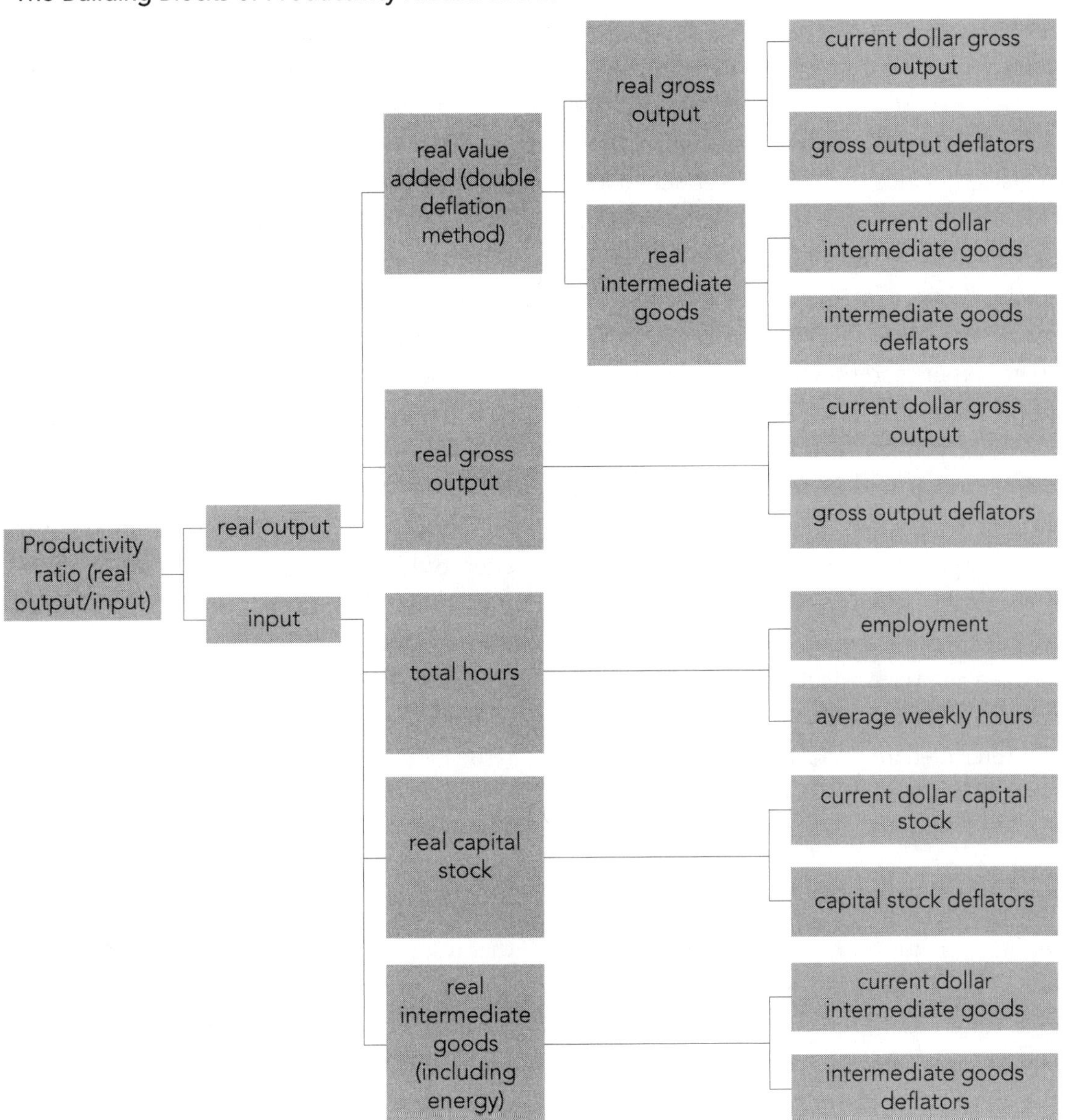

productivity, where real output is related to only one input, or a multifactor or total factor productivity measure where an index of real output is related to an index of more than one input. Inputs in addition to labour that have been included in multifactor productivity calculations are capital, including both fixed capital and inventories, and intermediate goods, including raw materials and energy.

Either of two real output measures can be used to construct productivity indexes — real value added and real gross output. The former defines output as the total incomes of the factors of production (basically, labour and capital) in an industry, sector or economy. The latter defines output as the physical output produced by an industry, sector or economy. At the industry or sectoral level, real gross output comprises real value added and real intermediate goods. At the aggregate level in a closed economy, real gross output is equivalent to real value added as intermediate goods are netted out.

The most appropriate output concept of industry productivity when labour or labour and capital are included as inputs is real value added. Use of real gross output may bias the results because of substitution, in the production process, between intermediate goods and labour or capital.[3] On the other hand, the most appropriate output concept when intermediate goods are included as an input is real gross output.

Real value added is calculated through a double-deflation procedure whereby real intermediate goods are subtracted from real gross output. Real gross output is calculated through the deflation of current-dollar gross output by gross output deflators. Real intermediate goods are calculated in a similar manner, from current-dollar intermediate goods and intermediate goods deflators.

Turning to the input side, labour input, most appropriately measured as total hours worked, is determined by employment and actual average weekly hours. The real capital services arising from the capital stock (fixed capital and sometimes inventories) are derived from current-dollar capital stock estimates and capital stock deflators.

From the above discussion, five basic building blocks of productivity measurement can be identified: estimates of labour input, including both employment and average weekly hours; estimates of current-dollar capital stock; estimates of current-dollar intermediate goods; estimates of current-dollar gross output; and estimates of product price indices. These product price indices are, in turn, used to derive deflators for gross output, capital stock and intermediate goods.

Productivity statistics are plagued by a number of measurement problems, the most important of which are outlined below.

Price Indices, Quality Adjustment and Hedonics

Price indices for goods and services are crucial for deflating the current value of output to produce real output and hence productivity estimates. But quality changes in goods and services over time must be integrated into price indices if true changes in real output are to be captured.[4]

The Panel to Review Productivity Statistics (1979) identifies three types of quality change. Type 1 is the change in the quantity of costly resources used to produce a product, such as the addition of a remote-control device to a television set. Type 2 occurs when a technological innovation raises the quality of a product without any increase in current resource inputs, such as when new models of computers have more memory and greater processing ability but cost the same or less than the models they replace. Type 3 quality change refers to any design change in durable goods that results in higher or lower operating costs, holding constant both the quantity of services provided by the good and the wages and prices of the inputs used in its operation. An example is the redesign of an engine to improve fuel efficiency.

Until the 1980s, statistical agencies made adjustments for Type 1 quality change but largely ignored Types 2 and 3. Since then, there has been growing recognition of the importance of these latter types of quality change, as represented by computers and more energy-efficient consumer durables, respectively, and attempts to adjust for them. The most common method of adjustment is known as hedonics. This involves the application of a statistical regression to the different models of a given type of product available in two or more years, where the dependent variable is the price of each model and the independent variables are its measured characteristics.

The application of hedonics has produced very large decreases in the quality-adjusted price indices for computer hardware and, to a lesser degree, telecommunications equipment, leading to enormous increases in real output and hence productivity growth in these sectors. Indeed, the computer hardware sector has accounted for a highly disproportionate share of output and productivity growth in the United States and to a lesser degree in Canada, where the sector is less important. In principle, productivity-growth comparisons across countries can be greatly affected by differences in the use of hedonics by national statistical agencies. In reality, this factor does not appear to account for significant international differences in aggregate productivity growth rates, although sectoral growth rates can be affected (Pilat 2001).

Non-marketed Output

A key requirement for the development of productivity estimates is that output be measured independently of inputs. If output is measured by the quantity of inputs, productivity growth will by definition be zero. In sectors where output is not marketed, it is not possible to deflate the nominal value of output to produce real output and hence productivity estimates. This means that there are no reliable estimates of productivity growth for these sectors — primarily public administration and the publicly funded components of the education and health sectors. It is therefore best to exclude these sectors from aggregate productivity measures.

For this reason, the business sector is the most appropriate category for analysing productivity trends at the aggregate level and the sector for which official productivity statistics are produced. The wide availability of data for total employment and real GDP does mean that productivity estimates for the total economy are often referred to, although, because of the lack of measured productivity growth in the non-marketed sectors, these estimates have a downward bias.

It is in theory possible to develop productivity growth estimates for the non-business sector by measuring, in physical units, the output of the sector. Possible physical indicators include the number of graduates of the education system, the number of procedures performed in hospitals and the number of cheques processed by a government office. But such indicators may represent only part of the output of the sector and, more importantly, may exhibit significant quality changes over time. The development of reliable productivity growth estimates for the non-marketed sector is still in its early stages.

The Underground Economy

The issue of the underground economy often arises in discussions of productivity trends. It is pointed out that the underestimation of real output because of unrecorded underground activity, not offset by a commensurate underestimation of inputs, will produce a downward bias to productivity level estimates. Estimates of the size of the underground economy vary widely. The most authoritative (and lowest) estimate is that by Statistics Canada (1994), which found that the underground economy represented around 3 percent of GDP in Canada in 1992. A key reason for the small size of the underground economy relative to GDP is that Statistics Canada is aware, through various sources, that many transactions in certain sectors, such as construction, are not reported to the tax authorities; the agency can therefore make imputations for this unreported economic activity in the national accounts.

It should also be noted that it is not the existence of the underground economy per se that produces bias in productivity growth rates, but rather changes in its relative size over time. If the size of the underground economy remains stable, productivity levels may be underestimated but productivity growth rates will be unaffected. Of the many measurement issues facing national accountants and productivity analysts, bias associated with the underground economy is certainly not the most serious.

Conceptual Problems in the Definition of Output

In certain industries in the business or marketed sector, the definition of what actually constitutes output poses conceptual problems that affect productivity estimates. For example, is the output of the banking sector the intermediation function the banks serve (as proxied by the value of the spread between what the banks earn and what they pay out in interest, net of expenses), or is it the services provided by the sector (number of accounts maintained, number of cheques processed, convenience provided by ATMs, etc.)? Other industries with conceptual problems include insurance, gambling and brokerage houses.

These conceptual issues are gradually being worked out, with the result that productivity estimates for these industries are becoming more reliable. For example, statistical agencies have changed the definition of output in the banking sector, from the first definition noted above to the second, with the result that measured productivity growth in the sector has increased.

Quality Adjustment of Inputs

A key issue in productivity research is whether inputs such as labour and capital should be adjusted for quality changes, just as output is adjusted. Statistical agencies certainly produce and release unadjusted estimates of labour and capital inputs. They also often adjust inputs for quality changes in the compilation of productivity estimates, particularly TFP estimates.

With quality adjustment, quality improvements increase the growth rate of the input and hence its contribution to output. This means that the size of the residual or TFP is reduced, shedding more light on the sources of growth. This is considered by many to be the main advantage of adjustment. The advantage of non-adjustment is that the conceptual and methodological difficulties inherent in adjustment are avoided and the productivity numbers are easier to interpret and understand.

The Importance of Statistical Revisions

Statistical agencies revise, on a regular and periodical basis, the economic series they produce. As productivity estimates draw upon a wide range of economic data, including estimates of employment, hours, nominal output, prices and capital stock, they are subject to frequent — and often significant — revisions. Indeed, these revisions are the scourge of productivity analysts, but a necessary evil since the most recent data must be used. Unfortunately, the revision of productivity data can result in the rewriting and reinterpretation of productivity trends.

Two examples illustrate this point. In May 2001, Statistics Canada released its Aggregate Productivity Measures data which showed that output per hour in the business sector advanced at a 1.2-percent average annual growth rate between 1995 and 2000, a performance characterized as weak by productivity analysts. Later that same month, Statistics Canada released new estimates of the national accounts using, for the first time, the Fisher chain index and capitalizing software expenditures. These changes boosted productivity growth by a very significant 0.5 percentage points, to 1.7 percent per year for the same period, and forced productivity analysts to change their characterization of productivity growth over this period.

In July 2001 the US Bureau of Labor Statistics revised its estimates on business-sector output per hour based on new national accounts data from the Bureau of Economic Analysis. Instead of increasing 2.8 percent per year over the 1995-2000 period, as originally reported earlier in the year, productivity growth was revised downward to 2.4 percent. This indicated that the acceleration in productivity growth was less than previously believed.

PRODUCTIVITY TRENDS AND DEVELOPMENTS

This section of the paper highlights a number of the developments that have characterized productivity growth in the post-war period in OECD countries and in Canada. The international trends discussed are: the post-1973 productivity slowdown, the post-war productivity convergence phenomenon, lagging productivity growth in certain service sectors, and the post-1995 productivity growth acceleration in the United States. The Canadian trends examined are: the relative decline of Canada's productivity performance, the growing Canada-US manufacturing productivity gap and sectoral productivity trends.

Three distinct productivity trends or stylized facts can be identified in the post-war

period for the United States and two for other developed economies, including Canada. From 1945 to 1973, developed countries experienced a golden age of productivity growth, with labour-productivity growth advancing at a rate of 3 percent or more per year. After 1973, virtually all developed countries entered a period of slower productivity growth. The failure of productivity to pick up in the first half of the 1990s despite the introduction of information technologies led observers to coin the term "productivity paradox." Since 1995, the United States has been in a period of much stronger productivity growth, resolving the productivity paradox as least for that country.

45

The Post-1973 Productivity Slowdown

The most important productivity development in the post-war period has been the slowdown in labour and total factor productivity growth, a phenomenon that affected virtually all industrial countries and most industries. According to official Statistics Canada estimates, growth in output per hour in the business sector fell by nearly two-thirds, from 4.0 percent per year in the 1946-73 period to 1.4 percent in the 1973-2001 period (Table 1 and Chart 2). Growth in output per hour in the business sector averaged 1.4 percent per year in 1973-81, fell slightly to 1.1 percent in 1981-89 and rose to 1.6 percent after 1989.

The post-1973 productivity slowdown affected most sectors of the Canadian economy (Table 2). Of the 10 one-digit SIC industries for which official data are available, eight experienced significantly lower growth in output per hour after 1973 (agriculture; fishing and trapping; logging and forestry; mining, quarrying and oil wells; manufacturing; transportation and storage; communications and other utility industries; and retail trade). The two exceptions were construction and wholesale trade, both of which have seen an improvement in productivity growth since 1973.

After more than 20 years of debate, there is still no consensus among economists on the causes of the productivity slowdown. The view that appears to be gaining the largest number of adherents is that the slowdown reflected the ebbing or withering away of the impact of the historically unprecedented factors that came together to boost productivity growth in the immediate post-war period (e.g., the shift of the workforce out of low-productivity agriculture, increased international trade, rapid capital accumulation and diffusion of the stock of technologies and know-how built up but unexploited during the Great Depression and the Second World War). The productivity experience in the post-1973 period in North America can be seen as a return to the long-run historical trend of around 1.5 percent per year.

The implications of the productivity slowdown are well recognized by government. For example, in 1994 the federal Department of Finance (1994) released the document *A New Framework for Economic Policy* (the Purple Book), which states: "At the root of the economic problem has been the failure of *productivity* to increase at the rates that prevailed during the post-war years to the mid-1970s" (p. 15).

Post-War Productivity Convergence in OECD Countries

The United States has been the world technological leader in the post-war period, with the highest level of productivity among industrial countries. On the other hand, it has experienced (until recently) one of the slowest rates of productivity growth. Economists believe this is not an accidental situation but rather reflects the dynamics of international productivity growth. Technological catch-up or convergence is seen as the major reason why most OECD countries experienced faster productivity growth than the United States in the post-war period.

Through technological catch-up, low-productivity countries have the potential of enjoying rapid (although declining) productivity growth until their productivity levels begin to converge on that of the leader. Indeed, a number of countries in the developed world have effectively exploited this potential in the post-war period. The average unweighted level of output per hour worked in OECD countries excluding the United States went from 44 percent of the US level in 1950 to 83 percent in 2001 (see Table 5 below).

CHART 2

Output Per Hour in the Business Sector, Canada (Average Annual Rates of Change)

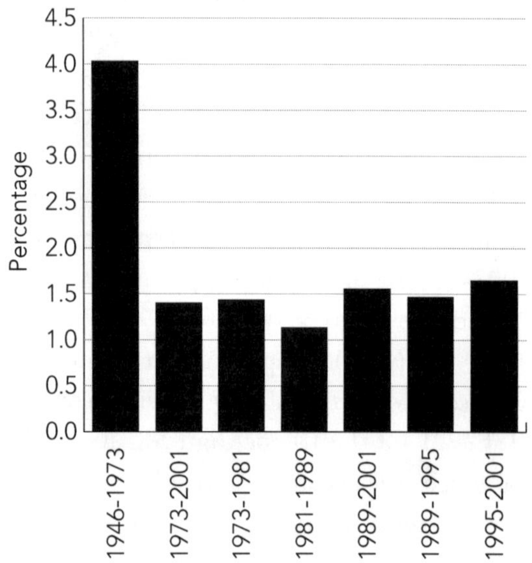

Source: Aggregate Productivity Measures, Statistics Canada, August 2002. For 1989 onwards, data are from the quarterly Aggregate Productivity Measures series, CANSIM II v1409153, July 2001.

TABLE 2

Trends in Labour Productivity, Output Per Hour Worked by Industry, Canada, 1961-2000

	Average annual rates of change in output per hour					
	1961-1973	1973-1981	1981-1989	1989-2000	1989-1995	1995-2000
Business Sector	3.8	1.6	1.1	1.6	1.5	1.8
Agriculture	5.9	6.6	2.4	4.6	4.3	5.0
Fishing & Trapping	2.6	-0.4	-3.0	-0.7	-1.4	0.2
Logging & Forestry	3.9	1.9	3.4	-0.1	-2.0	2.2
Mining, Quarrying & Oil Well	6.1	-6.1	3.1	1.5	3.5	-0.8
Manufacturing	4.2	1.8	2.4	2.3	3.3	1.0
Construction	0.5	3.9	-0.4	-0.6	-0.5	-0.7
Transportation & Storage	5.2	-0.5	2.7	1.8	2.1	1.4
Communication & other Utility Industries	5.8	3.1	1.7	2.3	1.3	3.5
Wholesale Trade	2.3	1.6	4.6	1.6	1.2	2.1
Retail Trade	3.6	1.3	1.1	2.0	0.3	4.0

Notes: Statistics Canada has updated the business sector and manufacturing series to 2001 consistent with the regular annual revision. All other industries will be updated later in the fall of 2002 on the basis of the North American Industry Classification System.

Source: Aggregate Productivity Measures, Statistics Canada, August 2002.

The convergence hypothesis is based on four advantages productivity laggards may exploit (Abramovitz and David 1996). (1) These countries can make use of state-of-the-art technology produced by the technological leader. (2) Because these countries have low capital-labour ratios, the marginal product of capital is high. (3) Less developed countries have considerable opportunities to shift resources out of low-productivity activities. (4) These countries can benefit from economies of scale as their markets grow.

However, there is no mechanism by which the productivity levels of poor countries automatically converge on that of the leader. Indeed, outside the industrial countries, there has been little convergence towards US productivity levels, with the exception of a number of countries in East Asia. Persistent national characteristics can inhibit laggard countries from exploiting the advantages of backwardness. These include poverty of natural resources; small domestic markets; barriers to trade; forms of economic organization or systems of taxation that reduce rewards for effort, enterprise or investment; and deeper elements of national culture that limit responses of people to economic opportunities. Throughout the Third World, deep-rooted political constraints imposed on social capability have prevented convergence, but when these constraints are removed, as has happened in East Asia, the potential for convergence can be realized.

Lagging Productivity Growth in Certain Service Industries

In general, productivity growth in the service sector has lagged behind that in the goods sector, although a number of service-sector industries, such as communications and trade, have posted respectable rates of productivity growth.[5] Service-sector productivity growth has been held back by the financial, insurance and real estate sector and, more importantly, by community, personal and business services. Indeed, Sharpe et al. (2002) show that the education and health sectors recorded negative measured labour-productivity growth in both Canada and the United States in the 1990s, which dragged down aggregate productivity growth.

For example, between the 1989 cyclical peak and 1998, output per hour in the service sector fell 1.3 percent per year, after falling 0.5 percent per year during the 1980s. This decline in the absolute level of productivity affected all industries within the sector: accommodation, food and beverage (-1.9 percent per year); amusement and recreation services (-1.4 percent); business services (-1.1 percent); health services (-1.0 percent); education and related services (-0.6 percent); and personal, household and other services (-0.5 percent). As the service sector accounts for more than one quarter of total hours worked in the business sector, this development exercised a significant downward influence on total business-sector productivity.

One explanation for the slower productivity growth in the service sector is the greater inherent difficulty of increasing productivity in certain service industries. For example, the non-tangible nature of services limits the possibilities for mechanization, while the one-to-one personal nature of many services, such as health care — where output depends on interaction with the user — makes standardization difficult. A second explanation is that official measures of service-sector output have a serious downward bias, greater than in the goods sector. Indeed, productivity growth in the service sector, if properly measured, may not be inferior to that in the goods sector.

Specific problems in the measurement of real output and hence productivity in market-ed service industries include: conceptual difficulties in the definition of output in sectors such as banking and insurance; improvements or deterioration in quality of output that are not captured by the price indices; absence of appropriate service-sector data for productivity measurement (data coverage is much better for goods industries); difficulties incorporating completely new services into existing price indices; and the extreme heterogeneity of transactions in certain service industries, such as legal and health services, which makes price systems non-linear and not directly linked to what is received by the customer.

Post-1995 Acceleration in US Productivity Growth

Since 1995, productivity growth has picked up significantly in the United States. Between 1995 and 2001, output per hour in the business sector advanced at a 2.4-percent average annual rate, up nearly a full percentage point from the 1.5 percent of the 1989-95 period. This development has been taken by many as *prima facie* evidence of a new economy characterized by higher trend productivity growth based on information technologies (IT). Research has shown that the productivity pickup, while greatest in the IT-producing sector, has also spread to the IT-using industries, including those in the service sector, supporting the view that IT is now having a pervasive impact on productivity (Stiroh 2001). Some economists, such as Robert Gordon (2000), argue that a significant component of this acceleration is transitory, related to the cyclical factors and the investment boom of the second half of the 1990s, and that productivity growth will be slower in the medium term. Others, such as Martin Baily (2002), believe that most of the acceleration is of a permanent nature.

Unlike the United States, the other industrial countries show no evidence of a post-1995 acceleration in productivity growth. In Canada, for example, business-sector output per hour advanced at a 1.7-percent average annual rate between 1995 and 2001 — barely above the 1.5 percent experienced over the 1989-95 period. With the acceleration in productivity growth in the United States in the second half of the 1990s, the productivity leader forged ahead of the followers and increased the productivity gap. This represents a situation of productivity divergence, in contrast to the productivity convergence of the pre-1995 period.

Canada's Relative Productivity Decline

From an international perspective, Canada has suffered a relative deterioration in its productivity performance in recent years. Data have been compiled by the Groningen Growth and Development Centre at the University of Groningen in the Netherlands. In 1973, Canada ranked second out of 22 OECD countries in terms of output per person, with 92.1 percent of the output per person employed, relative to that of the United States, the leader (Table 3). By 2001, Canada had fallen to fifth place, at 79.7 percent, behind Belgium, France, Ireland, Norway and of course the United States. In GDP per capita, Canada also fell from second to fifth over the period (Table 4). Canada's relative decline in terms of output per hour was even greater — from second to 13th place — because of the fewer hours worked per year in most European countries (Table 5). Canada's relative productivity decline largely reflects the pick-up of productivity growth in Europe, where productivity levels converged towards, and in a number of cases — Belgium, France, the Netherlands and Norway — surpassed US levels on a per-hour basis.

Data prepared by the Centre for the Study of Living Standards on Canada's aggregate labour productivity performance show that the greater deterioration relative to the United States was particularly abrupt in the second half of the 1990s. In 1976, GDP per person employed in Canada was 88.1 percent of that in the United States. In 1995, it was 85.0 percent. By 2001, however, it had fallen to 82.5 percent (Table 6 and Chart 3). The relative decline between 1995 and 1999 reflects the acceleration of productivity growth in the United States, as Canadian productivity growth has not fallen in absolute terms.

49

TABLE 3

Relative GDP Per Person Employed in OECD Countries

	US=100 in all years				
	1950	1973	1989	1995	2001
Australia	76.1	73.5	76.6	80.2	79.5
Austria	36.1	70.7	82.0	79.1	78.6
Belgium	63.2	82.1	98.6	100.5	94.2
Canada	91.4	92.1	88.0	85.7	79.7
Denmark	65.8	73.5	76.6	80.8	77.8
Finland	37.8	59.4	72.2	77.5	76.3
France	47.2	77.8	91.0	91.2	84.6
Unified Germany	n/a	n/a	80.8	81.5	76.5
West Germany	53.2	83.7	94.7	90.2	n/a
Greece	26.4	58.1	62.8	59.7	61.4
Ireland	37.5	51.3	75.6	82.6	90.2
Italy	39.9	67.9	80.1	85.0	77.6
Japan	19.4	59.1	74.5	74.2	69.9
Netherlands	77.0	94.5	84.7	80.6	73.4
New Zealand	n/a	79.6	66.0	64.3	57.7
Norway	52.3	64.6	77.6	86.8	81.5
Portugal	21.6	45.8	49.6	52.2	49.5
Spain	25.4	60.0	80.3	84.3	74.5
Sweden	58.9	70.0	69.0	73.9	71.6
Switzerland	85.5	93.2	83.5	78.2	73.6
Turkey	11.8	21.1	27.1	29.5	28.8
UK	65.9	66.3	71.8	74.0	70.9
US	100.0	100.0	100.0	100.0	100.0

Source: Groningen Growth and Development Centre & The Conference Board, June 13, 2002. www.eco.rug.nl/ GGDC/index-dseries.html

TABLE 4

Relative GDP Per Capita in OECD Countries

| | US=100 in all years | | | | |
	1950	1973	1989	1995	2001
Australia	78.5	76.6	74.0	76.9	77.6
Austria	41.4	71.9	75.4	77.2	74.6
Belgium	60.4	77.1	76.8	77.6	75.9
Canada	81.9	87.3	87.5	81.6	77.9
Denmark	75.3	86.6	82.1	83.6	80.7
Finland	45.7	68.2	75.4	65.8	71.5
France	53.2	75.9	74.2	72.4	69.7
Unified Germany West	n/a	n/a	81.4	75.5	69.7
Germany	54.5	89.6	89.2	81.9	n/a
Greece	22.1	50.7	48.2	46.0	47.2
Ireland	38.1	43.5	49.9	61.5	82.1
Italy	38.5	67.1	73.0	72.9	69.1
Japan	20.2	68.8	78.2	80.3	72.9
Netherlands	62.9	78.9	72.9	75.1	75.1
New Zealand	88.8	75.3	61.2	59.8	55.8
Norway	56.5	66.7	78.0	85.8	84.0
Portugal	22.2	45.1	46.0	48.8	49.8
Spain	26.2	54.8	53.5	54.5	56.4
Sweden	70.9	81.3	76.7	71.5	71.0
Switzerland	100.6	115.7	96.9	88.3	81.9
Turkey	16.3	19.3	18.9	20.1	17.8
UK	71.0	70.8	70.0	69.1	68.2
US	100.0	100.0	100.0	100.0	100.0

Source: Groningen Growth and Development Centre & The Conference Board, June 13, 2002. www.eco.rug.nl/GGDC/index-dseries.html

TABLE 5

Relative GDP Per Hour Worked in OECD Countries

| | US=100 in all years | | | | |
	1950	1973	1989	1995	2001
Australia	81.5	73.6	77.4	81.4	82.7
Austria	37.3	70.4	89.0	93.2	96.7
Belgium	57.0	78.3	106.9	112.6	113.3
Canada	94.7	91.2	88.2	89.0	83.3
Denmark	68.9	87.5	92.9	99.1	94.3
Finland	40.3	65.5	77.0	84.6	87.0
France	50.0	79.2	106.3	109.1	102.6
Unified Germany West	n/a	n/a	91.4	96.3	93.3
Germany	48.6	85.3	106.0	108.2	n/a
Greece	24.6	51.8	60.1	57.1	59.0
Ireland	33.3	44.3	71.7	82.9	99.2
Italy	44.1	70.4	87.6	95.7	88.7
Japan	21.5	54.4	68.6	73.5	72.6
Netherlands	77.4	104.0	109.0	108.7	101.8
New Zealand	n/a	n/a	68.2	66.4	61.3
Norway	55.6	72.7	98.6	112.9	110.6
Portugal	20.2	42.9	48.5	52.7	52.6
Spain	26.8	56.3	80.7	85.5	76.3
Sweden	62.6	80.2	81.4	84.3	82.4
Switzerland	88.5	93.2	91.1	90.0	86.5
Turkey	11.0	18.8	25.9	28.2	27.7
UK	67.6	65.0	76.6	81.6	80.2
US	100.0	100.0	100.0	100.0	100.0

Source: Groningen Growth and Development Centre & The Conference Board, June 13, 2002. www.eco.rug.nl/GGDC/index-dseries.html

The factors behind Canada's relative productivity decline are vigorously debated. Certainly, from an accounting perspective, the deterioration in its productivity performance in the IT sector compared to that in the United States can explain the lion's share of the decline in recent years (Rao and Tang 2001).

The Widening Canada-US Manufacturing Productivity Gap

Canada's relative performance in manufacturing productivity has been equally poor. Since 1981, Canada has had by far the weakest productivity growth among the G7 countries in this sector. Growth in output per hour has averaged 2.1 percent per year, compared to the G7 unweighted average of 3.3 percent (Table 7 and Chart 4). In the period 1995 to 2000, Canada's productivity performance was even worse, averaging 0.9 percent per year compared to the G7 average of 2.8 percent.

These developments have produced a widening gap in Canada-US manufacturing productivity, most notably in the second half of the 1990s. Manufacturing output per hour fell from 87.5 percent of the US level as recently as 1993 to a low of 67.3 percent in 2001 (see Table 6). Manufacturing productivity has been

TABLE 6

Productivity Levels, Canada Relative to the US

	US=100 in all years	
	Real GDP per Employed Person	Output per Hour in Manufacturing
1976	88.1	90.9
1977	89.1	92.1
1978	89.0	92.5
1979	88.7	91.4
1980	87.9	89.8
1981	86.8	89.6
1982	88.1	86.3
1983	87.2	87.5
1984	87.4	92.3
1985	87.6	91.3
1986	86.0	88.7
1987	86.5	82.7
1988	86.4	79.7
1989	85.6	82.9
1990	84.7	83.2
1991	84.0	83.1
1992	83.4	85.1
1993	84.0	87.5
1994	85.1	87.0
1995	85.0	83.2
1996	84.7	80.1
1997	83.8	79.5
1998	83.3	76.1
1999	82.6	72.3
2000	82.6	69.3
2001	82.5	67.3

Source: Output per hour series based on an estimate of 79.5 for the 1997 benchmark year by Bart van Ark, Inklaar and Timmer (2000), applied to data from *International Comparisons of Manufacturing Productivity and Unit Labour Costs*, April 5, 2001, News, Bureau of Labor Statistics, US Department of Labor; and Aggregate Productivity Measures for Canada. Output per worker is from the CSLS income and productivity database, August 2002.

largely driven by trends in IT-producing industries such as manufacturers of electronic and other electrical equipment and industrial machinery and equipment in the United States. This sector is relatively more important in the United States than in Canada and, in addition, has experienced a faster growth rate (Chart 5). This situation alone accounts for the widening gap in Canada-US manufacturing productivity (Sharpe 1999; Rao and Tang 2001).[6]

Variance in Sectoral Productivity Levels and Growth[7]

Productivity levels and growth rates vary greatly across industries. Industry-level differences in output per hour reflect a number of factors, including differences in capital intensity of production, quality of human capital, the existence of resource rents and competitive conditions. Industry-level differences in productivity growth rates reflect the pace of technological change in the sector, the ability to mechanize production, the pace of investment in both physical and human capital and competitive conditions.

In the 1989-2000 period, agriculture enjoyed the most rapid growth in output per hour (see Table 2), at an average 4.6 percent per year, followed by communications (2.3 per-

CHART 3

Labour Productivity Trends, Canada Relative to the US, 1976-2001

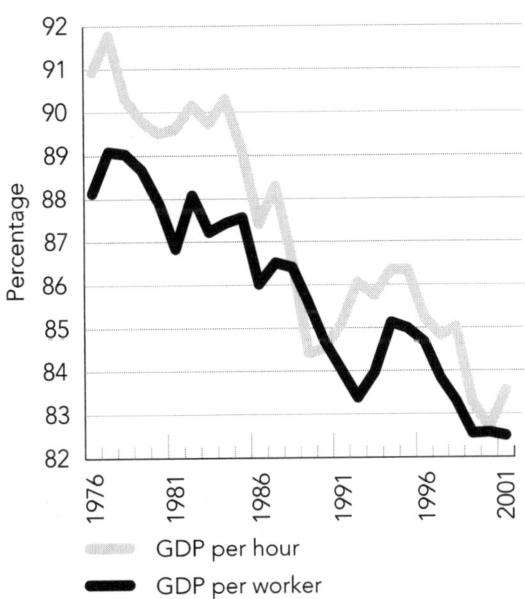

Source: CSLS income and productivity database, based on data from the National Accounts and Labour Force Survey for Canada and the National Income and Product Accounts and Current Population Survey for the United States; August 2002.

cent); manufacturing (2.3 percent); retail trade (2.0 percent); transportation and storage (1.8 percent); wholesale trade (1.6 percent) and mining, quarrying and oil wells (1.5 percent). Three sectors experienced negative productivity growth in the 1990s: logging and forestry (-0.1 percent per year); construction (-0.6 percent); and fishing and trapping (-0.7 percent).

PROSPECTS FOR PRODUCTIVITY GROWTH

52

As noted in the introduction to this paper, the shift from a 1.0-1.5-percent trend productivity world to a 2.0-2.5-percent world would have implications for a large number of economic and social variables. Real wages and incomes would be higher, as would tax rev-

CHART 4

Output Per Hour in Manufacturing, Selected OECD Countries, 1981-2000 (Average Annual Growth Rates)

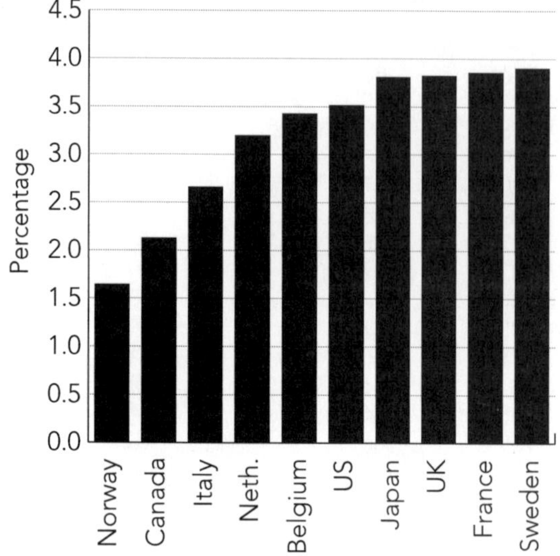

Source: International Comparisons of Manufacturing Productivity and Unit Labour Costs Trends, April 2002, Bureau of Labor Statistics, US Department of Labor.

TABLE 7

Growth in Output Per Hour in Manufacturing, Industrial Countries

	Average annual rates of change				
	1981-1989	1989-2000	1989-1995	1995-2000	1981-2000
Canada	2.25	2.03	3.00	0.88	2.12
US	3.25	3.71	2.93	4.64	3.51
Japan	3.89	3.74	3.85	3.62	3.81
France	3.74	3.93	3.76	4.14	3.85
UK	5.28	2.77	3.31	2.12	3.82
Italy	3.08	2.35	3.38	1.13	2.66
Germany (Unified)	n/a	n/a	n/a	2.85	n/a
G7 average	3.58	3.09	3.37	2.77	3.30
Belgium	4.13	2.91	2.63	3.25	3.42
Denmark	1.02	n/a	n/a	n/a	n/a
Netherlands	4.08	2.55	3.36	1.59	3.19
Norway	2.69	0.88	1.26	0.43	1.64
Sweden	3.15	4.45	4.58	4.29	3.90

Note: Only the 1995-2000 average includes Germany. Data on Unified Germany is only available beginning in 1991.
Source: International Comparisons of Manufacturing Productivity and Unit Labour Costs Trends, April 2002, Bureau of Labor Statistics, US Department of Labor.

enues, allowing expansion of social programs — political circumstances permitting. If we were all collectively richer, fewer tradeoffs between competing economic and social ends would be necessary.

From 1995 to 2001, the business sector in the United States enjoyed output-per-hour growth of 2.4 percent per year, up 1 percentage point from the 1973-95 period but below the 3.3 percent of the 1947-73 period. The million-dollar question for productivity analysts is whether the post-1995 acceleration is a permanent or temporary development. Opinions differ on this issue, depending in large part on how one views the causes of the acceleration. For economists such as Robert J. Gordon, who believe that much of the improvement in productivity growth is due to the strong cyclical conditions in the second half of the 1990s, and who see productivity growth narrowly concen-

CHART 5

Selected Industries Real GDP Share in
Manufacturing, Canada-US Comparison

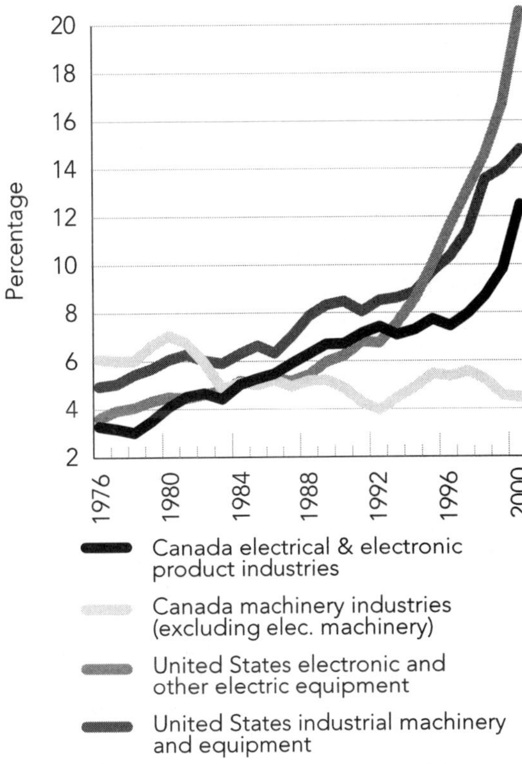

Canada electrical & electronic
product industries

Canada machinery industries
(excluding elec. machinery)

United States electronic and
other electric equipment

United States industrial machinery
and equipment

Source: Statistics Canada, GDP by Industry, and the
National Income and Product Accounts, US Bureau of
Economic Analysis.

trated in IT-producing industries with minimum productivity gains arising from investment in IT-using industries, the outlook for
productivity is not rosy. They see productivity growth reverting to 1.5 percent, just slightly above the trend of the 1973-95 period. On
the other hand, economists such as Dale
Jorgenson and Martin N. Baily, who believe
something fundamental happened to change
productivity behaviour and raise trend productivity in the mid-1990s, and believe this
change was associated with IT, the outlook for
productivity growth is more favourable,
although down somewhat from the unsustainable pace in the second half of the 1990s. Baily
(2002) projects annual productivity growth in

the range of 2.2-2.7 percent for the remaining
years of this decade.

There was virtually no acceleration in productivity growth in the second half of the 1990s
in Canada, at least relative to the first half of the
decade. Business-sector output per hour
advanced 1.6 percent, well below that recorded
in the United States. The issue for Canada is
whether it will follow the US lead and see a pick-
up in productivity growth. Again, economists
are divided on the issue. For example, Sharpe and
Gharani (2002) project business-sector output-
per-hour growth of a minimum of 2 percent per
year this decade, based on the view that Canada
tends to lag behind the United States and that
the productivity-augmenting effect of IT investment will finally have a payoff, just as it did in
the United States in the late 1990s. In other
words, technological catch-up will provide the
basis for stronger productivity growth in Canada.
Wilson and Dungan (2002), on the other hand,
foresee little acceleration in productivity growth,
arguing that the smaller size of the IT sector in
Canada will prevent this country from enjoying
US growth rates.

CONCLUSION

This paper has presented an overview of
productivity concepts, measurement issues, and
productivity trends and prospects in a Canadian
context. This material provides background for
an understanding of productivity issues addressed
in the papers in this volume. A number of messages or themes emerge. (1) Productivity is a
complex, nuanced concept with several dimensions, including such aspects as the different
types of productivity and the distinction between
growth rates and levels. (2) For a number of reasons, the measurement of productivity is fraught

53

with problems and the methodologies chosen to construct productivity estimates can greatly influence those estimates. (3) The determinants of productivity growth are multi-faceted, and include both economic and social variables. (4) Canada's productivity performance in recent years has been mediocre, particularly compared to that of the United States. (5) The interests of all Canadians converge on the importance of productivity growth as it is the basis of sustained real-income growth. (6) Productivity should not be oversold as a panacea for society's problems. Productivity growth and the additional income it generates are necessary conditions, but not the only ones, for improving the quality of life and increasing the well-being of Canadians.

NOTES

The author would like to thank Someshwar Rao, Daniel Schwanen, France St-Hilaire, an anonymous referee and participants in the 25-26 January 2002 IRPP-CSLS authors' workshop for comments on an earlier version of the paper. He would also like to thank Jeremy Smith for excellent research assistance. The paper draws on earlier work by the author in the productivity area, including Sharpe (1998, 2002*a*), Rao and Sharpe (2002), and Osberg and Sharpe (1998, 2002*a* and 2002*b*).

1 It should be noted that with the recent adoption by Statistics Canada of chain-Fisher indexes, the components of real GDP no longer add up exactly to real GDP.

2 The construction of PPPs requires comparisons of prices across countries. Internationally consistent surveys on the prices of goods and services in expenditure categories have been carried out by the OECD on a regular basis, so estimates of PPPs for GDP and consumer expenditure are available. However, there are no surveys of product prices, so estimates of PPPs for industry output are much harder to compile.

3 Of course, if materials in addition to labour and capital are used as inputs, the bias disappears.

4 Nordhaus (1997) provides a fascinating account of the history of the price of light, showing that on a quality-adjusted basis it has experienced an enormous long-term decline. When the quality-adjusted price of light is integrated into price indexes, he finds, over the 1800-1992 period living standards have increased by between 40 (low-bias assumptions) and 190 (high-bias assumptions) times instead of the conventionally estimated factor of 13. The implications of quality adjustment for the quantification of trends in living standards are very great.

5 See the volumes edited by Griliches (1992) and Diewert et al. (1999) for papers on productivity trends in a number of service industries.

6 For discussion of additional factors affecting the Canada-US manufacturing productivity gap, see papers from the CSLS conference on the Canada-US manufacturing productivity gap posted at www.csls.ca under past events.

7 In July 2002, the Centre for the Study of Living Standards updated its comprehensive productivity database on the basis of the North American Industry Classification System (NAICS), replacing earlier estimates based on the 1980 Standard Industrial Classification (SIC). Using Statistics Canada data on labour input, capital stock and output data, this database provides estimates of labour productivity levels (both output per worker and output per hour), capital productivity levels and TFP indexes for the years 1976-2001 inclusive for Canada (1976-98 on a 1980 SIC basis and 1987-2001 on a NAICS basis) and 1984-2001 for the 10 provinces (1984-98 on a 1980 SIC basis and 1997-2001 on a NAICS basis), giving as much industry disaggregation as confidentiality rules permit. This data base (www.csls.ca) is freely accessible to the public.

REFERENCES

Abramovitz, M., and P.A. David. 1996. "Convergence and Deferred Catch-up: Productivity Leadership and the Waning of American Expectionalism." In *The Mosaic of Economic Growth*, ed. R. Landau, T. Taylor, and G. Wright. Stanford, CA: Stanford University Press.

Baily, M.N. 2002. "The New Economy: Post Mortem or Second Wind?" *Journal of Economic Perspectives* 16(2):3-22.

Boskin, M., and L.J. Lau. 1992. "Capital. Technology and Economic Growth." In *Technology and the Wealth of Nations*, ed. N. Rosenberg, R. Landau, and D. Mowery. Stanford, CA: Stanford University Press.

Denison, E. 1962. *The Sources of Economic Growth in the United States and Alternatives Before Us*. Washington: Brookings Institution.

Department of Finance. 1994, October. *A New Framework for Economic Policy*. Ottawa: Department of Finance.

Diewert, E., A. Nakamura, and A. Sharpe. 1999. *Service Sector Productivity and the Productivity Paradox, Special Issue of the Canadian Journal of Economics*, April.

Easterlin, R.A. 1974. "Does Economic Growth Improve the Human Lot? Some Empirical Evidence." In *Nations and Households in Economic Growth*, ed. P.A. David, and M.W. Reder. New York: Academic Press, pp. 89-125.

—— 1995. "Will Raising the Incomes of All Increase the Happiness of All?" *Journal of Economic Behaviour and Organization* 27(1):35-48.

Gordon, R. 2000. "Does the 'New Economy' Measure Up to the Great Inventions of the Past?" *Journal of Economic Perspectives* 14(4): 49-74.

Griliches, Z. ed. 1992. *Output Measurement in the Service Sectors*. NBER Studies in Income and Wealth, Vol. 56. Chicago: University of Chicago Press.

Harris, R.G. 1999, December. "Determinants of Canadian Productivity Growth: Issues and Prospects." Discussion paper #8. Ottawa: Industry Canada.

Landau, R., T. Taylor, and G. Wright. 1996. "Introduction." In *The Mosaic of Economic Growth*, ed. R. Landau, T. Taylor, and G. Wright. Stanford, CA: Stanford University Press.

Lipsey, R.G., and K. Carlaw. 2000. "What Does Total Factor Productivity Measure?" *International Productivity Monitor* 1:31-40. Available: www.csls.ca

Nordhaus, W. 1997. "Do Real Output and Real Wage Measures Capture Reality? The History of Light Suggests Not." In *The Economics of New Goods*, ed. T. Bresnahan, and R.J. Gordon. NBER. Chicago: University of Chicago Press.

Osberg, L. 1985. "The Measurement of Economic Well-Being," In *Approaches to Economic Well-Being*, ed. D. Laidler. Research Vol. 1, MacDonald Royal Commission. Toronto: University of Toronto Press.

Osberg, L., and A. Sharpe. 1998. "An Index of Economic Well-Being for Canada." Research report 99-1, Applied Research Branch, Strategic Policy. Ottawa: Human Resources Development Canada.

—— 2002a. "The Index of Economic Well-Being." *Indicators: The Journal of Social Health*, 1(2): 24-62.

—— 2002b. "An Index of Economic Well-Being for Selected OECD Countries." *Review of Income and Wealth*, September.

Panel to Review Productivity Statistics. 1979. *Measurement and Interpretation of Productivity*. Washington, D.C.: National Research Council.

Pilat, D. 2001. "Productivity Growth in the OECD Area: Some Recent Findings." *International Productivity Monitor* 3:32-43. Available: www.csls.ca

Putnam, R.D. 2001. *Bowling Alone: The Collapse and Revival of American Community*. New York: Touchstone.

Rao, S., and A. Sharpe, eds. 2002. *Productivity Issues in Canada*. Calgary: University of Calgary Press.

Rao, S., and J. Tang. 2001. "The Contribution of ICTs to Productivity Growth in Canada and the United States in the 1990s." *International Productivity Monitor* 3:3-18. Available: www.csls.ca

Romer, P. 1990. "Endogenous Technical Change." *Journal of Political Economy* 98:S71–S102.

Sharpe, A. 1998. *Productivity: Key to Economic Success*. Centre for the Study of Living Standards for the Atlantic Canada Opportunities Agency. Ottawa and Moncton, NB: CSLS and ACOA. Available: www.csls.ca

—— 1999. "What Do the Canada-US Productivity Numbers Mean?" *Policy Options* May:29-34.

—— 2001. "Determinants of Trends in Living Standards in Canada and the United States, 1989-2000." *International Productivity Monitor* 2:3-10. Available: www.csls.ca

—— 2002a. "Recent Productivity Developments in the United States and Canada: Implications for the Canada-US Productivity and Income Gaps." *International Productivity Monitor* 4:3-14. Available: www.csls.ca

—— 2002b. "The Contribution of Productivity to Economic Well-Being." In *Productivity Issues in Canada*, ed. S. Rao, and A. Sharpe. Calgary: University of Calgary Press.

Sharpe, A., and L. Gharani. 2002. "Trend Productivity and the New Economy." In *Productivity Issues in Canada*, ed. S. Rao, and A. Sharpe. Calgary: University of Calgary Press.

Sharpe, A., S. Rao, and J. Tang. 2002. "Perspectives on Negative Productivity Growth in Service Sector Industries in Canada and the United States." Paper presented at the Services Productivity Workshop, Brookings Institution, Washington, D.C.

Solow, R. 1957. "Technical Change and the Aggregate Production Function." *Review of Economics and Statistics* 39(3):312-320.

Statistics Canada. 1994. *The Size of the Underground Economy in Canada*. Cat. 13-603. Ottawa: Statistics Canada.

Stiroh, K. 2001. "Is IT Driving the US Productivity Revival?" *International Productivity Monitor* 2:31-36.

Van Ark, B., R. Inklaar, and M. Timmer. 2000. "The Canada-US Manufacturing Productivity Gap Revisited: New ICOP Results." Groningen Growth and Development Centre.

Wilson, T., and P. Dungan. 2002. "Productivity in the New Economy." In *Productivity Issues in Canada*, ed. S. Rao, and A. Sharpe. Calgary: University of Calgary Press.

The Long View: Labour Productivity, Labour Income and Living Standards in Canada

Tony Fisher and Doug Hostland

Over long periods of time, productivity is the single most important determinant of a nation's living standard or its level of real income.

(Harris 2002, 166)

Thus, trends in productivity are the key determinants of long-run trends in both absolute and relative living standards. The fall-off in real income growth in Canada and other developed economies since 1973 is a direct result of slower productivity growth.

(Sharpe, this volume)

INTRODUCTION

Higher productivity growth is generally believed to result in higher real income and thereby raised living standards. This is supported by the cross-country comparison reported in Harris (2002, Figure 1), which shows a strong correlation between labour productivity and real wages across countries. Casual observation of Table 1 suggests that labour productivity (GDP per hour worked) and the aggregate real wage (labour income per hour worked) in Canada

have moved together since the mid-1950s.[1] This is reflected in annual growth rates averaged over several years. Labour productivity growth averaged 1.87 percent over the period 1956-2001, while average real wage growth was only slightly lower at 1.84 percent.[2] On this basis, the Canadian experience over the past 46 years appears to support the conventional wisdom that advances in labour productivity eventually get reflected in real wage gains at the aggregate level.

Recent developments in Canada, however, bring into question the stability of the relationship. Chart 1 shows that labour productivity and the aggregate real wage diverged in the

TABLE 1

Labour Productivity and the Aggregate Real Wage (Average Annual Growth Rates)

Period	Labour Productivity (GDP per hour worked)	Aggregate Real Wage (Labour income per hour worked)
1957–2001	1.87	1.84
1957-1973	2.81	2.95
1974-1993	1.19	1.18
1994-2001	1.56	1.11

CHART 1
Labour Productivity, the Aggregate Real Wage and Real GDP Per Capita

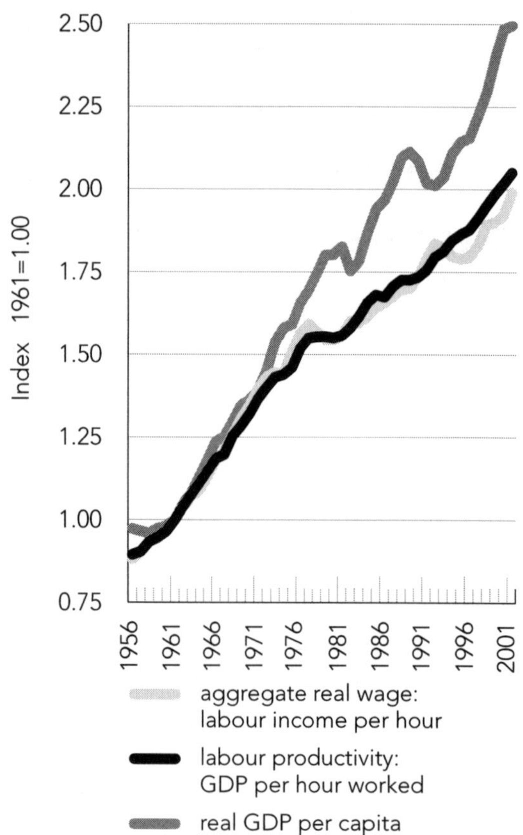

mid-1990s. Labour productivity growth has averaged 1.56 percent since 1994, while the aggregate real wage grew by an average rate of only 1.11 percent. Thus, advances in labour productivity (GDP per hour worked) over the past eight years have exceeded real wage gains (labour income per hour worked) by a substantial margin. This implies that labour income has declined as a proportion of GDP, suggesting that workers have not received the full benefits of labour productivity gains.

This paper examines the developments outlined above from a historical perspective and considers the implications for living standards. The following section examines shifts in labour and non-labour income shares of GDP over the period 1926-2001. The next section discusses the implications for living standards of shifts between labour and non-labour income shares. The final section draws a few policy conclusions from the analysis.

A NATIONAL ACCOUNTING PERSPECTIVE ON HISTORICAL TRENDS

The measure of labour productivity referred to above is defined as GDP per hour worked, while the aggregate real wage is labour income per hour worked. The two measures have the same denominator — hours worked. The ratio of the two measures — the aggregate real wage/labour productivity — is therefore equivalent to labour income/GDP. We focus on labour income as a percentage of GDP mainly because data on hours worked are available beginning in 1956 only, whereas labour income and GDP are available back to 1926. This is also convenient from an accounting perspective, because it enables us to analyse shifts in labour income versus other components of national income.

Labour Income

It is generally believed that real wage gains can be sustained over the long run only if supported by advances in labour productivity (other things being equal). The standard neoclassical model predicts that labour productivity growth (increases in the marginal product of labour) will be reflected in real wage growth (increases in the marginal cost of labour) in the long run.[3] In other words, labour productivity and the aggregate real wage should move together over long periods. Or, equivalently, the labour income share of GDP should tend to revert to its mean.

Before examining this prediction, let us draw attention to a few issues that arise in measuring labour income. The bottom line in Chart 2 shows that wages and salaries[4] increased from under 45 percent of GDP in 1926 to over 55 percent in the mid-1970s. The upward trend largely reflects migration of workers from farms and unincorporated businesses (UBs) into the paid labour force. Chart 3 shows that farm and UB income declined from about 19 percent of GDP in the mid-1940s to about 5 percent in the 1980s. While the agricultural sector continued its decline through to 2001, the income share of the UB sector rose by two percentage points beginning in the early 1980s, largely due to an increase in self-employment. These developments have tended to offset one another, such that the farm and UB income share of GDP has been stable since the early 1980s (see Chart 4).

We modify labour income to take into account changes in the share of farm and UB income as follows: We first calculate the average share of wages, salaries and supplementary labour income as a percentage of GDP less farm and UB income (57 percent over the period 1926-2001).[5] We then apply the constant proportion to divide farm and UB income into a labour and non-labour income component.[6] This section of the paper focuses on before-tax measures of household and corporate income. We consider the implications of changes in taxes less transfers to persons for living standards in the following section.

Chart 2 illustrates the definition of labour income defined above as a percentage of GDP over the period 1926-2001. The series exhibits large, persistent deviations from its historical mean, lasting over a decade during some episodes. For example, the labour income share of GDP was below its mean throughout the 15-year period

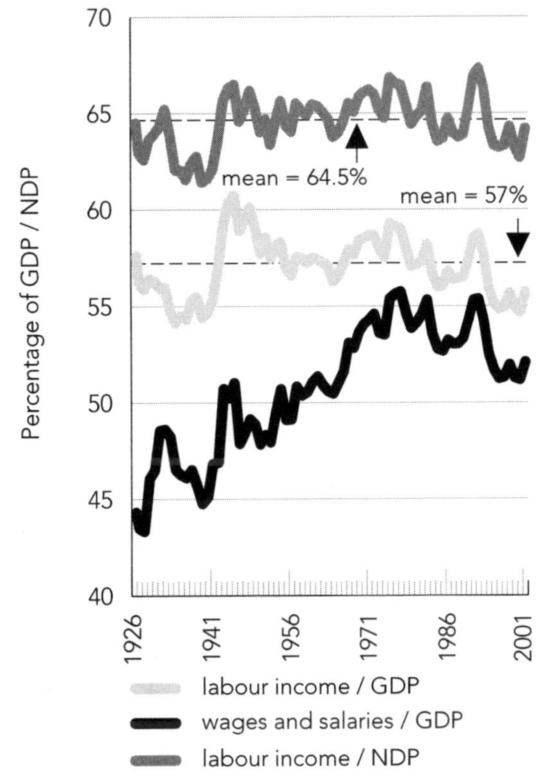

1927-41 and above its mean throughout the 12-year period 1966-77.

More rigorous econometric methods can be used to test whether the labour income share of GDP has tended to revert to its mean over the historical period. A Chow test provides evidence of a shift in the mean in 1994 at the 6 percent level of significance.[7] There is little evidence of a shift, however, when we test for a structural shift at an unknown breakpoint — one cannot reject the null hypothesis of a constant mean even at the 10-percent level of significance. Similarly, unit root tests provide weak evidence that the labour income share of GDP is mean-stationary. This finding contrasts with the results obtained by Hostland (1996). The conflict can be reconciled by the fact that the unit root tests are

CHART 3

Farm and Unincorporated Business Income as a Percentage of GDP

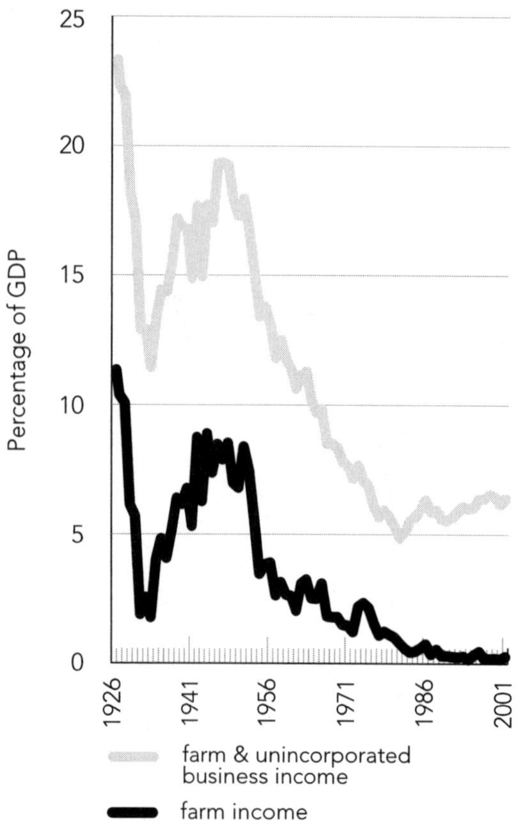

conducted over different sample periods. One can reject the unit root hypothesis at the 1-percent level over the period 1950-94, which corroborates the results reported in Hostland. The evidence in support of mean-stationarity diminishes, however, when the sample period is extended to 2001. One can reject the unit root hypothesis at only the 7-percent level over the period 1950-2001. These results indicate that the decline in the labour income share in 1994 brings into question its tendency to revert to its mean over time. Hence, we conclude that formal statistical tests are inconclusive about whether one can expect the labour income share of GDP to revert to its mean in the future.

Non-Labour Income

Labour income is but one source of household income. Many households receive income from interest and investment earnings. Moreover, retained earnings by corporations are a potential source of income for those households that hold equity (either directly or indirectly, in mutual funds and pension plans). One must also take into account the non-labour component of income earned by farms and UBs. In order to maintain consistency with the before-tax measure of labour income examined above, we include corporate profits before taxes in non-labour income.

Chart 4 illustrates the following three components of non-labour income as percentages of GDP:

> corporate profits before taxes

> interest and investment earnings

> the non-labour component of farm and UB income

Corporate profits as a percentage of GDP declined substantially during the Great Depression in the 1930s and again during the recession in the early 1990s. There was a strong rebound in the mid-1990s, raising corporate profits to an average level of 11 percent of GDP over the period 1995-2001, which is equal to its historical average over the post-war period. The decline in the labour income share of GDP in 1994 therefore cannot be attributed to a rise in corporate profits. Interest and investment income increased from 4 percent of GDP in the early 1970s to a peak of 10 percent in 1982, and then subsequently declined to an average of 5 percent over the four-year period 1998-2001.

Chart 4 shows that many of the shifts in the components of non-labour income have tended to offset one another. Non-labour income exhibited a tendency to revert

CHART 4

Non-Labour Income as a Percentage of
GDP / NDP

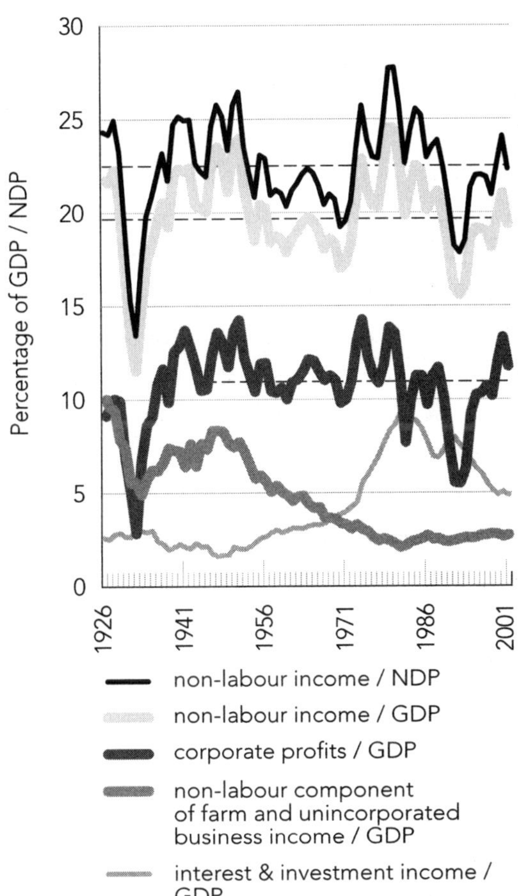

to its mean of about 20 percent of GDP over the period 1926 to 2001. This is supported by unit root tests, which indicate that the non-labour income share of GDP is mean-stationary.[8] The non-labour income share of GDP nonetheless exhibits large, persistent deviations from its mean, some lasting several years.

Other Components of National Income

We now examine components of national income that are not included in the measures of labour and non-labour income examined above. We focus on the following four main components, depicted in Chart 5:

> inventory valuation adjustment (IVA)

> net investment payments to non-residents

> indirect taxes less subsidies

> capital consumption allowances (CCA)

Chart 5 shows that there were sizeable fluctuations in each of these components over the historical period. The IVA share of GDP fluctuated substantially during the inflationary episodes in the 1970s. Net investment payments to non-residents increased from 1.5 percent of GDP in the mid-1970s to 3.5 percent in the early 1990s. Both of these components have shown little change over the past decade, however. Indirect taxes increased considerably from a low of 9.1 percent in 1980 to a peak of 13.4 percent in 1993, before declining to 11.7 percent in 2001. Indirect taxes therefore cannot account for the decline in the labour share of GDP in 1994.[9]

Changes in the CCA income share of GDP play a key role in our analysis. To illustrate, Charts 2 and 4 show labour and non-labour income shares of Net Domestic Product (NDP), defined as GDP less CCA. Both labour income and non-labour income exhibit much smaller fluctuations as shares of NDP versus GDP. Moreover, labour income as a percentage of NDP is only slightly below its historical mean in the 1990s. This indicates that the decline in labour's share of GDP in 1994 can be largely attributed to an increase in CCA. This is supported by formal statistical tests. For example, unit root tests provide strong evidence that the labour income and non-labour income shares of NDP are mean-stationary.

61

CHART 5
Other Components of National Income

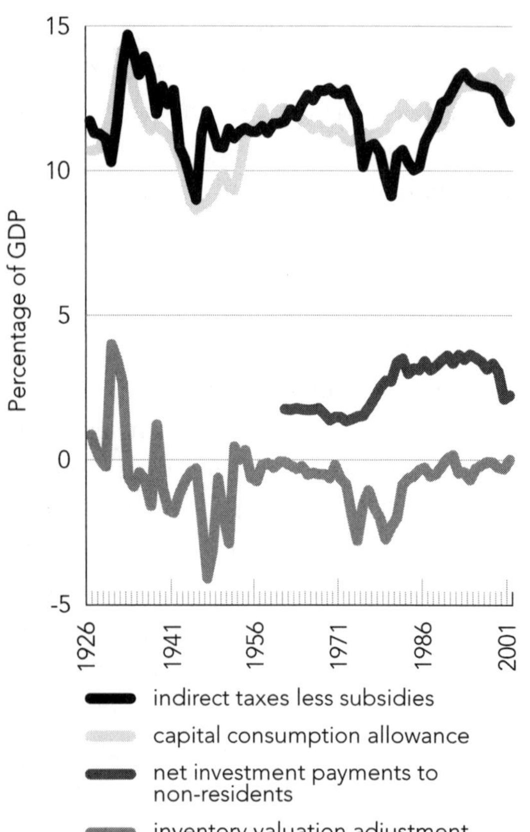

IMPLICATIONS FOR LIVING STANDARDS

We now address the methodological question of whether labour productivity growth in excess of real wage growth necessarily curtails the advancement of living standards.

Consider the case where there is a shift between labour and non-labour income. Since the household sector as a whole owns UBs and corporate equity, income from interest and investments, farms and UBs, and corporate retained earnings augment household wealth. Since not all households have these assets, there can be important implications for the distribution of wealth across house-

holds. The overall effects on living standards are unclear.

Now consider the implications of shifts between labour income and the "other income" components of GDP, namely CCA, IVA and net investment payments to non-residents. An increase in any of these income components clearly reduces household wealth. In particular, the gradual increase in CCA as a percentage of GDP after the 1970s implies that a growing proportion of national income is needed to replace depreciating capital, and hence less income is available to households and corporations for a given level of production. For this reason, NDP (GDP less CCA) per capita is a better measure of living standards than the more conventional GDP per capita measure. Similarly, the reduction in net payments to foreigners as a percentage of GDP since the mid-1990s implies that proportionally more income is retained by domestic households. One should also take this into account when measuring advances in living standards.

Taxes and Living Standards

Chart 6 shows that tax revenues from all sources less transfers to persons[10] increased from 20 percent of GDP in the mid-1980s to an average level of 25 percent over the period 1997-2001. This implies a five-percentage-point reduction in after-tax income as a percentage of GDP. The implications of an increase in the overall tax burden for living standards is complicated by several factors.

Taxes are used to fund fiscal expenditures, which benefit households and businesses. There is strong public support for public expenditures in many areas, health care and education being prime examples. Moreover, public investments in developing physical infrastructure (airports, roads, water, sewerage, public transportation,

CHART 6

The Tax Burden (Total Taxes less Transfers as a Percentage of GDP)

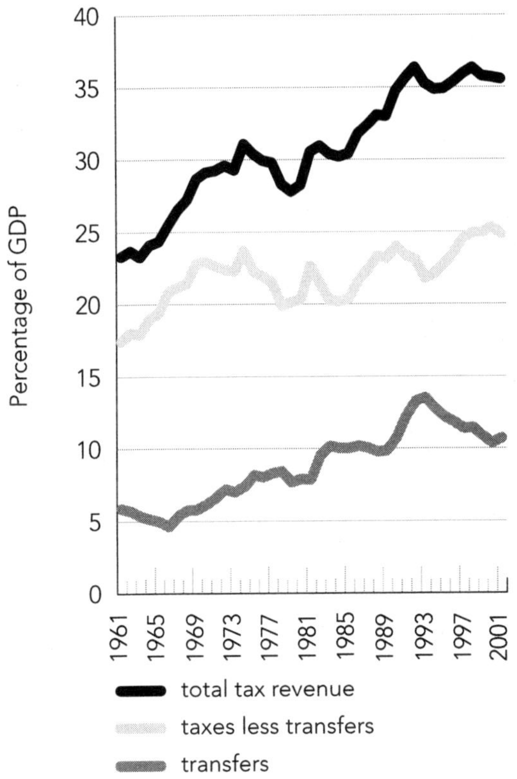

etc.) can boost productivity. Productivity growth can also be enhanced by public investments in research and innovation. On the other hand, high marginal tax rates reduce incentives to work, save and invest, which act to reduce labour supply, capital accumulation and productivity growth. High marginal tax rates can also raise compliance costs associated with tax evasion and avoidance (resulting in more activity in the underground economy, for example). In order to assess the implications of a rising tax burden for living standards, one must weigh the benefits derived from public expenditures against the distortion costs incurred by having to raise tax revenues.

The intertemporal nature of public debt also plays an important role in these calcula-tions. Net public debt increased substantially, from 14 percent of GDP in 1974 to 88 percent in the mid-1990s.[11] From a simple accounting perspective, this reflects a growing fiscal imbalance with expenditures on program spending and debt-service costs exceeding total tax revenues. Net public debt declined to 66 percent of GDP in 2000, a decline of 22.5 percentage points over five years. Higher tax revenues and lower program spending were needed to cover the rising debt-service costs and reduce the debt burden to a sustainable level. The build-up in net public debt from the mid-1970s to the mid-1990s and subsequent decline had an important influence on intertemporal alloca-tion of after-tax incomes. The implications for household wealth are unclear, however, because an increase in net public debt implies higher future tax liabilities.

Changes made to the Canada Pension Plan (CPP) in the mid-1990s are a good exam-ple of this. Increases in CPP contributions were introduced to reduce future unfunded liabili-ties of the plan. In addition, the "pay-as-you-go" funding scheme was modified to include partial funding. These changes have implica-tions for the intertemporal allocation of CPP contributions for individuals, and for inter-generational equity as well, but do not affect household wealth at the aggregate level. The increase in CPP contributions has reduced after-tax incomes, but the implications for national living standards are ambiguous.

The national-income accounting frame-work also falls short in measuring advances in liv-ing standards in other important dimensions. For instance, capital gains earned on real and finan-cial assets are not captured by the national accounts. As a consequence, the above analysis does not include the substantial increase in house-hold wealth arising from the dramatic rise in equity prices in the late 1990s. Similarly, the analysis does not take into account capital gains associated with the effect of unanticipated changes in inflation on the real value of outstanding long-term bonds. In short, the definition of non-labour income outlined above provides an incomplete measure of household wealth.

The analysis also fails to take into account changes in relative consumer versus producer prices that affect the real purchasing power of households. A decrease in consumer prices relative to producer prices implies that households can consume more in real terms for a given level of production. Chart 7 shows that the Consumer Price Index (CPI) declined relative to the GDP price deflator from the early 1930s to the late 1970s, raising the real purchasing power of households. The CPI has subsequently increased relative to the GDP price deflator, eroding the real purchasing power of households. These relative price changes reflect several underlying factors such as movements in the relative price of traded versus non-traded goods. In particular, the depreciation of the Canada-US exchange rate beginning in the mid-1970s raised the prices of imported goods, which make up a larger component of the CPI than the GDP price deflator. It is worth pointing out here that productivity advances abroad can lead to lower import prices and thereby raise the real purchasing power of domestic consumers. For example, technological innovations in the production of semiconductors in the United States over the past decade have led to dramatic reductions in the real price of information and communication technology (ICT) equipment in Canada. This is an example of productivity advances abroad raising the domestic standard of living but having no direct effect on the producer real wage.[12]

CHART 7

Consumer vs. Producer Price Level
(CPI / GDP Price Deflator)

It should also be noted that the measure of labour productivity examined above is defined as GDP per hour worked, whereas advances in living standards are typically measured as GDP per capita. Changes in hours worked per capita therefore lead to a divergence between labour productivity and living standards. Chart 8 shows that hours worked per capita increased throughout the 1960s and 1970s. This reflects changes in demographic factors, as well as labour market developments. Maturing of the baby boom generation over this period raised the working-age component of the population. There was a dramatic increase in the participation of women in the labour force at the same time. These trends were partially offset by a decrease in average weekly hours worked during the 1960s, along with an increase in the unemployment rate in the 1970s. Large cyclical fluctuations in the unem-

CHART 8

Average Annual Hours Worked Per Capita

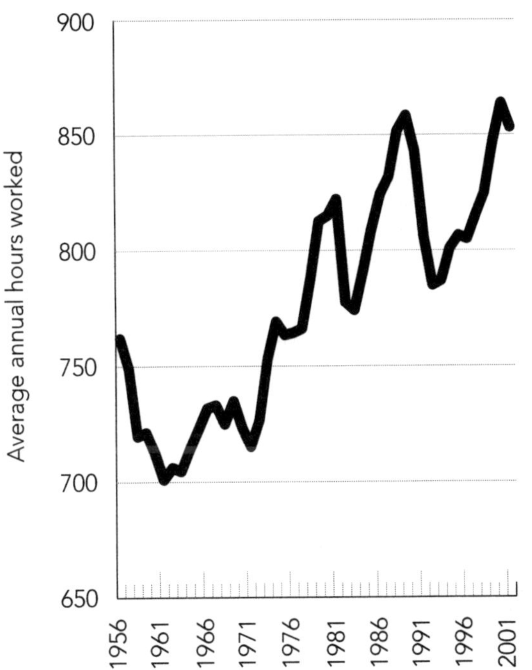

ployment rate throughout the 1980s and 1990s also had a major influence. Overall, the upward trend in hours worked per capita since the 1970s has raised living standards in excess of advances in labour productivity. This is illustrated in Chart 1, which compares indices of GDP per capita versus GDP per hour worked. GDP per capita grew at an average annual rate of 2.0 percent over the period 1971-2001, while GDP per hour worked grew at an average annual rate of only 1.4 percent.

CONCLUSIONS

Our analysis of national income shares indicates that the decline in the labour income share in 1994 can be largely attributed to an increase in capital consumption allowances (CCA). Casual observation and formal statisti-

cal tests indicate that labour income and non-labour income shares of NDP (GDP less CCA) tended to revert to their respective means over the historical period 1926-2001. Deviations can last for periods of several years, however. Hence, one can expect labour productivity growth and real wage gains to diverge for several years at a time.

The implications for living standards are unclear, however. Shifts between labour and non-labour income have little if any effect on household wealth at the aggregate level. The implications of changes in taxes and transfers for persons for living standards are complicated by several factors. Both before-tax and after-tax measures of income can give a misleading impression of advances in living standards. Analysing shifts in national income shares can provide valuable insights into underlying economic developments but does not provide reliable measures of advances in living standards over time or across countries. Several important aspects of living standards are not captured by the national income accounts, including changes in capital gains, relative consumer versus producer prices, and hours worked per capita. Moreover, the national income framework is not amenable to addressing issues such as the distribution of income, which often play a prominent role in assessing policy options.

We conclude that policy-makers should not be concerned with the recent divergence between labour productivity growth and real wage gains. This is not to imply that labour productivity is unimportant for policy analysis. On the contrary, real wage gains can only be sustained by advances in labour productivity, other things being equal. Labour productivity growth has been the chief source of advances in living standards over the historical period (Harris 2002; Sharpe, this volume).

65

Looking to the future, we cannot count on further increases in hours worked per capita to raise living standards. There is little scope for a continued rise in the labour force participation of women. Moreover, impending demographic trends will act to reduce the working-age component of the population and put downward pressure on labour force participation rates as the baby boom generation retires over the next few decades. Advances in labour productivity will be needed just to maintain living standards.

On a final note, we want to stress that NDP per capita provides only a rough measure of our standard of living. Economic progress has several more dimensions. We believe that policy analysis should be based on more meaningful measures of economic progress that take into account changes in household consumption, wealth and the distribution of income. Recent developments by Osberg and Sharpe (2001, 2002) and Sharpe (2002) on measuring "economic well-being" using these kinds of indicators represent a step in this direction. Further analysis along these lines will result in better measures of economic progress over time and across countries, and thereby provide a more reliable basis for policy decisions.

NOTES

The views expressed in this paper are those of the authors and not those of the Department of Finance. The authors would like to thank Pierre Fortin, Craig Riddell and Andrew Sharpe for several valuable comments.

1 This paper focuses on labour productivity and labour income in the total economy (the business and government sectors combined). Labour *income* can be more accurately described as labour *compensation*, because it includes wages, salaries and supplementary labour income. We also focus on the *producer* real wage so that labour income is deflated using the GDP price deflator. The implications of changes in consumer versus producer prices are considered later in the paper. A detailed description of the data is available upon request.

2 The statistics reported in the text and in Table 1 are calculated by averaging annual growth rates. Similar results are obtained by calculating compounded growth rates.

3 This relationship can be derived in the short run using a Cobb-Douglas production function with perfect competition in product and factor markets. The relationship can be derived in the long run under much more general assumptions.

4 More precisely, wages, salaries and supplementary labour income.

5 Average of (wages, salaries and supplementary labour income) / (GDP - farm and UB income).

6 Labour income = wages, salaries and supplementary labour income + 0.57 (farm and UB income).

7 Detailed results obtained from all statistical tests are available upon request.

8 These results are available upon request.

9 Since the components of national income sum to one, by definition, the decline in the labour and non-labour income share of GDP in the early 1990s is equivalent to the increase in the "other income components" listed above.

10 Direct taxes include taxes paid on labour and investment income, corporate income and capital gains, as well as contributions to the Employment Insurance (EI) program and the Canada and Quebec Pension Plans (CPP/QPP). Indirect taxes include taxes on production and imports. Transfers include all transfers made to persons and businesses.

11 This refers to net debt at the federal, provincial and local levels combined on a national accounts basis.

12 The relative consumer/producer price decline would be reflected in a divergence between the consumer real wage and the producer real wage.

REFERENCES

Harris, R. 2002. "Determinants of Productivity Growth: Issues and Prospects." In *Productivity Issues in Canada*, ed. S. Rao and A. Sharpe. Calgary: University of Calgary Press.

Hostland, D. 1996. "Real Wages, Labour Productivity and Employment in Canada: A Historical Perspective." Applied Research Branch HRDC Research Paper W-96-5E. Ottawa: Human Resources Development Canada.

Osberg, L., and A. Sharpe. 2001. "Trends in Economic Well-Being in Canada in the 1990s." In *The Review of Economic Performance and Social Progress 2001: The Longest Decade: Canada in the 1990s*, ed. K. Banting,

A. Sharpe and F. St-Hilaire. Montreal and Ottawa: Institute for Research on Public Policy and Centre for the Study of Living Standards.

Osberg, L., and A. Sharpe. 2002. "An Index of Economic Well-Being for Selected OECD Countries." *Review of Income and Wealth*, 48(3): 291-316.

Sharpe, A. 2002. "The Contribution of Productivity to Economic Well-Being in Canada." In *Productivity Issues in Canada*, ed. S. Rao and A. Sharpe. Calgary: University of Calgary Press.

Understanding Productivity and Income Differentials Among OECD Countries: A Survey

Bart van Ark

INTRODUCTION

The growth experience in the period 1995-2001 in OECD countries represents a major break from the slow growth performance of the previous two decades or so. First, in the mid-1990s economic growth in most OECD countries, notably in the United States, greatly accelerated. Second, across OECD countries the variation in output growth, and more specifically in productivity performance, increased substantially. And third, despite the slowdown in growth during the years 2000 and 2001, the underlying trend in productivity growth begun in 1995 held up. Indeed the United States experienced only a minor slowdown in productivity growth in 2001, whereas Europe and Canada continued along a path of slow productivity growth beginning in the mid-1990s.

An analysis of these trends and an explanation for differences over time and across countries are important for several reasons including the study of social progress. Productivity measures the effectiveness with which inputs (materials, capital and labour) are transformed into output. This transformation process is accommodated for by continuous improvements in the quality of inputs, such as a rise in educational attainment, the creation of knowledge, organizational changes within firms or the setting up of societal networks. All of these factors, which I refer to as intangible investments in the economy, facilitate allocation of inputs to their most productive uses.

Productivity — in this paper, more specifically labour productivity — is important for social progress for two reasons. The first and more obvious reason is that, together with a greater use of labour, productivity positively contributes to per capita income, which is a reasonable proxy for living standards in a country.[1] The second reason is that labour-productivity growth often reflects the accumulation of intangible capital, which itself contributes to social progress, as workers become equipped with more human capital, more knowledge and access to networks, and which may ultimately even lead to the creation of more social capital.[2]

This paper is intended to contribute to our understanding of the link between economic performance and social progress, by reviewing some of the reasons for differences in growth and levels of productivity and per capita income in OECD countries. Figure 1 presents a conceptual framework for studying sources of growth and productivity differentials. This framework is rooted in a traditional growth accounting framework but has several crucial extensions. For instance, it shows the importance of both productivity and increased labour participation in driving growth in per capita income. The next section documents the most recent evidence on this with preliminary estimates up to 2001. It shows that much of the recent growth in per capita income in Europe (and Canada) is driven by a rise in employment/population ratios, although partly offset by a decline in the number of average annual working hours per person. The strong rebound in employment growth in Europe beginning in the mid-1990s has been quite welcome after many years of relatively low rates of labour force participation. But the expansion takes place along a track of slow productivity growth. In contrast, the United States seems to have embarked on an expansion along a high productivity growth path in combination with greater labour utilization.

To investigate the forces behind productivity growth, one can adopt one of two approaches or — ideally — a combination of the two. The first is to look at the sources of growth from the perspective of factor inputs, in particular capital, and their contribution to productivity at the aggregate level. The second is to investigate the contribution of industries to productivity growth, which may be the result of either productivity advances within industries or shifts of resources from low-productivity to high-productivity industries.

Various authors have argued that the recent American productivity advances are due to large investments in information and communications technology (ICT) goods and services and to productivity advances in the ICT-producing sector of the economy (Jorgenson and Stiroh 2000; Oliner and Sichel 2000; Jorgenson 2001). This paper discusses the sparse results available so far on the contribution of ICT capital *vis-à-vis* other physical capital to productivity growth across countries. The evidence suggests an acceleration of ICT investment in most OECD countries, but the contributions of ICT capital to output and productivity growth are generally lower in Europe (and Canada) than in the United States. Unfortunately, for most countries we still lack sufficient data on ICT capital at the industry level to investigate whether the differences in ICT-capital contributions are not at least partly due to differences in industry composition, such as the United States having a larger ICT production sector.

We therefore proceed by looking at the contributions to aggregate labour-productivity growth from the perspective of three subgroups of industries: those classified as producers of ICT goods and services, those that typically are intensive users of ICT, and those that are less intensive users of ICT. The results suggest substantial differences in the productive use of ICT. It also appears that the strong employment growth in European economies is concentrated in industries that are typically not regarded as big users of ICT. Productivity in this group of less-intensive ICT users grows more slowly than elsewhere in the economy, particularly in European countries compared to the United States. Differences in ICT investment and intensity are therefore unlikely to account for the whole story on cross-country productivity differentials.

FIGURE 1

Analytical Framework of Sources of Growth

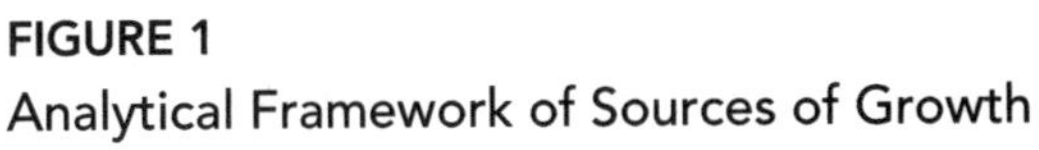

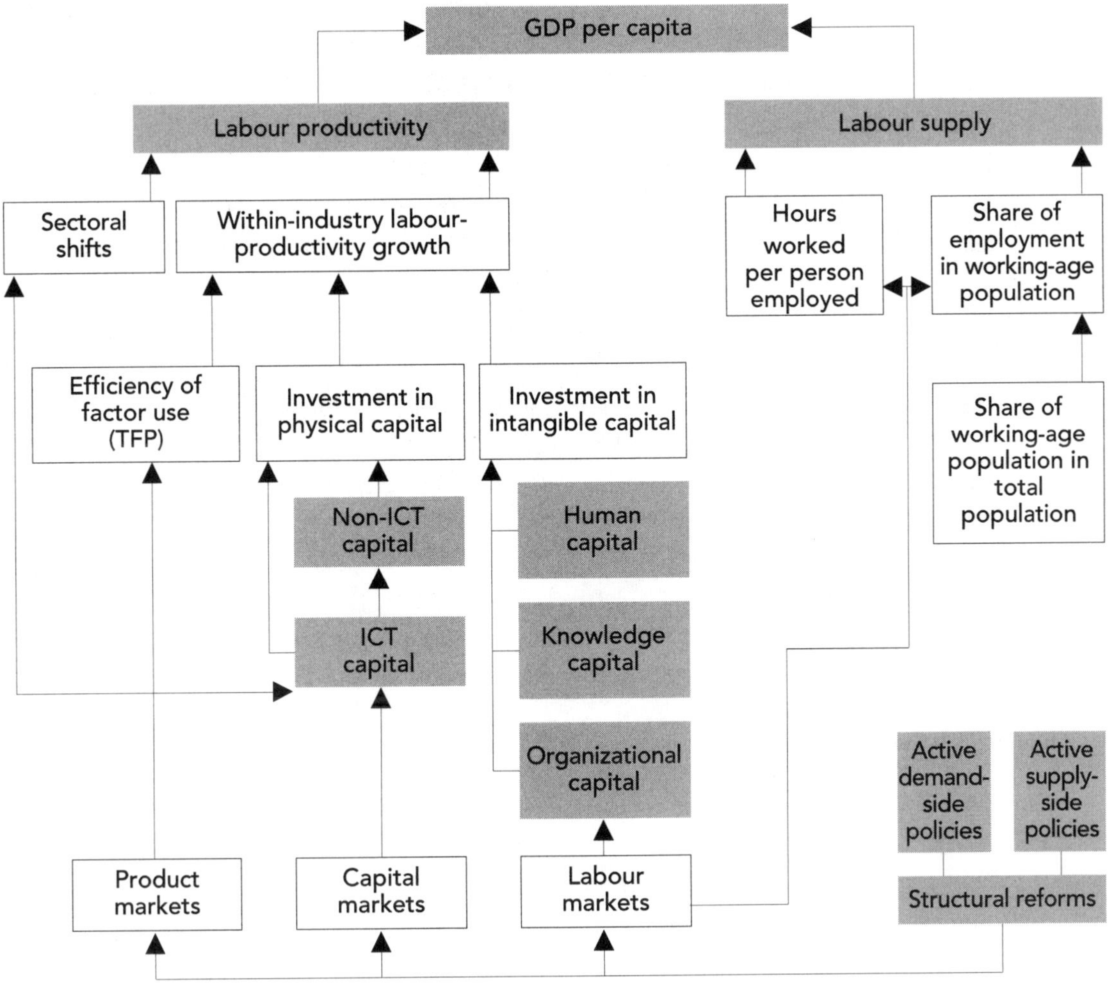

Figure 1 shows that within-industry productivity growth is driven by a second type of investment, namely that in intangible capital. The final section of the paper focuses on differences in the creation of intangible capital that may account for some of the cross-country differentials in productivity growth and levels. Although other classifications are possible, I distinguish among human capital, knowledge capital and organizational capital as components of intangible capital. Using recent numbers from the OECD, which include those components of intangible capital that are easiest to quantify (software, formal higher education, R&D), I find only a weak relation between intangible expenditures and either productivity growth or productivity levels. However, I also argue that a larger effect of intangibles is likely to be found in the organizational component of intangible capital. In the conclusion, I summarize the implications for the link between productivity and social progress and I briefly outline the agenda for further research.

LABOUR PRODUCTIVITY AND INCOME PERFORMANCE IN OECD COUNTRIES

Labour productivity and per capita income are two key measures of economic performance. Per capita income is a reasonable (but incomplete) proxy for living standards. The attractive feature of this measure is that it can be easily linked to labour productivity, thereby opening up the comprehensive framework for investigating the sources of growth by way of growth accounting. Table 1 summarizes per capita income and productivity growth rates for Canada, the United States and the European Union for the periods 1990-95 and 1995-2001.[3] It shows that all three experienced a substantial improvement in per capita income growth in the latter period. In 2001, output growth collapsed across the OECD, but the

TABLE 1

Summary Growth Rates of Per Capita Income, Labour Productivity and Total Hours Worked, Canada, European Union and United States

	Canada	European Union[1]	United States
Per Capita Income Growth (%)			
1990-1995	0.3	1.0	1.4
1995-2001	1.9	2.1	2.6
of which:			
1995-2000	2.2	2.3	3.1
2000-2001	0.3	1.5	0.2
Change in growth rates			
1995-2001 over 1990-1995	1.5	1.1	1.3
2001 over 1995-2000	-1.9	-0.7	-3.0
Labour-Productivity Growth (%)			
1990-1995	1.3	2.5	1.1
1995-2001	0.9	1.3	2.0
of which:			
1995-2000	1.0	1.4	2.0
2000-2001	0.2	0.6	1.8
Change in growth rates			
1995-2001 over 1990-1995	-0.4	-1.2	0.9
2001 over 1995-2000	-0.9	-0.8	-0.2
Total Hours Worked (%)			
1990-1995	0.2	-1.0	1.2
1995-2001	2.2	1.2	1.6
of which:			
1995-2000	2.5	1.2	2.0
2000-2001	0.7	1.1	-0.7
Change in growth rates			
1995-2001 over 1990-1995	2.1	2.2	0.3
2001 over 1995-2000	-1.9	-0.1	-2.7

[1] European Union is weighted average for 14 EU member countries, excluding Luxembourg
Source: Groningen Growth & Development Center & The Conference Board. See McGuckin and van Ark (2002). Based on OECD National Accounts, Economic Outlook, Employment Outlook and Labour Force Statistics, with GDP converted to US$ at 1996 EKS PPPs.

United States appears to be the hardest hit. When the focus is labour-productivity growth, however, the changes in growth rates differ greatly across countries. Whereas the United States experienced a strong acceleration, in both Canada and the European Union productivity growth began to slow down in the mid-1990s.[4] Furthermore, during 2001 productivity slowed much less in the United States than in Canada and Europe.

Differences among countries in terms of growth or relative levels of per capita income and labour productivity are determined by differences in the number of annual working hours per person employed and the share of the population at work. For example, even when two countries have the same productivity levels, a less intensive use of labour — fewer hours of work, more unemployment, lower labour participation rates — can cause one country to have lower per capita income than the other. This relationship can be conveniently expressed in a decomposition linking differences in per capita income and productivity. First, the relative difference in per capita income (O/P) between two countries (X and US) is expressed as the relative difference in labour productivity times the relative difference in labour input per person (H/P):

$$O/P^{\,x\text{-}us} = (O/H)^{\,x\text{-}us} * (H/P)^{\,x\text{-}us} \quad (1)$$

Then, the differences in working hours per person are decomposed into differences in hours worked per person employed (H/E) and the share of employment in the total population (E/P):

$$H/P^{\,x\text{-}us} = (H/E)^{\,x\text{-}us} * (E/P)^{\,x\text{-}us} \quad (2)$$

The employment/population ratio (E/P) can be further broken down into the number of persons employed relative to the total labour force (E/L) (i.e., employed persons plus registered unemployed persons), the ratio of the labour force to all persons aged 15 to 64 ($L/P1564$) (i.e., the working-age population) and the share of the working-age population in the total population ($P1564/P$) (see van Ark and McGuckin, 1999):

$$(E/P)^{\,x\text{-}us} = (E/L)^{\,x\text{-}us} * (L/P1564)^{\,x\text{-}us}$$
$$*(P1564/P)^{\,x\text{-}us} \quad (3)$$

Table 2 shows the relative levels of GDP per capita and labour productivity in 2001. The countries are ranked according to level of per capita income. These estimates are based on the most recent but still preliminary estimates for GDP, employment and hours derived from OECD national accounts and labour force statistics. GDP is converted from national currency to US dollars at 1996 purchasing power parities.[5]

The estimates show that the United States has by far the highest per capita income. Norway comes next, at 17 percentage points (or 5,500 US$) behind the United States. The European Union as a whole is 33 percentage points (or 11,000 US$) behind the United States. Canada is 23 percentage points (or 7,500 US$) behind the United States.

Productivity differences between the United States and most follower countries are considerably smaller than the per capita income differences. In fact, as many as four countries have a higher level of GDP per hour than the United States, namely Belgium (4.5 US$ per hour higher), Norway (3.5 US$), and the Netherlands and France (about 0.5 US$). Indeed the productivity level of the European Union as a whole falls only 13 percentage points (4.5 US$) behind that of the United States, which is 20 percentage points less than the distance between EU and US levels in terms of per capita income. Some 12 percentage points of the 20-percentage-point difference between the EU/US productivity gap and the

73

TABLE 2

Reconciliation of GDP Per Capita and Labour Productivity, OECD Countries, 2001 (preliminary estimates)

	GDP Per Hour Worked[1]		Effect of Working Hours[1]	Effect of Employment Share in Total Population (in % points)				GDP Per Capita	
	in 1996 US$	as % of US	in % points	Unemploy-ment[2]	Labor Force to Population (15-64 yrs)	Population (15-64 yrs) to Total Population	Total[3]	in 1996 US$	as % of US
United States	36.97	100.0	0.0	0.0	0.0	0.0	0.0	33,538	100.0
Norway	40.55	109.7	-28.9	1.0	3.1	-1.6	2.5	27,940	83.3
Ireland	36.36	98.4	-8.8	0.6	-9.7	1.0	-8.1	27,318	81.5
Switzerland	31.73	85.8	-12.8	2.1	5.5	0.6	8.2	27,236	81.2
Denmark	34.58	93.5	-16.4	0.1	2.4	0.4	2.9	26,857	80.1
Canada	30.53	82.6	-3.5	-2.1	-1.2	1.5	-1.8	25,923	77.3
Australia	30.32	82.0	-3.1	-1.7	-1.7	1.5	-1.9	25,818	77.0
Belgium	41.54	112.4	-18.9	-2.1	-15.4	-0.7	-18.2	25,252	75.3
Netherlands	37.32	100.9	-28.1	1.5	-1.1	1.3	1.7	24,989	74.5
Austria	35.46	95.9	-17.9	0.8	-6.3	1.5	-4.0	24,828	74.0
Japan	26.64	72.1	-2.7	-0.1	1.4	1.7	3.0	24,267	72.4
Finland	31.92	86.3	-10.7	-3.4	-2.2	0.9	-4.7	23,795	71.0
Sweden	30.22	81.7	-10.7	-0.3	1.7	-2.0	-0.5	23,636	70.5
Germany	34.20	92.5	-16.6	-2.5	-5.1	1.0	-6.6	23,247	69.3
France	37.63	101.8	-17.8	-3.6	-9.6	-1.6	-14.8	23,176	69.1
Italy	32.53	88.0	-11.0	-4.1	-5.2	0.9	-8.4	22,991	68.6
United Kingdom	29.40	79.5	-9.2	-0.2	-1.8	-0.6	-2.7	22,696	67.7
Spain	27.93	75.6	-1.8	-6.6	-12.2	0.9	-18.0	18,723	55.8
New Zealand	22.49	60.8	-3.6	-0.3	-0.7	-0.8	-1.9	18,560	55.3
Korea	15.18	41.1	13.6	0.4	-8.4	3.3	-4.7	16,747	49.9
Portugal	19.25	52.1	-3.1	0.3	-1.1	1.2	0.4	16,548	49.3
Greece	21.64	58.5	2.4	-3.9	-10.9	0.7	-14.1	15,696	46.8
Czech Rep.	14.43	39.0	3.2	-1.5	-3.0	2.0	-2.5	13,346	39.8
Hungary	17.44	47.2	-1.8	-0.5	-10.8	1.0	-10.4	11,730	35.0
Poland	11.90	32.2	2.7	-4.8	-4.2	1.1	-7.9	9,021	26.9
Mexico	12.13	32.8	3.0	0.9	-9.6	-2.7	-11.5	8,156	24.3
Turkey	10.16	27.5	1.1	-0.9	-10.2	0.2	-10.9	5,933	17.7
European Union[4]	32.30	87.4	-12.1	-2.4	-6.0	0.2	-8.2	22,511	67.1
OECD excl. US	24.87	67.3	-2.8	-1.5	-7.0	0.1	-8.4	18,818	56.1

[1] Calculated on basis of actual hours worked per person per year.
[2] Calculated on basis of standardized unemployment rates from OECD.
[3] Sum of previous columns plus rounding differences.
[4] European Union is weighted average for 14 EU member countries, excluding Luxembourg.
Source: Groningen Growth & Development Center & The Conference Board. See McGuckin and van Ark (2002). Based on *OECD National Accounts, Economic Outlook, Employment Outlook* and *Labour Force Statistics*, with GDP converted to US$ at 1996 EKS PPPs.

EU/US income gap can be explained by fewer working hours per person employed in the European Union (1,609 hours) than in the United States (1,868 hours). Another nine percentage points are due to the ratio of employed persons *vis-à-vis* the total population, 0.43 percent in the

TABLE 3

Growth of GDP Per Capita and Labour Productivity and Differences in Labour Market Indicators, Canada, European Union and United States

	GDP/Capita (US 1990=100)			GDP/Hour Worked (US 1990=100)		
	Canada	European Union[1]	United States	Canada	European Union[1]	United States
1990	85.2	70.2	100.0	87.4	85.4	100.0
1991	82.5	70.6	98.5	88.9	88.1	101.0
1992	82.3	71.3	100.4	91.8	90.4	104.0
1993	83.4	70.7	102.0	92.1	92.3	104.3
1994	85.7	72.4	105.1	92.0	95.0	105.4
1995	86.5	73.9	107.0	93.4	96.6	105.8
1996	86.7	74.9	109.8	92.9	97.7	108.2
1997	88.0	76.5	113.6	94.4	99.7	109.9
1998	89.9	78.5	117.3	95.8	100.5	112.0
1999	93.1	80.2	121.0	97.2	101.5	114.3
2000	96.4	82.7	124.9	98.3	103.5	117.1
2001[2]	96.7	84.0	125.1	98.5	104.2	119.2

	Hours Per Person Employed			Employment/Population (15-64) Share		
	Canada	European Union[1]	United States	Canada	European Union[1]	United States
1990	1799	1657	1819	0.468	0.429	0.475
1991	1764	1637	1808	0.455	0.423	0.466
1992	1736	1633	1799	0.447	0.417	0.464
1993	1760	1624	1815	0.445	0.408	0.466
1994	1789	1624	1825	0.449	0.406	0.472
1995	1771	1621	1840	0.452	0.408	0.475
1996	1789	1619	1838	0.451	0.409	0.477
1997	1782	1616	1848	0.452	0.410	0.483
1998	1766	1620	1864	0.459	0.417	0.486
1999	1772	1617	1872	0.467	0.422	0.489
2000	1789	1609	1879	0.474	0.429	0.491
2001[2]	1789	1609	1868	0.475	0.433	0.486

[1] European Union is weighted average for 14 EU member countries, excluding Luxembourg.
[2] Preliminary estimate.
Note: US hours based on total working hours from BLS Productivity Database divided by total numbers of employed persons from BLS CPS; Canadian hours from CSLS Productivity Database. European average hours from GGDC Total Economy Database.
Source: Groningen Growth and Development Center & The Conference Board (http://www.eco.rug.nl/ GGDC/index-dseries.html). See McGuckin and van Ark (2002).

European Union and 0.49 percent in the United States. Most of the difference in the employment/population ratio is a result of the share of the labour force in the working-age population ($L/P1564$).

In the case of Canada, the productivity gap is 18 percentage points and the per capita income gap is 23 percentage points, for a difference of five percentage points. Three of those percentage points are due to Canada's fewer working hours per person (1,789 hours) and two are due to its lower employment/population ratio (E/P), with some offsetting effects between higher unemployment ($1-E/L$) and lower labour force participation ($L/P1564$) on the one hand and a somewhat larger working-age population share in the total population on the other ($P1564/P$).

CHART 1

Reconciliation of GDP Per Capita and Labour Productivity, Canada, US and European Union

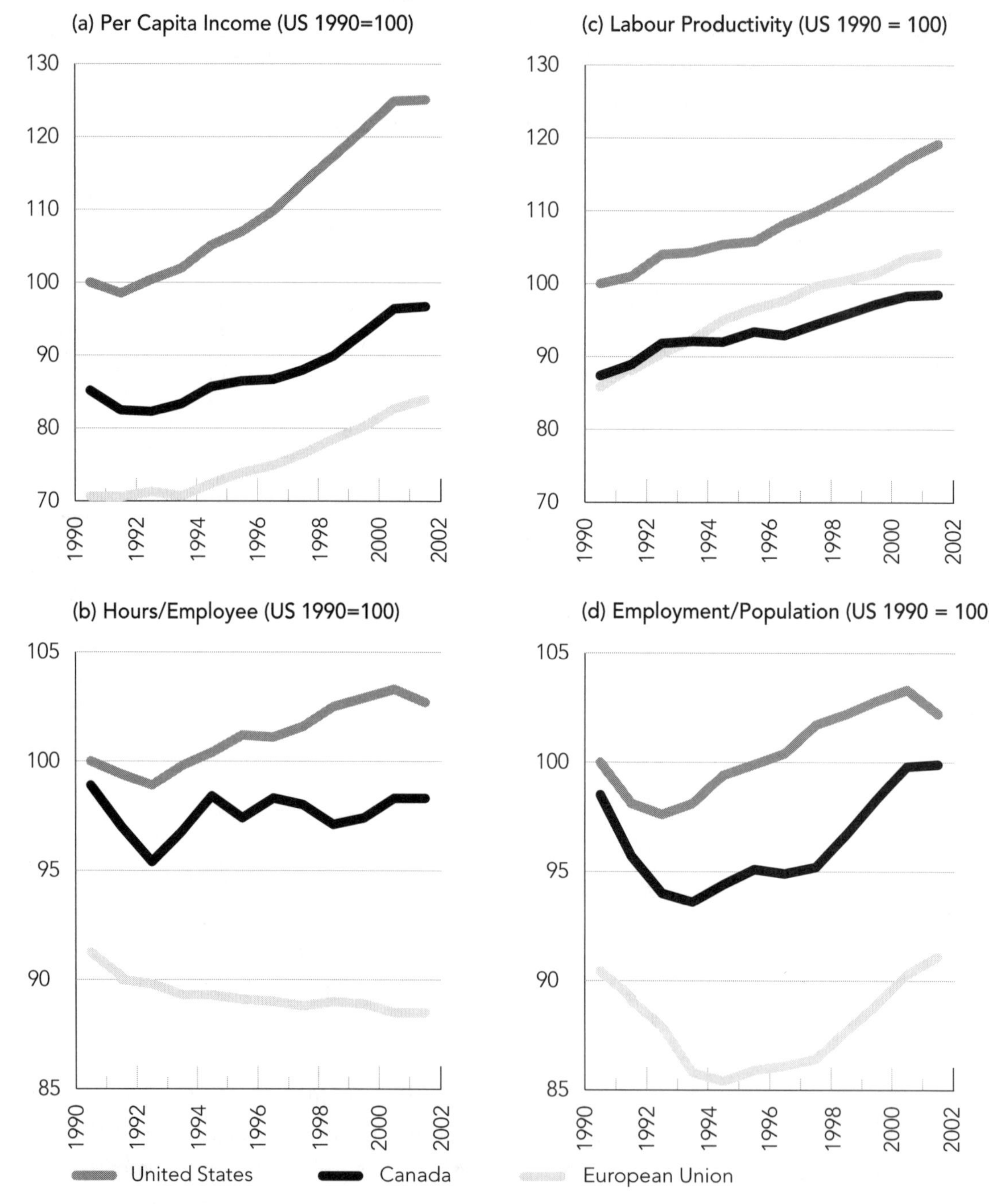

The lower levels of working hours and labour force participation in both the European Union and Canada relative to the United States in 2001 are characteristic of the 1990s (and indeed of the two preceding decades). Until 1997, labour force participation and working hours increased at a much slower rate in these countries than in the United States (Table 3 and Chart 1). In contrast, until about the same time productivity in the follower countries increased faster than in the United States, reflecting their long run process of catching up after the Second World War. Since 1997, however, labour force participation has increased more rapidly in Europe and Canada than in the United States. Yet it still has not led to a further narrowing of the income gap, for two reasons. First, working hours per person continued to decline, particularly in Europe, because of labour time shortening schemes (such as in France and Germany) and the creation of many part-time jobs (such as in the Netherlands). Second, since 1995 productivity growth in the United States has zoomed ahead of both Europe and Canada, which is the main topic of the next section.

In conclusion, at least two factors may have contributed to slower income growth in Europe and Canada relative to the United States during the 1990s. The first is different labour market arrangements, leading to underutilization of the labour potential in Europe and Canada. This explanation dominated the differences in income trends until the mid-1990s. The second factor is slower productivity growth in Europe and Canada. This has been the main explanation for better income performance in the United States in the 1995-2001 period. The search for an explanation for recent differences in per capita income performance should therefore concentrate on the reasons for the differences in productivity growth in 1995-2001.

THE ROLE OF ICT CAPITAL

The rapid increase in ICT investment is seen by many as a key explanation for the acceleration of productivity growth in the United States (OECD 2000*a*, 2001*a*). Some stress that this acceleration is to a large extent due to improved productivity growth in the ICT-producing sector (Jorgenson and Stiroh 2000; Jorgenson 2001). Others point to the increasingly productive use of ICT goods and services elsewhere in the economy (Oliner and Sichel 2000; Baily and Lawrence 2001). Most authors, however, agree that investment in ICT has been heavy and widespread in the United States.[6]

Although the international evidence on the impact of ICT capital on growth is still sparse, there are some comparative growth accounting studies that compile ICT investment as a separate factor input. These studies mostly derive information on ICT expenditure from (private) data sources (e.g., Schreyer 2000; Goldman Sachs 2000; Daveri 2001). The latter include consumer expenditure, which needs to taken out on the basis of crude assumptions to arrive at proxies for ICT investment.

Only recently have attempts been made to obtain genuine investment series for ICT (Colecchia and Schreyer 2001; ECB 2001). The top panel of Table 4 compares the acceleration of real investment growth in ICT in the United States, Canada and five European countries (Finland, France, Germany, Italy and the United Kingdom) for the periods 1990-95 and 1995-99.[7] ICT investment includes IT goods, communications equipment and software. The figures show that throughout the 1990s growth in ICT investment was quite high, and not only in the United States. Canada even experienced a faster rise in ICT investment than the United States during the second half of the 1990s. Moreover, many countries have experienced a greater acceleration of ICT investment than the United States: Canada,

77

TABLE 4

Growth of ICT Investment[1] and Contribution of ICT to Output Growth, Canada, US and Selected European Countries

	Canada	United States	Euro-5[2]	Finland	France	Germany	Italy	UK
			Growth of ICT investment in constant prices					
1990-1995	12.0	13.5	11.6	9.4	14.4	8.8	6.9	18.9
1995-2000[3]	22.8	21.3	17.6	21.0	15.7	17.7	16.3	19.8
Acceleration	10.8	7.8	5.9	11.6	1.2	8.9	9.4	0.9
			Share of ICT investment in total non-residential investment					
1990	13.2	22.5	12.3	13.2	9.4	13.9	13.7	10.1
1995	16.8	26.1	13.7	16.8	10.8	13.3	14.4	15.6
2000	21.4	29.9	15.8	24.1	14.4	16.2	16.3	15.0
			Contribution of ICT services to output growth					
1990-1995	0.30	0.43	0.25	0.24	0.18	0.30	0.21	0.27
1995-2000[3]	0.57	0.87	0.38	0.62	0.33	0.35	0.36	0.47
Acceleration	0.27	0.44	0.13	0.38	0.15	0.05	0.15	0.20

[1] Includes information technology, communications equipment and software.
[2] Five European countries, which are the only ones available from Colecchia and Schreyer (2001), are weighted at ICT-investment shares from Mulder et al. (2001).
[3] For Finland and Italy data are available only up to 1999.
Source: Calculated from Colecchia and Schreyer (2001) and Mulder et al. (2001).

Finland, Germany and Italy all show greater improvement in ICT investment than the United States.

To estimate the contribution of ICT to productivity growth, one must transform the ICT investment numbers into a measure of ICT capital. This is usually done by cumulating the investment figures over the years and applying certain assumptions about the service lives and scrapping patterns of the assets (the "perpetual inventory method"). Service lives of ICT capital goods are substantially shorter than those of other capital goods, which raises the pace at which old capital goods are replaced by new capital goods. Following Schreyer (2000) and Colecchia and Schreyer (2001), output growth (Q) can decomposed into:

$$\hat{Q} = s_L \hat{L} + s_{KC} \hat{K}_C + s_{KN} \hat{K}_N + \hat{A} \qquad (4)$$

where L is labour input, K_c is ICT capital, K_N is all other physical capital and A represents total factor productivity, with the latter being measured as a residual (the hats on the variables indicate percentage rates of change). Labour and capital services are weighted at the share of their respective revenues in total factor income.[8] The bottom panel of Table 4 shows the contribution of ICT capital (K_c) to output growth. Colecchia and Schreyer find a higher ICT contribution for the United States than for the other countries, with the exception of Finland.[9] Indeed the larger share of ICT investment in expenditure (also shown in Table 4), not the faster growth rate of ICT investment, accounts for the greater contribution from ICT capital in the United States. Daveri (2001), who covers a larger group of countries but uses adjusted ICT expenditure proxies for investment, largely confirms these results. He finds that the contribution of ICT capital to GDP growth in

European countries varied between 0.31 and 0.64 percentage points over the period 1991-99, compared to 0.94 percentage points in the United States. In an earlier version of his paper, Daveri (2000) also produced estimates for non-European countries, including Australia and Canada, which showed ICT contributions as large as those for the leading group of European countries such as the United Kingdom and the Netherlands.[10]

In this paper we do not go into many of the methodological details concerning the calculation of the contribution of factor inputs to growth, and the interpretation of total factor productivity that emerges as a residual from any growth accounting study. These have been the subject of a long debate that is well summarized in a recent survey article by Hulten (2001). From the perspective of using ICT as a separate capital good in the production function, one of the fundamental problems is the constant returns that characterize the production function and that assume there can be no "supra-normal" returns from ICT beyond that of other capital goods.[11]

Another issue concerns the assumption of Hicks-neutral technical change, which implies that technological progress increases output without changing the proportional distribution among the factor inputs. This viewpoint can be challenged for at least two reasons. First, a distinction can be made between the fraction of investment that is required to keep the capital/output ratio constant (given the state of technology) and the fraction that is induced by the innovations themselves. The latter represents the part of investment that contributes to the outward shift of the production function and therefore represents technological change rather than accumulation.[12] Second, it is generally asserted that ICT is not neutral to the use of factor inputs, as it is typically characterized by high capital-skills complementarity (Berman, Bound and Machin 1998). Although the latter issue is relevant from the perspective of investment in intangible capital, which will be discussed in the last section, I have not tried to resolve the links between the factor inputs that go beyond measuring to also explain productivity differentials among countries.

At this stage suffice to note that the figures reported in Table 4 suggest that ICT investment is one of the causes of slower productivity growth in Europe and Canada compared to the United States. However, even though for most countries the contribution of ICT to output growth is lower than that of the United States, one would expect at least some acceleration in labour-productivity growth (Table 1). Instead, despite the acceleration of ICT investment, labour-productivity growth in many European countries and Canada actually decelerated.

THE ICT-USE DIFFERENTIAL

As many countries still lack the necessary statistics, disaggregation of ICT investment by industry is not possible in the framework of international comparison. An alternative approach is to focus on labour productivity, which requires only output and employment data by industry. Van Ark (2001b) compares the contributions to overall labour-productivity growth of three groups of industries: ICT-producing industries; intensive ICT-using industries; and industries that use ICT less intensively, hereafter referred to as "non-ICT" industries. This approach can shed light on the role of ICT in growth, for several reasons. First, a strong presence of ICT-producing industries (i.e., hardware and software producers), as is the case in the United States and Finland, is in itself an explanation for a greater contribution of ICT investment to growth. Second, a large ICT-producing sector may facilitate the process of diffusing ICT to industries that are major users. Third, some industries in the economy are much more intensive ICT users than others. Particularly intensive users are in found in business and producer services (McGuckin and Stiroh 2001). These are relatively large industries in which most of the employment creation of the past decade was concentrated and which therefore are key to the acceleration of productivity growth. This also implies that a sectoral composition biased against those industries may be a reason for slower productivity growth at the aggregate level.

The precise shares of the three ICT categories in total output depend on the definition of ICT-producing industries and on the empirical distinction between ICT-using industries and non-ICT industries. ICT-producing industries as defined by the OECD include computer hardware and software producers, computer services, and telecommunications equipment and services (OECD 2000*b*). For the definition of ICT-using industries, van Ark (2001*b*) used estimates of ICT investment/output ratios by industry as well as the industry shares of ICT capital for two countries, the United States and the Netherlands.[13] About one third of industries with the highest ICT intensity and/or the highest shares in ICT capital stock are defined as ICT-using industries.

The first two columns of Table 5 show that the output shares of the ICT-producing sector are quite low across the board. Even for the United States the share of ICT production in total economy output is less than 7.5 percent of current-dollar GDP in 1999. With the exception of Finland, the shares of the ICT-producing sector in nominal output increased only slightly. The differences in output shares are mainly due to larger shares of ICT manufacturing industries in Japan, the United States and Finland.

The third and fourth columns of Table 5 show the shares of ICT-using industries in GDP. The United States is again characterized by larger output shares than all the other OECD countries except the Netherlands. However, the differences in output share of the ICT-using sector are smaller than for the ICT-producing sector. The differences in shares between the ICT-using sector are due to differences in industry composition across countries. For example, the relatively high output share for the Netherlands is due to the larger share of chemicals in ICT-using manufacturing and of business services in ICT-using services. To measure the contribution of the ICT producing sector, the ICT-using sector and the non-ICT sector to the growth of labour productivity, a traditional shift-share analysis was employed. This implies that labour productivity for the total economy (P) can be perceived as the sum of the productivity contributions of three sectors (i) distinguished above weighted at their labour share ($L_i/L=S_i$):[14]

$$P = \frac{Y}{L} = \sum_{i=l}^{n} (\frac{Y_i}{L_i})(\frac{L_i}{L}) = \sum_{i=l}^{n} (P_i S_i)$$

Table 6 shows the contribution of the ICT-producing sector, the ICT-using sector and the non-ICT sector to the growth of labour productivity from 1990 to 1999, with the period being divided into two sub-periods, 1990-95 and 1995-99.[15] In the United States, the ICT-producing sector and the ICT-using sector together accounted for almost two-thirds of labour-productivity growth during the latter period (0.6 + 1.4 as a share of 2.5). In all other countries except Finland the combined contri-

TABLE 5

Output Shares of ICT-producing, ICT-using and Non-ICT Industries, Selected OECD Countries, 1990 and 1999 (as % of GDP at current basic prices)

	ICT-producing Industries as % of Total Economy[1]		ICT-using Industries as % of Total Economy[2]		"Non-ICT" Sector as % of Total Economy	
	1990	1999	1990	1999	1990	1999
Canada[3]	4.2	4.8	20.3	20.9	75.5	74.3
Denmark	4.3	4.7	18.5	19.2	77.2	76.1
Finland	4.6	9.6	16.3	16.3	79.1	74.1
France[4]	5.0	5.3	19.6	19.4	75.4	75.3
Germany[5]	5.4	5.3	21.0	20.8	73.6	73.9
Italy	4.4	5.0	21.2	21.6	74.4	73.4
Japan[4]	6.0	6.3	22.0	21.4	72.0	72.3
Netherlands	4.5	5.5	22.9	25.4	72.6	69.1
United Kingdom	5.7	7.0	21.6	22.4	72.7	70.6
United States	6.5	7.3	21.0	25.0	72.5	67.7

[1] The ICT-producing sector consist of IT hardware, radio, television and communication equipment, medical appliances and instruments and appliances for measurement (together the ICT industry) and telecommunication and computer services (together ICT services).
[2] The distinction between intensive ICT-using industries and "non-ICT" industries is largely based on studies by McGuckin and Stiroh (2001) and the National Science Foundation (2000) for the United States, making use of ICT investment/output ratios and ICT capital stock shares by industry.
[3] For Canada, value added at current prices for 1999 is derived by extrapolating 1996 current price estimate to 1999 with index in constant prices and using average deflators for 1990-1996.
[4] For France and Japan for 1998.
[5] For Germany for 1991 and 1998.
Source: Van Ark (2001*b*).

bution of ICT production and ICT use was lower in absolute terms.[16] Table 6 also shows that in almost all countries ICT production (with the exception of Denmark) and ICT use (with the exception of Italy and to a lesser extent Japan and the United Kingdom) contributed positively to *acceleration* in labour-productivity growth during the second half of the 1990s compared to the first half. However, in several European countries, notably Denmark, Finland, Germany, Italy, the Netherlands and the United Kingdom, the non-ICT sector contributed negatively to labour productivity acceleration, offsetting the positive effects of ICT production and ICT use. The mirror-image of the slowdown in productivity growth in the non-ICT sector is the rapid acceleration in employment growth in this part of the economy during 1995-99. Only in the United States did employment expansion go together with a substantial gain in labour productivity. These effects may relate to differences in the pace of structural reforms in labour and product markets (McGuckin and van Ark 2001).

In conclusion, despite a somewhat smaller role for ICT-producing industries and a moderate positive growth effect from intensive ICT-using industries, the core of the productivity problem in Europe, Canada and Japan seems to lie as much in the non-ICT sector of the economy as in the intensive ICT-using industries. In Europe the recent employment expansion has not been accompanied by the creation of employment in sectors with rapid productive growth in the way that it has in the United States. Hence we now shift our focus to another type of investment, one that is cur-

TABLE 6

Contribution by Sector to Labour-Productivity Growth, Selected OECD Countries, 1990-1995 and 1995-1999 (in percentage points)

	ICT-producing Sector	ICT-using Sector	Non-ICT Sector	Total Economy
Canada (1990-1995)	0.2	0.3	0.7	1.2
Canada (1995-1999)	0.3	0.4	0.3	1.0
Acceleration/deceleration	0.1	0.1	-0.4	-0.2
Denmark (1990-1995)	0.3	0.2	1.6	2.0
Denmark (1995-1999)	0.2	0.6	0.2	1.0
Acceleration/deceleration	-0.1	0.4	-1.4	-1.0
Finland (1990-1995)	0.6	0.1	2.7	3.3
Finland (1995-1999)	1.4	0.6	0.7	2.7
Acceleration/deceleration	0.8	0.5	-2.0	-0.6
France (1990-1995)	0.2	0.2	0.8	1.1
France (1995-1998)	0.4	0.2	0.7	1.3
Acceleration/deceleration	0.2	0.0	-0.1	0.2
Germany (1991-1995)	0.1	0.5	1.5	2.1
Germany (1995-1998)	0.4	0.5	0.7	1.7
Acceleration/deceleration	0.3	0.0	-0.7	-0.4
Italy (1990-1995)	0.2	0.5	1.1	1.8
Italy (1995-1999)	0.3	0.2	0.1	0.6
Acceleration/deceleration	0.1	-0.3	-1.0	-1.2
Japan (1990-1995)	0.3	0.4	0.1	0.8
Japan (1995-1998)	0.4	0.3	0.1	0.8
Acceleration/deceleration	0.1	-0.1	0.0	0.0
Netherlands (1990-1995)	0.1	0.3	0.9	1.3
Netherlands (1995-1999)	0.5	0.6	-0.2	0.9
Acceleration/deceleration	0.4	0.3	-1.1	-0.3
United Kingdom (1990-1995)	0.4	0.6	1.5	2.5
United Kingdom (1995-1999)	0.6	0.5	0.1	1.2
Acceleration/deceleration	0.2	-0.1	-1.4	-1.3
United States (1990-1995)	0.3	0.3	0.5	1.2
United States (1995-1999)	0.6	1.4	0.5	2.5
Acceleration/deceleration	0.3	1.1	0.0	1.3

Source: Van Ark (2001b) and McGuckin and van Ark (2001).

rently seen as an important engine of growth, the creation of intangible capital.

INTANGIBLE CAPITAL: THE MISSING LINK?

The creation of a knowledge-based economy is now at the top of the economic policy agenda in many industrialized nations. For example, the Lisbon Declaration of the European Union in spring 2000 identified the knowledge-based economy as key to the creation of a competitive economy.[17] Policy-oriented organizations such as the OECD have made the investigation of knowledge creation a priority on their research agenda.[18] The academic literature has also given renewed attention to the contribution of intangible capital to growth, even though the topic is not at all new.[19] The renewed urgency to deal with the issue is partly related to the rise of ICT. ICT is a typical general purpose technology, characterized by its broad scope of applications across the economy and its ability to generate a continuous stream of cost-reducing innovations (Bresnahan and Trajtenberg 1995). Its successful diffusion is facilitated by investment in human capital, knowledge capital and organizational capital, together labelled "investment in intangible capital" (Brynjolfsson and Hitt 2000).

Despite its acknowledged importance, the problems concerning the conceptualization of intangible capital, and its measurement and integration into a production function or growth accounting framework, are still huge and largely unresolved. Various definitions of intangible capital are possible with different coverage, but most are offsprings of Schumpeter's (1934) classification, including the development of new products and production processes, organizational change, management, marketing and finance. A distinction can be made between narrow and broad concepts of intangible capital. The narrow concept deals mainly with human capital and knowledge capital (see Figure 2). With the rise of "new growth theory" in the 1980s and 1990s, these components are now well rooted in mainstream neoclassical growth theory. New growth models have improved the modelling of increasing returns and interactions among input variables that are typical of intangible assets. The broad concept of intangible capital emphasizes the facilitative role of intangible capital in the search for new technologies. It assigns a clear role to the attributes of the entrepreneur and his or her ability to raise organizational capital.[20]

From the growth accounting perspective that is pursued in this paper, the narrower concept of intangible capital is more attractive

because of its roots in the production function and its focus on measurement of human capital and knowledge capital at the macroeconomic or industry level.[21] Howitt (1996) argues that knowledge creation can be treated as capital formation because it "can be produced, exchanged and used in the production of other goods, or in the production of itself. It can also be stored, although subject to depreciation, as when people forget or let their skills deteriorate, and subject also to obsolescence, as when new knowledge comes along to supersede it" (99-100). Diewert (2001) clearly defines knowledge in the context of production theory as "the set of input and output combinations that a local establishment could produce…[in a] given time period t" (93). Hence, investment in knowledge capital refers to an outward shift of the traditional production function referred to above in the section on the role of ICT capital.

For both Howitt (1996) and Diewert (2001), the inherent measurement problems of intangible capital go beyond those of tangible capital, despite their similar characteristics. Howitt classifies these measurement problems as follows:

The knowledge-input problem. This concerns the measurement of the resources devoted to the creation of knowledge, which often cannot be distinguished unambiguously from other inputs, such as labour and capital.

The knowledge-investment problem. This refers to the output of the process of knowledge creation, which typically is not measured at all because knowledge does not for the most part produce a commodity or service.

The quality-improvement problem. This relates to the need to pick up on improvements in goods and services that result from knowledge creation. It is an inherent part of the criticism of official statistical measures of prices and real output

---

FIGURE 2

Classification of Intangible Capital

a) **Human capital**
      a-1 Formal education
      a-2 Company training

b) **Knowledge capital**
      b-1 Research and development
      b-2 Patents
      b-3 Licences, brands, copyrights
      b-4 Other technological innovations,
           not related to b1, b2 and b3
      b-5 Software
      b-6 Mineral exploration
      b-7 Experience

c) **Organizational capital**
      c-1 Engineering design
      c-2 Organization design
      c-3 Construction and use of databases
      c-4 Remuneration of innovative ideas

d) **Marketing of new products**

e) **Social capital**

Source: Based on Vosselman (1998) and Young (1998).

---

growth and has induced major statistical programs to improve their measurement methods.[22]

The obsolescence problem. This refers to the need, with any type of capital, to find a measure of depreciation, which is very difficult for intangible capital measures.

So far there has been little attempt to measure intangible capital beyond human capital.[23] Measures of knowledge capital have not gone much beyond the accumulation of R&D expenditure combined with some rough assumptions about its price and depreciation pattern (Griliches and Cockburn 1988). To my knowledge there are no available international comparisons of organizational capital. Moreover, it is difficult to distinguish investment from operating expenses on intangibles. Finally, measurement problems also arise because intangible investments relate to services rather than goods. In conclusion, then, the stock or flow of intangible assets is not easily measured.

The latest international comparisons of intangible expenditure — as opposed to investment or capital — were conducted under the auspices of the OECD by Croes (2000) and Khan (2001). But even Khan, whose work probably represents the state of the art in this area, applies a fairly narrow concept of intangible capital, which includes measures of investment in higher education (including private expenditure), R&D (including the capital expenditure component) and software.[24] Khan adjusted the estimates for the overlap in some expenditure categories, such as that between investment in higher education and R&D, between higher education and software, and between R&D and software.

One simple way to observe the extent to which international differences in investment in intangible capital relate to diversity in productivity performance is to compare rankings of productivity estimates, the share of ICT-producing and ICT-using industries in GDP, and the share of knowledge investment shown in Table 7 of this paper. As discussed in an earlier section, minor differences in relative levels should not be reflected as different rankings. The rankings in Table 7 are therefore indifferent for between-country differences in productivity of less than 2.0 percentage points, differences in the combined ICT production and use share of less than 1.0 percentage points, and differences in the share of knowledge expenditure in total GDP of less than 0.2 percentage points.

The United States ranks second in terms of intangible-investment intensity and between third and sixth in terms of productivity (i.e., its productivity ranking cannot be distinguished from that of France, the Netherlands or Ireland).

TABLE 7

Rankings of Labour Productivity and Income levels, ICT Output Shares and Knowledge Investment/Output Ratios, OECD Countries

	Labour Productivity		Output Share of ITC Producers and Users		Investment in Knowledge as % of GDP (1998)				
	2001 (1996 US$)	rank[1]	%-share 1999	rank[2]	R&D	software	higher education	total	rank[3]
Belgium	112.4	1			1.9	1.4	0.4	3.7	13-16
Norway	109.7	2			1.7	1.2	1.0	4.0	9-14
France	101.8	3-4	24.7	9	2.2	1.2	0.8	4.1	9-14
Netherlands	100.9	3-4	30.9	2	2.0	1.7	0.7	4.3	9-11
United States	100.0	3-6	32.3	1	2.6	1.5	1.9	6.0	2
Ireland	98.4	5-6			1.4	0.5	1.1	3.1	17-18
Austria	95.9	7			1.8	0.9	0.8	3.5	15-17
Denmark	93.5	8-9	23.9	10	1.9	1.5	1.1	4.6	6-8
Germany	92.5	8-9	26.1	6-8	2.3	1.2	0.7	4.2	9-12
Italy	88.0	10-11	27.1	4-5	1.0	0.5	0.6	2.1	20-21
Finland	86.3	10-12	25.9	6-8	2.9	1.2	1.1	5.2	3-4
Switzerland	85.8	11-12			2.8	1.5	0.5	4.8	5-8
Canada	82.6	13-15	25.7	6-8	1.6	1.6	1.5	4.7	6-8
Australia	82.0	13-15			1.5	1.2	1.2	3.9	11-15
Sweden	81.7	13-15			3.8	1.9	0.8	6.5	1
United Kingdom	79.5	16	29.4	3	1.8	1.3	0.8	3.9	11-15
Spain	75.6	17			0.9	0.5	0.8	2.2	20-21
Japan	72.1	18	27.7	4-5	3.0	1.1	0.6	4.7	6-8
New Zealand	60.8	19							
Greece	58.5	20			0.6	0.2	0.9	1.7	22-23
Portugal	52.1	21			0.6	0.4	0.8	1.8	22-23
Hungary	47.2	22			0.7	1.0	0.8	2.6	19
Korea	41.1	23			2.6	0.4	2.2	5.2	3-4
Czech Republic	39.0	24			1.3	1.2	0.8	3.3	16-18
Mexico	32.8	25			0.4	0.4	0.7	1.5	24
Poland	32.2	26							
Turkey	27.5	27							
OECD	76.5				2.2	1.2	1.2	4.7	
European Union[4]	87.4				1.8	1.0	0.7	3.6	

[1] Countries within a 2%-point productivity range were ranked the same.
[2] Countries within a 1%-point ICT-share range were ranked the same.
[3] Countries within a 0.2%-point knowledge-intensity range were ranked the same.
[4] European Union is weighted average for 14 EU member countries, excluding Luxembourg.
Note: Knowledge investment includes R&D (including capital expenditure), higher education (including private expenditure) and software, and is adjusted for overlap between investment in higher education and R&D, between higher education and software, and between R&D and software.
Source: GGDC Total Economy Database, van Ark (2001b), Khan (2001), OECD Science, Technology and Industry Scoreboard, 2001.

The US measure is particularly high because of its expenditure on higher education (1.9 percent, against 1.2 percent for the OECD as a whole and 0.7 percent for the European Union). Moreover, the United States also stands out in terms of its share (the largest) of ICT-producing and intensive ICT-using industries in total GDP. But the relation between relative productivity levels and intangible investment is far from perfect. Indeed the country with the highest level of intangible capital, Sweden, ranks between 13th and 15th in terms of productivity. Moreover, the two countries with productivity levels similar to Sweden's (Canada and Australia) rank much lower in knowledge intensity. Sweden's high R&D intensity is the main reason for its high ranking, which can also be said of Finland and Korea. Canada's sixth to eighth position on the ladder of intangible expenditures is — as with the United States — due to its high expenditure on higher education.

Table 8 looks at the dynamics of the relation among the acceleration in productivity growth, the combined contribution of ICT production and ICT use to labour-productivity growth, and the growth in knowledge expenditure. At first sight this picture looks somewhat better than that for levels. Greece and Ireland, which are among the countries with the greatest accelerations in labour productivity during the second half of the 1990s, also show the fastest growth in intangibles. However, Greece and Ireland are typical catching-up countries, so their rapid growth on both indicators — starting from relatively low levels — comes as no surprise. The United States, which ranks between fifth and seventh in terms of productivity acceleration, ranks between ninth and 15th in terms of growth in knowledge expenditure. Sweden, Finland and Denmark score high on growth in knowledge expenditure, all ranking between third and eighth, but much lower on acceleration of productivity growth during the second half of the 1990s.

It can be concluded that the crude comparisons shown here do not suggest a clear-cut story on the role of intangibles in explaining the recent growth differentials among OECD countries. However, it should be emphasized that these measures relate only to those components of intangible capital that are easy to quantify (R&D, software, education). More importantly, these measures are likely to be most strongly related to tangible investment in new high-tech equipment, such as IT and communications equipment, which complicates the explanatory growth story — an issue briefly touched upon earlier in this paper.

The measures for intangible expenditure used so far do not include various other components of the broad definition of intangible capital, especially organizational capital. Indeed micro research suggests that the successful implementation of ICT is greatly facilitated by investment in organizational capital. For example, a 1996 Danish study showed that the growth in productivity brought about by ICT is four or five times greater if it also involves changes in work-floor methods. Norwegian research has shown that the returns on physical capital are 50 percent higher if the investment in ICT is accompanied by a comprehensive ICT strategy within the particular organization (UNICE 2001). A recent study by Brynjolfsson and Hitt (2000) of 800 US firms found that the overall expenditure on non-material capital that firms must make when introducing ICT is at least 10 times greater than the expenditure on ICT itself.

More recently, Yang and Brynjolfsson (2001) argue that the omission from the growth accounts of expenditures associated with the creation of intangible assets is a main reason for the productivity slowdown which began in 1973. If these expenditures relative to ICT investment have remained constant, then the recent productivity surge may have been underestimated. To make their case, Yang and

TABLE 8

Rankings of Labour-Productivity Growth and Acceleration, Acceleration of ICT Contribution to Productivity Growth and Growth in Knowledge Investment, OECD Countries

	Change in Growth Rate of GDP Per Hour Worked		Contribution of ITC Producers and Users to Acceleration of Labour Productivity (percentage points)		Growth in Knowledge Investment	
	1995-2001 over 1990-95	%-share rank[1]	1995-99 over 1990-95	rank[1]	1991-98	rank[2]
Mexico	3.1	1				
Czech Republic	2.2	2				
Greece	1.9	3			10.1	1-2
Ireland	1.5	4			10.2	1-2
United States	0.9	5-7	1.4	1-2	3.9	9-15
Austria	0.8	5-7			6.3	4-8
Switzerland	0.8	5-7			3.2	10-16
Turkey	0.0	8-14				
Japan	0.0	8-14	0.0	7-10	2.6	14-17
Australia	-0.1	8-14			4.0	9-14
Belgium	-0.1	8-14				
Netherlands	-0.2	8-17	0.7	3	3.8	9-15
Poland	-0.2	8-17				
Sweden	-0.2	8-17			7.6	3-4
New Zealand	-0.3	10-19				
Finland	-0.3	10-19	1.3	1-2	6.8	3-5
Canada	-0.4	12-19	0.2	4-9	2.6	14-17
France	-0.5	12-19	0.2	4-9	3.0	11-17
Hungary	-0.5	12-19			1.6	17-18
United Kingdom	-0.8	20	0.1	4-9	3.6	9-15
Denmark	-1.2	21-22	0.3	4-8	5.9	4-8
Korea	-1.4	21-23				
Portugal	-1.6	22-25			5.4	5-8
Norway	-1.7	23-25			5.6	5-8
Germany	-1.7	23-25	0.3	4-8	2.2	15-18
Spain	-2.2	26-27			4.3	9-13
Italy	-2.3	26-27	-0.2	9-10	-0.6	19
European Union[3]	-1.2				3.1	
OECD	0.1				3.4	

[1] Countries within a 0.2%-point range of productivity acceleration were ranked the same.
[2] Countries within a 0.2%-point knowledge-intensity growth range were ranked the same.
[3] European Union is weighted average for 14 EU member countries, excluding Luxembourg.
Note: Knowledge investment includes R&D (including capital expenditure), higher education (including private expenditure) and software, and is adjusted for overlap between investment in higher education and R&D, between higher education and software, and between R&D and software. See Khan (2001), Figure 6, for a breakdown by subcategory.
Source: GGDC Total Economy Database, van Ark (2001*b*) and Kahn (2001).

Brynjolfsson combine traditional growth accounting with the q-theory of investment. In this way the market valuation of the assets rep-resents their tangible and intangible value. This methodology has not yet been applied to international comparisons.

CONCLUSIONS

We have reviewed some of the reasons for differences in growth performance and changes in the income and productivity gaps among OECD countries. The United States has continued to enjoy the highest per capita income of all OECD countries. Despite their faster GDP growth, most countries have seen little or no narrowing of the per capita income gap between them and the United States over the past decade (see Chart 1). Before the mid-1990s the reasons for the failure to narrow this gap were related to the underperformance of the labour market, which offset the catch-up effects in terms of productivity growth in the follower countries. However, for the period 1995-2001 sluggish productivity growth seems to one of the main causes of slower growth in Europe, Japan and Canada.

Using a conceptual framework, which is rooted in a traditional growth accounting framework — but with several extensions — we focused on two sources of growth differentials. First we looked at the role of the "new economy," in the sense that ICT has been a source of faster productivity growth in the United States. Then we looked at the impact of the creation of intangible capital, which has been identified as a necessary condition for exploiting the productivity advantages of ICT investment.

The analysis suggests that differential realization of the potential to generate productivity accelerations from ICT has contributed to the differential economic growth performance among OECD countries. At the same time, it is difficult to precisely measure the contribution of the various factors at the macroeconomic level. One may even argue that the traditional methods for analysing and measuring the relation between inputs and output at the macroeconomic level are, increasingly, failing to describe the processes that drive changes and differences in growth performance between firms. Nevertheless, the past several years have seen significant advances in growth theory and improvements in measurement methods, even though it is probably true that formal theory is ahead of conceptual clarity and reliable measurement (Howitt 1996). This paper has identified some areas for further research, such as the need to improve the measurement of ICT capital as well as the analysis of its contribution to growth, to extend measures of intangible capital to organizational capital, and to disaggregate input and output measures to the level of industries.

Macroeconomic analysis and measurement of sources of growth remain crucial to our understanding of the relation among economic growth, improvement in living standards and social progress. Per capita income is a reasonable — though imperfect — proxy for living standards, one that is fairly comparable across countries. Many sources of economic growth are themselves direct contributors to improvements in living standards and social progress. For example, the creation of human capital and the creation of knowledge are important determinants of social progress, and income growth provides feedback on the demand for such assets. Efficient allocation of such scarce resources is essential for full exploitation of this potential in order to raise living standards and drive social progress.

NOTES

This paper was written while I was a Visiting Fellow at the Economic Growth Center at Yale University. Parts of the paper are based on earlier work, including van Ark (2001*a*, 2001*b*), van Ark and McGuckin (1999), and McGuckin and van Ark (2001, 2002). I am grateful to Thomas Rymes, Andrew Sharpe and other participants at the IRPP-CSLS workshop "Productivity and Social Progress in Canada: Perspectives and Prospectives" for their helpful comments.

1   See, for example, various issues of the United Nations *Human Development Report*. See also Banting, Sharpe and St-Hilaire (2001).

2   See van Ark (2001*a*) for a more extensive discussion.

3   The 2001 numbers are preliminary figures based on estimates of output and employment from *OECD Economic Outlook* (December 2001).

4   It should be noted that the productivity growth rates for Canada differ from other estimates, which show that productivity growth rates in the Canadian business sector have not decelerated since the mid-1990s (see, e.g., Sharpe's contribution in this volume). The estimates in Table 1 and throughout the remainder of this paper refer to the total economy.

5   For all underlying data and a complete description of sources, see the GGDC Total Economy Database (http://www.eco.rug.nl/ggdc/*index-dseries.html*). All dollar-based estimates are expressed at 1996 price levels. This price measure is preferable because all national currency estimates are converted to US dollars on the basis of purchasing power parities (PPP) for 1996 (OECD 1999). It should be emphasized that exact rankings of these estimates are hazardous given the margin of error involved. Countries within a range of 1-2 percent in terms of productivity and per capita income cannot really be distinguished. See also the final section and Tables 7 and 8. There can be slight differences between the data used here and the data from national statistical offices. Our measures are largely derived from OECD sources (national accounts and labour force statistics). These are most comparable internationally but can differ from national sources because the OECD numbers may be less current or somewhat differently defined. For example, in the case of Canada, mainly because of a lower GDP growth estimate for 2001, the productivity growth rates from the GGDC database are lower than those from Statistics Canada for the period 1995-2001, and therefore show somewhat greater deceleration compared to the early 1990s.

6   However, there are also those who argue that ICT does not have the potential to increase growth by as much as the great innovations of the early 20th century, such as electricity and the combustion engine (Gordon 2000). In addition, Gordon stresses that part of the growth acceleration in the United States is due to pro-cyclical productivity in the upward phase of the business cycle during the second half of the 1990s. Indeed, it is only after a complete cycle has passed that one can fully evaluate the growth impact of ICT.

7   There are as yet no studies available on ICT investment and its contribution to growth for the whole of the European Union. See Daveri (2001) for a study of proxy estimates of ICT investment based on expenditure information. See van Ark et al. (2002) for provisional estimates of ICT investment in 12 out of 15 EU member states.

8   In principle, equation (3) can also be rearranged to obtain the rate of change of labour productivity: $\hat{Q} - \hat{L} = s_{KN}(\hat{K}_N - \hat{L}) + s_{KC}(\hat{K}_C - \hat{L}) + \hat{A}$. It should be recognized that K_C and K_N represent the annual services that ICT capital and other capital goods deliver to output growth, which are weighted at the user cost of individual assets. The latter consist of the gross rate of return times the current price of the given asset. Gross rates of return on ICT capital are typically high to compensate for the rapid price declines of ICT goods. Hence the rapid growth of individual capital services from ICT and the rapidly increasing weights at which these enter the overall measure of capital services account for the increasing contribution of ICT capital to growth (see Schreyer 2000; Colecchia and Schreyer 2001).

9   Finland is a special case, however, as the production of communications equipment is a dominant feature of its manufacturing sector.

10   See van Ark (2002) for a review. At the national level, except for the United States, growth accounting studies with ICT as a separate input, and based on actual investment data instead of reworked expenditure data, were carried out for Finland (Jalava and Pohjola 2001), France (Cette, Mairesse and Kocoglu 2001), the Netherlands (van der Wiel 2001) and the United Kingdom (Oulton 2001). The overall picture suggests that most countries show somewhat lower contributions of ICT to economic growth than the United States, the one exception being Finland.

11   As a result, if there are any supra-normal returns on ICT capital, these end up in the TFP residual. See Schreyer (2000) and Stiroh (2002) for a discussion of this issue.

12   Here, one speaks of an assumption of Harrod-neutral technical change, keeping the capital-output ratio rather than the capital-labour ratio constant. More specifically, following the Harrod-Rymes concept of technical change, the larger investment in ICT will not reduce growth of total factor productivity, but rather will raise it, as ICT improves the efficiency by which the capital goods themselves are produced.

13   The distinction between intensive ICT-using industries and non-ICT industries is largely based on studies by McGuckin and Stiroh (2001) and the National Science Foundation (2000) for the United States. See Table 4 in van Ark (2001*b*) for the exact classification used here. Even though ICT-producing industries are also ICT-

using industries (as the producers themselves also invest heavily in ICT), ICT-producing industries are excluded from the ICT-using sector in the analysis below. The distinction between ICT-using industries and non-ICT industries has two limitations. First, even though we use one and the same classification for all countries, ICT investment-output ratios and ICT capital shares are not necessarily distributed in the same way across countries. For example, even though retailing is within the non-ICT category in the classification used here, it would in fact fall within the ICT-using category in the United States. Second, ICT investment intensity may not always be the best criterion for determining the potential impact of ICT on productivity. In some industries even a small amount of ICT can generate high returns because of its leverage on existing activities. For example, in the oil-extraction industry a small investment in ICT has fundamentally changed the methods by which this industry explores new oil reserves (see Olewiler's contribution in this volume). Obviously the classification used here can be further tested for its sensitivity for other distributions, which is a topic for further research. See van Ark, Inklaar and McGuckin (2002) for a more refined classification and wider ranger of countries.

14   In fact seven sectors instead of three are distinguished in the weighting scheme: ICT-producing manufacturing, ICT-producing services, ICT-using manufacturing, ICT-using services, other manufacturing, other services, and remaining sectors (such as agriculture, mining, construction and public utilities). See van Ark (2001*b*).

15   For France, Germany and Japan the last period ended in 1998; for Germany the first period started in 1991.

16   In Denmark, Italy, Japan, the Netherlands and the United Kingdom the *relative* contribution of ICT production and ICT use was higher than the two-thirds contribution in the United States, but overall labour-productivity growth in these countries was much slower. The relatively rapid productivity growth in Finland is largely accounted for by ICT production.

17   See http://ue.eu.int/Newsroom/LoadDoc.asp?BID=76&DID=60917&LANG=1

18   For example, the OECD Growth Project has targeted knowledge creation as a pillar of sustainable growth. See also the OECD's *Science, Technology and Industry Scoreboard 2001* and STI Review #27 (2001).

19   See Ducharme (1998) for an overview of theory related to intangible capital, which is rooted in human capital theory, theory on technical change, intellectual capital and new growth theory. See Hill (1999) for classification issues. Howitt (1996) and Diewert (2001) deal with the conceptualization of knowledge capital in a production function framework. Mortensen (2000) also discusses the growth accounting work related to intangible capital.

20   The latter is more firmly rooted in evolutionary theory (see, e.g., Clement, Hammerer and Schwarz 1998). Recently, the literature on the sources of growth has moved a step further by looking at the creation of organizational capital not only within the firm but also within the society as a whole, so-called social capital (see, e.g., Helliwell 2001; OECD 2001*b*). Here I abstain from dealing with social capital as the problems concerning its conceptualization and measurement go beyond what can be achieved in the analytical framework I am using. It should be noted, however, that as far as OECD countries are concerned, the empirical work has so far not shown large differences in the effect of social capital on growth (Temple 1999).

21   See Mortensen (2000) for an overview of growth accounting work including intangibles.

22   Much of the criticism of official accounts, particularly price index measurement, stems from the work of Griliches (1992, 1994) and the US Advisory Commission to Study the Consumer Price Index in 1996. Recent attempts by the Bureau of Labor Statistics and the Bureau of Economic Analysis in the United States, supported by a range of studies at the Brookings Institution, as well as new work by national statistical office across the OECD and by Eurostat, have contributed to many improvements in the measurement of prices and real output to deal with quality issues, even though many issues remain unresolved. See Dean and Harper (2001) for a review of work in the United States. See van Ark (2002) for references to other work, in particular in Europe.

23   See OECD (1998) for a review of international comparisons of human capital. Kendrick (1976) is one of the first encompassing studies to measure intangible capital beyond human capital; see also Kendrick (1994).

24   Croes (2000) uses a broader concept including expenditure on private and secondary education and marketing.

REFERENCES

Baily, M.N., and R.Z. Lawrence. 2001. "Do We Have a New Economy?" NBER Working Paper #W8243. Cambridge, MA: National Bureau of Economic Research.

Banting, K., A. Sharpe, and F. St-Hilaire, eds. 2001. *The Review of Economic Performance and Social Progress 2001: The Longest Decade: Canada in the 1990s*. Montreal and Ottawa: Institute for Research on Public Policy and Centre for the Study of Living Standards.

Berman, E., J. Bound, and S. Machin. 1998. "Implications of Skill-Biased Technological Change: International Evidence." *Quarterly Journal of Economics* 113(4): 1245-1280.

Breshnahan, T., and M. Trajtenberg. 1995. "General Purpose Technologies: Engines of Growth." *Journal of Econometrics* 65(1):83-108.

Brynjolfsson, E., and L.M. Hitt. 2000. "Beyond Computation: Information Technology, Organizational Transformation and Business Performance." *Journal of Economic Perspectives* 14(4):23-48.

Cette, G., J. Mairesse, and Y. Kocoglu. 2001. "Diffusion des technologies de l'information et de la communication et croissance économique : le cas de la France sur une longue période (1980-2000)." Mimeograph. Paris: INSEE.

Clement, W., G. Hammerer, and K. Schwarz. 1998. "Intangible Capital from an Evolutionary Perspective." In *Measuring Intangible Investment*. Paris: OECD. Available: http://www.oecd.org/pdf/m00032000/m00032553.pdf

Colecchia, A., and P. Schreyer. 2001. "ICT Investment and Economic Growth in the 1990s: Is the United States a Unique Case? A Comparative Study of Nine OECD Countries." STI Working Paper #2001/7. Paris: OECD.

Croes, M.M. 2000. *Data for Intangibles in Selected OECD Countries*. The Hague: OECD and Ministry of Economic Affairs, Statistics Netherlands.

Daveri, F. 2000. "Is Growth an Information Technology Story in Europe Too?" Mimeograph. Parma: University of Parma and IGIER.

—— 2001. "Information Technology and Growth in Europe." Mimeograph. Parma: University of Parma.

Dean, E.R., and M.J. Harper. 2001. "The BLS Productivity Measurement Program." In *New Developments in Productivity Analysis*, ed. C.R. Hulten, E.R. Dean and M.J. Harper. Chicago: University of Chicago Press.

Diewert, E. 2001. "Which (Old) Ideas on Productivity Measurement Are We Ready to Use?" In *New Developments in Productivity Analysis*, ed. C.R. Hulten, E.R. Dean and M.J. Harper. Chicago: University of Chicago Press.

Ducharme, L.-M. 1998. "Introduction: Main Theories and Concepts." In *Measuring Intangible Investment*. Paris: OECD. Available: http://www.oecd.org/pdf/m00032000/m00032552.pdf

European Central Bank. 2001. "New Technologies and Productivity in the Euro Area." *Monthly Bulletin* (July), pp. 37-48.

Gordon, R.J. 2000. "Does the 'New Economy' Measure Up to the Great Inventions of the Past?" *Journal of Economic Perspectives* 14(4):49-77.

Goldman Sachs 2000. "The IT Revolution – New Data on the Global Impact," *Global Economics Weekly*, October 18, pp. 3-21.

Griliches, Z., ed. 1992. *Output Measurement in the Service Sectors: Studies in Income and Wealth*, Vol. 56. Cambridge, MA, and Chicago: National Bureau of Economic Research and University of Chicago Press.

—— 1994. "Productivity, R&D, and the Data Constraint." *American Economic Review* 84(1):1-23.

Griliches, Z., and I. Cockburn. 1988. "Industry Effects and Appropriability Measures in the Stock Market's Valuation of R&D and Patents." *American Economic Review* (Proceedings Issue) 78(2):419-423.

Helliwell, J. 2001. "Social Capital, the Economy and Well-Being." In *The Review of Economic Performance and Social Progress 2001: The Longest Decade: Canada in the 1990s*, ed. K. Banting, A. Sharpe, and F. St-Hilaire. Montreal and Ottawa: Institute for Research on Public Policy and Centre for the Study of Living Standards.

Hill, P. 1999. "Tangibles, Intangibles, and Services: A New Taxonomy for the Classification of Output." *Canadian Journal of Economics* 32(2): 426-446.

Howitt, P. 1996. "On Some Problems in Measuring Knowledge-Based Growth." In *The Implications of Knowledge-Based Growth for Micro-Economic Policies*, ed. P. Howitt. Calgary: University of Calgary Press.

Hulten, C.R. 2001. "Total Factor Productivity: A Short Biography." In *New Developments in Productivity Analysis*, ed. C.R. Hulten, E.R. Dean, and M.J. Harper. Chicago: University of Chicago Press.

Jalava, J., and M. Pohjola. 2001. "Economic Growth in the New Economy: Evidence from Advanced Economies." Discussion Paper #2001/05. Helsinki: United Nations University WIDER.

Jorgenson, D.W. 2001. "Information Technology and the U.S. Economy." *American Economic Review* 91(1): 1-32.

Jorgenson, D.W., and K.J. Stiroh. 2000. "Raising the Speed Limit: U.S. Economic Growth in the Information Age." *Brookings Papers on Economic Activity* 1:125-235.

Kendrick, J.W. 1976. "The Formation and Stocks of Total Capital." General Series 100. New York: National Bureau of Economic Research.

—— 1994. "Total Capital and Economic Growth." *Atlantic Economic Journal* 1:1-18.

Khan, M. 2001. *Investment in Knowledge*. STI Review #27. Paris: OECD.

Lev, B. 2001. *Intangibles: Management, Measurement and Reporting*. Washington: Brookings Institution.

McGuckin, R.H., and K.J. Stiroh. 2001. "Do Computers Make Output Harder to Measure?" *Journal of Technology Transfer* 26(4): 295-321.

McGuckin, R.H., and B. van Ark. 2001. *Making the Most of the Information Age: Productivity and Structural Reform in the New Economy*. Perspectives on a Global Economy series. Report R-1301-01-RR. New York: Conference Board.

——— 2002. *Productivity 2001: Productivity, Employment and Income in the World's Economies*. New York: Conference Board.

Mortensen, J. 2000. "Intellectual Capital: Economic Theory and Analysis." In *Competitiveness and the Value of Intangible Assets*, ed. P. Buigues, A. Jacquemin and J.-F. Marchipont. Cheltenham: Edward Elgar.

National Science Foundation. 2000. *Science and Engineering Indicators 2000*. Arlington, VA: National Science Foundation.

OECD. 1998. *Human Capital Investment: An International Comparison*. Paris: OECD.

——— 1999. *Purchasing Power Parities and Real Expenditures: 1996 Results*. Paris: OECD.

——— 2000a. *A New Economy? The Changing Role of Information Technology in Growth*. Paris: OECD.

——— 2000b. *Measuring the ICT Sector*. Paris: OECD.

——— 2001a. *The New Economy: Beyond the Hype: The OECD Growth Project*. Paris: OECD.

——— 2001b. *The Well-Being of Nations: The Role of Human and Social Capital*. Paris: OECD.

Oliner, S.D., and D.E. Sichel. 2000. "The Resurgence of Growth in the Late 1990s: Is Information Technology the Story?" *Journal of Economic Perspectives* 14(4):3-22.

Oulton, N. 2001. *ICT and Productivity Growth in the UK*. London: Bank of England.

Schreyer, P. 2000. *The Contribution of Information and Communication Technology to Output Growth: A Study of the G7 Countries*. STI Working Papers 2000/2. Paris: OECD.

Schumpeter, J.A. 1934. *The Theory of Economic Development*. Cambridge, MA: Harvard University Press.

Stiroh, K.J. 2002. "Are ICT Spillovers Driving the New Economy?" *Review of Income and Wealth* 48(1): 33-58.

Temple, J. 1999. "Growth Effects of Education and Social Capital in the OECD Countries." Economics Department Working Paper #263. Paris: OECD.

UNICE. 2001. *The ReNEWed Economy: Business for a Dynamic Europe*. Brussels: Industrial and Employers' Confederations of Europe.

Van Ark, B. 2001a. "Productivity, Technology and Growth: A Matter of Investment?" English translation of lecture given on the occasion of the inauguration of the chair in The Economics of Productivity and Technology Policy, Faculty of Economics, University of Groningen. Available: http://www.eco.rug.nl/medewerk/ark

——— 2001b. *The Renewal of the Old Economy: Europe in an Internationally Comparative Perspective*. STI Working Paper #5. Groningen: University of Groningen. Available: http://www.eco.rug.nl/medewerk/ark

——— 2002. "Measuring the New Economy: An International Comparative Perspective." *Review of Income and Wealth* 48(1): 1-14.

Van Ark, B., and R.H. McGuckin. 1999. "International Labor Productivity and Per Capita Income." *Monthly Labor Review* 122 (7):33-41.

Van Ark, B., van, R. Inklaar, and R. H. McGuckin. 2002. "Changing Gear: Productivity, ICT and Service: Europe and the United States." Mimeograph. Groningen and New York: University of Groningen and The Conference Board.

Van Ark, B., J. Melka, N. Mulder, M.P. Timmer, and G. Ypma. 2002. "ICT Investment and Growth Accounts for the European Union, 1980-2000." Mimeograph. Groningen and Paris: University of Groningen and CEPII.

Van der Wiel, H. 2001. "Does ICT Boost Productivity Growth?" CPB Document #016. The Hague: Netherlands Bureau for Economic Policy Analysis, CPB.

Vosselman, W. 1998. "Initial Guidelines for the Collection and Comparison of Data on Intangible Investment." In *Measuring Intangible Investment*. Paris: OECD. Available: http://www.oecd.org/pdf/ m00032000/m00032582.pdf

Yang, S., and E. Brynjolfsson. 2001. "Intangible Assets and Growth Accounting: Evidence from Computer Investments." Mimeograph. New York and Cambridge, MA: New York University/MIT.

Young, A. 1998. "Towards an Interim Statistical Framework: Selecting the Core Components of Intangible Investment." In *Measuring Intangible Investment*. Paris: OECD. Available: http://www.oecd. org/pdf/m00032000/m00032583.pdf

The Impact of Productivity on Social Well-Being: The Cases of Government Fiscal Balances and Environmental Sustainability

The Impact of Productivity Growth on Government Fiscal Balances

Peter Dungan

INTRODUCTION

The task of this paper is to investigate the sensitivity of Canadian government fiscal balances to alternative long-run productivity growth rates. By implication, the larger the incipient fiscal balances, the greater the scope for the financing of social programs. Whether larger incipient fiscal balances would indeed be used for the financing of social programs, or would instead be used for tax reduction or for paying down government debt, is beyond the scope of this paper. But, clearly, determining the sensitivity of fiscal balances to alternative productivity growth rates is at least an initial step in determining whether alternative productivity growth rates would affect the provision of social programs.

Briefly, we examine the sensitivity of fiscal balances using elements of the FOCUS macroeconometric model of the Canadian economy, maintained at the Institute for Policy Analysis of the University of Toronto, and a "base case" projection of the Canadian economy, and of its fiscal detail, through the year 2030. The simulation strategy, the base case, and the many important assumptions and judgements that had to be made in doing the calculations are described in the following section.

The results of the calculations, both for the main alternatives and for selected variations, are presented in the subsequent section. Briefly, we find that even minor changes in long-run productivity growth rates can cumulate over nearly 30 years to form huge differences in the absolute fiscal resources available to governments, but smaller differences result when these fiscal resources are measured as a share of the achieved GDP.

METHOD: MODELLING FISCAL SENSITIVITY TO ALTERNATIVE LONG-RUN PRODUCTIVITY GROWTH RATES

The first part of this section examines the simulation strategy used to measure the sensitivity of fiscal indicators to alternative productivity growth rates. The second part reviews the base case on which the calculations are made, while the third catalogues the important assumptions and judgements that were required in order to produce the calculations.

The simulation strategy employed here parallels, in part, the technique used by the finance department in recent budgets and fiscal statements in estimating the implicit size of the fiscal dividend — see, for example, the November 2001 *Budget* (Finance Canada 2001) and the November 2000 Fiscal Statement (Finance Canada 2000). For these exercises, the finance department had either three or four macroeconometric modelling groups (of which the Policy and Economic Analysis Program was one) tie their models to a common consensus view of the performance of the economy over a five-year horizon. It then asked the groups to calculate, using their models, federal revenues and endogenous expenditures (that is, those driven by economic indicators, such as employment insurance payouts). In effect, only parts of each macro model were used — namely, the fiscal modules. These were not full-model simulations, as much economic behaviour — for example, the evolution of inflation, real growth, interest rates and the exchange rate — was tied to a common set of numbers.

For the current exercise, we begin with a base-case projection of the Canadian economy through the year 2030 developed by the Policy and Economic Analysis Program at the Institute for Policy Analysis. A projection this far into the future will naturally draw considerable attention, and probably criticism, as discussed in the section immediately below. However, the base case and what it says about the long-term fiscal future of Canada are not the emphasis of this paper. Instead, we are concerned with the *sensitivity* of this projection to alternative productivity growth paths.

Alternative productivity growth paths can occur for wide variety of reasons and can have many different implications.[1] As we explore several of the variations, it seems sensible — indeed necessary — to simplify the exercise and to make some strong assumptions about what alternative productivity growth paths would look like. For example, what is one to assume about the shares of aggregate demand under a lower (or higher) productivity growth path? A higher productivity path might or might not involve higher investment expenditure. In this case, and in many others, we have made a simplifying assumption — that the base-case values will persist. A list of these assumptions and judgements is provided below. The important point here is that much of the macro model has been turned off in developing the alternative productivity growth path — just as in the finance department fiscal dividend exercises. We use only the revenue and expenditure blocks of the FOCUS model.

The Base Case to 2030

The calculations begin with a projection for the Canadian economy through the year 2030. We make no pretence about this projection being the definitive analysis of the long-term future of the Canadian economy. There are many outstanding issues requiring further research — notably, the most likely productivity growth rate and the impact of the aging of the baby boom generation on government revenues and expenditures; much work remains to be done in examining all of these issues (on the issue of demographics and its effect on fiscal balances, see, e.g., King and Jackson 2000). The projection presented and briefly examined here is intended as no more

TABLE 1

Base Case: Selected Economic Indicators, 2000-2030

	2000	2005	2010	2015	2020	2025	2030
Real GDP (billions $2000)	1056	1227	1413	1580	1740	1903	2071
Population (millions)	30.7	32.1	33.3	34.4	35.5	36.5	37.2
Real GDP Per Capita (thousands $2000)	34.3	38.2	42.4	45.9	49.0	52.2	55.7
Real GDP Growth Rate (%)	4.4	3.6	2.6	2.1	1.8	1.8	1.7
Population Growth Rate (%)	0.9	0.8	0.7	0.7	0.6	0.5	0.3
Unemployment Rate (%)	6.8	6.5	6.2	6.2	6.2	6.2	6.2
Employed (millions)	14.9	16.1	16.9	17.3	17.4	17.4	17.3
Employment Growth Rate (%)	2.6	1.6	0.7	0.3	0.0	-0.1	0.0
Real GDP/Employed (thousands $2000)	70.8	76.3	83.5	91.5	100.2	109.7	119.6
Productivity Growth Rate (%)	1.8	1.9	1.8	1.8	1.8	1.8	1.7
CPI Inflation Rate (%)	2.7	1.8	1.8	1.8	1.8	1.8	1.8
Gov't of Canada 10-year Bond Rate (%)	5.9	5.8	6.0	6.0	6.0	6.0	6.0
Compound Growth Rates (%)		2000-2010	2010-2020	2020-2030		2000-2030	
Real GDP		3.0	2.1	1.8		2.3	
Population		0.8	0.6	0.5		0.6	
Employment		1.3	0.3	0.0		0.5	
Productivity		1.7	1.8	1.8		1.8	

than a reasonable starting point for the analysis of fiscal sensitivities.

Basic indicators for the projection are presented in Table 1. Included are actual data for the year 2000 (the latest available at the time the projection was prepared) and snapshots at five-year intervals into the future.

As can be seen from the table, the population increases through 2030 but at an ever-decreasing rate.[2] The story is somewhat different for employment. We project that the unemployment rate will settle in the second half of the current decade at slightly higher than 6 percent. While this figure may seem a trifle low to some and high to others, this matters relatively little for the underlying base case; the main point is that the unemployment rate will *stabilize*, which means that it is labour force growth which determines the number of employed persons. In contrast to total population growth, which will continue to be positive (if only barely) through 2030, employment growth is projected to touch zero, and even to become negative, by about the year 2020. The reason for this projection is, of course, the aging of the baby boom generation and the passing of this large cohort into their retirement years.

The base case features a relatively optimistic assumption about productivity growth over the next three decades. Productivity growth, by the way, is measured in the model in the simplest way possible — as the ratio of real GDP to the number of persons employed.[3] As can be seen, we project that productivity growth, in terms of output per worker, will grow an average of about 1.8 percent per year for the next 30 years. This contrasts with the 1.5-percent rate of growth achieved in the 1990s, and with lower figures still for the

1980s and the latter half of the 1970s. Despite this recent historical performance, however, we anticipate that information technology and its gradual dissemination throughout the economy, together with a more educated workforce and the projected relatively high level of investment, will serve to push the average productivity growth rate higher than it has been in the last 20 years. The validity of this assumption is addressed in other papers in this volume.

The combination of relatively strong productivity growth and rapidly diminishing employment growth yields the real GDP values and growth rates seen in Table 1. Measured in year 2000 dollars, real GDP rises from just over $1 trillion in the year 2000 to slightly over $2 trillion by 2030. In per capita terms there is also a significant increase, with a rise of just over 60 percent over the 30-year span. While not all of this extra output goes to consumption, as the projection features strong investment and net export growth, it is still the foundation of a significant increase in the average standard of living.

Finally, note that the CPI inflation rate stabilizes at just under 2 percent throughout the 30-year horizon. We assume that the Bank of Canada will maintain an inflation target of 2 percent, plus or minus 1 percent, for the next three decades, and that prudent behaviour on the part of the central bank will have the inflation rate fall slightly below the 2-percent target on average. With inflation thus stabilized, it is not surprising that longer-term bond yields are also very stable. Our projection for the 10-year bond rate shows a real rate of 4.2 percent — somewhat high by historical standards but in line with strong productivity growth — and therefore high returns on investment in Canada, the United States and much of the world.

Tables 2 through 4 detail the major fiscal indicators of the base case by level of government, while Table 5 shows all governments combined (and with major intergovernmental transfers netted out). It should be noted at the outset that all figures in these tables are calculated on a National Accounts basis, not the more commonly reported Public Accounts basis. The National Accounts measure is consistent with the other components of National Accounts, like GDP and its components, used throughout the FOCUS macroeconometric model.

TABLE 2

Base Case: Federal Government Fiscal Indicators, 2000-2030 (National Accounts Basis)

Fiscal Indicators	2000	2005	2010	2015	2020	2025	2030
In Billions $2000:							
Revenues	194	199	214	234	252	273	295
Program Expenditures	131	156	176	200	223	247	272
of which: Transfers to Provinces	32	38	45	55	64	73	84
Interest on Debt	44	38	34	30	26	22	20
Balance	19	5	4	4	3	3	3
Debt	544	465	401	346	297	254	217
As a Percentage of GDP:							
Revenues	18.4	16.2	15.2	14.8	14.5	14.3	14.2
Program Expenditures	12.4	12.7	12.5	12.7	12.8	13.0	13.1
of which: Transfers to Provinces	3.0	3.1	3.2	3.5	3.7	3.9	4.0
Interest on Debt	4.2	3.1	2.4	1.9	1.5	1.2	1.0
Balance	1.8	0.4	0.3	0.2	0.2	0.2	0.1
Debt	51.6	37.9	28.4	21.9	17.1	13.4	10.5

Table 2 shows the projected fiscal performance of the federal government. (All figures are in dollars with year 2000 purchasing power — that is, inflation effects have been removed.) As can be seen, in the year 2000 the federal government ran a surplus of about $19 billion — the difference between revenues of $194 billion and program expenditures of $131 billion — with an extra $44 billion for interest payments on the national debt. These revenues amounted to over 18 percent of GDP, while federal debt, again on a National Accounts basis, was just over 50 percent of GDP. Our projection assumes that the federal government will, on average, run surpluses, but not as large as those seen at the end of the last decade. Interest on the debt declines steadily as small amounts are paid off each year, while interest rates remain stable. The debt itself gradually declines as GDP grows steadily; thus as a percentage of GDP it is approximately 10 percent in 2030. After the

tax cuts recently put in place, and some further cutting that we project for the second half of the current decade, federal revenues are projected to fall from 18 percent of GDP in 2000 to something close to 14 percent by 2020 and beyond. Program expenditures, however, will actually rise slightly as a share of GDP compared to the year 2000. The primary reason for this, of course, is the declining level and share of interest on the debt, which leaves room for other expenditures even with fixed or falling revenues.

Table 3 shows fiscal indicators for provincial and local governments. On a National Accounts basis, the provinces and territories also ran a surplus in the year 2000, and we project smaller surpluses for most of the years to come. Just as at the federal level, revenues as a share of GDP are projected to decline from 2000 levels during the first half of our projection, largely on the basis of tax cuts already in place or being phased in by a

TABLE 3

Base Case: Provincial, Territorial and Local Government Fiscal Indicators, 2000-2030
(National Accounts Basis)

Provincial/Territorial Governments Fiscal Indicators	2000	2005	2010	2015	2020	2025	2030
In Billions $2000:							
Revenues	230	246	269	292	318	346	376
of which: Federal Transfers	32	38	45	55	64	73	84
Program Expenditures	190	215	242	280	299	329	362
of which: Transfers to Local Governments	32	36	40	45	50	56	63
Interest on Debt	29	26	22	19	16	14	12
Balance	11	5	4	4	4	3	3
As a Percentage of GDP:							
Revenues	21.7	20.0	19.0	18.5	18.3	18.2	18.2
of which: Federal Transfers	3.0	3.1	3.2	3.5	3.7	3.9	4.0
Program Expenditures	18.0	17.5	17.1	17.7	17.2	17.3	17.5
of which: Transfers to Local Governments	3.0	2.9	2.8	2.8	2.9	3.0	3.0
Interest on Debt	2.7	2.1	1.6	1.2	0.9	0.7	0.6
Balance	1.0	0.4	0.3	0.2	0.2	0.2	0.1
Local Governments							
Revenues and Expenditures in billions $2000	79	90	101	113	125	138	151
Revenues and Expenditures as % of GDP	7.5	7.3	7.2	7.2	7.2	7.3	7.3

number of provinces and additional cuts that will be made in the second half of the current decade. However, the reduction in revenues is less pronounced for the provinces than for the federal government. At the same time, increases in expenditures are not as large for the provinces as for the federal government, partly because interest on the debt for the provinces is lower to start with and declines at a slower rate. However, it should be noted that part of the increase in federal expenditures represents increased transfers to the provinces as health-care and education needs predominate in the decades to come.

Local governments are assumed to run balanced budgets, on average, and their revenues and expenditures are therefore almost identical. As can be seen, we project that the size of local government as a share of GDP will remain largely unchanged over the next three decades.

Finally, Table 4 shows the fiscal indicators of the combined Canada and Quebec Pension Plans. Included in the table is an estimate of the cumulative balance or assets of the two plans. The effects of the large increases in pension plan contribution rates over the last several years can be clearly seen in the projection of pension plan revenues and in the large annual balances racked up by the two plans in the middle years of the three-decade span. From 2005 through 2020 the annual balance of the plans exceeds 1 percent of GDP, and the cumulative balances accumulate rapidly — rising from 5.4 percent of GDP in 2000 to a maximum of around 18 percent by about 2025. As the bulk of the baby boomers retire after 2020, there is a pronounced growth in expenditures relative to revenues, although our projection shows the pension plans still running a modest surplus in 2030.

Naturally, the projections for the pension plan balances and cumulative assets are sensitive to both the underlying economic growth rate (which is the focus of this study) and the payout rate. The latter will depend on the extent of disability and non-retirement payments — partly a political decision — and on the increase in the number of benefit claims by women, as this cohort, which showed an enormous increase in labour force participation in the 1960s and 1970s, reaches retirement age. Each of these elements is difficult to estimate.

Assumptions and Judgements Behind the Simulations

In order to run the alternative productivity growth simulations, we had to make a number of major assumptions and judgements. These are described below.

TABLE 4

Base Case: CPP/QPP Fiscal Indicators, 2000-2030 (National Accounts Basis)

Fiscal Indicators	2000	2005	2010	2015	2020	2025	2030
In Billions $2000:							
Revenues	30	43	52	61	69	76	81
Program Expenditures	26	30	35	43	52	64	75
Balance	4	13	17	18	17	12	6
Cumulative Balance (Assets)	57	104	169	238	300	342	353
As a Percentage of GDP:							
Revenues	2.8	3.5	3.7	3.9	4.0	4.0	3.9
Program Expenditures	2.5	2.5	2.5	2.7	3.0	3.3	3.6
Balance	0.4	1.1	1.2	1.1	1.0	0.6	0.3
Cumulative Balance (Assets)	5.4	8.5	11.9	15.1	17.2	18.0	17.0

Source of the change in productivity growth. We assumed that the change in productivity growth originated solely in a different rate of total factor productivity (TFP) growth, not from any contribution of capital. For the moment we leave open the question of whether there is a corresponding increase in the rest of the world or whether the change is confined to Canada.

Components of aggregate demand. A different productivity growth rate may or may not change the underlying shares of aggregate demand — and this, in turn, will have fiscal implications, since some categories of final demand (e.g., consumption) have a greater tax burden than others (e.g., investment or exports). It is difficult to know if a society will translate higher productivity growth into a larger share of consumption or a larger share of investment ("more jam today" or "more jam tomorrow"). A higher productivity growth rate might mean increased competitiveness and higher net exports, but this depends on whether higher productivity growth also occurs in the rest of the world.

In light of these uncertainties it seemed best to assume a neutral stance: in the simulations, all shares of final demand (except government spending) are increased or decreased proportionately to the change in GDP resulting from higher or lower productivity growth.

Unemployment and labour force participation rates. As noted above, the base case has the unemployment rate steady at just above the full-employment rate. Higher or lower productivity growth might conceivably change the latter rate, but the evidence is not compelling either way.[4] In terms of the labour force, both the size of the population and the labour force-participation rate could conceivably change. A higher productivity growth rate, for example, might serve to raise immigration rates, but this is essentially a policy decision. A higher productivity growth rate, and the resultant higher real wage (see below), might increase labour force participation — but it might also decrease it, as some of the higher real-wage returns are taken in the form of leisure or early retirement by households.[5] In the light of all these possibilities, the simplest assumption is to maintain the base-case unemployment and labour force participation — and therefore employment — rates under the alternative productivity growth scenarios.

Prices and exchange rate. While higher or lower productivity growth rates might make the Bank of Canada's job of achieving its inflation targets somewhat easier (or harder), we have little doubt that the net result would be virtually no change in the average inflation rate, since 2 percent is the Bank's inflation target no matter what the underlying productivity growth rate might be. We have therefore not allowed average prices to change from the base case.

As for the exchange rate, changes in Canada's relative competitiveness would depend, as noted above, on whether the productivity growth rate change to be simulated is also occurring in the rest of the world. They would also depend on how Canadians choose to adjust to their own changed productivity path — for example, they might choose to increase their purchases of imported goods, in which case even a higher relative Canadian productivity growth rate would not translate into an appreciation of the Canadian dollar. Once again, the simplest assumption seems to be to keep the exchange rate as it is in the base case.

Real wages. In the FOCUS model, changes in labour productivity show up in changes in

TABLE 5

Base Case: Combined Government[1] Fiscal Indicators, 2000-2030
(National Accounts Basis)

Fiscal Indicators	2000	2005	2010	2015	2020	2025	2030
In Billions $2000:							
Revenues	469	504	551	600	650	703	757
Program Expenditures	362	418	470	536	585	648	714
Interest on Debt (Fed+Prov)	73	64	56	49	42	36	31
Balance	34	22	26	26	24	18	12
As a Percentage of GDP:							
Revenues	44.4	41.0	39.0	37.9	37.4	37.0	36.5
Program Expenditures	34.3	34.0	33.3	33.9	33.6	34.1	34.5
Interest on Debt (Fed+Prov)	6.9	5.2	4.0	3.1	2.4	1.9	1.5
Balance	3.2	1.8	1.8	1.6	1.4	1.0	0.6

[1] Net of intergovernmental transfers.

real wages after a lag of several years. In a long-term simulation the lag becomes unimportant, but we have kept the FOCUS principle that real wages will reflect changes in labour-productivity growth. In the alternative simulations, therefore, the growth rate of real *private-sector* wages is changed by the same amount as the assumed change in labour-productivity growth. The net result of this assumption, and of the assumption of no change in overall employment, means that there is also very little change in the share of wage and salary income in GDP, and in most other income shares, under the alternative productivity growth scenarios.

Nominal interest rates. Nominal interest rates are, of course, simply the sum of real interest rates plus expected future inflation. In the alternative simulations, there is no change in the underlying inflation rate that is anchored by the Bank of Canada's target inflation policy. Whether there would be a change in real interest rates is a more open question. If the productivity growth is assumed to occur in Canada only, it is unlikely that real interest rates would change very much, since these are primarily determined in world capital markets. However,

if the alternative productivity growth is assumed to reflect a worldwide phenomenon, there might indeed be a change in the real interest rate — but by exactly how much remains unclear. Of course, the issue of what happens to interest rates is important for determining the fiscal effects of alternative productivity growth rates. Higher interest rates mean higher payouts of interest on government debt too, which can have important effects in long-term simulations. At the same time, however, there could be higher earnings by the public pension plans on their accumulated assets.

Our initial assumption will be that interest rates in Canada do not change — which would reflect either the fact that the alternative productivity growth rate is confined to Canada or the fact that world real rates are insensitive to the relatively small changes in productivity growth rates that we will be examining. We will, however, develop an alternative scenario in which the real interest rate and the nominal interest rate are changed by some relatively arbitrary amount in response to a change in the productivity growth rate.

Government-sector wages. It is generally recognized that productivity growth is extremely difficult to measure in the public sector and other non-commercial sectors. When goods and services are sold through the market, there is an observable difference between the price at which they are sold and the cost of producing them. National income accountants therefore have at least some chance of determining whether there has been a change in productivity. Government outputs, however, are not sold, and therefore national accounts have no way of determining their market value. According to national accounting conventions, therefore, the value of government output is equal to the value of the inputs — largely labour and government capital stock. Thus productivity growth is unlikely to show up in the public sector under standard national income accounting. If information technology, for example, permits 10 workers in a government office to perform the same functions that previously were performed by a hundred workers, the government output is deemed to have fallen, since the inputs have fallen.

What this all means is that the market competition mechanism that normally passes productivity improvements through to real wages in the private sector is not automatically at work in the public sector. Nonetheless, government still competes for workers with the private sector and, it might be argued, an increase in general labour productivity in the economy will still show up as higher wages in the government sector. On the other side, it might be argued that the greater security of government jobs, and the continual pressure on governments to provide more services and cut taxes, might cause government-sector wages to be much less sensitive than private-sector wages to changes in productivity growth — as has been the case in recent decades.

Our initial assumption in the simulations below is that government wages do indeed change to the same extent as private-sector wages. That is, if we assume a higher productivity growth rate we must also assume a higher rate of wage growth in the public sector — which can add significantly to government-sector costs and blunt the fiscal impact of stronger productivity. (Note that currently approximately 75 percent of government spending on goods and services is wage-based, and this type of spending is just under half of all government spending, which also includes transfers and interest on the public debt.) We will also conduct an alternative simulation in which the pass-through of changes in productivity to government wages does not occur, but this is an extreme alternative. If government wages do not follow the private sector fully, then most likely they will follow it at least partially — but we have no way of knowing by how much. We therefore present a polar case with the caution that government wages are unlikely to be completely unaffected by productivity-based changes in private-sector real wages.

Government spending and taxation. One of the last specifications for the simulations to be conducted is perhaps the most important: what will be the spending or taxation reaction of the government sector? Borrowing on the experience gained during the "fiscal dividend" exercises for the finance department, we make three assumptions. First, government real spending on goods and services is set the same as in the base case. It is true that a scenario of higher or lower productivity growth may very well cause a change in the growth path of government spending, but there are no agreed-upon rules by which this change might occur. We intend to measure the growth or decline in fiscal "room to manoeuvre" that a change in productivity might yield, instead of prejudging how that room to manoeuvre will be used up. Second, we similarly assume that tax rates are unchanged from the base case. Once again, to do otherwise would be to prejudge what governments will do as the room to manoeuvre on the fiscal side becomes smaller or larger. Third, and this might seem unusual, we assume also that governments will pursue the same fiscal balances as they do in the base case. In other words, surpluses or deficits are assumed to be unchanged from the base case. Behind this last assumption is the notion that, in the longer term, governments will avoid deficits, but also that they will see little political gain in running anything above modest surpluses. Should spending needs or taxation change, rather than balances adjusting, corresponding adjustments will be made in other categories of spending or taxation.

Nonetheless, under alternative productivity growth rates, there will clearly be changes in tax revenues, transfer payments and endogenous spending components. Where, then, do these go? Again using the experience of the "fiscal dividend" exercise, it is assumed that they go into *non-taxable* transfers to persons — or, equivalently, a lump-sum change in personal income taxes.

This assumption turns out to be the most neutral in terms of effects on the rest of the economy. To assume that the endogenous responses in taxation, transfers and spending would show up in changes in current spending on goods and services distorts the shares of GDP. Worse still, to assume that they would show up in the fiscal balance is in fact not neutral, because a change in the fiscal balance causes a change in government debt and therefore interest payments on the debt. Because this effect can accumulate rapidly over a long-term

simulation, it gives a false picture of the change in the fiscal room to manoeuvre available to governments. In a high-productivity scenario, for example, government revenues would increase. If these were devoted to debt paydown, interest on the debt would be lower in future years and the fiscal room to manoeuvre would be larger still. However, part of this increase in fiscal room to manoeuvre would simply be the result of the decision to use the initial productivity increase and its effect on revenues to pay down the debt, instead of making some other change in policy. In a scenario of lower productivity growth, it might be expected that fiscal balances would be smaller and debt higher, and therefore that interest payments on the debt would be higher. But again, if governments responded by raising taxes or reducing spending elsewhere, and leaving the fiscal balance unchanged, there would be no change in debt or in interest payments on the debt, and the fiscal room to manoeuvre, while still negative, would be lower than in a case of reduced surpluses and increased debt.[6]

In sum, therefore, the lesson of the fiscal-dividend exercise is that it is better to put incipient changes in fiscal balances into non-taxable transfers to persons rather than into debt paydown or changes in tax rates or government spending — and that is the practice followed here. When the tables for the various simulations report on the fiscal impact by level of government, what they are reporting is this calculation of what would need to be changed in transfers to persons in order to keep the fiscal balance from deviating from the base case.

There is one exception to this rule. For the public pension plans, a change in the productivity growth rate is permitted to change the fiscal balance — and it likely will, since contributions are based on wages that will change with productivity, while payouts are based on inflation, which we assume will not change. Over the next 30 years, higher or lower collections or earnings by the pension plans likely will not significantly alter the currently legislated contribution or payout rates (unless disaster appears imminent). However, the accumulated surplus of the plans likely will vary, and this does, of course, have implications for earnings and balances later in the simulation period.

Intergovernmental transfers. In the wild and wonderful Canadian federal system, large sums of money flow between levels of government. As can be seen in Tables 2 and 3, the federal government transferred about $32 billion to the provinces in 2000, and the provinces transferred almost an equal amount to local governments. While the treatment of intergovernmental transfers does not affect the calculation of the fiscal impact of alternative productivity growth rates for the combined government sector, clearly it does affect the measure of fiscal impacts by different levels of government.

Most of the simulations assume that federal transfers to the provinces will change in proportion to any change in the productivity growth rate — that is, if the economy improves and the federal government collects higher taxes, political pressures will push it in the direction of increasing transfers to the provinces by a proportional amount. However, other outcomes are possible, and one simulation that assumes no change in federal transfers will be presented to gauge the sensitivity of this issue.

Local governments are assumed to balance their budgets on average, with the balancing factor being transfers from the provinces. A change from the base case that tends to increase local spending will therefore cause increased transfers from the provinces to the municipalities, while a rise in local tax collections, all else being equal, will tend to reduce provincial transfers. In this way, the fiscal impact on local governments of alternative productivity growth rates generally ends up as a fiscal impact on the provinces.

RESULTS: FISCAL IMPACTS UNDER HIGH AND LOW PRODUCTIVITY GROWTH RATES

A total of five simulations are presented in this section. The first, and principal, simulation shows the impact of assuming a relatively modest addition of 0.3 percent to the annual productivity growth rate from 2004 through 2030. For this simulation it is assumed: first, that public-sector real wages follow productivity-based increases in real wages in the private sector; second, that federal transfers to the provinces are increased at the same rate as productivity growth; and third, that the interest rates of the base case do not change under the higher assumed productivity growth.

The second simulation follows the first but simply reverses the assumed productivity change to a reduction of 0.3 percent per year (or to a level of roughly 1.5 percent per year through the simulation period). All other assumptions follow Simulation 1.

Simulation 3 assumes an increase in productivity identical to Simulation 1 but assumes no response in public-sector real wages. Simulation 4 again follows Simulation 1, but assumes no response of federal transfers to the provinces. Finally, Simulation 5 also follows Simulation 1 but assumes that interest rates rise an (arbitrary) 0.3 percent in line with higher productivity.

Simulation 1: 0.3-Percent Increase in Productivity Growth

Results for Simulation 1 are displayed in Table 6. The results are depicted in several forms: some — for example, the Productivity Growth Rate or Federal Government Revenues — are the solution levels for this simulation. Note again that all dollar values are expressed in terms of year 2000 dollars, to remove inflation distortion. Other results show the change from the base-case projection described in the second section of the paper. For example, line 2 of the table reminds us that in this simulation the productivity growth rate is 0.3 percentage points above that in the base projection. These changes are sometimes shown in levels (as for the productivity growth rate) and sometimes as a percentage of the base-case projection. Finally, the fiscal impact of the change in productivity growth is shown not only in levels form (in $2000) but also as a percentage of the relevant government expenditures in the base case. The table offers snapshots of the results at five-year intervals from 2005 through 2030, but most of the discussion will focus on results for the last year shown.

The first panel of Table 6 shows the impact of an assumed 0.3-percentage-point higher productivity growth on real GDP and GDP per capita. As can be seen, a relatively small change in productivity growth, if sustained for a long interval, can have large cumulative effects in terms of outcomes. With productivity growth increasing by 0.3 percent between 2004 and 2030, by the year 2030 real GDP would be higher by $171 billion, or a little over 8 percent higher than in the base case, while real GDP per capita would be just over $60,000, and $4,600 above the base-case projection.

For the federal government, the higher productivity growth rate increases revenues by $28 billion by 2030. This is an increase of approximately 9.5 percent above the base case, which is slightly above the 8.3-percent increase in GDP in the simulation. Not surprisingly, the revenue elasticity of the federal government in the model is somewhat greater than one.

Since the federal balance is assumed not to change from base in the simulation, the increase in revenue must be exactly matched by changes in expenditure. Two increases occur automatically, given the assumptions behind this particular simulation: "Other Induced Changes in Expenditures" amount to $6 billion in 2030 and are largely the result of increased payments to federal employees as the federal government must match the real-wage increases gained by private-sector workers under the higher productivity gains. A further $7 billion goes in increased transfers to the provinces, under the assumption that these will move in proportion to higher productivity growth and increased GDP.

What remains, about $15 billion in 2030, is the true fiscal impact of the higher productivity growth — an amount equalling about 5.5 percent of total federal expenditures in the base case. This is the amount that could be used for further tax cuts, new or expanded expenditure programs, or more aggressive debt reduction. (If debt reduction were to be selected, there would, of course, be a compound effect on the fiscal impact, as interest payments on the debt would also be reduced over time — as discussed in the second section.) Note that, because some of the increased federal revenue from higher productivity growth is diverted to higher real wages and higher transfers to the provinces,

TABLE 6

Simulation 1: Productivity Growth 0.3-Percent Increase Per Year — Public-Sector Real Wages Respond (Federal Transfers Respond; Base Interest Rates)

Economic and Fiscal Indicators	2005	2010	2015	2020	2025	2030
Productivity Growth Rate (%)	2.2	2.1	2.1	2.1	2.1	2.0
Change from Base	0.3	0.3	0.3	0.3	0.3	0.3
Real GDP (billions $2000)	1235	1443	1637	1830	2030	2242
Change from Base	7	29	57	89	127	171
% Change from Base	0.6	2.1	3.6	5.1	6.7	8.3
Real GDP Per Capita (thousands $2000)	38.5	43.3	47.5	51.5	55.7	60.3
Change from Base	0.2	0.9	1.6	2.5	3.5	4.6
Federal Government						
Revenues (billions $2000)	200	219	244	267	294	323
Change from Base	1	5	10	15	21	28
Fiscal Impact of Prod'ty Change (billions $2000)						
(after change in transfers to provinces)	1	3	6	9	12	15
Fiscal Impact as % of Base Expenditures	0.6	1.9	3.0	3.9	4.8	5.5
Change in Transfers to Provinces (billions $2000)	0	1	2	3	5	7
Other Induced Changes in Expenditures (billions $2000)	0	1	2	3	5	6
Provincial/Territorial Governments						
Revenues (billions $2000)	248	276	306	339	375	415
Change from Base	2	7	13	21	29	39
Fiscal Impact of Prod'ty Change (billions $2000)						
(after changes in federal and local transfers)	1	4	7	10	14	18
Fiscal Impact as % of Base Expenditures	0.4	1.4	2.3	3.2	4.0	4.7
Change in Transfers to Local Gov't (billions $2000)	0	1	2	3	4	6
Other Induced Changes in Expenditures (billions $2000)	1	2	5	7	11	15
Local Governments						
Revenues (billions $2000)	90	103	116	129	144	159
Change from Base	0	1	3	4	6	8
Fiscal Impact of Prod'ty Change (billions $2000)						
(excluding change in provincial transfers)	0	0	1	1	1	2
Fiscal Impact as % of Base Expenditures	0.1	0.3	0.6	0.8	1.1	1.3
Induced Changes in Expenditures (billions $2000)	0	1	3	4	6	8
Canada and Quebec Pension Plans						
Revenues (billions $2000)	44	53	63	73	82	90
Change from Base	0	1	2	4	6	9
Fiscal Impact of Prod'ty Change (billions $2000)	0	1	2	4	6	9
Fiscal Impact as % of Base Expenditures	0.5	2.6	4.9	7.2	9.6	12.3
Combined Government						
(Net of Intergovernmental Transfers)						
Revenues (billions $2000)	508	566	628	694	765	840
Change from Base	3	13	24	37	53	71
Fiscal Impact of Prod'ty Change (billions $2000)	2	8	15	23	32	42
Fiscal Impact as % of Base Expenditures	0	2	3	4	5	6
Induced Changes in Expenditures (billions $2000)	1	5	9	15	21	29

the federal fiscal impact, as a percentage of base expenditures, rises *less* than in proportion to the increase in GDP.

For the provincial governments, the increase in revenues by 2030 is about $39 billion — or slightly more than 10 percent above

108

base revenues — again, in excess of the 8.3-percent increase in GDP. Of course, these revenue increases include the $7 billion in transfers from the federal government that rose fully with the productivity increase. Again, since provincial balances are assumed not to change, the revenue increase is fully matched by increases in expenditures. First, induced expenditures resulting from higher real wages rise by $15 billion — significantly more than for the federal government, as at the provincial level a larger share of expenditure is allocated to wages. A further $6 billion is transferred to local governments to keep their balances from moving into deficit — on which more immediately below. This leaves $18 billion as the final fiscal impact of the productivity increase, which, at about 4.7 percent of base expenditures, represents a slightly smaller proportional impact than that for the federal government. Again, these funds could be used to cut taxes further, to increase real expenditures or to reduce public debt (with the last having a further compounding effect through reduced interest charges).

Local governments, with a relatively inelastic tax base, show a much smaller proportional revenue increase than the federal or provincial governments. Of the $8 billion in extra revenue in 2030, fully $6 billion results from increased transfers from the provinces and only $2 billion from higher productivity growth. This is the fiscal impact at the local level, and it amounts to only a little over 1 percent of base local expenditures by 2030. However, local governments are also major employers, and we have assumed that public-sector wages will increase in line with productivity improvements in the private sector. Local governments therefore need to pay out an additional $8 billion by 2030 in induced wage expenditures. To do this, they must, in effect, use up their own $2 billion of fiscal impact and obtain an additional $6 billion in transfers from the provincial governments.

For the Canada and Quebec Pension Plans, the dynamics and results differ somewhat from those of the three levels of government. First, the pension plans have no change in induced expenditures to speak of, since they employ few workers of their own and since pension payouts are calibrated on inflation (which has not changed), not on current real wages — although this situation could change with significant real-wage variation in the economy. Second, the balance of the pension plans is not assumed to be fixed, as it is for the three levels of government. Higher productivity growth serves to increase revenues much more than expenditures and leads to larger surpluses and more asset accumulation — and these extra assets themselves also contribute to earnings. By 2030, revenues are above base by $9 billion, or over 12 percent of base expenditures of the pension plans. The percentage increase in revenues is greater than that in GDP, because the higher contributions from wages earlier in the simulation increase the assets of the pension plans and so compound into higher earnings on assets. As can be seen in Table 6, the percentage improvement in fiscal impact steadily widens relative to the percentage change in GDP, reflecting compounding through investment earnings of the pension plans.

Finally, the last panel in Table 6 aggregates the levels of government and nets out intergovernmental transfers. It is estimated that by 2030 aggregate government revenues will have increased by $71 billion, of which $29 billion goes to induced wage expenditures in the public sector and $42 billion, or roughly 6 percent of government expenditures in the base case, are available for tax cuts, expenditure enhancement or debt reduction.

Simulation 2: 0.3-Percent Decrease in Productivity Growth

Simulation 2 is simply Simulation 1 in reverse — productivity growth is assumed to be 0.3 percent lower than in the base case, which is about the average attained by the Canadian economy in the 1990s. The most important thing to note about the simulation is that the results are not simply those of Simulation 1 with changed signs (see Table 7). Compounding matters: 0.3 percent less growth per year does not reduce GDP over 30 years as much as 0.3 percent more growth enhances it. After 30 years, GDP is 7.6 percent below base, while in Simulation 1, with 0.3 percent extra growth, GDP is 8.3 percent above base. There are corresponding proportional effects through the remainder of the results.

While we need not go through the results in detail, one item to note is that the factor of "induced expenditures" works to mitigate the negative impacts of lower productivity growth. For the combined government sector, a 0.3-percent reduction in the productivity growth rate means $66 billion less revenue by 2030, but of this amount $27 billion is "saved" in the form of lower wage expenditures. Nonetheless, there is still a fiscal-impact shortfall of $39 billion, which will have to made up in the form of higher taxes, lower expenditures or less debt paydown. And, as noted in Simulation 1, there is no "induced" effect on the public pension side. Table 7 shows that pension plan revenue would be reduced by $9 billion in 2030 under the assumed lower productivity growth rate. In the base case (see Table 4), the pension plan surplus is only $6 billion in 2030. This would translate into a deficit of $3 billion under the assumed lower productivity growth rate. While this picture does not indicate insolvency — since the pension plans still have large accumulated assets at this point — it does indicate the relative sensitivity of the pension plan system to the underlying productivity growth rate.

Simulation 3: 0.3-Percent Increase in Productivity Growth — No Response of Public-Sector Wages

Simulation 3 assumes the same increase in productivity growth as Simulation 1, but with no response of public-sector wages. As can be seen in Table 8, induced expenditures, aside from the wage response, are very small; therefore, in this simulation virtually all of the increased revenue from higher productivity growth translates into fiscal impact at the combined government level.

Of the government levels, the chief beneficiary of assuming a low wage response is the provincial level. Under the assumptions for this simulation, the federal government is still obliged to increase transfers to the provinces when productivity growth improves, and the federal government — due to transfers and interest payments on the debt — has a smaller share of wage expenditure. Thus, the federal fiscal impact in this simulation increases from $15 to $20 billion — a substantial improvement but much smaller than that at the provincial level, where the impact increases from $18 to $41 billion. Not only do the provinces "save" the expenditure they would have had to make

TABLE 7

Simulation 2: Productivity Growth 0.3-Percent Decrease Per Year — Public-Sector Real Wages Respond (Federal Transfers Respond; Base Interest Rates)

Economic and Fiscal Indicators	2005	2010	2015	2020	2025	2030
Productivity Growth Rate (%)	1.6	1.5	1.5	1.5	1.5	1.4
Change from Base	-0.3	-0.3	-0.3	-0.3	-0.3	-0.3
Real GDP (billions $2000)	1220	1384	1525	1655	1784	1912
Change from Base	-7	-29	-55	-85	-119	-158
% Change from Base	-0.6	-2.0	-3.5	-4.9	-6.3	-7.6
Real GDP Per Capita (thousands $2000)	38.0	41.6	44.3	46.6	48.9	51.4
Change from Base	-0.2	-0.9	-1.6	-2.4	-3.3	-4.3
Federal Government						
Revenues (billions $2000)	198	209	224	238	253	269
Change from Base	-1	-5	-10	-14	-20	-26
Fiscal Impact of Prod'ty Change (billions $2000)						
(after change in transfers to provinces)	-1	-3	-6	-8	-11	-14
Fiscal Impact as % of Base Expenditures	-0.6	-1.9	-2.9	-3.7	-4.5	-5.1
Change in Transfers to Provinces (billions $2000)	0	-1	-2	-3	-5	-6
Other Induced Changes in Expenditures (billions $2000)	0	-1	-2	-3	-4	-6
Provincial/Territorial Governments						
Revenues (billions $2000)	244	262	279	299	319	340
Change from Base	-2	-7	-13	-20	-27	-36
Fiscal Impact of Prod'ty Change (billions $2000)						
(after changes in federal and local transfers)	-1	-4	-7	-10	-13	-16
Fiscal Impact as % of Base Expenditures	-0.4	-1.4	-2.2	-3.0	-3.7	-4.4
Change in Transfers to Local Gov't (billions $2000)	0	-1	-2	-3	-4	-6
Other Induced Changes in Expenditures (billions $2000)	-1	-2	-5	-7	-10	-14
Local Governments						
Revenues (billions $2000)	89	100	111	121	132	144
Change from Base	0	-1	-2	-4	-6	-7
Fiscal Impact of Prod'ty Change (billions $2000)						
(excluding change in provincial transfers)	0	0	-1	-1	-1	-2
Fiscal Impact as % of Base Expenditures	-0.1	-0.3	-0.6	-0.8	-1.0	-1.2
Induced Changes in Expenditures (billions $2000)	0	-1	-2	-4	-6	-7
Canada and Quebec Pension Plans						
Revenues (billions $2000)	43	51	59	65	70	72
Change from Base	0	-1	-2	-4	-6	-9
Fiscal Impact of Prod'ty Change (billions $2000)	0	-1	-2	-4	-6	-9
Fiscal Impact as % of Base Expenditures	-0.5	-2.6	-4.8	-7.0	-9.1	-11.6
Combined Government (Net of Intergovernmental Transfers)						
Revenues (billions $2000)	500	537	573	609	645	679
Change from Base	-3	-13	-23	-36	-50	-66
Fiscal Impact of Prod'ty Change (billions $2000)	-2	-8	-14	-22	-30	-39
Fiscal Impact as % of Base Expenditures	0	-2	-3	-4	-5	-5
Induced Changes in Expenditures (billions $2000)	-1	-5	-9	-14	-20	-27

on their own employees but, because local governments do not have to increase their wage payments (relative to Simulation 1), the provinces need not increase their transfers to the local level. In fact, because the local governments gain some additional revenue and

TABLE 8

Simulation 3: Productivity Growth 0.3-Percent Increase Per Year — No Response of Public-Sector Wages (Federal Transfers Respond; Base Interest Rates)

Economic and Fiscal Indicators	2005	2010	2015	2020	2025	2030
Productivity Growth Rate (%)	2.2	2.1	2.1	2.1	2.1	2.0
Change from Base	0.3	0.3	0.3	0.3	0.3	0.3
Real GDP (billions $2000)	1235	1443	1637	1830	2030	2242
Change from Base	7	29	57	89	127	171
% Change from Base	0.6	2.1	3.6	5.1	6.7	8.3
Federal Government						
Revenues (billions $2000)	201	219	244	268	294	323
Change from Base	1	5	10	15	21	28
Fiscal Impact of Prod'ty Change (billions $2000)						
(after changes in federal and local transfers)	1	4	8	12	16	20
Fiscal Impact as % of Base Expenditures	0.7	2.4	3.9	5.2	6.4	7.4
Change in Transfers to Provinces (billions $2000)	0	1	2	3	5	7
Other Induced Changes in Expenditures (billions $2000)	0	0	0	1	1	1
Provincial/Territorial Governments						
Revenues (billions $2000)	248	276	306	339	376	415
Change from Base	2	7	14	21	30	39
Fiscal Impact of Prod'ty Change (billions $2000)						
(excluding change in federal transfers)	2	8	14	22	31	41
Fiscal Impact as % of Base Expenditures	0.8	2.8	4.9	6.9	8.9	11.0
Change in Transfers to Local Gov't (billions $2000)	0	0	-1	-1	-1	-2
Other Induced Changes in Expenditures (billions $2000)	0	0	0	0	0	0
Local Governments						
Revenues (billions $2000)	90	101	113	125	138	151
Change from Base	0	0	0	0	0	0
Fiscal Impact of Prod'ty Change (billions $2000)						
(excluding change in provincial transfers)	0	0	1	1	1	2
Fiscal Impact as % of Base Expenditures	0.1	0.3	0.6	0.8	1.0	1.2
Induced Changes in Expenditures (billions $2000)	0	0	0	0	0	0
Canada and Quebec Pension Plans						
Revenues (billions $2000)	44	53	63	73	82	90
Change from Base	0	1	2	4	6	9
Fiscal Impact of Prod'ty Change (billions $2000)	0	1	2	4	6	9
Fiscal Impact as % of Base Expenditures	0.5	2.6	4.8	7.1	9.4	12.0
Combined Government (Net of Intergovernmental Transfers)						
Revenues (billions $2000)	507	565	625	690	760	833
Change from Base	3	13	24	38	54	72
Fiscal Impact of Prod'ty Change (billions $2000)	3	13	24	37	53	70
Fiscal Impact as % of Base Expenditures	1	3	4	6	8	10
Induced Changes in Expenditures (billions $2000)		0	0	0	1	1

the provinces are committed to keeping the local governments in balance, the provinces are actually able to slightly reduce their transfers to the local level. Of course, the huge fiscal impact for the provinces could well end up in increased transfers to local governments, which might be used to increase expenditures (or lower taxes) at the local level, but this would be a discretionary change.

Finally, note that for the public pension plans the results of this simulation are almost identical to those of Simulation 1. The smaller wage payouts at the government level lead to somewhat reduced pension-plan contributions, but the difference in the fiscal dividend as a percentage of expenditures in 2030 is only 0.3 percent.

Simulation 4: 0.3-Percent Increase in Productivity Growth — No Change in Federal Transfers

Simulation 4 is identical to Simulation 1 except that federal transfers to the provinces are not increased in proportion to the assumed higher growth rate. The net result is a change only in the outcomes for the federal government and the provinces (see Table 9). The results for the combined government, local governments and pension plans are the same as in Simulation 1.

In Simulation 1, the fiscal impacts for the federal and provincial governments are very close as a percentage of base-case expenditures (5.5 percent for the federal government vs. 4.7 for the provinces). In Simulation 4 the balance changes dramatically in favour of the federal government. With no change in transfers to the provinces, the extra 0.3-percent productivity growth results in a fiscal impact equal to 8 percent of base expenditures in 2030, versus an impact of only 2.9 percent at the provincial level.

Simulation 5: 0.3-Percent Increase in Productivity Growth — Interest Rates +0.3 Percent

The final simulation assumes that higher productivity growth is a worldwide phenomenon that increases real interest rates. An arbitrary 0.3-percent increase has been chosen. There is no change in the impact on GDP, compared to Simulation 1, but the results (see Table 10) show a varied impact by level of government.

Since it holds the largest debt at the starting point, the federal government is the most negatively affected. The larger interest payments resulting from the higher interest rates serve to increase induced expenditures and make the fiscal impact of the higher productivity growth path slightly negative in 2005. However, as time passes, the higher cumulative output caused by higher productivity growth generates more and more additional revenue, while the effect of higher interest rates on debt payments actually decreases (since debt is gradually reduced in the base case). By 2030 the fiscal impact on the federal government is 5 percent of base expenditures, instead of the 5.5 percent when interest rates did not change. The primary impact of higher interest rates, therefore, is "up front" and fades over time.

The provinces also have public debt charges that are increased by higher interest rates, but, compared to the federal government, these are smaller in proportion to revenues and expenditures. The fiscal impact of higher productivity growth is reduced from 0.4 to 0.2 percent of base expenditures in 2005, and thereafter fades further. By 2030 the assumed higher interest rates have reduced the fiscal impact as a share of base expenditures from 4.7 to 4.6 percent.

As the local governments have little debt, higher rates make almost no difference to their fiscal profile. To the extent there is

TABLE 9

Simulation 4: Productivity Growth 0.3-Percent Increase Per Year — No Change in Federal Transfers (Public-Sector Real Wages Respond; Base Interest Rates)

Economic and Fiscal Indicators	2005	2010	2015	2020	2025	2030
Productivity Growth Rate (%)	2.2	2.1	2.1	2.1	2.1	2.0
Change from Base	0.3	0.3	0.3	0.3	0.3	0.3
Real GDP (billions $2000)	1235	1443	1637	1830	2030	2242
Change from Base	7	29	57	89	127	171
% Change from Base	0.6	2.1	3.6	5.1	6.7	8.3
Federal Government						
Revenues (billions $2000)	200	219	244	267	294	323
Change from Base	1	5	10	15	21	28
Fiscal Impact of Prod'ty Change (billions $2000)						
(after changes in federal and local transfers)	1	4	8	12	17	22
Fiscal Impact as % of Base Expenditures	0.7	2.4	3.9	5.4	6.7	8.0
Change in Transfers to Provinces (billions $2000)	0	0	0	0	0	0
Other Induced Changes in Expenditures (billions $2000)	0	1	2	3	5	6
Provincial/Territorial Governments						
Revenues (billions $2000)	248	276	306	339	375	415
Change from Base	2	7	13	21	29	39
Fiscal Impact of Prod'ty Change (billions $2000)						
(excluding change in federal transfers)	1	3	5	7	9	11
Fiscal Impact as % of Base Expenditures	0.3	1.0	1.7	2.2	2.6	2.9
Change in Transfers to Local Gov't (billions $2000)	0	1	2	3	4	6
Other Induced Changes in Expenditures (billions $2000)	1	3	7	11	16	21
Local Governments						
Revenues (billions $2000)	90	103	116	129	144	159
Change from Base	0	1	3	4	6	8
Fiscal Impact of Prod'ty Change (billions $2000)						
(excluding change in provincial transfers)	0	0	1	1	1	2
Fiscal Impact as % of Base Expenditures	0.1	0.3	0.6	0.8	1.1	1.3
Induced Changes in Expenditures (billions $2000)	0	1	3	4	6	8
Canada and Quebec Pension Plans						
Revenues (billions $2000)	44	53	63	73	82	90
Change from Base	0	1	2	4	6	9
Fiscal Impact of Prod'ty Change (billions $2000)	0	1	2	4	6	9
Fiscal Impact as % of Base Expenditures	0.5	2.6	4.9	7.2	9.6	12.3
Combined Government **(Net of Intergovernmental Transfers)**						
Revenues (billions $2000)	508	566	628	694	765	840
Change from Base	3	14	26	41	58	78
Fiscal Impact of Prod'ty Change (billions $2000)	2	8	15	23	32	42
Fiscal Impact as % of Base Expenditures	0	2	3	4	5	6
Induced Changes in Expenditures (billions $2000)	1	6	11	18	26	36

any change at all, it is positive, as interest earnings rise slightly.

Finally, the public pension plans gain from higher real rates as their accu-

mulated surpluses earn higher returns. By 2030, the fiscal impact of higher productivity with higher interest rates is 12 percent of base expenditures, as opposed to

TABLE 10

Simulation 5: Productivity Growth 0.3-Percent Increase Per Year — Interest Rates 0.3-Percent Increase (Public-Sector Real Wages Respond; Federal Transfers Respond)

Economic and Fiscal Indicators	2005	2010	2015	2020	2025	2030
Productivity Growth Rate (%)	2.2	2.1	2.1	2.1	2.1	2.0
Change from Base	0.3	0.3	0.3	0.3	0.3	0.3
Real GDP (billions $2000)	1235	1443	1637	1830	2030	2242
Change from Base	7	29	57	89	127	171
% Change from Base	0.6	2.1	3.6	5.1	6.7	8.3
Federal Government						
Revenues (billions $2000)	201	220	244	267	294	322
Change from Base	2	6	10	15	21	27
Fiscal Impact of Prod'ty Change (billions $2000)						
(after changes in federal and local transfers)	0	2	5	7	10	13
Fiscal Impact as % of Base Expenditures	-0.3	1.1	2.3	3.3	4.2	5.0
Change in Transfers to Provinces (billions $2000)	0	1	2	3	5	7
Other Induced Changes in Expenditures (billions $2000)	2	3	4	5	6	7
Provincial/Territorial Governments						
Revenues (billions $2000)	248	276	306	339	375	415
Change from Base	3	8	14	21	29	39
Fiscal Impact of Prod'ty Change (billions $2000)						
(excluding change in federal transfers)	0	3	6	10	13	17
Fiscal Impact as % of Base Expenditures	0.2	1.2	2.1	3.0	3.8	4.6
Change in Transfers to Local Gov't (billions $2000)	0	1	2	3	4	6
Other Induced Changes in Expenditures (billions $2000)	2	4	6	8	11	15
Local Governments						
Revenues ($2000 Bill)	90	103	116	129	144	159
Change from Base	0	1	3	4	6	8
Fiscal Impact of Prod'ty Change (billions $2000)						
(excluding change in provincial transfers)	0	0	1	1	1	2
Fiscal Impact as % of Base Expenditures	0.2	0.4	0.6	0.9	1.1	1.3
Induced Changes in Expenditures (billions $2000)	0	1	3	4	6	8
Canada and Quebec Pension Plans						
Revenues (billions $2000)	44	54	64	74	84	93
Change from Base	0	1	3	5	8	12
Fiscal Impact of Prod'ty Change (billions $2000)	0	1	3	5	8	12
Fiscal Impact as % of Base Expenditures	0.7	3.6	6.6	9.6	12.5	15.7
Combined Government (Net of Intergovernmental Transfers)						
Revenues (billions $2000)	509	567	629	696	767	843
Change from Base	5	14	26	39	55	73
Fiscal Impact of Prod'ty Change (billions $2000)	0	7	14	22	32	43
Fiscal Impact as % of Base Expenditures	0	1	3	4	5	6
Induced Changes in Expenditures (billions $2000)	5	8	12	17	23	30

only 9 percent when real rates did not change. In 2030 also, the positive impact on the pension plans is actually slightly greater than the negative impact of higher interest charges at the federal and provincial levels, and the combined government account shows a slight increase in the overall fiscal impact.

CONCLUDING OBSERVATIONS — AND WORK TO BE DONE

The simulations described above indicate that even relatively small changes in productivity growth rates can cumulate over several decades into large changes in GDP and living standards, and can significantly alter the fiscal room to manoeuvre of the federal and provincial governments and the public pension plans. This is true whether we are contemplating higher productivity growth rates or lower ones.

Of the sensitivities tested, the most important one turned out to be the response of government-sector wages to changes in private-sector real wages that would likely occur under alternative productivity growth rates. If higher productivity growth passes through to higher public-sector wages (as would seem likely), then the fiscal impact of higher productivity growth is muted. Under higher productivity growth, some of the increased government revenues simply go to pay higher public-sector wages. If, on the other hand, productivity growth is lower than thought, then the negative impact on government is partly offset by a reduction in government-wage rates. This effect is important for the provincial level of government, somewhat less so for the federal level and barely discernable for the public pension plans.

If real interest rates move with higher or lower productivity growth rates, the fiscal impact is on average very small. An interest-rate response mutes the impact of changes in productivity growth for the federal and provincial governments, primarily in the near term. On the other hand, the fiscal impact on the public pension plans is amplified by an interest-rate response.

This study is only the beginning of an inquiry into the interconnections between productivity and fiscal policy. At least two groups of issues remain to be addressed.[7]

First, we have discussed only how productivity growth affects the fiscal room to manoeuvre. Undoubtedly fiscal policy also has important feedbacks for productivity growth. How the fiscal room to manoeuvre is used can make a significant difference: some tax cuts or expenditure increases could raise productivity growth, through either improved technology or capital accumulation, while some badly designed new social programs could serve to reduce incentives and productivity growth. Also, feedback from fiscal policy to productivity becomes more important the further out the projections go. The possibilities are too numerous, and the connections to productivity too imprecise, to be included in a macroeconometric model, but the problem is an important one. The question also arises: What is the best use of fiscal room in order to further raise productivity growth? Clearly, though, this represents a large and separate research agenda.

Second, the issue of whether a productivity change is confined to Canada or is universal also has implications that cannot be modelled. In particular, a general increase in productivity could lead to extended fiscal room to manoeuvre in many countries, some of which would likely be used — especially in the United States — to lower tax rates. Canada might well be obliged to devote some of its fiscal room to manoeuvre to matching such tax cuts, thereby reducing the amount of the extra room to manoeuvre that is truly discretionary and that could be devoted to social programs.[8]

115

NOTES

I would like to thank Andrew Sharpe and an anonymous referee for extremely useful comments on an earlier draft. Any remaining errors are my own.

1   For a discussion of some of these issues about future alternative productivity growth paths, see Dungan and Wilson (2002) and other papers in the same volume.

2   The projection was prepared before the release of census 2001 data; while the population figures may seem high compared to the census figures released in early 2002, it must be kept in mind that the latter will eventually be inflated by an under-reporting factor by Statistics Canada before they become the official population figures.

3   Output per hour is a superior productivity measure when available, but reliable and consistent long-term time series data have been difficult to obtain for the model.

4   The argument is sometimes made that higher productivity growth pushed down the full-employment unemployment rate in the second half of the 1990s, especially in the United States. However, it could be that we simply did not know what the rate was before then, after the early 1990s recession and recovery, and that it had been lower than we thought all along. This is certainly the author's opinion about the Canadian full-employment rate, which, to the extent that it did decline, did so for reasons of an aging work force and a stiffening of Employment Insurance qualifications and reduced payout rates.

5   Theoretical macroeconomics makes labour supply a function of the real wage, but the empirical evidence is slim. In the FOCUS macroeconometric model, labour force participation is a function of employment availability, and, for some age/sex groups, leniency of EI regulations and relative cohort size, but it is not a function of the real wage.

6   The discussion here is the proper measure of the fiscal room to manoeuvre, not how to make use of it. The compounding effect of early debt paydown is a strong argument in favour of using some fiscal room to manoeuvre for this purpose. There is, however, a re-entry problem to be kept in mind: the more rapidly one approaches an "optimal" debt/GDP level (whatever it might be), the more rapidly fiscal policy must be switched to tax cuts or expenditure increases, with potentially wrenching effects on the industrial make-up and skills set of the economy.

7   I am indebted to an anonymous referee for much of what follows.

8   The dilemma, of course, is greater still if the productivity increase occurs in other countries and not in Canada, leading to pressures to cut taxes with no compensating additional fiscal room.

REFERENCES

Dungan, P., and G. Jump. 1998. *FOCUS: Quarterly Forecasting and User Simulation Model of the Canadian Economy: Version 97A*. Toronto: Institute for Policy Analysis, University of Toronto.

Dungan, P., and S. Murphy. 2002. "National Projection Through 2025." Policy and Economic Analysis Program Policy Study #2002-1. Toronto: Institute for Policy Analysis, University of Toronto.

Dungan, P., and T.A. Wilson. 2002. "Productivity in the New Economy." In *Productivity Issues in Canada*, ed. Someshwar Rao and Andrew Sharpe. Calgary: University of Calgary Press.

Finance Canada. 2000. *Economic Statement and Budget Update*. Ottawa: Finance Canada.

———. 2001. *Budget*. Ottawa: Finance Canada.

King, P., and H. Jackson. 2000. "Public Finance Implications of Population Ageing." Working Paper #2000-08. Ottawa: Finance Canada.

Natural Capital, Sustainability and Productivity: An Exploration of the Linkages

Nancy Olewiler

INTRODUCTION: THE ROLE OF NATURAL AND ENVIRONMENTAL RESOURCES IN THE CANADIAN ECONOMY

The goals of this paper are to explore potential relationships among natural capital, sustainability and productivity. Three questions are posed. First, how important is natural capital in sustaining natural resource production in the Canadian economy over time?[1] Second, does the omission of natural capital in estimates of productivity growth bias these estimates? And finally, has the role of natural capital changed over time as a result of three factors: its depletion, its degradation (declining quality) and technological change? Available data will be analysed with a view to providing an overview and suggested interpretation of what are very complex relationships. The paper begins by defining natural capital and discussing its link to sustainability. It presents trends in natural capital over the past 20 to 30 years. Links between natural capital and productivity are explored, focusing first on labour productivity and then on multifactor productivity of Canada's natural resource sectors. Next, the possible role of technological change in these sectors is examined, with specific examples for coal, copper, petroleum and forestry. The impact of omitting natural capital from productivity estimates is examined by looking at cases in which environmental resources are factored into the calculation. The paper concludes with observations on possible connections between productivity estimates and sustainability.

The economy's goods and services are produced with factor inputs, traditionally identified as land, labour and capital. Land has been a proxy for the stocks of natural resources — land and soils, timber, minerals, energy, water and the capacity of the natural environment to absorb or neutralize the waste products of production and consumption, protect organisms from excessive ultraviolet radiation, support ecosystem sustainability and much more. Economic modelling during much of the 20th century typically focused on the roles of labour and capital, implicitly assuming that natural and environmental resources were so abundant that they could be treated as "free" goods. Of course, most economists recognized that natural resources used as inputs were not free — capital and labour had to be used to extract or harvest them — but because of the relative abundance of natural resources they were routinely ignored in productivity studies and other aggregate analyses of the economy. It is typically when market or implicit prices of natural resources are particularly high — for example, during the "energy crisis" of the 1970s when petroleum prices skyrocketed — that natural resources enter into estimations of production functions and productivity.[2] The late 1960s and early 1970s also ushered in an awareness of the increasing scarcity of environmental resources, because pollution levels began to have a noticeable impact on human and ecosystem health.

The stock of natural and environmental resources is known as natural capital — capital in the sense that the resources are assets that yield services over time but can also depreciate. Depreciation of natural capital results from depletion and degradation (declining quality) of these stocks. Degradation may have a greater impact on production than depletion. When quality declines as a natural resource is extracted or harvested, the costs of extraction typically rise unless the decline is offset by technology. Data on quality are difficult to obtain and at the aggregate level would necessarily combine positive and negative quality changes. In this paper, quantity serves as an imperfect proxy for both attributes. Natural capital consists of three components: (1) natural resource capital — stocks of renewable and non-renewable resources, (2) ecosystems or environmental capital — systems that provide essential environmental goods and services, and (3) land — the space in which human activities take place. Measurement of Canada's natural capital has focused thus far on stocks of land, energy, mineral and timber.[3] The natural capital embodied in environmental resources is very difficult to conceptualize, let alone measure. However, even for the resources whose natural capital is more readily measurable, there is very little in the way of empirical estimation of natural capital's contribution to productivity. Research on how changes in the stocks of natural resources affect the sustainability of resource extraction or harvesting, and ultimately the sustainability of the economy, is limited but growing.[4]

Sustainability, broadly defined, is the ability of the economy to maintain the flow of production necessary to ensure non-decreasing per capita consumption indefinitely, so that future generations can have a standard of living equal to or better than that of present generations. To sustain production, the economy needs a constant supply of the inputs that are essential in the sense that without them there would be no output. The relationship between natural capital and sustainable output, then, depends on whether natural capital is essential — that is, the substitution possibilities between factor inputs. Some forms of natural capital, such as water and our atmosphere, are clearly essential. If the protective stratospheric ozone layer is lost, the amount of ultraviolet radiation reaching the earth's surface will be sufficient to exterminate most plant and animal life. Other types of natural capital — specific non-renewable or renewable resources (oil, timber) and even some of the waste assimilation processes of the natural environment — may not be essential. Natural gas, oil products extracted from tar sands or biofuels can be substituted for conventional oil in most uses. It is energy that is the key input in this case, not the specific type of energy input that is essential for production. Water and sewage treatment plants (reproduced capital) can substitute for the waste absorption capacity of rivers and lakes.

The concepts of weak and strong sustainability reflect the *essentialness* of natural capital to the economy and the environment. Weak sustainability means that an aggregate stock of capital (natural, human and reproduced) is maintained at a level necessary to ensure indefinite production. All of the forms of capital aggregated under weak sustainability must therefore be perfectly substitutable for each other. Strong sustainability means that specific forms of natural capital are essential (they do not have substitutes) and that stocks of these resources must be kept intact to ensure continued production. The challenge is to discover what forms of natural capital are essential and how to sustain the stocks necessary to ensure non-decreasing production, consumption and, hence, human survival. We do not have good estimates of how much natural capital we need. Our knowledge is particularly weak when it comes to understanding the complex roles of ecosystems in sustaining the hydrological cycle, climate, biodiversity, soil productivity and other natural processes. We also tend to look at forms of natural capital independently rather than as part of an integrated, multiple-input and -output system. Natural capital provides well-being directly to individuals along with yielding inputs used to produce other goods and services. Natural capital also occurs in the space where people live. Hence, its extraction or harvest affects people's quality of life, their employment, the long-term sustainability of their communities and their relationships with their ecosystems. Ideally, measurement of sustainability is directed to all the multiple uses of natural cap-

ital. This study is far more modest in scope. It explores linkages in aggregate and suggests many avenues for future work.

LONG-RUN TRENDS FOR CANADIAN NATURAL RESOURCE CAPITAL

Charts 1 and 2 illustrate trends in output from some natural resource industries and natural resource reserves — a measure of natural capital for timber, oil, natural gas and coal over the past 40 years.[5] Three patterns are apparent. The stocks of natural capital are either falling (timber and oil), in an inverted U-shape (gas) or rising in a nonlinear fashion (coal) (where the rate of increase has slowed in recent years). In all cases, however, production has been rising over time. Thus, the declining stocks of timber and oil do not appear to be

CHART 1
Timber Harvests and Assets, 1961-1997

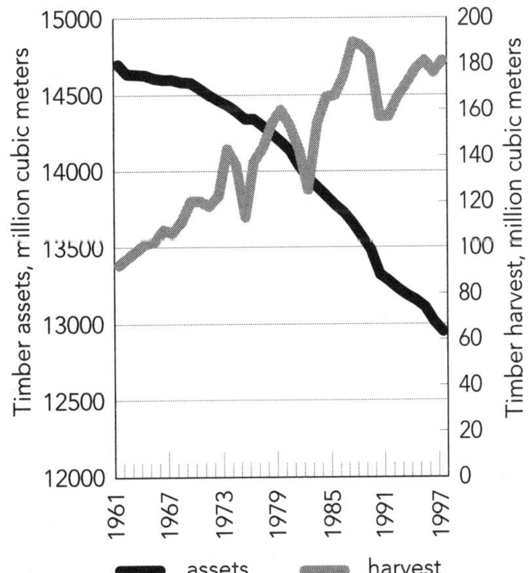

Source: Statistics Canada. Canada Timber Assets (Volume), Opening Stock, Table Number: 1530030. Timber Harvests, Table Number I530030.

CHART 2

Canadian Energy Reserves and Production, 1970-1998

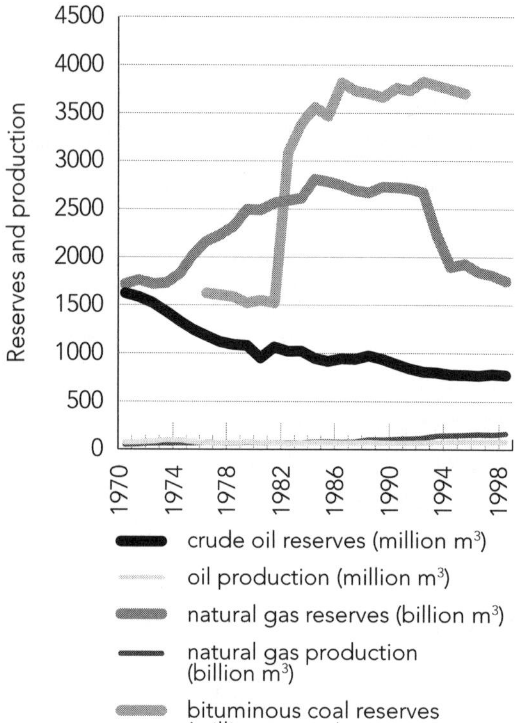

Source: Natural Resources Canada, *Energy in Canada 2000*. www.nrcan.gc.ca/es/ener2000.

restraining current production. Chart 2 indicates why this is so: some natural resource reserves (forests, coal and bituminous coal) are still many orders of magnitude larger than annual production.[6] Canada imports as well as exports all of these natural resources.

Measurement of natural resource reserves is sensitive to current prices in that it includes stocks that are economically recoverable — that is, extractable at the prevailing prices. Many natural resources have been generally falling in real prices over the past 20 years.[7] Long-run real prices of oil and gas trended downward from 1981 to 1998, as shown in Chart 3. Chart 4 illustrates that the real price of timber harvests, while cyclical, generally

declined over the period 1961–98. These data suggest that while conventional oil, gas and timber stocks have fallen over time due to extraction/harvesting in excess of new discoveries or regrowth, stocks are still high relative to annual production.[8] If markets are functioning perfectly, none of the resources examined are becoming scarcer in an economic sense, because their prices over the long term have not been rising.[9] This does not mean that declining reserves will not ultimately lead to rising prices: prices depend not only on Canadian supply but also on world supply and, of course, the total demand for the resources. Canadian depletion of many natural resources may simply be too insignificant to affect world prices. This is where the distinction between weak and strong sustainability is important. If specific types of natural capital have substitutes

CHART 3

Constant Dollar Prices of Crude Oil and Natural Gas Exports, 1981-1998 (1997 = 100)

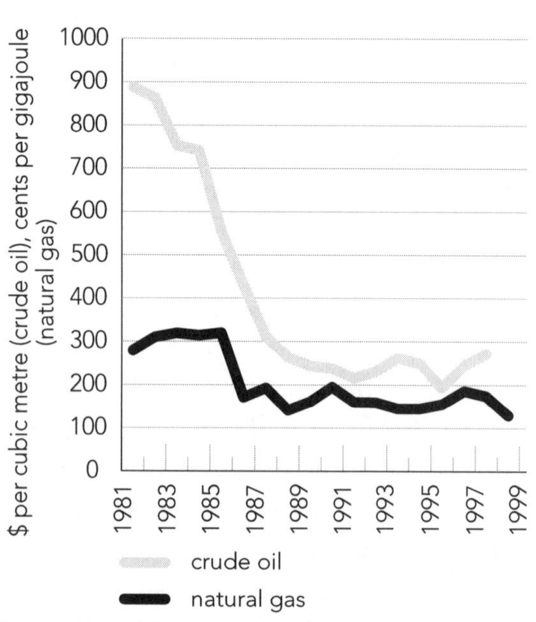

Source: Natural Resources Canada, *Energy in Canada 2000*. www.nrcan.gc.ca/es/ener2000.

CHART 4

Real Price of Timber, 1961-1998

(base year 1992)

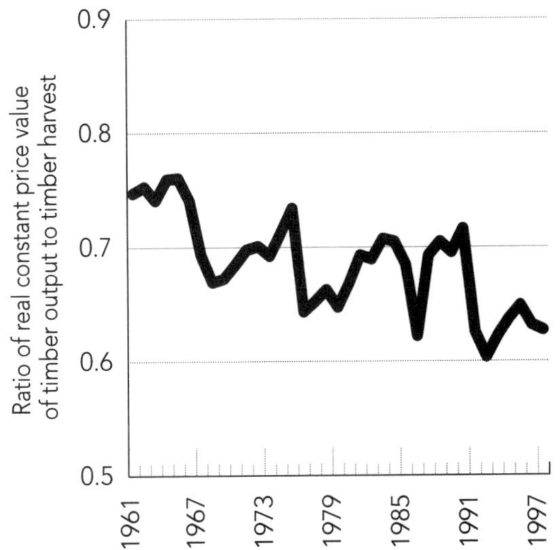

Source: Computed from Statistics Canada, Timber Harvests and Indexes of Real GDP in Logging and Forestry, Table Number: 1607603.

(the same type of natural capital from other sources, labour or reproduced capital), a decline in their stocks will not signal economic dislocation.[10]

Declining natural resource prices may also be the result of other factors. The composition of Canadian output may be changing over time. Technological changes and innovations and rising labour productivity (e.g., due to increases in human capital) can reduce the amount of natural capital required per unit output. That is, the economy may substitute for production that is natural resource-intensive, becoming less dependent on natural capital over time, in which case productivity will fall in the natural resource sectors as those industries decline. However, declining stocks of renewable resources can affect environmental capital such as biodiversity and ecosystem integrity, not to mention quality of life. Substitution may also take place in environ-

mental capital. For example, the use of pollution abatement and control technologies and recycling means that there is less use of the absorptive capacity of the natural environment (and, presumably, less stress on ecosystems). But there are limits to the amount of substitution that is possible with environmental capital. The challenge lies in defining these limits. Environmental resources are addressed again at the end of the paper.

One can get a rough picture of the relative contribution of natural resource capital to total output in the economy by examining changes in real output over time. Table 1 shows that output has risen for all resource sectors except (in 1980-97) fishing and trapping. Real GDP growth for all Canadian industries rose at an average annual rate of 6.5 percent from 1961 to 1980 and 2.6 percent from 1980 to 1997. In the latter period, only one resource industry, coal, exceeded the growth in real output of the aggregate economy.[11] The other sectors grew more slowly. The fishing and trapping industry is a special case; all the data and information available about fish stocks point to a significant decline in natural capital — major reductions in stocks due to harvesting and natural conditions.[12]

TABLE 1

Average Annual Percentage Change in Real Output for Natural Resource Industries

	% Change in Real Output	
	1961–1980	1980–1997
Agriculture	1.2	2.5
Fishing & Trapping	0.4	-0.9
Logging & Forestry	1.7	0.8
Mining	1.3	1.5
Coal	1.8	4.6
Oil & Natural Gas	2.4	2.5

Source: Statistics Canada, Indexes of Real Gross Domestic Product by Industry, 1992 = 100, Table Numbers: 1607601,1607602,1607603, 1607704,1607810,1607705.

Declining growth in most natural resource sectors implies that these sectors represent a smaller share of the value of total output over time. This is explained at least in part by the declining real prices of many resources. But one might also infer that there has been a reduction in the essentialness of natural capital in these sectors; put another way, the economy may be developing substitutes for some of its domestic natural capital. This view is supported by data on aggregate energy consumption in Canada over the past four decades. While energy consumption has risen in aggregate and per capita terms (by over 200 percent and 93 percent, respectively, from 1961 to 1997), energy consumed (in physical terms) per unit GDP has fallen by 12 percent (see Environment Canada). However, when one looks at specific energy products and examines total production relative to GDP, a somewhat different picture emerges. Recall from Chart 3 that the real prices of oil and gas fell between 1981 and 1997. The relative importance of energy may thus be even greater than suggested by the energy consumption-to-GDP ratio. Chart 5 shows the ratios to GDP (in constant 1992 dollars) of energy output in physical units for oil, gas and coal. The share of output for coal is rising; natural gas is U-shaped, rising since the late 1980s; and oil is falling. These trends may have implications for sustainability, especially when one considers environmental capital. Production of energy from fossil fuels generates pollution that can damage ecosystems and health.

As noted above, all the data presented in this paper are aggregated to the national level. Resource stocks and the importance of natural resources in provincial GDP vary across the country — for example, British Columbia and Alberta are much more resource-intensive than Ontario and Quebec. As well, changes in resource stocks may differ across the country — for example, timber reserves may be falling more quickly in British Columbia than in Quebec. Because of this variability, should one examine natural capital and sustainability at the national or regional levels? This paper focuses on the national level because natural resource capital from one part of the country can be substituted for that in another.[13] It may be argued that even the national level is too limited because natural resources from other countries can be substituted for declining natural capital stocks in Canada. This argument does not hold for environmental resources — one cannot substitute air quality in Regina for that in Toronto.

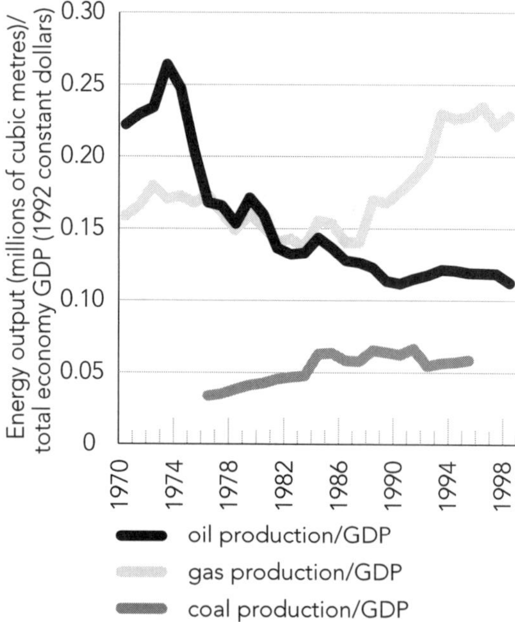

CHART 5

Physical Energy Output-to-GDP Ratios, 1970-1998

Source: Natural Resources Canada, *Energy in Canada 2000.* www.nrcan.gc.ca/es/ener2000, Statistics Canada, Gross Domestic Product at Factor Cost.

NATURAL CAPITAL AND PRODUCTIVITY GROWTH

Productivity growth may be linked to sustainability because it indicates scope for improvements in a country's living standards that are, in principle, sustainable through technological advances.[14] For example, technological advances in natural resource production can allow for more output from a given stock of the resource, or offset the natural decline in output or quality of the stock of the extracted resource as its reserves are depleted. Technological advances in oil extraction, for instance, allow for the recovery of more oil from a given pool than was possible 25 years ago; a tree now yields more useable fibre because of advances in harvesting and milling technology.[15] This gets at the heart of what constitutes recoverable reserves of a natural resource. Technology, along with prices and production costs, determines what is economic to recover. On the other hand, if depletion of a natural resource leads to increases in the marginal cost of extraction/harvesting, then, *ceteris paribus*, productivity ought to decline unless there are offsetting technological changes. For example, the marginal cost of pumping oil from a well rises as the oil in the pool is depleted because of a decline in the natural pressure. More capital and labour must be used to extract a given quantity of oil. The sustainability of a natural resource may therefore be connected to productivity. This is not to suggest that one need look only at productivity, because clearly there are many possible indicators of sustainability; the point is that productivity might be one of those indicators. The same concept could apply to environmental capital; however, we know so little about the relationships among environmental capital, productivity and sustainability that it is very difficult to make inferences. One would expect far less substitutability of manufactured and human capital for environmental capital than for natural resources. This is clearly a major research topic in itself.

Two measures of productivity growth are commonly used to gauge the ability of the economy to produce goods and services over time: labour productivity and multifactor or total-factor productivity (MFP or TFP). Labour productivity indicates how much is produced per worker and hence the real income available to the population. In this sense, it links well with sustainability, by showing how much sustainable consumption is possible. Multifactor productivity is used as a measure of technological change. It is the growth rate of output minus the growth rate of the inputs weighted by their input shares, where, generally, only two inputs are included — capital and labour. The "unexplained" portion of output growth is generally interpreted as technological change. It would more appropriately be interpreted as disembodied technological change (or a measure of our ignorance) because, as a residual, MFP is telling us what is not explained by the growth rates in measured inputs.[16] But natural capital is also an input into the production of goods and services and is not captured in most estimates of MFP, so MFP should be adjusted to reflect changes in natural capital. However, even if we could measure natural capital, we could not determine its input share without estimating production (or cost) functions; it is thus part of the residual. The contribution of natural capital to productivity growth has been estimated for individual industries (see Squires 1992; Repetto et al. 1996; Swinand 1999; Harchaoui and Lasserre 2001; Harchaoui et al. 2001; these papers will be discussed in more detail below).[17] Labour productivity and MFP for Canada's natural resource sectors are examined below.

Labour Productivity in Natural Resource Industries

Labour-productivity growth rates for the total economy versus the primary sectors in Canada and the United States are shown in Table 2, for several periods starting in 1989.[18] One can draw several conclusions from this table. Productivity growth in the primary sector as a whole significantly exceeds that in the total economy. While the growth rate for the primary sector dipped slightly in the late 1990s, it then rose almost to the 1989-95 level and remains more than twice as high as that for the total economy. In addition, while the United States has higher productivity growth overall than Canada, the productivity growth of the primary sector in Canada is about twice that of the United States. The positive productivity growth indicates that, over time, the economy becomes more efficient in turning inputs into outputs. If one combines productivity data with measurement of changes in natural resource stocks, it might be possible to draw some inferences about weak sustainability. If, for example, natural resource stocks are declining but labour productivity is rising, the suggestion is that other factor inputs are being substituted for natural resource capital. We cannot say if this process will continue, of course, and one would also want to examine other indicators of sustainability. As well, these inferences are based on aggregate data that obscure many different patterns amongst the primary industries.

Table 3 breaks down the primary sector in Canada into separate industries and

TABLE 2

Labour-Productivity Growth — Primary Sector Relative to the Total Economy, Canada and the United States

	Total Economy (%)		Primary Sector (%)	
	Canada	United States	Canada	United States
1989–1995	1.0	1.2	3.1	1.5
1995–2000	1.6	2.4	2.5	1.1
1989–2000	1.2	1.7	2.9	1.3

Note: Real GDP per worker, average annual percentage rate of change.
Source: Rao and Tang (2001, Table 2).

TABLE 3

Average Annual Labour-Productivity Growth Rates in Resource Industries , Canada

	1961–1973	1973–1981	1981–1989	1989–1997	1989–2000
Agriculture	2.2	2.1	1.3	2.6	5.5
Fishing & trapping	3.3	-0.7	-3.7	-0.6	-0.9
Forestry	2.2	1.3	3.0	-0.8	-0.8
Mining	2.4	-1.5	4.1	1.0	n/a
Coal	5.2	0.8	6.5	5.3	n/a
Oil & gas	1.4	-14.7	- 0.4	3.8	n/a

Note: Average growth rates are calculated from peak to peak to be cyclically neutral. Data are not available for mining, coal, and oil and gas beyond 1997.
Source: Statistics Canada, Indexes of Real GDP per Hour Worked, 1961–1997, 1961–2000, Table Numbers: 1610101, 1610102, 1610103, 1610204, 1610310, 1610205.

provides average annual rates of growth in labour productivity over the four decades starting in 1961. The chosen time periods are cyclically neutral — that is, they go from peak to peak in the business cycle. There is no clear pattern. While most resource industries show a slowdown in growth beginning in the 1970s (and for fishing and trapping, consistently negative growth), oil and gas had its highest labour-productivity growth in the 1990s. But even these average rates expressed per decade do not accurately indicate the longer-term trends in each industry.

Charts 6 and 7 show labour productivity for the renewable and non-renewable resource industries over the past 40 years. Chart 6 illustrates the diversity among the renewable resources. Labour productivity has been generally rising for agriculture[19] and forestry, but declining, since the late 1970s, for fishing and trapping. For the entire period, labour productivity in agriculture has grown by 313 percent and forestry by 158 percent, while fishing and trapping has declined by 0.2 percent. Recall from the previous section that over the past 40 years the stock of forest natural capital and most fish stocks have been declining, but labour-productivity trends are quite different for the two sectors. There are many possible explanations for this difference. The role of technological change is examined in the next two sections. The responses of each industry to changing prices may also be a factor. Industries with declining real prices over significant parts of the time series (timber and agriculture) may have restructured and consolidated their enterprises, thus improving labour productivity. But changes in natural

125

CHART 6
Labour Productivity in Renewable Resource Industries, 1961-2000

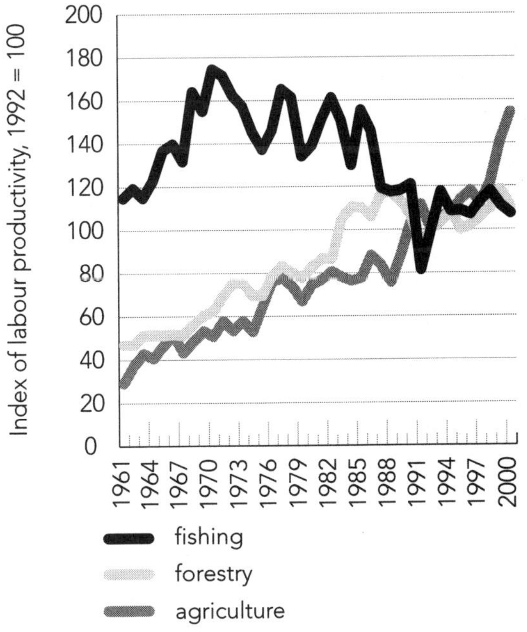

Source: Statistics Canada, Indexes of Real GDP per Hour Worked, Table Numbers: 1610101, 1610102, 1610103.

CHART 7
Labour Productivity in Non-Renewable Resource Industries, 1961-1997

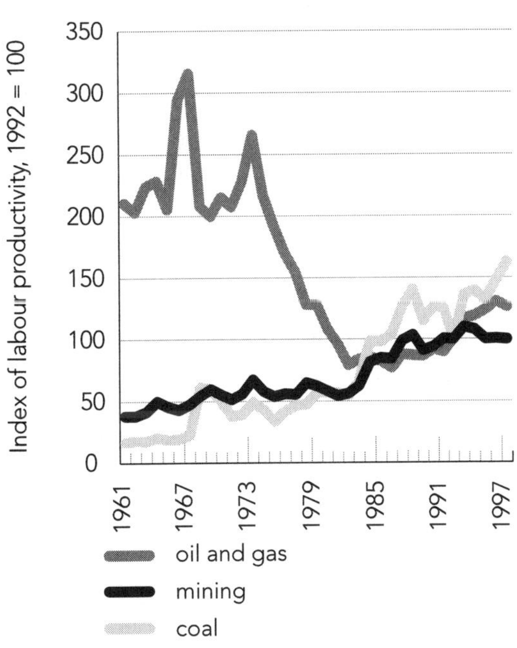

Source: Statistics Canada, Indexes of Real GDP per Hour Worked, Table Numbers: 1610204, 1610310, 1610205.

capital may also play a role. Natural capital in fisheries may have crossed a threshold below which sustainable production in the sector is not possible, despite an attempt to substitute other inputs for the declining stock of natural capital. Falling labour productivity is consistent with this argument. Theoretical models of open access and imperfectly regulated fisheries have predicted for many years that harvests exceeding the sustainable yield from the fishery will ultimately exhaust the fishery. Natural capital is clearly essential for this industry. One cannot substitute labour and capital indefinitely to sustain the harvest.

The decline in forest stocks reflects the harvesting of old-growth timber and its replacement with lower-yielding second growth. While the total stock has declined, labour productivity has not been adversely affected because annual harvests represent only a small percentage of the total stock. Annual harvests have risen from 0.6 to 1.4 percent of the timber stock.[20] While this suggests a relatively high "reserves-to-harvest" ratio, timber stocks are vulnerable to losses from natural phenomena such as fire, insect pests, disease, pollution and weather. For agriculture, data are available for measures of natural capital for 1981 and 1996. Total area in farms and land in crops has risen by 3.3 and 12.8 percent, respectively, while that in pasture and summerfallow has fallen by 1.3 and 35.5 percent. These data suggest no clear picture with regard to the impact of changes in agricultural capital on labour productivity in the sector.[21]

Chart 7 illustrates labour productivity for non-renewable resource industries in the period 1961-97. For coal and mining, labour productivity generally rose throughout the period, while for oil and natural gas the picture

is more complex, with productivity declining from the mid-1970s to the early 1980s and rising thereafter at a rate roughly comparable to that for mining (until the most recent years).[22] During the 1970s and early 1980s, exploration for new reserves was driven by increases in the real price of energy and was also affected by an export licensing requirement of a minimum reserves-to-extraction ratio. The more extensive and intensive drilling led to large increases in labour (and capital) but little in the way of incremental output. Recall from Chart 2 that reserves of oil were falling. This decline in natural capital would also help explain the drop in labour productivity. Declining stocks of natural capital may have played a role for oil, but not for natural gas. Gas reserves were rising over this period. The data for the mid-1980s indicate that once the reserve-ratio regulation was lifted, exploration activity was based on expected profits, falling when energy prices decreased. Labour productivity has been rising since the mid-1980s. Technological change is now playing a greater role (as will be discussed below). For coal, the reserves of natural capital are enormous relative to current extraction. Mining is an aggregate that obscures developments with individual minerals, and hence it is difficult to explain trends in labour productivity. Reserves (and prices) have declined for some minerals but not for all. In aggregate, however, labour productivity is rising. This suggests that these sectors are weakly sustainable. The important point is that labour productivity and, as seen below, MFP might be helpful adjuncts to the strictly physical indicators of sustainability. Productivity measures may provide insight into the degree of substitution of capital and labour for natural capital. The substitution may be stimulated by declining natural capital stocks and/or technological changes affecting the use of different inputs.

How does labour productivity in the resource industries in Canada compare to that in the United States? Parry (1999) looks at coal, petroleum, logging and copper. His estimates of labour productivity in the United States yield paths over time similar to those in Canada.

Multifactor Productivity in Natural Resource Industries

Charts 8 and 9 present MFP for renewable and non-renewable resource industries compared to that for all industries. As noted above, MFP gives us an estimate of the combined effects of technological change, changes in natural capital over time (if it is an excluded input) and other unexplained factors.[23] As illustrated in Chart 8, of the renewable resource industries, only agriculture shows a generally rising trend, with a rate of growth exceeding that of all industries combined. Forestry and fishing are somewhat more cyclical, but trending downward with rates falling below those of all industries after the early 1990s and with fisheries falling below the rate of the base year (1984). In the non-renewable sectors the trends are quite different, with rates above that of all industries after the early 1990s and rising between 1984 and 1993 — except for coal, which rose throughout the period, with accelerated growth after the early 1990s (see Chart 9).

127

CHART 8

Multifactor Productivity: Renewable Resources vs. All Industries, 1984-1998

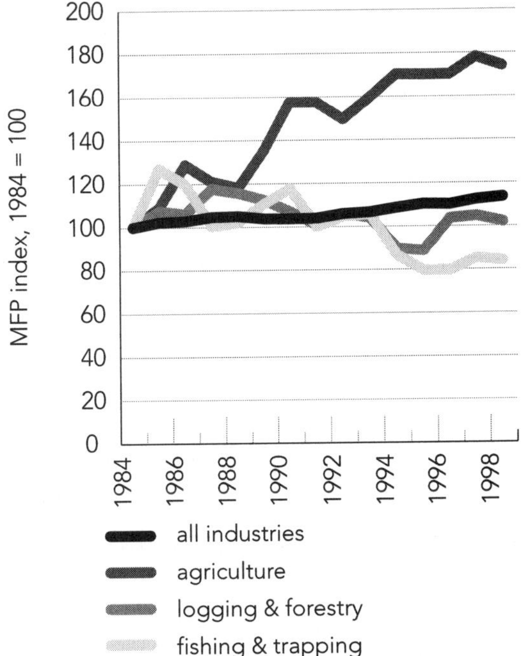

Source: Centre for the Study of Living Standards, based on Statistics Canada, *Labour Force Survey*, GDP, and Capital Stock Data, as cited in Natural Resources Canada, *Energy in Canada 2000*. www.nrcan.gc.ca/es/ener2000.

CHART 9

Multifactor Productivity: Non-Renewable Resources vs. All Industries, 1984-1998

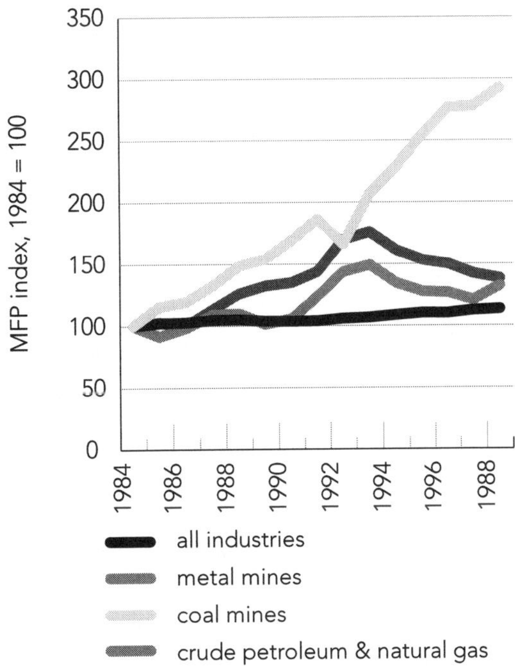

Source: Centre for the Study of Living Standards, based on Statistics Canada, *Labour Force Survey*, GDP, and Capital Stock Data, as cited in Natural Resources Canada, *Energy in Canada 2000*. www.nrcan.gc.ca/es/ener2000.

These estimates suggest very different roles of technological change and/or changes in natural capital in the renewable and non-renewable sectors. This subject is explored more fully below for the energy sector and forestry.

While labour-productivity trends in Canada are similar to those in the United States, MFP growth is somewhat different. Table 4 illustrates that Canada's MFP average annual growth was considerably higher than that of the United States over the period 1985 to 1994. Again, one must be careful in selecting a specific period if the trend has been cyclical, but the data for the 10-year period indicate that Canadian resource industries are healthier than their US counterparts. Is this because of greater technological change in Canada than in the United States? That is doubtful. The two economies are closely linked and one would expect technological change to readily flow between the countries. Because natural capital is omitted from the MFP calculation, an alternative explanation might be that declining natural capital had a greater impact on these sectors in the United States than in Canada. An examination of such a possibility is beyond the scope of this paper, but such an investigation is warranted.

It is generally expected that the growth rate of MFP will be lower than that of labour productivity, because the growth rate of the capital stock (or capital plus intermediate inputs) is typically higher than that of employment — that is, capital-labour ratios tend to rise over time. If we look at average annual growth rates in the two measures of productivity for Canadian resource industries, we find that they are highly variable year to year and that in a number of years MFP exceeds labour productivity. This variability suggests that omitting natural capital as an input in MFP measurement skews the estimates in an unexpected direction. This skewness may arise because the MFP estimates do not distinguish between impacts of changes in natural capital and those resulting from technological change. If natural capital is rising over time, traditional MFP estimates will overstate technological change and vice versa for a given level of output growth. Traditional MFP that is still rising while natural capital is declining might be an indication of weak sustainability, because technological change and substitution of other inputs may be occurring. When MFP declines consistently over time, concern about sustainability is warranted.

The relationship between MFP and labour productivity is exemplified by the fishing industry. A study of several fisheries in the United States shows that omitting natural capital from productivity measurement does bias the estimates. Squires (1992) measures total-factor productivity (TFP) in the open-access Pacific coast trawl fishery, explicitly accounting for changes in the abundance of fish stocks. TFP properly measured is "the residual after allocating the growth rate of output among changes in variable inputs, capital, and resource abundance" (Squires 1992, p. 225). Squires compares the conventional measure of TFP with the measure inclusive of natural capital. He finds that in years when

TABLE 4

Average Annual Growth in Multifactor Productivity (Percentage), 1985–1994

	Coal	Petroleum[1]	Logging
Canada	11.3	5.8	-1.8
United States	1.4	3.7	-2.1

[1] Includes natural gas in Canada.
Source: Parry (1999, Figure 5), Centre for the Study of Living Standards as cited in Natural Resources Canada, *Energy in Canada 2000.* www.nrcan.gc.ca/ es/ener2000.

fish biomass is declining, conventional TFP understates "true" TFP, which includes the resource stock, and that, analogously, in years when biomass is rising, conventional TFP overstates productivity growth adjusted for changes in natural capital. This is because in abundant years it is easier and hence cheaper to harvest fish, and excluding the resource stock makes it look as though technological change, not the increase in the resource stock, is the contributing factor to the increased outputs. In Squires's time series, productivity growth is on average about half that of measured TFP. Changes in the resource stock (and other variables such as capacity utilization and the catchability of the fish stock) are responsible for a significant portion of the measured productivity growth. Proper accounting for changes in natural capital (both quantity and quality) can thus be extremely important in providing an accurate picture of productivity growth and sustainability.

LINKS BETWEEN NATURAL CAPITAL, TECHNOLOGICAL CHANGE AND SUSTAINABILITY OF NATURAL RESOURCES

Multifactor productivity growth captures changes in natural capital and in technology and other unexplained factors, and, as we saw above, it is important to estimate natural capital inputs in order to accurately measure productivity growth. But natural capital and technological changes are not mutually independent. For example, depletion or degradation of natural capital may stimulate investment in research and development to increase the stock size. For non-renewable resources, improved exploration techniques may result in more discoveries of viable reserves. With renewable resources, genetic and selective breeding techniques may increase biomass (e.g., timber volume, fish weight and size, crop yields). New extraction or harvesting technologies may yield higher recovery of a given stock of total reserves. There are many examples: offsetting the natural decline in pressure for oil and gas deposits; finding more fish in the oceans due to satellite mapping of stocks; or recovering more usable timber from a given tree due to advances in harvesting and sawmilling technology.

129

A second factor may be regulation. This is particularly relevant for environmental resources. Government policies that require producers and consumers to reduce waste emissions may induce technological changes that reduce the amount of emissions per unit output, thus sustaining the stock of environmental capital. For example, less polluting inputs could be substituted for those that release high levels of waste, or technologies could be introduced that turn waste products into inputs that can be used on-site or by other businesses. Regulation also plays a role in natural resources. For example, regulation of open-access fisheries may induce firms to manage aquatic stocks in a more sustainable manner.

Innovation takes time, with regard to both the discovery of appropriate technologies and the diffusion of those technologies into a particular sector from other sectors or other countries. The innovations we see today may be the result of changes in natural capital that occurred some time ago, or that occurred elsewhere and have spilled over into Canada. Thresholds may have to be crossed wherein the decline in natural capital (relative to production and consumption) reaches a point where it pays to look for ways to augment the stock or recover more of the extracted resource per unit of stock. The precise relationships are difficult to determine. Several examples of technological change in natural resource industries might serve to illustrate some of the factors responsible.

Examples of Technological Change in Natural Resource Industries

The papers published in Simpson (1999) examine technological changes and innovations in four US natural resource industries: coal, petroleum, copper and forestry. Although the lessons learned are applicable to the Canadian counterparts, examples from the energy sector and forestry show that the technology transfer from the United States to Canada is incomplete. A snapshot of each industry may help to "explain" changes in productivity in these industries over the past 40 years and highlight the roles played by depletion of the natural capital and environmental regulation.

Coal. Coal is an "old" natural resource. It has been used as an energy source for hundreds of years and is also used in the manufacture of steel. Coal is a significant input into electricity generation in the United States, less so in Canada. As shown in Chart 2, Canada has enormous reserves of coal (this is also the case worldwide); there is no fear of depletion for the foreseeable future due to exhaustion of the natural capital stock.[24] Natural capital stocks are thus not a constraint on coal production. Labour productivity and MFP growth rates for coal have been very high in some time periods — among the highest of all the natural resources (as illustrated in Tables 3 and 4 and Charts 7 and 9). Labour-productivity growth averaged 4.1 percent in the United States over the period 1950 to 1995, compared to 3.1 per-

cent in Canada over the period 1961 to 1995.[25] Thus, technological changes in the United States have likely spilled over into Canada. The industry has seen a large decrease in labour intensity due to the adoption of new technologies.[26] For example, ever larger and more sophisticated equipment (e.g., large electrified draglines) have been deployed to extract ore in surface mining, while longwalling techniques have improved productivity in underground mines. The industry is pervaded with the use of remote-control computer processes and other information technology innovations. The capital intensity of the industry has increased considerably over the past 40 years, but MFP has also increased, suggesting continued and strong technological change. Recall, however, that if coal reserves are growing, MFP measures may be overstating technological change.

Innovation has also been stimulated by environmental and health and safety regulations introduced in the 1970s. For example, the US *Clean Air Act* legislated reductions in sulphur emissions from fossil fuel combustion in electric power plants, resulting in the development of new technologies to reduce sulphur. Labour productivity in the US coal industry fell by 1.9 percent during the 1970s. The regulations, along with periods of labour unrest and the entry of inefficient producers responding to high energy prices in the 1970s, were deemed responsible. But over the period 1980 to 1995 labour productivity grew at an average annual rate of 6.6 percent, a growth rate significantly above that of the pre-regulatory period (e.g., 4 percent between 1960 and 1969). Improvements in labour relations, falling coal prices, and increases in efficiency and new marketable by-products (sulphur and methane) recovered from pollution-abatement technologies are the reasons offered for the boost in productivity. In Canada, concerns over local and regional air pollution led to guidelines and regulations to reduce sulphur emissions from fossil fuel combustion and the adoption of the new pollution-abatement technologies by coal users (e.g., electric utilities in Alberta and Saskatchewan). Coal is thus an example where regulation-induced technological change has been a major factor in productivity growth, once the adjustment to capital acquisition and new technologies occurred.

Petroleum. In contrast to coal, with its vast stocks of natural capital, oil and gas reserves have been declining. Canadian conventional oil reserves in 1998 were approximately half of what they had been in 1970 (see Chart 2). In this sector incentives for the development of new technologies are therefore more likely to be based on the depletion and degradation of reserves. Innovations that support the discovery of new reserves of oil and gas, or greater recovery from existing reserves, help to keep extraction costs from rising as quickly as the stocks of reserves are drawn down. Recall as well that the real prices of petroleum resources fell over much of the period, intensifying the need to reduce costs to keep the North American industry viable. Given the fact that supply and demand are governed by a world price, North American producers compete with lower-cost suppliers such as those in the Middle East. Bohi (1999) identifies three innovations that have lowered the costs of exploration and development of deposits: three-dimensional seismology, horizontal drilling and deepwater drilling. Other innovations have improved the process of recovering oil from existing wells; for example, replacement of losses in natural pressure can increase the total reserves extracted from a given deposit. Oil production from oil sands and other "unconventional" sources represent

technological advances that have significantly lowered the costs of extraction and processing.[27] Environmental regulations, while inducing some technological change, are believed to be a less significant factor for petroleum than for coal (Simpson 1999).

Chart 7 shows a fall in Canadian labour productivity for the oil and gas industry between the mid-1970s and the mid-1980s. The United States also experienced this drop, even though it did not have the same regulatory environment, the reason being, according to Bohi, that the number of wells drilled was greatly reduced during the period — by the 1990s, drilling in the United States was half that seen prior to 1973 — with no corresponding reduction in labour inputs. In Canada, oil and gas exploration declined by 60 percent over the period 1983 to 1995. Helliwell et al. (1989) argue that the decline in the 1980s would have been even greater had the National Energy Plan not been introduced. Private R&D expenditures (in constant dollars) were essentially flat from the 1980s to the late 1990s but may now be increasing again (United States Department of Energy 2000). Government investment in energy R&D declined by 75 percent between 1984 and 2000. Over the same period electric-utility R&D increased steadily (2 percent per year), with a portion devoted to renewable energy resources. Canada is also a world leader in fuel-cell technology. Average annual productivity growth, after falling in the 1970s and 1980s, increased significantly in the 1990s. Canada also imports R&D, so the decline in domestic R&D may not be correlated with decreasing domestic innovation over time. Given the cyclicity in this sector, it is difficult to draw a general conclusion.

131

Copper. Copper mining is almost as old as human civilization. The industry in North America dates back to the 19th century. Although some discoveries have been made in the past 40 years, reserves in Canada and the United States were generally depleted by the 1970s to the point where the industry could no longer compete with lower-cost mines in other parts of the world. Copper prices remained low due to sufficient worldwide supplies and substitution away from copper inputs (e.g., fibre optic cable substituting for copper wire). In mining, extraction costs are affected by both the quantity and the quality of natural capital. The "best" ore bodies are typically extracted first. As depletion occurs, labour (and MFP) productivity decline, because poorer-quality deposits either reduce output per unit input or require more inputs per unit output. The situation facing US and Canadian producers was to either find innovative ways of recovering copper at costs that would allow for continued production, or shut down. There was essentially no productivity growth in the US copper industry from 1960 to 1975.[28]

In this industry major innovations did occur in response to depletion, degradation and lack of productivity growth. A notable example is the recovery of copper from mine tailings using a chemical process that required the development of new solvents.[29] Wastes are literally "re-mined" to extract copper not recovered using older, less efficient technologies, essentially allowing a higher percentage of metal to be ultimately recovered from an orebody. The process has cut the tonnes of waste per tonne of ore mined by over 35 percent; in 1995 output was 21 percent above 1970 levels and 72 percent above 1985 levels. Labour-productivity growth reflects this technological

boost, increasing by 50 percent between 1980 and 1986.[30] Re-mining has a limited life, however, and these deposits will be exhausted. By the 1990s, productivity growth, while still much higher than it had been in the 1960s and 1970s, had begun to flatten. Copper illustrates how technological change can extend the life of a non-renewable natural resource. Copper is not an essential resource for most of its uses. Unless further technological change occurs, therefore, productivity in this industry is expected to fall in the United States as the industry declines.

Forestry. Forests are a renewable resource, but, as in the case of the non-renewable commodities discussed above, their natural capital can be depleted, because old-growth forests often have far more wood volume per hectare than the secondary forests that replace them (whether these are the result of planting or natural regeneration). In the case of forestry, soil fertility is the depletable resource. Unless forestry companies invest in inputs to improve fertility, the productivity of the land will decline. Another factor is insufficient reforestation. This can occur when property rights to forest land are insecure: harvesters have no guarantee of being able to harvest, 30 to 80 years hence, a tree they plant today. The problem is clearly exacerbated by long growing periods for this "crop." Property rights may be insecure, even in North America, because of inconsistent government policy — for example, with regard to leasehold arrangements or bidding policies for harvesting rights on Crown lands. In the 19th and early 20th century, many forests were essentially open access, allowing harvesters to "cut and run." The industry can now be characterized as having depleted much of its high-quality timber. Most of the industry is harvesting secondary growth, and for the segment of the industry that is still cutting old growth the sites are increasingly inaccessible. As shown in Chart 1, over the past 40 years the stock of timber has steadily declined in Canada. Other factors contributing to the decline in forest natural capital are environmental regulations, land-use restrictions, and conversion of forested lands to other uses such as agriculture, housing and protected sites. This removal of land from timber production represents an interesting trade-off. The decrease in the supply of timber lands reduces natural capital, which could, in turn, lower productivity due to reduced input and potentially higher prices for the remaining land. On the other hand, greater scarcity of natural capital could stimulate R&D in intensive forestry technologies.

Charts 1, 4, 6 and 8 show that the Canadian forest industry is characterized by steadily declining natural capital (timber stocks), positive labour-productivity growth and, from 1986 to 1994, declining MFP. A closer look at the British Columbia industry reveals factors responsible for productivity changes and the potential for sustainable production (Sedjo 1999). Over the period 1970 to 1981, labour productivity in the BC industry was relatively flat; it rose by over 60 percent between 1981 and 1987, then fell by about 9 percent between 1987 and 1992. In the 1970s unit labour costs rose by 144 percent, reflecting a period of significant labour unrest, but after 1981 growth in labour costs sharply declined, to about 1 percent per year. Despite that earlier growth in labour costs, net logging costs[31] were essentially flat from 1975 to 1993. After the 1970s, total costs were held down through the introduction of labour-saving innovations such as a new means of attaching felled trees to cables to remove them from the site (grappling).

Innovations in sawmilling technology — for example, computer-guided systems to recover more usable wood per tree — have been adopted in part of the industry. In the 1990s, the province imposed new policies such as stricter standards for the construction and maintenance of logging roads, ostensibly for reasons of environmental protection. These regulations limit the use of the labour-saving grappling technology, hence increasing logging costs. Other regulations that restrict harvests on sites adjacent to recently cut areas may lead to extensive logging in more remote areas. This will further increase costs and could help explain the negative growth rates in labour productivity in recent years. Estimates of the impact on costs range from $220 million to $1.5 billion annually (see, e.g., van Kooten 1994; Binkley 1995).[32] New innovations do not appear to be emerging in the BC forest industry.[33]

In the United States, labour productivity increased until the mid-1980s, then slowed; average annual MFP growth was negative after the mid-1980s. Unlike Canada, the United States has essentially exhausted its old-growth forests. The decline in productivity could be a result of this loss of high-quality natural capital and its substitution with lower-quality secondary growth, which produces less output per unit input. These factors might be interpreted as reducing the sustainability of timber resources. However, the United States, helped by favourable geography and climatic conditions, has been moving towards a more intensive forestry practice: plantation forests. Timber production is being stepped up through innovations such as biotechnology and genetic selection for high-yield species, more intensive use of fertilizers and pesticides, and forest practices such as optimal thinning and irrigation. However, intensive forest management has environmental implications: monoculture and increased use of fertilizers and pesticides may adversely affect other industries and wildlife and may reduce biodiversity.

These four industries illustrate the diversity of responses to changing levels of natural capital and the impact of regulation. There is ample evidence of new technologies being adopted to mitigate or offset declining stocks of natural capital. What are the implications for sustainability? Two questions arise. First, are technological change and innovation necessary to ensure productivity growth in natural resource sectors? The answer appears to be yes for the cases discussed. There are no significant threats to the sustainability of production of these natural resources or the production of goods using them as inputs.[34] But it is clear that technological change has kept production levels from falling and/or costs from rising as much as they might. Second, how well can the past predict the future with regard to technological change and innovation? This brings us back to the issues of identifying which types of natural capital are essential to sustainable production and which sectors of the economy are at greatest risk with regard to dependence on natural capital. This is a topic that requires more research.

UNMEASURED FACTORS IN PRODUCTIVITY GROWTH: ENVIRONMENTAL SERVICES

The discussion has focused to this point on natural capital in the form of natural resources. Environmental resources are another type of natural capital. Unlike most of the examples above, environmental resources are essential to the sustained life of humans and all species. We can sustain consumption and production with a degraded natural environment — for example, lower air quality, a depleted stratospheric ozone layer, less biodiversity, fewer natural areas, and climate change that raises average temperatures and increases variability of weather events such as intense storms, flooding and unseasonable temperatures. There will be tradeoffs in the form of higher insurance and health costs, loss of enjoyment from natural areas, less outdoor recreation, and higher expenditures to mitigate and adapt to the effects of ecosystem degradation. Clearly we will not be sustaining the same quality of natural capital — clean air is replaced by dirty air. If people value clean air, they will view environmental degradation as a loss in their utility due to lower consumption of clean air. This loss in consumption is difficult to measure using market values; one must turn to non-market approaches.[35] Thus one must define the notion of sustainable consumption more carefully when addressing environmental capital. The loss in environmental capital could also show up in productivity measures. As ecosystem natural capital declines and/or the stock of accumulative pollutants builds up, productivity may begin to decline. Productivity measures may, however, lag behind other indicators of sustainability because of time lags or thresholds in people's perception of the impact of environmental degradation on them and on ecosystems.

We lack ecosystem degradation indicators sufficient to determine the impact of environmental natural capital on productivity. This is an area of active research and data collection by governments, NGOs and research institutes worldwide. One problem is that we have no comprehensive measure of environmental capital. There are many indicators — ambient air quality; emissions of specific air, water and land pollutants; amount of protected lands; crude measures of biodiversity; and so on. But what is one to do with these numbers? How can they be linked to productivity and, in turn, to the sustainability of consumption? Various organizations have compiled sustainability indices from the indicators of environmental capital (and other variables). The problem is that these are largely "black box" exercises that impose weights on each indicator to perform the aggregation. In principle, these weights should be the proportionate contribution of each indicator to the outcome variable (e.g., sustained production, quality of life). But in the absence of any sort of "production function" showing how the various environmental inputs are combined to produce output, the weights become arbitrary and, often, subjective. This does not mean that these exercises are without value. They are a start, and if construction of the index is transparent and consistently measured over time, they can help draw a picture of the role of environmental capital in sustaining economies.[36]

A more modest approach is to examine the contribution of environmental natural capital to productivity growth in the context of specific industries. The effect of leaving environmental capital out of estimates of productivity is analogous to that of leaving out natural resource capital. As environmental capital is used up, its price will rise if markets reflect the scarcity of environmental goods or if greater public awareness of the benefits of environmental goods leads to pressure for more regulation. If the price goes up and environmental capital is not included as an input, measured productivity growth will understate the extent of real productivity growth, with the divergence a function of the

amount of environmental capital as a proportion of total inputs. If environmental capital is an insignificant input, measured productivity will approximate actual productivity.

Several studies have tried to estimate the difference in MFP with and without environmental capital. Repetto et al. (1996) calculated MFP with and without environmental capital for US industries expected to use varying degrees of environmental capital. They impute a value to emissions of an industry based on estimates of damage from pollution. If pollution levels fall, the net value of output rises more rapidly than when pollution levels are not incorporated. As Kolstad (2000) notes, this is not quite the same as changing the price of the environment over time but is conceptually similar. Two industries, electricity generation and agriculture, illustrate their results for the period 1970 to 1990. As noted above, the US government introduced air-pollution regulations in the 1970s. This increased the cost to electrical utilities of using the natural environment but had little effect on agriculture. The traditional measure of MFP shows a decline in productivity growth of about 9 percent over the period. If environment is included as an input, however, productivity growth is around 12 percent over the period, relative to a base year of 1970. The divergence in MFP with and without environmental services is negligible for agriculture.

Conrad and Morrison (1989) also look at the impact of environmental regulation on productivity growth. They assume that pollution regulations are socially efficient in that they correctly balance the marginal damage caused by pollution with the marginal costs of abatement. This is unlikely to be the case in practice. They also assume that pollution abatement is entirely

135

a capital expenditure. This is also not the case, but it is not a bad proxy for many manufacturing industries (their data set). Looking at the United States, Canada and West Germany, they find that for a period when environmental regulations were minimal (1960-67), traditional productivity growth measures were approximately the same as an estimate of productivity inclusive of environmental inputs; but for a period during which many environmental regulations were introduced (1972-80), the traditional measure understated the environment-adjusted measure (annual average rates of 2.2 and 2.4 percent, respectively). The effects were less pronounced for Canada (a divergence of 0.06) and West Germany (a divergence of 0.14) than for the United States. During the period 1972 to 1980, Canada's environmental regulation was on average much less stringent that that of the United States. These results suggest that measured productivity growth is understated in periods when environmental regulations are tightening, to reflect growing scarcity of environmental quality.

Swinand (1999) calls MFP adjusted for changes in the level of pollution "total resource productivity" (TRP).[37] Estimating production functions for different regions of the United States, he calculates MFP and TRP for agriculture, using pesticide pollution as his environmental variable. His results corroborate those of Repetto et al. regarding the small impact of environmental regulation on agriculture. He finds that when growth in pollution levels exceeded growth in output, TRP was less than MFP and vice versa. For example, over the period 1989 to 1993 agricultural output was growing at an annual rate of 1.1 percent, pollution was falling by 29.5 percent and TRP exceeded MFP by 0.15 percent per year (1.36 versus 1.21 percent). His results illustrate the level of complexity needed to properly establish the relationship between MFP and TRP. Doing this at the level of the aggregate economy is a daunting task.

Harchaoui and Lasserre (2001) estimate the difference between MFP and TRP when emissions of greenhouse gases are included as an input into the production processes of the Canadian business sector.[38] Modelling the production structure (cost functions) of 37 industries over the period 1981 to 1996, they find that the private shadow value of reducing greenhouse gas emissions is significant for a number of industries. Once the value of greenhouse gas emissions as an input into production is included in productivity estimates, they find that for these industries TRP grows on average by half a percentage point a year faster than conventional MFP. The difference is that costs associated with emission reductions are interpreted as productivity losses in conventional TFP. TRP grows faster than MFP because a number of industries have reduced their greenhouse gas emissions (due to public pressure, anticipated regulation or other reasons). This represents an additional efficiency gain over that measured by conventional MFP.

Chart 10 presents a very crude estimate of the relationship between GDP and pollution for Canada, showing the ratio of GDP to ambient concentrations of the five air pollutants responsible for deterioration of urban and regional air quality. While the slopes of the curves vary considerably, the ratio is rising except for ground-level ozone (O_3).[39] Over the period 1979 to 1996 output growth does not appear to be at the expense of lower levels of aggregate air quality.[40] Thus, one would expect TRP for the aggregate economy to be above MFP if the environment as an input were explicitly taken into account. These numbers are only suggestive of a trend. Air pollutants are one indicator of environmental quality. Other indicators suggest a deterioration of environmental capital (e.g., declining water quality in some regions of the country, loss of ecosystems). The work on measuring MFP inclusive of natural capital is just beginning.

Do Productivity Estimates Help Predict Sustainable Economies?

This paper has examined productivity in Canadian natural resource industries in some detail in order to determine whether depletion of natural resource capital has affected productivity growth. It has also addressed, to a much lesser extent, the relationship between environmental natural capital and productivity growth. Limitations of data and lack of published studies preclude in-depth examination of all components of natural capital. Do any conclusions regarding sustainability follow from this discussion? Is Canada on a path of continued production and consumption, without the destruction of our natural environment? This we do not know. The good news and bad news can be summarized as follows.

On the positive side, it appears that for the non-renewable resource industries examined, changes in the stock of natural capital have not led to a sustained decrease in labour productivity or MFP. Technological change, whether induced by environmental regulation or depletion of the natural capital stock, appears to be contributing to continued productivity growth. Production of these natural resources has been weakly sustainable despite falling levels of natural capital. For the economy as a whole, it has been suggested that the natural resource inputs, with the exception of energy, may represent a smaller input

CHART 10

GDP-to-Pollution Ratios, Criteria Air Pollutants, 1979-1996

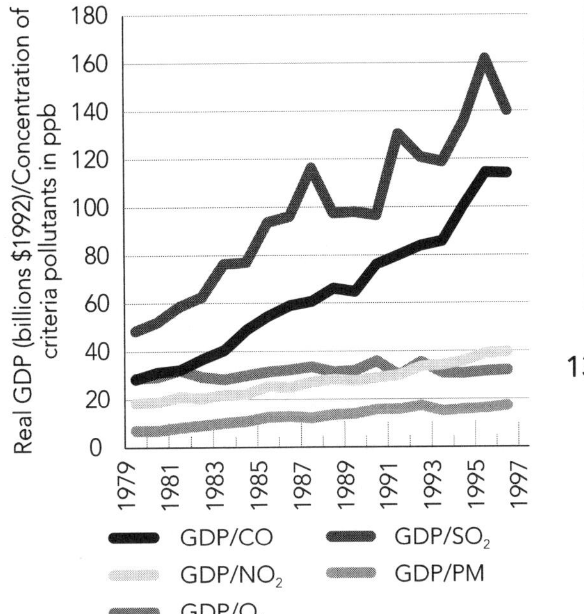

Source: Statistics Canada, Gross Domestic Product at Factor Cost. Environment Canada (1999) *State of the Environment, SOE Technical Supplement No. 99-1*, p. 5. *Urban Air Quality, Technical Appendix*, Spring 1999, www.ec.gc.ca/ind/English/Urb_Air/Tech_Sup/uasup5_e.cfm

share in aggregate production now than in the past. This changing composition of output also implies continued sustainability, because labour and human capital, reproduced capital and other materials appear to be substitutes for natural capital. Canada is a small, open economy, and as our stocks of natural capital diminish, inputs from other countries can take their place. This, too, may contribute to sustained productivity growth domestically (but may have adverse effects on the sustainability of foreign economies).

There is, however, a dark side, or at least a high degree of uncertainty about the contribution of natural capital to productivity growth and sustainability. The productivity measures for the renewable industries indicate declining sectors. This is consistent with other evidence of problems in these sectors. The fishing industry and fish stocks in general (and also some sport fisheries) are in trouble. These are predominately open-access resources where regulations have not been effective in ensuring sustainable stocks. Productivity (labour and MFP) has been falling over time. These resources are certainly not essential to continued production and consumption — people can substitute other food for fish — but these industries do affect the viability of many communities. There is also the growth of fish farming, a controversial issue in terms of its environmental impact. What we do not know are how the loss of a number of fish species will affect aquatic ecosystems and whether there will be other negative spillovers for society. Forest stocks are declining and MFP lies below that of the all-industry aggregate. Energy resources are another case in which it is not yet clear whether our path is sustainable. Productivity growth has helped sustain production of fossil fuels in recent years. Stocks of conventional oil and gas are declining, but technological changes may help to keep total oil reserves robust due to oil supplied from oil sands. In any event, there are substitutes for fossil fuels, and if markets are functioning properly and supplies do decline, rising prices for increasingly scarce fuels should accelerate the development of technologies to substitute alternative energy sources such as fuel cells. Fossil fuels are also major sources of pollution, so their use as natural resource inputs also has implications for stocks of environmental capital. This is where our ignorance about the state of our environmental capital and its impact on productivity and sustainability is evident. We do not know if we are passing thresholds (e.g., with climate change) that will lead to very high costs of mitigation or adaptation in the future, reduce

productivity and, hence, drive us onto a non-sustainable path. This uncertainty has led many researchers to advocate taking a precautionary path that requires the use of efficient environmental regulation as a complement to economic growth.

Estimating productivity changes for the Canadian economy, ideally adjusted to reflect changes in natural capital, is a worthwhile undertaking. Doing it properly requires more data and analysis at both aggregate and micro levels. Falling productivity in sectors that rely on natural capital suggests that technological change is not keeping up with depletion, that substitute inputs are not readily available and that regulation is not addressing the market failures that are associated with resource use (open access, pollution externalities). Reductions in productivity may be seen as a warning that production and consumption are moving onto a path of non-sustainability.

NOTES

1   Ideally, one would assess the importance of natural capital in the production of all goods and services. This is beyond the scope of this paper primarily because of data limitations, especially for ecosystem or environmental capital (defined below). Natural capital is clearly essential to the production of extracted natural resources. However, human capital, produced capital and technological changes affecting all aspects of natural resource production, from exploration to extraction, also play vital roles. It is the changes in the relative importance of these factor inputs over time that is a focus of the paper.

2   Examples are the so-called KLEM — capital, labour, energy and materials — production and cost functions that were estimated in the 1980s.

3   Some renewable resource stocks, namely fish and other wildlife, are difficult to observe in nature — for example, locating a migratory fish stock in the oceans. Natural capital data for these resources are very slim and are limited to studies of individual species. Aggregate data are not available.

4 Economic analysis of sustainability dates back to classic pieces such as Jevon's concern about using up coal resources in 19th-century England and Malthus's fears about the limits to food production. The 20th-century literature emanates from pieces such as Hotelling's (1931) theoretical model of non-renewable resource production, the open-access renewable resource model (e.g., Gordon 1954), Barnett and Morse's (1963, 1979) work on scarcity and growth, the Club of Rome's limits to growth (Meadows et al. 1972) and much theoretical literature spawned by these works. Economists have certainly been concerned for centuries about the contribution of natural capital to sustainability. But what is sparse is the systematic inclusion of natural capital into economic analyses of productivity growth and, in turn, the linkage of productivity growth to sustainability.

5 Reserves data are the most readily available estimates of natural capital. There are several ways of estimating reserves, each having advantages and disadvantages. The estimates presented in this paper are thus illustrative, not definitive. While coal reserves are shown on Chart 2, production of coal is not, because it would not show up on the scale presented. Estimates of other forms of natural capital — soil depth, arable land, fish stocks — are less readily available and hence not presented here. One can also obtain estimates of the value of the same natural resource stocks presented here. Values fluctuate more than physical stocks due to volatility of prices. Ideally, one would also want to know marginal costs of production, as this would be another indicator of scarcity and hence sustainability. Data on marginal costs are not available at a macro level. One would also like to compute sustainable yields of renewable natural resources. This could be done on a more disaggregated basis — for example, for a specific region or province.

6 Other Canadian reserves are much smaller — for example, oil and natural gas reserves are approximately 20 times current production. On the other hand, ultimate recovery of oil extracted from tar sands is estimated to be approximately 600 billion cubic metres, enough to last many decades at current rates of consumption. See Natural Resources Canada (2000).

7 This is the case for oil and gas, many minerals and timber (although timber is cyclical), but not for many types of fish.

8 For non-renewable resources, exploration and development is dependent on expected profits. Low oil and gas prices in the 1990s discouraged such investment. Recent price increases, combined with reductions in costs due to innovation, have stimulated drilling in recent years. For example, total wells drilled (dry, oil, gas) went from 10,000 in 1998 to approximately 18,000 in 2000, according to the Canadian Association of Petroleum Producers (2002).

9 A better measure of the scarcity of new stocks of a natural resource is the marginal cost of discovering new reserves, in the case of non-renewable resources, or the marginal cost of growing an incremental stock of renewable resources. This sort of data is not readily available for all natural resources and aggregate estimates may obscure significant differences across regions.

10 Substitution can thus come in many forms — for example, the same natural resource from other countries or recovered from more intensive recycling, or petroleum from oil sands rather than conventional sources.

11 For oil and gas and agriculture, the average annual growth rates are slightly below that of the aggregate economy. One should also be cautious about using specific end points for computing average annual growth rates.

12 The cod fishery is an example of how excessive harvesting has depleted the stock to the point where virtually no commercial harvests are viable and the stocks themselves may be irreversibly exhausted. Stocks of several Pacific salmon species also have declined significantly in recent years due to changes in water temperature, migration patterns, harvesting, disease and other factors that are not all clearly understood. Technological change may also be contributing to the depletion of fish stocks. For example, GPS and satellite tracking of fish stocks allows harvesters to accurately track a declining stock, thereby reducing increases in harvesting costs.

13 If one's focus is on sustainability of economic activity in a region — for example, resource-dependent locations — then, clearly, a national focus is inappropriate. This presents a dilemma for sustainability: at what scale should it be measured?

14 See Andrew Sharpe's paper in this volume for a more in-depth discussion of measures of productivity and what they mean for the economy and sustainability. See also Sharpe (2001) and Smith and Simard (2001).

15 More examples are provided later in the paper.

16 See, for example, Lipsey and Carlaw (2000) and Lipsey (2002) for critiques of TFP as a measure of technological change.

17 Note as well that even if natural capital is included in MFP, there may be unobserved factors in addition to technological change included in the residual.

18 All labour productivity figures for Canada represent the entire primary natural resource industry. This means they will include both production and non-production workers as well as those in initial harvesting or extraction plus some processing (e.g.,

sawmilling and pulp production, on-site concentrating of ores). Separating out the primary harvesting/extraction activities on their own would have to be done by province and most likely would involve micro-level studies.

19 One must be cautious with labour productivity measures for agriculture, because wage income is low relative to total income. Labour productivity overstates productivity in this sector. In all these estimates of labour productivity, labour is measured as hours worked.

20 Timber stocks have declined from 14.7 to 12.9 billion cubic metres, while harvests have risen from 92.2 to 181.2 million cubic metres.

21 A detailed examination of agriculture is beyond the scope of this paper. There are a number of estimates of agricultural production functions, and the role of natural capital in agriculture may be better gleaned from this work.

22 It is unfortunate that oil and gas are aggregated in Statistics Canada's series on labour productivity, because, as Chart 2 illustrates, their stocks of natural capital do not always move in the same direction.

23 One important barrier to using the quantity of natural capital as an indicator is that it is both the quantity and quality of natural capital stocks that affects their use. The absolute quantity of natural capital can be constant, but its quality can decline over time due to extraction and degradation. The declining quality may adversely affect productivity and also affect sustainability. For example, fish biomass may be constant over time, but salmon may have declined while bottom-feeders have risen. Salmon is a human food fish, while a number of bottom-feeders may be fit only for cat food and fertilizer. Similarly, forest biomass may be constant over time, but see a shift in age classes or types of timber. One must also be very careful with mineral reserve data, due to changes in quality of deposits.

24 Coal may be "economically depleted" if, due to environmental considerations and the development of less pollution-intensive energy sources, demand diminishes over time. It is possible that demand for coal as an energy input will effectively go to zero long before the stocks are depleted. If so, coal is clearly not an essential natural resource.

25 If Canadian labour productivity data were available back to 1950, Canadian numbers would probably be at least as high as those for the US.

26 Information about coal is taken from Darmstadter (1999). See also Ellerman et al. (2001) for an analysis of productivity in the US coal sector.

27 An example given by Syncrude (Clarke 1999) is that average costs of production fell by approximately two-thirds due to a variety of innovations, ranging from new types of scoops for extracting the raw material to the substitution of pipelines for conveyor belts for transporting the ore. However, more recent comments by the president of Suncor (see Cattaneo 2002) suggest that extraction costs for oil sands will be higher than previously estimated.

28 Tilton and Landsberg (1999) is the source for all the information on the US copper industry.

29 This is called solvent extraction electrowinning. Not all mines adopted this technology. Some had closed permanently and others did not have favourable conditions for its use.

30 The total labour force also fell sharply after the 1970s due to mine closures and capital deepening. Real wages also fell due to removal of unions at some mines.

31 These are total costs net of stumpage fees, royalties, depreciation and a rate of return on investment.

32 The current provincial government is in the process of changing provisions of the *Forest Practices Code*.

33 These comments are more applicable to coastal logging than interior production and reflect a host of factors in addition to the supply of natural capital — for example, US/Canada exchange rates and the softwood lumber dispute with the United States.

34 Recall that fisheries were identified in an earlier section as a renewable natural resource industry that appears to be unsustainable.

35 These could include contingent valuation, hedonic and revealed preference techniques.

36 See, for example, the sustainability indices produced by the World Economic Forum in collaboration with the Yale Center for Environmental Law and Policy and Columbia University's Center for International Earth Science Information Network. Two of their recent reports are *2002 Environmental Sustainability Index* and *Pilot Environmental Performance Index*, available at: www.ciesin.org/indicators/ESI/ESI2002_21MAR02tot.pdf and www.ciesin.org/indicators/ESI/EPI2002_11FEB02.pdf. See also Jones et al. (2002).

37 Swinand's work can also be found in Gollop and Swinand (2001). See also Acharya (1998), Smith (1998) and Weaver (1998) for discussion of the theoretical issues involved in incorporating pollution into productivity estimates.

38 This implies using the services of the natural environment as a waste depository.

39 Ground-level ozone is an input of urban smog and is associated with adverse health effects. The GDP to ozone curve is relatively flat over the period, showing neither continual improvement nor decline.

40   The data also obscure regional and daily variations in air quality. Average ambient air quality does not reflect spikes in pollutants that may occur within a given day. Days of poor air quality are correlated with higher death rates from lung and heart disease, a higher incidence of asthma attacks and other adverse events. While likely not affecting aggregate productivity, these variations in ambient quality are most definitely a quality-of-life concern to individuals.

REFERENCES

Acharya, G. 1998. "Valuing the Environment as an Input: The Production Function Approach." In *Environmental Valuation, Economic Policy and Sustainability*, ed. M. Acutt, and P. Mason. Cheltenham, UK: Edward Elgar.

Barnett, H. 1979. "Scarcity and Growth Revisited." In *Scarcity and Growth Reconsidered*, ed. V.K. Smith. Baltimore: Johns Hopkins Press.

Barnett, H., and C. Morse. 1963. *Scarcity and Growth: The Economics of Natural Resource Availability*. Baltimore: Johns Hopkins Press.

Binkley, C.S. 1995. "Designing an Effective Forest Research Strategy for Canada." *Forestry Chronicle* 71:589-595.

Bohi, D.R. 1999. "Changing Productivity in U.S. Exploration and Development." In *Productivity in Natural Resource Industries: Improvements Through Innovation*, ed. R.D. Simpson. Washington: Resources for the Future.

Canadian Association of Petroleum Producers. 2002. "Prospects for the Future: Implications of Tax, Environment, and Regulatory Policy." Presentation at C.D. Howe Policy Conference, May 29. Available: www.capp.ca

Cattaneo, C. 2002. "Rising Costs Hitting Oilsands, Suncor Warns." *Financial Post*, June 18: FP7.

Clarke, J.A. 1999. "How Syncrude Cut Costs from $40 to $13 per Barrel." *CA Magazine*, December.

Conrad, K., and C.J. Morrison. 1989. "The Impact of Pollution Abatement Investment on Productivity Change: An Empirical Comparison of the U.S., Germany, and Canada." *Southern Economic Journal* 55(1):684-697.

Darmstadter, J. 1999. "Productivity Change in U.S. Coal Mining." In *Productivity in Natural Resource Industries: Improvements Through Innovation*, ed. R.D. Simpson. Washington: Resources for the Future.

Ellerman, D., T.M. Stoker, and E. Berndt. 2001. "Sources of Productivity Growth in the American Coal Industry: 1972-95." In *New Developments in Productivity Analysis*, ed. C.R Hulten, E.R. Dean, and M.J. Harper. Chicago: University of Chicago Press.

Environment Canada. National Environmental Indicator Series, Canadian Consumption of Energy, 1961-1997, at www.ec.gc.ca/soer-ree/English/Indicators/Issues/Energy/Tables/ectb01_3.cfm

Gollop, F.M., and G.P. Swinand. 2001. "Total Resource Productivity: Accounting for Changing Environmental Quality." In *New Developments in Productivity Analysis*, ed. C.R Hulten, E.R. Dean, and M.J. Harper. Chicago: University of Chicago Press.

Gordon, H.S. 1954. "The Economic Theory of a Common Property Resource." *Journal of Political Economy* 62(2):124-142.

Harchaoui, T., D. Kabrelyan, and R. Smith. 2001. "Accounting for Greenhouse Gases in the Standard Productivity Framework." Unpublished manuscript. Ottawa: Statistics Canada.

Harchaoui, T., and P. Lasserre. 2001, October. "CO_2 Emissions, Shadow Prices and Productivity in Canada, 1981-1996." Unpublished manuscript.

Helliwell, J., M.E. MacGregor, R.N. MacRae, and A. Plourde. 1989. *Oil and Gas in Canada: The Effect of Domestic Policies and World Events*. Canadian Tax Paper #83. Toronto: Canadian Tax Foundation.

Hotelling, H. 1931. "The Economics of Exhaustible Resources." *Journal of Political Economy* 39(2): 137-175.

Jones, L., L. Fredricksen, and T. Wates. 2002. *Environmental Indicators, 5th Ed*. Fraser Institute Critical Issues Bulletin. Vancouver: Fraser Institute.

Kolstad, C. 2000. *Environmental Economics*. New York: Oxford University Press.

Lipsey, R.G. 2002. "The Productivity Paradox: A Case of the Emperor's New Clothers." *Isuma* 3(1): 120-126.

Lipsey, R.G., and K. Carlaw. 2000. "What Does Total Factor Productivity Measure?" *International Productivity Monitor* 1:31-40.

Meadows, D.H., D.L. Meadows, J. Randers, and W.W. Behrens III. 1972. *The Limits to Growth: A Report for the Club of Rome's Project on the Predicament of Mankind*. New York: Universe Books.

Natural Resources Canada. 2000. *Energy in Canada 2000*. Available: www.nrcan.gc.ca/es/ener2000

Parry, I.W.H. 1999. "Productivity Trends in Natural Resource Industries." In *Productivity in Natural Resource Industries: Improvements Through Innovation*, ed. R.D. Simpson. Washington: Resources for the Future.

Rao, S., and J. Tang. 2001. "The Contribution of ICTs to Productivity Growth in Canada and the United States in the 1990s." *International Productivity Monitor* 3:3-18.

Repetto, R., D. Rothman, P. Faeth, and D. Austin. 1996, October. *Has Environmental Protection Really Reduced Productivity Growth?* Washington: World Resources Institute.

Sedjo, R.A. 1999. "The Forest Sector: Important Innovations." In *Productivity in Natural Resource Industries: Improvements Through Innovation*, ed. R.D. Simpson. Washington: Resources for the Future.

Sharpe, A. 2001. "The Development of Indicators for Human Capital Sustainability." Working paper. Ottawa: Centre for the Study of Living Standards.

Simpson, R.D., ed. 1999. *Productivity in Natural Resource Industries: Improvements Through Innovation.* Washington: Resources for the Future.

Smith, R., and C. Simard. 2001. "A Proposed Approach to Environmental and Sustainable Development Indicators Based on Capital." Working paper. Ottawa: Centre for the Study of Living Standards.

Smith, V.K. 1998. "Should Pollution Reductions Count as Productivity Gains for Agriculture?" *American Journal of Agricultural Economics* 80(3):591-594.

Suires, Dale. 1992. "Productivity Measurement in Common Property Resource Industries: An Application to the Pacific Coast Trawl Fishery." *Rand Journal of Economics* 23(2): 221-236.

Swinand, G.P. 1999. *From Total Factor Productivity to Total Resource Productivity: Incorporating Trends in Pesticide Pollution into Productivity Growth Measures in U.S. Agriculture.* Ph.D diss., Boston College.

Tilton, J.E., and H.H. Landsberg. 1999. "Innovation, Productivity Growth, and the Survival of the U.S. Copper Industry." In *Productivity in Natural Resource Industries: Improvements Through Innovation*, ed. R.D. Simpson. Washington: Resources for the Future.

United States Department of Energy. 2000. *Energy Research and Development in Canada.* Available: http://energytrends.pnl.gov/ canada/ca002.htm

Van Kooten, G.C. 1994. *Cost-Benefit Analysis of B.C.'s Proposed Forest Practices Code.* Vancouver: Forest Economics and Policy Analysis Research Unit, University of British Columbia.

Weaver, R.D. 1998. "Measuring Productivity of Environmentally Interactive Technologies: The Case of Agriculture and the Environment." *American Journal of Agricultural Economics* 80(3):595-599.

Social Determinants of Productivity: Demographics, Human Capital and Social Diversity

Population Aging, Productivity and Living Standards

William Scarth

INTRODUCTION

The productivity challenge is gaining attention among policy-makers. One reason for this is that the deficit has been "defeated." The new finance minister can afford to shift the focus to other initiatives that address the same long-run objective — to increase the living standards of Canadians over time. A second reason is the warning issued by demographers. For example, Denton and Spencer (1998) note that the rate of growth of per capita GDP is certain to fall significantly over the coming decades unless either the immigration rate or the productivity growth rate increases rather dramatically. It is the aging of Canada's population that lies behind this concern. The purpose of this paper is to evaluate some of the economic analyses that have attempted to put the concern about aging into perspective. As we shall see, it is possible that aging will lead to increases in productivity growth — even if no policy initiative is taken. In other words, population aging may create both a problem and the solution to that problem.

In the remainder of this introduction I describe more fully the basis for the concern about aging. Then, in three separate sections, I summarize research that focuses on why it is reasonable to argue that our economy possesses mechanisms that insulate living standards (at least to some extent) from the adverse effects of an aging population. In the first section I consider how an aging population affects society's incentive to invest in physical capital accumulation. The focus then shifts to an open-economy setting, where variations in the level of foreign indebtedness are just as important as changes in the capital stock. Finally, I consider how aging affects investment in human capital. A brief appendix provides a fuller explanation of some of the material in the last section.

Demographers certainly do predict that there will be dramatic growth in Canada's elderly dependency ratio — the number of individuals over 65 years of age divided by the number between 15 and 64 years of age. This ratio will essentially double, from 19.2 percent in 1996 to 38.5 percent in 2040. The most common reaction to this development is that, with so few workers trying to support so many dependants, it is obvious that our living standards will have to fall. Indeed, many studies (such as a World Bank 1994 report) have referred to this development as a "crisis." Other studies (see, e.g., Emery and Rongve 1999; Mérette 2002) reach much more optimistic conclusions, sometimes referring to the aging-population phenomenon as "much ado about nothing." How are non-specialists to react when there is such a dispersion of views in the field?

First, it should be noted that Canadians have already experienced an *overall* dependency ratio that was just as high as the level to which overall dependency will rise in the coming decades. In the 1950s, when the baby boom generation was too young to work, the youth dependency ratio was extremely high. But that overall dependency ratio was pulled down by the fact that there were relatively few older Canadians. With the passage of time, and given the dramatic drop in birth rates (the so-called baby bust), things have been in the process of switching. The youth dependency ratio has been falling while the old-age dependency ratio has been rising. The overall dependency ratio fell as the baby boomers entered their working years, and now it is rising again as the boomers begin to retire. We managed to cope quite well with the high overall dependency ratio before. Optimists presume that we can do so again.

Less optimistic individuals stress the fact that it costs a lot more to provide health care to the elderly than to provide education for the young. Numerous studies (such as Office of the Auditor General of Canada 1998 and Robson 2001) have estimated that, when the baby boomers retire, Canadian governments will need another 3 percentage points of GDP in revenue to finance existing pro-

grams for the elderly — despite some savings on other programs. Since adequate health is needed for people to enjoy consumption goods, and since an aging population requires a shifting of resources away from the production of consumption goods and towards the health sector, there may well be grounds for concern about average living standards.

Despite these estimates, optimists draw attention to several factors. First, with increased life expectancy and growing acceptance of flexible working arrangements (such as job sharing), baby boomers may choose to remain in the work force to a more advanced age than their predecessors. In addition, Canadian immigration rates may rise. Both of these developments may limit the predicted labour shortage. Second, even if these developments do not occur, and labour does become scarce, that scarcity should cause the price of labour to rise. After all, with each scarce worker having more capital to work with, her productivity will be higher. The resulting increase in pre-tax wages may make it possible for governments to tax the generation that follows the baby boomers more (to cover the extra health and pension costs for the boomers) and still leave the young better off. The next section explains how economists evaluate this possibility.

AGING, RELATIVE FACTOR PRICES AND INVESTMENT IN CAPITAL

Economists use models of overlapping generations to estimate the effects of demographic changes on living standards. The simplest framework (Diamond 1965) involves just two generations living at any point in time, the "young" and the "old." The young work with the existing stock of capital to produce output, and they decide how much of their income to consume during their working years (and how much to save so that they can supplement the public pension benefits they will receive in their old age). Saving takes the form of capital accumulation, and the decision to save is affected by the after-tax return that the individual can expect when the capital is employed during retirement.

To derive numerical predictions from a model of this sort, economists need to specify how individuals make their consumption-savings choice and how firms make their labour-capital choice when producing goods. Household decisions depend on how impatient people are, how constrained they are in their attempts to borrow, and how accurately they can predict future wages and interest rates (the yield on capital). Decisions made by firms depend on how easily labour can be substituted for capital in production processes, how rapidly capital depreciates, and the degree of competition among firms. Standard practice is to consult the empirical studies on all of these issues and, using the results of those studies as a guide, select representative parameter values for the model economy. The model economy is then used to simulate various developments, and numerical estimates of what will occur are calculated.

Many economists have constructed model economies of this sort and reported simulation results. I summarize the results of one such study here, that by Scarth and Souare (2002). This study is relatively easy to understand since it uses the simplest, baseline version of the overlapping model to examine the aging phenomenon. Fortunately, its results are representative of many of the more involved studies. To simu-

late the aging population, we need a base for comparison. Initially, therefore, the model economy is in equilibrium, with each generation the same size as all the others. Then a larger cohort arrives, the baby boomers, so that the economy comprises more young than old for an entire generation. The post-boomer cohort is the same size as the pre-boomer cohorts, so when the baby boomers become the old generation the model economy goes through conditions that are designed to be representative of what Canadians will confront in the next few decades. What are the results?

147

When the baby boomers are young, their large numbers push down both pre-tax wages and the tax rates faced by each person. In most simulations, the former effect dominates the latter, so living standards for this cohort fall somewhat. The pre-baby boom generation is better off, however. Since they own the capital that has become relatively scarce when they are old, and since they also benefit from lower tax rates, their incomes and living standards rise. Overall, consumption of the average person rises by close to 2 percent. This analysis is consistent with what we observed in Canada from the mid-1970s to the mid-1990s, when baby boomers flooded the labour market and contributed to very slow growth in wages, and older Canadians enjoyed very high interest income.

When the baby boomers constitute the old generation in the model economy, capital is the relatively abundant factor of production, so interest rates fall and wage rates rise. As a result, the old suffer a drop in their living standards, while the young — the post-boomers — enjoy an increase in consumption. The model confirms the proposition that the wages of the young rise more than their taxes, so they should welcome the aging of the generation that has preceded them. Nevertheless, we should not make too much of this result, since — considering both young and old as one group — it turns out that average living standards fall by about 2 percent. Furthermore, when the baby boomers are retired they constitute the majority of the population and thus have the political power to increase the benefits paid to the old. In this way, part of the drop in their living standards can be passed on to the post-boomer generation. Overall, then, the main outcome is that average living standards fall by about 2 percent.

This set of results is surprisingly unaffected when major changes in the model economy are considered: whether households are liquidity-constrained, whether individuals within the model accurately anticipate demographic changes and their effects, and whether governments offer favourable tax treatment for household saving. This latter issue has been stressed in the literature (especially by Mérette 2002). As the baby boom generation ages, the RRSP system shifts from being an arrangement that can limit government revenue (when the majority of the population is working and receiving tax breaks by contributing to retirement savings plans) to one that can increase government revenue (when the majority of the population is retired and paying tax on the income generated by those savings). But the model economy has two important features: both government debt and per capita government spending are fixed. Thus, when government revenue would otherwise be affected by variations in the proportions of the population that are paying into and receiving payments from their RRSPs, tax rates are adjusted. This is one of the reasons why the predictions of the model economy are unaffected by a major spec-

ification difference such as the existence (or not) of tax-sheltered savings plans.

AGING AND FOREIGN INDEBTEDNESS

Other, rather different, versions of the overlapping-generations model support the general conclusion reported above. In some specifications, there are many generations alive at the same time. Instead of just two cohorts, the young and the old, with the period of analysis covering an entire generation (roughly 30 years), there are dozens of cohorts co-existing at each point in time (with a new cohort born every year). Scarth and Jackson (1998) use this version of the model economy to investigate an alternative way of increasing the old-age dependency ratio. Instead of a temporary, but long, period involving an older population (as discussed above), they consider a permanent reduction in the average retirement age. In this scenario, the aging population occurs because the average person spends a greater portion of her life in retirement. Another important feature of this analysis is that it is designed to represent a small, open economy.

The model economy discussed in the previous section assumes that the ratio of the wage rate to the interest rate is determined by the relative scarcity of labour and physical capital. There is no constraint that factor prices bear any relationship to what labour and capital earn elsewhere in the world. For this reason, that model is best applied to the entire North American economy. Since the Canadian and American old-age dependency ratios are increasing at roughly the same rate, this is a natural application of the model.

If we want to consider an analysis that applies exclusively to Canada, we must recognize that there are serious limits on how much the factor prices of any one small country can depart from what is observed elsewhere. In the modern, "globalized" world, capital is very mobile internationally. Indeed, many studies assume that the option of moving capital elsewhere makes it impossible for domestic interest rates to depart, in any lasting way, from the yield available in the rest of the world. With the most common specification for the input-output process, the fact that the interest rate is determined in the rest of the world is sufficient to make the wage level of the domestic economy determined in the rest of the world as well. Within this framework, then, it is possible to break the effect of a rising old-age dependency ratio on average living standards into two components, one that occurs because the domestic population is aging and one that occurs because the population in the rest of the world is aging. Only the second of these developments changes relative factor prices in the domestic economy.

An older population brings down the living standards, but — as with the simpler, closed-economy overlapping-generations specification discussed in the previous section — living standards decrease by a smaller percentage than does the labour force. In this setting, the cushion is provided partly by a change in factor prices and partly by a change in the economy's foreign indebtedness. In simulations using Scarth and Jackson's specification, living standards are reduced by a little over 4 percent if the retirement age falls sufficiently to increase the dependency ratio by what we anticipate for the several decades after 2030. Faced with the prospect of a longer retirement, individuals save more. As a result, the country pays off some of

its pre-existing foreign debt. Since higher savings mean less consumption for a while, there is "short-term pain." Eventually, though, with smaller interest-payment obligations to foreigners, individuals can consume more and there is "long-term gain." This gain counteracts — at least partially — the drop in living standards that occurs when there is less labour available to produce consumption goods. Living standards fall by 3 percent if an aging population occurs in the domestic economy only. The additional 1 percent drop occurs if there is an equivalent increase in the dependency ratio in the rest of the world (an event that causes the domestic interest rate to fall). Some readers may find this last outcome surprising, since it is usually assumed that lower interest rates are "good" for the economy.

It is true that lower borrowing costs make it profitable for firms to hire more capital, and more capital to work with makes labour more productive. But this favourable effect on domestic incomes competes with an unfavourable effect. With lower interest rates, individuals choose to save less. As a result, foreign debt (and the associated level of interest-payment obligations) is higher. In short, GDP is higher but the ratio of GNP to GDP is lower. Since domestic income is GNP, not GDP, this unfavourable effect cannot be ignored. It turns out that the unfavourable effect *dominates*.

Before ending this section, I touch on two issues. The first is that aging will affect the economy in ways other than by raising the dependency ratio. The second is that other important developments, such as government debt reduction, will likely continue as aging proceeds. Also, we indicate how estimates of *one-time* effects on the *level* of living standards can be converted to equivalent changes in the productivity *growth rate*.

One of the reasons for an aging population is increasing life expectancy. The models discussed above have been used to examine this aspect of aging, and favourable effects have emerged. People who live longer have an increased incentive to save. Individuals acquire more capital and achieve lower foreign indebtedness as a result, and (other things being equal) these developments raise living standards.

An additional feature of an aging population is a falling birth rate, since a population with a large proportion of old people has a correspondingly smaller proportion of individuals in the child-bearing phase of life. As a result, Canada's population growth rate is expected to fall.

According to standard growth theory, low population growth is associated with high living standards — since less of each year's output must be withheld from consumption and used to provide each worker with an adequate supply of capital. There is tension between this proposition and recent discussions of our aging population. For example, the Office of the Auditor General of Canada (1998) predicts a large drop in government revenue (and therefore in the living standards of those who are dependent on government transfers) when lower population growth causes GDP growth to fall. Scarth (2001) examines these competing effects using a small, open-economy version of a standard growth model — with overlapping generations, lifecycle features, and both forward-looking and liquidity-constrained consumers — and finds that the "rich" are better off with lower population growth (as predicted by standard theory), while the "poor" are worse off (as predicted by analysts such as the Auditor General). The model permits us to calculate the present value of all gains and losses. The conclusion is that the rich gain much more than the poor lose. Thus — as long as the rich and the poor are given equal weight, and the economist's standard rule for evaluating alternatives, the hypothetical compensation criterion, is applied — the analysis supports the proposition that lower population growth is "good."

So, the lower-population-growth dimension of the aging population is cause for optimism regarding how *average* living standards will fare as the population ages. Nevertheless, the incomes of those who are dependent on government transfers will be squeezed slightly, and income redistribution may become increasingly difficult in a global economy where mobile "rich" individuals can escape taxes that exceed international norms. Furthermore, since skilled-biased technical change will likely continue to increase the inequality of pre-tax-and-transfer incomes, it would be imprudent to give too much weight to this consideration. In short, in the face of rising demands for governments to address growing inequality, both within Canada and throughout the world, policy-makers may feel constrained to increase immigration rates by enough to avoid a significant drop in overall population growth.

There is a big difference between the model-economy simulations that have been discussed and Canada's future economy. The simulations assume that the aging population is the only shock to hit the economy, but other significant developments will very likely be occurring simultaneously as Canada's population ages. One such development is government debt reduction. Many studies (such as Scarth and Jackson) have found that if the federal debt-to-GDP ratio continues its downward trend and reaches its post-war low of about 20 percent, we can expect average living standards to increase by some 3 percent.

This is roughly what is needed to allow Canadians to shift resources from the production of consumer goods to the provision of health care for the elderly — a requirement that is not included in the simulations. Thus, the two excluded considerations essentially cancel off one another. Debt reduction can give governments just the room their budgets need to cope with rising health-care costs.

Nevertheless, the mechanisms that insulate living standards from the aging phenomenon are still incomplete. We are left with something like a 3 percent reduction in average living standards (since this is the average of the 2 percent estimate discussed in the preceding section and the 4 percent estimate discussed in this section, and since all of the simulations exclude the two effects that cancel off).

We close this section by indicating how one-time *level* effects on the standard of living can be converted to equivalent *rate of growth* effects. The following calculation might put the finding of a 3 percent one-time reduction into a productivity-growth-rate perspective. Growth in real per capita income of 2.1 percent per year for 30 years results in a rise in living standards by a factor of 1.865. Growth at one-tenth of one percentage point less (that is, by 2 percent per year) for the same period results in living standards that are higher by a factor of 1.811 — an outcome that is 3 percent lower than achieved with the higher growth rate. Thus, one way of summarizing the simulation results is to say that the aging population can be expected to reduce the annual growth rate in living standards by one-tenth of one percentage point. Many Canadians may regard this loss as fairly modest, especially considering that it will be even smaller if it is assumed that immigration rates will not be increased.

AGING AND INVESTMENT IN HUMAN CAPITAL

The economic analyses discussed in previous sections have one particularly limiting feature. They assume that labour productivity can be increased only if labour has more physical capital with which to work. But recent advances in growth theory have stressed the fact that individuals can and do invest in education and training, so that their productivity is higher even if they work with no additional amount of physical capital. If labour is expected to be the relatively scarce input as the population ages, we can expect that the return to investment in human capital will rise. Thus, by excluding this option for increasing labour productivity, the simulations have *overestimated* the threat to our living standards that is posed by aging. In this section I will attempt to explain how economists have tried to estimate the magnitude of this overestimate.

Unfortunately, the studies that focus on aging and human-capital investment are based on model economies that are more complicated than those discussed above. No study has applied the simplest version of the human-capital, endogenous-productivity growth-rate model (the textbook model) to the aging-population question. In the appendix, I show how this can be done; only the essence of the approach and the results are described here in the body of the paper.

The analysis is an extension of the many-overlapping-generations framework. Households continue to save for their retirement; the main difference is that they have two options for investing their savings — in physical capital and in human capital. There are two sectors of the economy: the goods-producing sector, which produces both consumption goods and physical capital, as before; and the education sector, which produces knowledge (human capital, which raises each individual's productivity). The education sector uses human capital more intensively in the production of knowledge than the manufacturing sector uses human capital in the production of goods. In the simplest version of the analysis, physical capital is not needed at all in the education sector, so it is employed only in the manufacturing sector. It is the fact that knowledge is a man-made input in the production process, in this extended analysis, that makes the nation's productivity *growth rate* dependent upon both demographic events and government policy.

The details concerning the structure and empirical calibration of this model economy are provided in the appendix. Since we continue to assume that government debt reduction will make room, in government budgets, for rising health-care expenditures, we limit the reported experiments to the following three:

> *An increase in the old-age dependency ratio.* Since individuals plan to spend more time in retirement, this development induces each person to save more and to re-evaluate how much of her time she spends in training. These responses at the individual level have a positive effect on the growth of living standards. However, there is a reduction in aggregate human capital, since more individuals are retired, and this has a negative effect. The simulations show that these competing influences almost exactly cancel off. The net effect on the growth rate of per capita consumption is positive, but is too small to be relevant.

> *An increase in life expectancy.* This development induces competing effects as well, but the specifics are different. The incentive for increased saving is more pronounced, so there is, on balance, a noticeable increase in the annual productivity growth rate — roughly an additional one-tenth of one percentage point in the annual growth rate, for an increase in life expectancy of four years.

> *A decrease in the population growth rate.* Just as favourable income-level effects accompany this dimension of aging in the models that abstract from human capital, favourable productivity *growth rate* effects accompany it when investment in human capital is highlighted. A drop of one percentage point in annual population growth yields an increase of about one-third of one percentage point in the annual productivity growth rate.

Do these results call for a modification of the conclusions reached in the previous sections? In one sense, no modification is required. There is additional support for the proposition that the falling-population-growth-rate dimension of an aging population is good news for *average* living standards. Nevertheless, there is still the concern that governments will have difficulty meeting the likely rising demand for income redistribution in a global setting. Since lower population growth hurts those who are dependent on government transfers — even though it raises the average income level rather dramatically — governments may want to override this dimension of the aging population by increasing immigration quotas. Thus, as argued in the previous section, it is prudent to identify, but not to count on, this good-news dimension of an aging population.

Nevertheless, there is one reason why a modified conclusion is called for. In this analysis of human capital, rising life expectancy can be expected to have a positive effect on a productivity growth rate that is small, yet large enough to compensate for the unfavourable one-time level effect of aging seen in previous sections. Overall, then, a rather benign view of aging is supported. If it is assumed that policy-makers will adjust immigration rates to keep population growth roughly constant, there are likely to be neither large negative nor large positive effects on growth in productivity or in average living standards. If it is assumed that population growth will fall, we can expect to see an increase in the growth rate of living standards.

Before concluding this section, it is worth considering how we might develop confidence regarding the finding that a focus on human capital investment does not affect the results dramatically. This is particularly worthwhile since there is disagreement on this finding in the literature. On the one hand, Devereux and Love's (1994) simulation results concerning tax changes are consistent with the small effects reported here for changes in the dependency ratio. On the other hand, Fougère and Mérette's (2000) simulations involve large effects accompanying both demographic and tax changes. A full evaluation of these alternative specifications of training and education is beyond the scope of this paper. Thus, I provide perspective in another way — by considering the following "back of the envelope" calculations (which are discussed in more detail in Scarth 2000, 259).

Consider shifting resources away from current consumption and into education. Assume that the rate of return on education is 10 percent; a shift of 1 percent of GDP would lower annual consumption by this much. What would be the payoff? This reallocation is equivalent to society annually buying an equity that pays a dividend of 10 percent. If the initial year's GDP value is unity, the present value of the first "equity purchase" is $(.01)(.10)(1/(r\text{-}n))$, where r and n denote the discount rate and the GDP growth rate respectively. Since this permanent shift of resources involves the equivalent of buying such an equity every year, the total benefit is $(0.1)(.10)(1/(r\text{-}n)^2)$. The present value of the cost is $(.01)(1/(r\text{-}n))$, so the net one-time percentage increase in living standards is $(.01)[(.10/(r\text{-}n))\text{-}1]$, which equals 0.04 if $r=.04$ and $n=.02$.

In Canada, public expenditure on education is about 5 percent of GDP, so an increase of one percentage point is a significant initiative. Roughly speaking, the reasoning in the above paragraph suggests that the net benefit is equivalent to a one-time increase in consumption of 4 percent. What increase in the annual growth rate brings the same one-time equivalent benefit? If the interest rate is 4 percent, the answer is an increase in n from 0.02 to 0.02078. I therefore conclude that a significant investment in education can be expected to generate an increase in the growth rate of the economy of about one-thirteenth of one percentage point. It would seem that scepticism is warranted whenever formal growth models show more than a modest growth-rate effect following from variations in the size of the education sector.

CONCLUSIONS

I have summarized several approaches used by economists to analyze how an aging population might affect the growth rate of per capita consumption. I have focused on basic versions of each approach so that non-specialists can better appreciate why there are competing effects. A second reason for highlighting the simulation results from several simple model economies is so that our comparison of the numerical results can be interpreted as a bold test of the robustness of some conclusions. It is noteworthy that from this approach a fairly general conclusion has emerged. It appears that the aging population will probably lead to rather modest changes in the growth rate of our living standards, and that the net effect could even be a favourable one.

APPENDIX

To highlight the role of training in the growth process, I follow Uzawa (1965) and Lucas (1988), and focus on a simple model economy with two sectors. I start with the simplified treatment in Barro and Sala-i-Martin (1995) and Turnovsky (1995), and extend it to overlapping generations by using Nielsen's (1994) extension of Blanchard's (1985) analysis of household savings behaviour. As long as household utility depends on private consumption and government-provided goods in a separable fashion, private consumption is proportional to broadly defined wealth (the sum of physical and human capital). The factor of proportionality is the sum of each individual's rate of impatience, m, and the (constant) probability of death, p. More than one newborn appears to replace each individual as she dies, so the overall population grows (at rate z).

One sector uses physical capital and labour to produce goods, and these goods can be either consumed by households or used by firms as additional capital in future periods. The second sector involves just labour; it is the education sector that produces human capital. Individuals are more productive in the goods sector when they have more human capital. The production processes are a Cobb-Douglas function in the goods sector (with capital's share equal to a) and a linear function in the training sector. Net of depreciation, the increase in human capital equals B times the amount of human capital, H, that is employed in that sector. Parameters b, p and f are the fraction of non-retired individuals who are employed in the manufacturing sector, the annual death probability faced by each individual and the retirement age. As a result, the fraction of the population that is working in the training sector is $(1-b)(1-e^{-pf})$.

Long-run equilibrium exists when the growth rate for all per capita variables is the same — that is, when per capita consumption, per capita output, per capita physical capital and per capita human capital all grow at one rate, n, which I use to denote the growth rate in living standards. The model is used to determine how a reduction in the retirement age, f, an increase in life expectancy (a fall in p) and a reduction in the population growth rate, z, affect the growth rate in living standards, n.

Parameter B indicates the gross yield on human capital, since it indicates how much "output" follows from employing one unit of "input" in the training sector. It is assumed that both physical and human capital wear out with the passage of time at the same depreciation rate, d. Thus, the net return on human capital is $r^* = B-d$. Equilibrium requires that the pre-tax return on physical capital, r, generate the same net return, $r^* = r(1-t)$, where t is the tax rate. With firms in the manufacturing sector hiring physical capital so that its marginal product is just equal to its rental cost, we have $(Y/K)=(r+d)/a$, where Y and K denote manufacturing output and physical capital.

The full-equilibrium version of the human capital accumulation identity is:

$$n+z+d=B(1-b)(1-e^{-pf}) \qquad (1)$$

The physical capital accumulation identity, when combined with the resource constraint (that output equals the sum of private consumption, C, government programs and investment in physical capital), the government budget constraint (that government spending equals tY), and the (Y/K) expression given above, implies:

$$z+x+n-d(1-t)(1-a)/a=r^*/a \qquad (2)$$

where $x=C/K$. Finally, as derived in Nielsen (1994), the full-equilibrium version of the consumption function is

$$n=r^*-m-[(p+z)(p+m)]/x+q(Y/K)/x \qquad (3)$$

where

$$q=[p(p+m)(1-a)(1-t)(1-e^{-r^*f})]/[r^*(e^{pf}-1)] \quad (4)$$

The total differential of these four equations, along with the definitions of r, r^* and the expression for (Y/K) given in the previous paragraph, are used to determine the changes in n, x, r, r^*, b, q and Y/K that result when changes in life expectancy $(1/p)$, the population growth rate (z) and the retirement age (f) are specified.

The model ensures that the discussion of these issues is internally consistent. While it is deliberately simplified, the model can be used to illustrate the quantitative effects of these developments. For this purpose, representative parameter values that are suitable if each period is interpreted as one year have been selected. The initial values for private consumption, government spending and investment in physical capital (as proportions of measured [manufactured goods] output) are assumed to be 0.55,

0.27 and 0.18. Physical capital's share of output in the manufacturing sector is 0.33; capital's depreciation rate is 0.04; the net-of-tax yield on capital is 6 percent; and the initial growth rate of the population and per capita living standards is 0.02 ($n=z=0.02$). All other parameter values are determined by the equations of the model. The numerical results are reported in the body of the paper.

NOTE

Without implication, I thank participants at the CSLS-IRPP workshop, in particular Marcel Mérette, Andrew Sharpe, Daniel Schwanen, and Malick Souare for helpful comments. Also, the able research assistance of Krishna Sen Gupta and financial support from the SEDAP research program are gratefully acknowledged.

REFERENCES

Barro, R., and X. Sala-i-Martin. 1995. *Economic Growth*. New York: McGraw-Hill.

Blanchard, O. 1985. "Debt, Deficits, and Finite Horizons." *Journal of Political Economy* 93(2):223-247.

Denton, F., and B. Spencer. 1998. "Population, Labour Force and Long-Term Economic Growth." *Policy Options*: 19(1): 3-9.

Devereux, M., and D. Love. 1994. "The Effects of Factor Taxation in a Two-Sector Model of Economic Growth." *Canadian Journal of Economics* 27(3):509-536.

Diamond, P. 1965. "National Debt in a Neoclassical Growth Model." *American Economic Review* 55(5):1126-1150.

Emery, H., and I. Rongve. 1999. "Much Ado About Nothing? Demographic Bulges, the Productivity Puzzle, and CPP Reform." *Contemporary Economic Policy* 17:68-78.

Fougère, M., and M. Mérette. 2000. "Population Aging, Intergenerational Equity and Growth: An Analysis With an Endogenous Growth Overlapping Generations Model." In *Using Dynamic General Equilibrium Models for Policy Analysis*, ed. G. Harrison, S. Jensen, L. Pedersen and T. Rutherford. Amsterdam: North Holland.

Lucas, R. 1988. "On the Mechanics of Development Planning." *Journal of Monetary Economics* 22(1):3-42.

Mérette, M. 2002. "The Bright Side: A Positive View on the Economics of Aging." *Choices* 8(1). Montreal: Institute for Research on Public Policy.

Nielsen, S. 1994. "Social Security and Foreign Indebtedness in a Small Open Economy." *Open Economies Review* 5:47-63.

Office of the Auditor General of Canada. 1998. "Population Aging and Information for Parliament: Understanding the Choices." *Report of the Auditor General to the House of Commons – 1998*. Available at www.oag-bvg.gc.ca/domino/reports.nsf/html/98menu_e.html

Robson, W.B.P. 2001. "Will the Baby Boomers Bust the Health Budget? Demographic Change and Health Care Financing Reform." *Commentary* no. 148. Toronto: C.D. Howe Institute.

Scarth, W. 2000. *Economics: The Essentials*. Toronto: Harcourt.

——. 2001. "Population Growth and Average Living Standards." (mimeo).

Scarth, W., and H. Jackson. 1998. "The Target Debt-to-GDP Ratio: How Big Should It Be? And How Quickly Should We Approach It?" In *Fiscal Targets and Economic Growth*, ed. T. Courchene and T. Wilson. Kingston, ON: John Deutsch Institute for the Study of Economic Policy.

Scarth, W., and M. Souare. 2002. "Baby-Boom Aging and Average Living Standards." SEDAP Research Paper No. 68. Hamilton, ON: SEDAP (Social and Economic Dimensions of an Aging Population), McMaster University.

Turnovsky, S. 1995. *Methods of Macroeconomic Dynamics*. Cambridge, MA: MIT Press.

Uzawa, H. 1965. "Optimal Technical Change in an Aggregative Model of Economic Growth." *International Economic Review* 6:18-31.

World Bank. 1994. *Averting the Old Age Crisis: Policies to Protect the Old and Promote Growth*. Oxford: Oxford University Press.

Working Smarter: Education and Productivity

Arthur Sweetman

THE REVIEW OF ECONOMIC PERFORMANCE AND SOCIAL PROGRESS | 2002

INTRODUCTION

Issues related to a "skills" strategy, or perhaps more accurately a "high skills" strategy, appear to be near the top of the public policy agenda. Internationally, for example, the United Kingdom's Chancellor of the Exchequer, Gordon Brown, indicated recently that he was "very much focused on the problems that arise for productivity and social cohesion if there is not a sufficient opportunity for people to get the skills necessary" (Riddell and Webster 2002). This statement was followed a few days later by the largest real increase in educational spending to occur in the UK in a few decades together with programs to increase both quality and accessibility. In Canada a similar argument seems to be motivating several public initiatives. The skills and learning agenda of the federal government's innovation strategy "rests on the principle that in the knowledge economy, prosperity depends on innovation which, in turn, depends on the investments that we make in the creativity and talents of our people."[1] Underpinning these policies is the idea that skills, produced in large part through formal education, are crucial to increasing productivity and economic competitiveness.[2]

Despite this clear policy direction, there are challenges to the value placed on education by both the individual and the country. After clarifying a few conceptual issues, I will evaluate these challenges and explore the evidence for them in relation to recent research on the link between education and productivity. I will address three sets of evidence. First, from a microeconomic perspective, I will consider the causal impact of education on individual-level earnings, which has long been considered a measure of at least marginal productivity. Then I will look at the impact of education on national productivity as reflected in economic growth per capita. Finally, I will turn to issues related to the Canadian education system (or systems, as there really are many). Since the education system generates the skills that are — barring the above-mentioned challenges — believed to be determinants of productivity, issues surrounding it are of direct relevance. Given that the focus of this paper is productivity, the discussion that follows will centre on economic/financial measures of the return on education. This discussion can thus be seen as addressing a small set of topics, since much research argues that education has many other benefits, such as reducing incarceration rates, improving health, and developing parenting skills. Education also has pure consumption — or enjoyment — value.

Overall, education is found to have a real impact on productivity at both the individual and the national level. In particular, educational quality has a significant impact on labour market outcomes and per capita economic growth. Further, the Canadian education system, with the evidence being mostly at the elementary and secondary levels, produces students with very high outcomes by international standards, which in turn has positive implications for future productivity growth. Unfortunately, there is little evidence at the post-secondary level (which is not to say that the quality is poor, only that the evidence is lacking). There is also a lack of evidence on whether the education system is operating efficiently, which raises questions about whether educational resources are being allocated in an economically efficient manner.

BACKGROUND

Canadians are concerned about the income that they, and their communities, receive from employment, and the standard of living experienced as a result. Most aspire to real earnings increases over time as a means to improve their standard of living. Most economists argue that, for an industrialized society, the primary determinant of increasing real income per person in the long term is increasing productivity. At the level of society, pro-

ductivity is commonly measured as the value of output per unit of input — for example, GDP per worker or GDP per worker hour.[3]

What we really want, to use a catchphrase, is to "work smarter." Our great-grandparents worked at least as hard as we do — certainly they worked longer hours and far more strenuously on average — but their material well-being was lower. Increased productivity has greatly increased society's standard of living. Fogel (1999) estimates that, for the United States (and Canada is not very different in this respect), the poverty line today is at a level that was met by only the top 10 percent of society a century ago. This increase is a direct result of productivity increases, and education has played a central role in raising productivity.

Working smarter involves issues not only at the individual and firm levels, but also at the national level, such as how society is organized (both formal and informal institutions), governance, government policies and property rights. These societal factors interact with those at the individual and firm levels (e.g., human capital accumulation and the willingness and ability to innovate). Education, which produces human capital, affects all levels and is a crucial determinant of productivity growth in both the medium and long terms; it is a key element of working smarter. Education allows workers to use existing physical capital more efficiently, and it drives the development and diffusion of new technologies.[4] However, it also represents a costly and far from homogeneous investment, which implies that it is possible to over- or under-invest in education, or to invest in more or less economically viable forms of human capital. Therefore, the details of the operation of the education "industry" and the quality of its output have a noticeable impact on productivity growth.[5]

THE VALUE OF EDUCATION — SOME CHALLENGES

While most pundits and policy-makers appear to believe it commonsensical that education is good for both individuals and the country, and that more is better, there are many challengers to the accepted wisdom, especially in academic and policy-development circles. Evidence supporting the "more is better" view that holds up against the arguments presented below has until recently been hard to come by and sometimes controversial. The issue is not whether education has benefits but, rather, the magnitude of its "true" benefits, the benefits relative to the costs, and the distribution of costs and benefits. There are concerns about whether common estimates of the return to education are too high, in which case society may be over-investing in this area. Other challengers ask whether the social return on education exceeds the private return sufficiently to justify increased (or sustained) subsidization, and whether the education system is being run efficiently. A sample perspective on these policy concerns comes from the UK Department of Education and Employment, which argues that there is "a limit to how many extra graduates the economy can absorb before the increased productivity they generate starts to decline" (Carvel 1997).

Is It Worth Getting More Education?

A traditional argument is that the average value, or economic return, attributed to education by policy-makers and researchers is higher than it ought to be. This view stems from the longstanding belief that the ubiquitous positive correlation observed between education and earnings is biased upwards because of "unobserved ability." The argument is that those with higher education have, on average, higher innate earning potential or "ability."[6] Their higher ability is posited to cause both higher education and higher earnings, so that some of the high earnings observed for those with higher education really result from this innate (and unobserved) ability.[7] While the value of education is rarely argued to be zero, common estimates are seen as markedly high. However, if the "true" return is low, education has serious limitations as a viable policy lever to aid disadvantaged groups, since it does not really boost earnings much. Further, a low return raises questions about the value of additional investment more generally. Among the popular proponents of extreme versions of this argument are Richard Herrnstein and Charles Murray (1994), authors of *The Bell Curve*.

A related but distinct argument that implies Canada has too many highly educated people is put forward by David Livingstone (1999) of the University of Toronto.[8] The fact that his book won the John Porter Memorial Book Award of the Canadian Sociology and Anthropology Association lends credit to Livingstone's views. He argues that Canadians are overeducated and/or underemployed relative to current employer needs. Harvey Krahn (1997) makes a similar argument. He observes that in survey data many people report that their skills are underutilized in their jobs: they are overeducated relative to labour market demand. Krahn does not, however, believe there is public support for a policy of cutting back on education (for example, reducing the number of places in post-secondary institutions), thus lending support to a policy of creating more "upper end" jobs to soak up the excess of educated workers. In a related vein, some European researchers — for example, contributors to a collection of essays edited by Borghans and de Grip (2000) — suggest that a form of crowding out, or "bumping down," is occurring. The argument is that, increasingly, highly skilled workers are taking jobs traditionally held by less-skilled workers and that skills are being wasted. Further, they argue that this has a negative impact on the less-educated.[9]

Does a More Educated Country Benefit from the Investment?

The macroeconomic literature addresses similar issues. In an empirical study for the World Bank, Pritchett (1996) compares a number of countries and provocatively asks whether it is possible "to explain the surprising finding that more education did not lead to faster economic growth." He finds that increased educational attainment within the labour force does not affect the growth rate of output per worker. As will be discussed in a later section, a number of other studies have failed to find a robust relationship between country-level measures of either educational attainment or inputs that are correlated with per-capita economic growth, which results from productivity increases.

Are Educational Resources Allocated Appropriately?

An equally controversial issue is the allocation of resources, especially government resources, within the education and training sectors (and in public research, since it is hard to disentangle the two at the university level). For example, Paul Kedrosky (2002), of the University of British Columbia School of Business, argues in a newspaper editorial that the distribution of funding across fields of

study within universities is not optimal in that it oversubsidizes fields that have low value in the labour market.[10] Much more importantly, if the education system falls short of its potential, the reduced productivity of its graduates will stay with them throughout their entire lives. Such losses in productivity, summed over a lifetime, can be substantial.

CONCEPTUAL CLARIFICATIONS

Some conceptual clarifications should be made at the outset of this discussion.

(1) In developing realistic education policies, the debate is, or should be, not about whether the *average* return on education is sufficiently large to justify the entire existing educational infrastructure, but about the value to society of incremental changes in the resources allocated for a particular educational purpose — marginal changes and *marginal* benefits.[11] What is the value to society, and to the individuals directly involved, of a 1- or 2-percent change in public spending on some aspect of education? Note that each policy change will have its own marginal benefit and cost. Further, the test of each allocation decision is not whether it has a positive value, but whether the value is greater than the next best use of the resource, which might be in health care, social services or some other part of the education system. In short, the value of the investment must exceed its opportunity cost. In its extreme form, this test cannot be implemented given our lack of knowledge about the value of all possible alternatives.[12] If we care about produc-

tivity growth, however, or good management more generally, it remains a useful guide in allocating resources across alternatives.

(2) We should be interested in *causal impacts* as well as *outcomes*. While these terms can have alternative definitions, in this context an impact is the value added, or the causal result, of a particular educational program or "treatment" (e.g., an expansion in computer science enrolment). In contrast, an outcome is simply a measurement of some variable we care about and observe following the treatment. An outcome may be caused, perhaps in part, by the program in question, but it may also be caused by factors unrelated to it. The concept of an impact implies a causal link and answers a specific question such as: How much has this program caused employment or job satisfaction to *increase* for those who participated? This is quite different from an outcome, which answers a more general question such as: What is employment, or job satisfaction, following participation? An impact measures, for example, how a program has changed the average wage or unemployment rate of its graduates. An outcome, on the other hand, simply measures the graduates' average wage or unemployment rate following the program, without saying anything about whether the program caused the ensuing outcome.[13]

In general, there is no reason why a program that graduates individuals with "good" outcomes need also have "good" impacts: those graduates might have had good outcomes even in the absence of the program; alternatively, graduates with poor outcomes might have had even worse ones without the program. Programs targeting children at risk may have graduates with "normal" or even "below normal" outcomes. However, the program's impact will be quite large if those same children would otherwise have had very poor outcomes. Although we can never know the impact of a program on an individual, average impacts can be estimated for those treated, or for subgroups of the same, and benchmarks and similar proxies for impacts can be employed. In general, estimating impacts is difficult; nevertheless, keeping the concept in mind can help in evaluating programs and policies, which is a fundamental issue in maximizing productivity growth.[14] Remarkably, although it is better to inform policy using causal impacts, many programs continue to be justified without even an estimate/assessment of their outcomes.

(3) A distinction must be made between the value of education to an *individual* and to *society* as a whole. Since education in Canada is highly subsidized — all (net) taxpayers bear the costs — we must consider both the private value and the social value of education. Of course, though we consider only economic/financial factors here, the return on education is not entirely financial.

(4) It is also useful to distinguish between *partial* and *general* equilibrium effects. This point is closely related to points (1) and (3) but I separate it out for emphasis. A policy with a particular impact on a small fraction of the population may have less impact if implemented on a large scale. Graduates of an accounting program may have high outcomes, but if the pro-

gram is expanded the average return to its graduates will almost certainly fall should demand remain constant. More generally, as a higher percentage of the population acquires a post-secondary education, the increase in supply will bid down the value of that education in the labour market, unless demand is also increasing simultaneously (as seems to be occurring in some technology fields).

162 EVIDENCE ON THE VALUE OF EDUCATION FOR THE INDIVIDUAL

The last decade has seen much research on estimating the "causal" impact of education on the labour market. Motivating this work has been a belief, held by many researchers and policy-makers, that the observed return on education in the labour market is much greater than the causal one. Individuals with high earnings potential both acquire more education and achieve higher wages because of their high level of pre-education ability. The observed difference in labour market outcomes, then, arises from *both* sources: the pre-existing skills, and the learned skills associated with schooling. It is difficult to identify each independently, and ignoring one makes the other appear too significant as a determinant of outcomes.[15]

A related issue is the "signalling" or "filtering" models of education where, in extreme versions, education is assumed to have no causal impact on future productivity. As discussed by Weiss (1995), in this view of the world, education serves to filter or screen people according to their pre-existing ability. Filtering may have some value to society in that it identifies high-ability workers and allows them to be assigned to appropriate jobs, but it does not have an impact on skills. Complex models of this sort allow schooling to have both signalling and human capital augmenting aspects. If the filtering component of the return to education is large, then increasing public subsidization may reduce the quality of the filter and decrease the return on education. The empirical estimates of causal impacts discussed below implicitly address this issue.

The causal impact of education in the labour market is a central issue in the study of the impact of education on productivity. While few believe that a person's gross wage for a particular hour's work reflects her productivity for that hour, in the aggregate the economic return on education reflects the value of the output associated with that education. Since this "causal impact of education" literature estimates the impact on gross wages for population subgroups, it tells us something about the increase in output — the productivity — of education.

Most estimates of outcomes come from simple ordinary least squares (OLS) multivariate regressions that take into account factors such as years of work experience and region of residence. But because they cannot be measured (or because it is impractical to measure them on a large scale), these do not include motivation or other unobserved and pre-existing factors that might cause an increase in both schooling and wages. These types of analyses suggest that the return on a year's education, in terms of employment earnings, is in the range of 7 to 15 percent, with many estimates clustering around 10 percent and women usually showing a higher return than men[16] — that is, an additional year of schooling increases pre-tax wages by about 7 to 15 percent each and every year of a person's working life. This is a sizeable real rate of return on investment. A causal impact that is much smaller, however, puts severe limitations on education as a policy lever in generating higher standards of living and addressing equity issues.

A sizeable literature has evolved, much of which is surveyed and interpreted by Card (1995, 1999), that uses various exogenous sources of variation in educational attainment to estimate the causal impact of education using instrumental variables and statistical/econometric techniques. In this context, an instrument is some mechanism, frequently a policy or policy change, that induces people to get more (or less) education than they otherwise would. Many of the instruments follow from changes in institutional features of the education system, such as compulsory schooling laws, that cause some segment of the population to get more schooling than they otherwise would. In particular, the extra education is not correlated with the person's characteristics. This is frequently referred to as a "natural" or quasi-experiment, in contrast to a "true" random assignment experiment such as a random assignment drug trial in the medical context, which is the standard for determining causality. As Card points out, this approach builds on a long tradition in econometrics: it uses a supply-side shock to identify demand-side parameters.

Early results of this line of research were remarkable and unexpected. Point estimates of the causal impact of education were found to be at least as high as the OLS estimates, although the instrumental variable estimates usually had large standard errors and could not be said to differ statistically from the OLS ones. Importantly, however, the estimates were not lower than the OLS ones. Although many studies of this type

have been conducted across both developed and developing countries, with broadly consistent results, there have been very few in the Canadian context. A notable exception is Card and Lemieux (2001). They use the post-Second World War Canadian *Veterans Rehabilitation Act* (VRA) to explore the effect of "extra" education on a cohort of workers for decades after completing school. Canadian veterans who served overseas were eligible for substantial subsidies to pursue advanced education. However, take-up of the program was close to zero among French Canadians in Quebec, because of low rates of overseas military service and a less flexible post-secondary system, whereas take-up was substantial in Ontario. The authors look at the impact of this reduction in education costs on education levels and subsequent earnings in Ontario, using Quebec as a comparison group. Sizeable increments in education are observed for the affected birth cohorts in Ontario, but not for adjacent birth cohorts in Ontario nor for the same cohorts in Quebec. Further, this spike in education is associated with a spike in earnings. Card and Lemieux estimate a causal return on the extra education in the order of 10 to 15 percent.

One interpretation of these findings is that by using instrumental variable techniques, researchers are correcting not only for the upward ability bias but also for measurement error, which causes a bias towards zero — a case of two wrongs counterbalancing each other. Thus the ability bias exists, but its impact is roughly equal to and opposite in direction from the effect of measurement error. However, Card (1995, 1999) points to a model encompassing an additional, more subtle, interpretation. If every individual has their own unique return on education and there is substantial diversity in this return, then the instrumental variables estimate will deviate from the OLS one since it represents the average causal return among those affected by the instrument; the OLS estimate, in contrast, reflects that average correlation in the entire population.

Thus, for example, if the instrument is derived from compulsory schooling laws, it affects individuals differently. It forces some to obtain more schooling than they otherwise would, but does not affect those who would complete high school regardless of the law (see Angrist and Krueger 1991). The instrumental variables estimate is, then, the estimated causal return on education (correcting for measurement error) for those people who would have dropped out of school under the old regime but are constrained to remain in school longer by the raised compulsory schooling age. A high instrumental variables estimate implies that the subgroup in question has a high causal return on schooling but tells us little if anything about the return for other individuals, or the average for the population. In the Card and Lemieux (2001) case, the observed rate of return on the education obtained by Second World War veterans because of the *VRA* tells us only about the economic return for those who obtained the extra education as it affected them over their lifetimes. Still, a large number of such studies using different sources of variation (different supply-side policy changes) that affect different parts of the population can, together, paint a picture.

While the estimates from the instrumental variables line of research tend to be imprecise, there is little evidence that the returns are lower than the OLS ones. This implies a larger role for educational policy levers in the long run than previously believed. It appears that, for individuals, the causal private economic return is substantial. In response to work such as that by Livingstone or by Krahn mentioned earlier, while some people may feel overqualified for their jobs, *on average* education is a solid investment, and it increases productivity in the labour market.

It is worth looking at the correlation between education and three important labour market outcomes, taking into account the above discussion on the difficulties in interpreting these outcomes causally. The data are from Statistics Canada's monthly labour force surveys for the year 2000, and the variables are defined as in the survey. In Tables 1 through 3, education is presented by age group according to the highest level attained: grades 0 to 8 (i.e., less than high school), some (incomplete) high school, high-school graduate, some post-secondary, post-secondary certificate or diploma, bachelor's degree, and master's or Ph.D degree.

Table 1 presents average hourly wages by age and educational level for each gender. For both males and females, wages increase significantly with education; consistent with much previous research, the increase is greater for women than men — though the female wage level is lower. Wages also increase with age until 50 or 55, and then decline. The decline coincides with the onset of retirement; some people are, therefore, very selectively, not in the sample.

In addition to wages, employment is a crucial issue if one is concerned about output per capita. Table 2 looks at employment, either part-time or full-time, in the survey week of each of the 12 months in the sample. It is clear that the likelihood of employment increases with education for each gender and all age groups. The relationship is remarkably steep for women,

TABLE 1
Hourly Wages by Education and Age

Age\Educ	Grd 0-8	Some HS	HS Grad	Some PS	Cert	Bach	M.A./Ph.D	Total
Females								
25-29	8.81	9.80	11.66	11.98	13.57	17.05	18.49	14.19
30-34	11.02	10.26	12.92	14.37	15.38	20.12	22.37	16.00
35-39	9.84	10.94	13.50	14.82	16.32	21.99	23.25	16.30
40-44	10.23	11.26	14.08	15.31	16.55	22.08	24.27	16.27
45-49	10.13	11.80	14.59	15.46	16.82	22.40	26.03	16.82
50-54	11.02	11.79	14.79	15.41	16.80	23.26	26.14	16.94
55-59	10.38	12.04	13.89	14.40	16.78	21.90	25.41	15.77
60-64	10.03	11.81	14.43	14.11	16.33	21.07	26.73	14.87
65-69	9.58	10.79	12.75	13.22	13.26	14.50	21.61	12.96
70+	10.15	9.11	13.97	11.34	11.36	11.70	16.13	11.85
Total	**10.35**	**11.27**	**13.76**	**14.51**	**15.93**	**20.65**	**23.40**	**16.00**
Males								
25-29	13.97	13.30	14.45	13.97	16.12	19.54	21.36	16.14
30-34	13.12	14.08	16.36	16.96	18.41	22.71	24.40	18.54
35-39	14.02	15.14	17.78	18.34	20.23	25.36	26.82	20.04
40-44	14.43	16.49	18.84	19.63	21.37	26.31	28.15	20.94
45-49	15.73	17.27	20.24	22.09	22.15	27.89	29.85	22.37
50-54	16.16	17.68	20.42	22.55	22.51	28.06	31.62	22.76
55-59	16.08	17.21	20.39	19.66	21.60	25.44	31.72	21.31
60-64	14.83	16.83	19.29	21.11	20.34	25.08	30.52	20.03
65-69	12.26	12.82	15.85	19.85	16.22	22.33	23.67	16.36
70+	11.73	14.87	15.03	11.73	15.64	18.01	25.29	15.81
Total	**15.00**	**15.90**	**18.07**	**18.49**	**20.07**	**24.52**	**27.90**	**20.07**

Note: Sample sizes are 239,133 females and 251,629 males.
Source: Calculations by the author from all of Statistics Canada's 2000 labour force surveys (LFSs).

TABLE 2
Proportion Employed by Education and Age

Age\Educ	Grd 0-8	Some HS	HS Grad	Some PS	Cert	Bach	M.A./Ph.D	Total
Females								
25-29	0.23	0.47	0.70	0.68	0.81	0.83	0.83	0.75
30-34	0.40	0.53	0.72	0.70	0.79	0.83	0.85	0.75
35-39	0.39	0.60	0.73	0.72	0.80	0.81	0.85	0.75
40-44	0.47	0.63	0.76	0.77	0.82	0.82	0.83	0.76
45-49	0.45	0.60	0.74	0.75	0.81	0.84	0.90	0.75
50-54	0.37	0.52	0.68	0.71	0.74	0.81	0.84	0.67
55-59	0.28	0.42	0.54	0.56	0.58	0.61	0.70	0.50
60-64	0.13	0.23	0.28	0.31	0.35	0.25	0.45	0.26
65-69	0.03	0.06	0.07	0.13	0.09	0.16	0.26	0.07
70+	0.01	0.01	0.02	0.02	0.03	0.05	0.09	0.02
Total	**0.14**	**0.36**	**0.58**	**0.61**	**0.67**	**0.76**	**0.79**	**0.55**
Males								
25-29	0.59	0.73	0.86	0.77	0.89	0.87	0.85	0.84
30-34	0.66	0.73	0.88	0.83	0.91	0.92	0.90	0.87
35-39	0.63	0.77	0.88	0.86	0.91	0.92	0.91	0.87
40-44	0.63	0.80	0.88	0.86	0.90	0.93	0.93	0.87
45-49	0.60	0.79	0.87	0.88	0.90	0.91	0.93	0.87
50-54	0.63	0.75	0.83	0.82	0.85	0.87	0.92	0.82
55-59	0.54	0.67	0.71	0.64	0.74	0.75	0.74	0.69
60-64	0.37	0.38	0.44	0.45	0.46	0.46	0.62	0.44
65-69	0.09	0.17	0.14	0.19	0.17	0.22	0.29	0.16
70+	0.04	0.06	0.06	0.07	0.06	0.10	0.15	0.06
Total	**0.31**	**0.59**	**0.75**	**0.73**	**0.79**	**0.81**	**0.79**	**0.70**

Note: Sample sizes are 529,726 females and 486,711 males.
Source: Calculations by the author from all of Statistics Canada's 2000 labour force surveys (LFSs).

whereas men are much more attached to the labour market.

Employment is a very coarse measure in that it does not address the quantity of time supplied. Table 3 addresses this issue by looking at hours per week. In sharp contrast to the employment numbers, which represent the *probability of having a job*, hours per week *conditional on having a job* are not sensitive to educational attainment. It appears that education is associated with hourly wages and the probability of having a job, but those who have a job show very similar mean hours across education categories.

EDUCATION AND ECONOMIC GROWTH — A MACROECONOMIC PERSPECTIVE

One way of considering the total economic impact of education on society, as opposed to just the private return, is to look at the relationship between education and growth in the national economy on a per capita basis, which is a measure of productivity growth. There are many externalities, or spillovers, from education that might cause the individual and national (private and social) return to differ.

A Positive Externality from Education

One such positive externality derives from living and working in an environment with more highly educated workers. Moretti (1998) estimates the causal impact of living in cities that comprise different average levels of education. He finds that a 1-percent increase in the share of university-educated workers in a US city raises the wages of high-school dropouts in the same city by 2.2 percent. High-school graduates, those with some university education and university graduates all experience wage increases of just over 1 percent. While this externality is substantial, macroeconomists have focused on a broader picture still.

Endogenous Growth Models

An emphasis in macroeconomics for over a decade has been endogenous growth models, which see human capital leading to innovations and to the implementation of those innovations. The production and diffusion of innovation are, in turn, perceived to be central factors in the growth of a country's economy and standard of living. The central point is that if education can have even a small impact on the growth rate of living standards, over a number of years these benefits compound and generate huge increases. As we have seen, despite the posited central role of human capital in these theoretical models, most empirical researchers within this field have until recently found (at best) mixed evidence supporting the hypothesis. Most of the evidence comes from studies that use measures of the average level of schooling across countries and/or changes in schooling within countries, and then look for relationships with growth in GDP per capita (all such measures discussed below are per capita).[17] The hope is that higher levels or growth rates in education will be associated with higher growth rates in output. Of course, these studies also control for a small number of other variables, since, as noted by Hall and Jones (1997), factors such as intellectual and physical property rights remain the primary drivers of economic success levels across countries.[18]

TABLE 3
Usual Total Hours Per Week by Education and Age

Age\Educ	Grd 0-8	Some HS	HS Grad	Some PS	Cert	Bach	M.A./Ph.D	Total
Females								
25-29	34.9	34.1	35.0	33.9	35.5	36.7	37.6	35.6
30-34	34.6	33.5	34.8	34.2	34.9	35.8	36.7	35.1
35-39	35.8	33.8	34.6	34.4	34.6	34.8	36.6	34.7
40-44	35.5	35.1	35.0	34.9	35.1	35.1	36.4	35.1
45-49	37.0	35.0	35.9	35.5	35.1	35.6	36.9	35.6
50-54	35.3	34.5	35.1	34.9	34.4	35.1	36.8	34.9
55-59	33.3	32.6	33.5	34.8	33.5	33.3	34.8	33.5
60-64	33.1	30.4	32.0	33.1	32.7	30.3	33.2	32.1
65-69	29.6	29.8	28.6	24.0	25.1	25.1	26.5	27.1
70+	24.6	22.4	25.0	17.1	21.3	25.5	22.5	22.9
Total	**34.5**	**33.9**	**34.8**	**34.4**	**34.7**	**35.4**	**36.5**	**34.9**
Males								
25-29	42.9	41.8	41.7	39.9	41.2	39.9	41.0	41.0
30-34	44.6	42.7	42.6	42.0	42.3	40.9	41.7	42.1
35-39	43.0	43.3	43.3	42.7	42.3	41.1	42.3	42.5
40-44	43.3	43.4	43.2	42.6	42.4	41.6	42.9	42.7
45-49	44.1	44.1	43.0	42.3	42.4	41.6	43.0	42.7
50-54	44.1	43.7	42.1	42.3	42.0	41.4	42.8	42.4
55-59	43.3	42.6	41.6	40.6	41.5	41.6	41.3	41.8
60-64	40.8	41.5	40.8	40.6	39.8	39.7	40.5	40.5
65-69	40.0	36.2	33.3	31.7	31.6	34.2	33.9	34.6
70+	36.5	32.4	31.8	38.4	33.1	35.2	34.0	34.3
Total	**42.7**	**42.8**	**42.5**	**41.7**	**41.9**	**41.0**	**42.0**	**42.0**

Note: Sample sizes are 529,726 females and 486,711 males. Sample sizes are 280,396 females and 328,564 males.
Source: Calculations by the author from all of Statistics Canada's 2000 labour force surveys (LFSs).

Correctly measuring an economy's human capital is the central empirical problem in this exercise. Studies that have failed to find an impact for education have tended to use educational attainment, enrolment rates, or educational spending and related inputs as measures of a country's human capital. Extensive effort is put into measuring human capital. For example, Barro and Lee (1993) tried to develop better measures of educational attainment in a number of countries, but this did not give much support to the prediction that countries with a larger stock of human capital will experience higher rates of economic growth. Barro (1991) tried to include real school resources in an effort to measure quality differences, but this approach was also unsuccessful. These measures turn out to be poor proxies.

Recent empirical approaches have, however, increased critics' confidence in the empirical validity of endogenous growth models. One strand of research uses direct measures of quality and provides reasonably convincing evidence that a country's human capital is indeed an important determinant of growth. Hanushek and Kimko (2000) use measures of school quality from standardized tests administered in many countries as a method for quantifying the country's educational stock. Their data are from six sets of science and math tests written between 1965 and 1991.[19] Once these measures of actual labour force skills — that is, educational outputs — are used instead of educational inputs or credentials, the data show a substantial, and remarkably precise, correlation between human capital and growth. Economic outcomes seem to be strongly affected by the types of factors that can be measured by standardized (though not necessarily multiple-choice) testing, but are much less affected by degrees or school spending.

Barro (2001) compares two approaches. First he focuses on a very simple measure of schooling, the fraction of each gender with completed high school or greater, and attempts to correct for measurement error in the education data by using an instrumental variables approach. He finds that the male education rate has a modest impact on the growth rate of the economies in his sample, but that the female education rate has no impact. The lack of an impact for the female variable could be the result of sizeable discrimination in many of the countries in the sample, or it could be the result of his including fertility rates in the model — female education and fertility rates are so closely related that it is hard to identify the independent effects of each. However, Barro then follows Hanushek and Kimko and introduces international standardized test-score results into the regressions. Barro's test score data differ, however, in that he uses a literacy score in some specifications, whereas Hanushek and Kimko exclusively used math and science scores since they believed them to be more internationally comparable.[20] Barro concludes: "The results suggest that the quality and quantity of schooling both matter for growth but that quality is much more important" (2001, 15).[21] Using his estimates, he then does a "back of the envelope" calculation and argues that a one-standard-deviation increase in educational attainment (about one year), where that year is of "average" quality, is associated with an annual increase in GDP

of 0.44 percent. This implies a real social rate of return on education of about 7 percent.

There are, however, several arguments suggesting that 7 percent is "too big" — that it exceeds the causal impact of education.

First, as noted by Topel (1999), it is not clear that a country with very high levels of per capita income will continue to have rates of return as high as countries with low income levels. Topel does note, however, that in 1950 Canada had the world's third-highest per capita income and between 1950 and 1990 the Canadian annual economic growth rate averaged a very respectable 2.6 percent, while that of the Philippines, for example, was only 1.6 percent. So it is unclear whether there are really important diminishing returns — Romer (1990) argues that there may not be traditional diminishing returns for innovations.

Second, Hanushek and Kimko are concerned that the observed relationship between education and growth may be larger than the causal impact because the correlation could reflect both the causal impact of education on growth and causality in the other direction. This issue remains open and the exact size of the relationship is not known, but Hanushek and Kimko investigate the issue by looking at US data. In estimating the economic return on schooling in the US labour market of immigrants educated before emigrating, they observe the same positive relationship between (source-country) school quality and (US) labour market earnings. The magnitude of the relationship is somewhat reduced, however. (They also perform tests to ensure that their results are not driven by a small number of Asian countries with high growth and educational levels.) Thus it might be wise to remember that Barro's 7-percent estimate has confidence limits and is probably slightly larger than the "true" causal impact. Also, this number comes from cross-country comparisons and represents a multi-country average that may not be the actual number for any given country.

Nevertheless, the educational quality or content embodied in a country's labour force appears to have implications for productivity, and through it growth.[22] Interestingly, the earlier inability to find a relationship is itself informative when taken together with the findings in the later work using direct measures of test scores. First, and perhaps obviously, educational content as it is valued by the labour market and as a determinant of productivity is harder to measure than first thought. High-school or university completion is far from a homogeneous good. Second, educational quality, more so than inputs or credentials, appears to matter for national economic outcomes. Also, there appears to be little evidence at the international level that school resources are highly correlated with the quality, or skill level, of the labour force. We will cover this issue in more detail when discussing the domestic economy.

GENERAL EQUILIBRIUM EFFECTS AND POLICY IMPLICATIONS — A CAVEAT

The "causal impact of education" literature supports the notion that there is a substantial private return on education. This might suggest that there is room for expanding the education sector from the perspective of the student or potential student. Heckman, Lochner and Taber (1998*a*, 1998*b*), however, point to a caveat with regard to the return across individuals. In brief, they argue that the empirical literature on causal impacts focuses exclusively on *partial* equilibrium effects — that is, it examines the impact of small changes in education on small subgroups of the population. Using primarily simulation methods as evidence, they argue that were a nation to embark on a massive program of educational upgrading, the return on education would be bid down substantially as the supply increased. This implies a nuanced interpretation of research findings in the field of causal impact.

Some evidence for the general-equilibrium impact of education on rates of return is provided by Murphy, Riddell and Romer (1998), who compare the dramatic rise in the (non-causal) return on education in the United States in the 1980s and 1990s to the relatively flat profile in Canada over the same period. They find that most of the deviation between the two rates of return, in the face of similar changes in the availability of new technology, can be explained by the much larger increases in post-secondary enrolment in Canada. The price of skilled labour was bid down by a more rapidly increasing supply in Canada. From the perspective of the Canadian government this combination might lead to policy that is in keeping with Canadian values. A large-scale increase in educational enrolment can increase the national standard of living while reducing inequality — or at least preventing an increase in inequality. This is particularly important in the face of growing demand for highly educated workers. One side effect of this policy is that some highly skilled workers will undoubtedly migrate out of Canada to jurisdictions with a lower supply of, and higher wage rates for, educated workers. The fight against inequality inevitably generates conditions that foster a "brain drain." This should be seen as a cost of

169

a high-skills policy. Of course, the magnitude of the cost is not clear at this point.[23]

Chart 1 presents Canadian enrolment rates from 1976 to 2000 for 15- to 29-year-olds. It is clear that overall, as well as at the college and university level, the last quarter of a century has witnessed a massive increase in school attendance. Riddell and Sweetman (2000) document the same phenomenon, pointing out that this increase in supply has not decreased the wage premium associated with higher education, which has remained relatively constant in Canada.

Related work on education and wage inequality is Bedard and Ferrall's (forthcoming) comparison of wage and test-score dispersion across 11 industrialized countries. Looking at the test scores of cohorts of 13-year-olds in 1962 and 1982, they find that wider test-score dispersion in a country is correlated with greater wage inequality later in life. To my knowledge, this is the first study that looks at the dispersion of pre-labour market schooling outcomes in relation to wage inequality. It is not clear that this relationship is entirely causal; it might reflect, in whole or in part, a nation's underlying tolerance for inequality, which is reflected in the observed inequality in both education and the labour market. However, it seems reasonable to suspect that a school system, in focusing on the elite or providing extra resources to those facing educational challenges, will have a substantial influence on the inequality experienced by its society over the lifecycle of its students. Bedard and Ferrall also show that reductions in test-score dispersion within countries are associated with reductions in wage dispersion for the relevant cohorts. A particularly interesting new policy aimed at reducing inequality is Quebec's policy of providing extra resources to schools with students of low socio-economic status; see Hô (2002) for details.

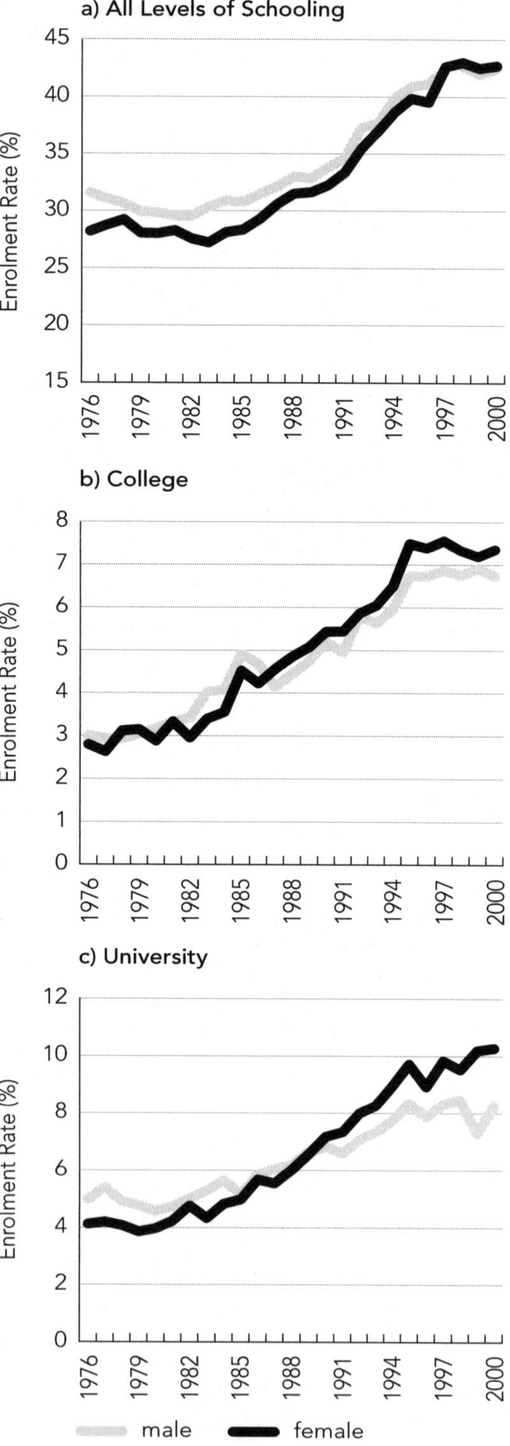

CHART 1

Full-Time Enrolment Rates for Those Aged 15-29

Source: Statistics Canada's Labour Force Survey microdata; tabulations by the author.

Of course, the actual level of productivity growth also depends on factors other than, and interacting with, education. An issue that has not been sufficiently studied is the interaction between human and physical capital accumulation. Beaudry and Green (2001) argue that, compared to the United States and European countries, Canada is accumulating human capital relatively faster than physical capital, which results in decreased relative real wage growth and increased inequality. It could be argued that the increase in human capital experienced by the Canadian economy needs a concomitant increase in physical capital to allow the value of the human capital to be fully exploited and to achieve more of the potential productivity gains.

THE CANADIAN EDUCATION SYSTEM, THE LABOUR MARKET AND THE ALLOCATION OF RESOURCES

What do the above two threads of the economics literature have to say about the educational policies Canada should be pursuing if we believe that increased productivity is an important policy goal? From the causal impact literature we can deduce that individuals, on average, gain substantially from increasing their education. At the macroeconomic level it appears that educational content has a substantial impact on economic growth, but the exact magnitude of the effect for Canada's economy is far from understood. Perhaps the most significant finding is that educational content, or quality, apparently matter decisively for the macroeconomy. It appears that productivity, especially in the long run, depends upon

the education system operating efficiently and allowing students to reach high skill levels. Given that education has a large impact on the wages of individuals and the output of the nation, and that the quality of education matters, the process by which educational quality is achieved becomes a prime concern for improving the nation's standard of living.

Quality Matters

Canadian microeconomic research strongly supports the "quality matters" result in the macroeconomic literature. Two recent individual-level studies of the Canadian labour market are Charette and Meng (1998) and Green and Riddell (2001). Using different Canadian sources of literacy and numeracy scores, both find that these measures explain a large fraction of earnings differences across workers, and account for a substantial fraction of the value of formal educational credentials in the Canadian labour market. Green and Riddell (2002) provide a useful discussion of the issues. Notwithstanding the importance of such skills, however, a very large fraction of earnings differentials remains unexplained. This is not overly surprising at the individual level since these tests are generic and much education is field-specific. In a somewhat different vein, Heckman and Rubinstein (2001) argue, using evidence from US data with both a battery of test scores and information on high-school equivalency status for individuals, that non-cognitive skills explain a substantial fraction of the variance in earnings. These non-cognitive skills appear to be associated with time spent in the classroom. Skills — and school quality — matter, but skills are more than that which is captured in simple numeracy and literacy tests.

Canada Has a Good (But Expensive) Education System

Since both education and its quality matter for productivity and economic growth, Canada is fortunate: it has good educational outcomes at the elementary and secondary levels. Tables 4 and 5 show Canada's rank in the Third International Math and Science Survey (TIMSS): led by Quebec, Alberta and British Columbia, it scores remarkably well in these international standardized tests. Table 6 presents material from a recently released OECD study of 15-year-olds. Canada has among the best results in the world, again with Alberta, British Columbia and Quebec leading the other provinces. It should be noted that even the provinces that score below the Canadian average do remarkably well by international standards.

One concern with the previous surveys is that they focus on high school, and the quality may not be sustained through the post-secondary level. Table 7 looks at prose literacy using results from the International Adult Literacy Survey (IALS). In looking at young adults and older adults, an interesting pattern emerges: the younger group scores higher than the older one. Moreover, consistent with the results in Tables 2 through 4, the younger group has very high scores by international standards. In contrast, the older adults score lower than the comparison countries. Canadian outcomes appear to have improved over time relative to those of other countries. However, post-secondary education supposedly involves a lot more than basic literacy and numeracy, and as far as I know there are no international comparisons of skills at the post-secondary level. Of course Canada's education system has many advantages; in particular its students are relatively healthy and have access to numerous learning resources.[24]

Some authors, such as Riddell (2001), have commented that Canada's good showing is a natural consequence of its heavy investment in education. In terms of both dollars per student and spending on education as a fraction of GDP, Canada spends perhaps the most on education of all OECD countries. Despite Canada's low productivity growth relative to the United States over the 1990s, this would appear to be a good investment for the future. However, there is little evidence that we are spending our education dollars optimally. For a detailed international comparison of education expenditures, see OECD (2001).

Improving Educational Quality

Unlike the United States, Canada has seen little debate on the allocation of resources, and the level of outcomes, within its education system.[25] Perhaps this is because the Canadian system appears to have much better outcomes on average, at least at the primary and secondary levels. It is common in discussions on quality improvements for the topic to quickly turn to resource limitations. However, it is interesting to note that there is little correlation across provinces in test-score outcomes and total spending. Although some spending is location-specific (e.g., heating, busing), one wonders how some jurisdictions attain such good outcomes with fewer resources;[26] there is also a lack of a correlation for spending on classroom instructors. Moreover, at the high-school level Quebec has among the largest class sizes in Canada, yet among the highest scores. If class size matters greatly, why is this the case? Similarly, spending on different educational resources varies widely by province. We do not really understand the effects of this spending.[27] More work needs to be done to ensure that we are using resources within the system optimally. Further, research is

TABLE 4

Average Score on Mathematics Test by Jurisdiction, Grade 8 Students TIMSS-99

Results Significantly Higher than Canada's		Results as Good as Canada's		Results Significantly Lower than Canada's	
Singapore	60	Netherlands	54	Latvia	51
Korea	59	Slovak Republic	53	**Newfoundland**	**50**
Taiwan	59	Hungary	53	United States	50
Hong Kong	58	**CANADA**	**53**	England	50
Japan	58	Slovenia	53	New Zealand	49
Quebec	**57**	**Alberta**	**53**	Lithuania	48
Belgium (Flemish)	56	Russia	53	Italy	48
		Australia	53	Cyprus	48
		British Columbia	**52**	Romania	47
		Finland	52	Moldova	47
		Czech Republic	52	Thailand	47
		Malaysia	52	Israel	47
		Ontario	**52**	Tunisia	45
		Bulgaria	51	Macedonia	45
				Turkey	43
				Jordan	43
				Iran	42
				Indonesia	40
				Chile	39
				Philippines	35
				Morocco	34
				South Africa	28

Note: TIMSS-99 is the Third International Math and Science Survey. The international average score is 49. "Significantly" implies statistical significance at the 95% level.
Source: *TIMSS-Canada Report*, Robitaille and Taylor (2001).

TABLE 5

Average Score on Science Test by Jurisdiction, Grade 8 Students TIMSS-99

Results Significantly Higher than Canada's		Results as Good as Canada's		Results Significantly Lower than Canada's	
Taiwan	57	Netherlands	55	United States	52
Singapore	57	**British Columbia**	**54**	**Newfoundland**	**51**
Alberta	**56**	Australia	54	New Zealand	51
Hungary	55	**Quebec**	**54**	Latvia	50
Japan	55	Czech Republic	54	Italy	49
Korea	55	England	54	Malaysia	49
		Finland	54	Lithuania	49
		Slovak Republic	54	Thailand	48
		Belgium (Flemish)	54	Romania	47
		Slovenia	53	Israel	47
		CANADA	**53**	Cyprus	46
		Hong Kong	53	Moldova	46
		Russia	53	Macedonia	46
		Ontario	**52**	Jordan	45
		Bulgaria	52	Iran	45
				Indonesia	44
				Turkey	43
				Tunisia	43
				Chile	42
				Philippines	35
				Morocco	32
				South Africa	24

Note: TIMSS-99 is the Third International Math and Science Survey. The international average score is 49. "Significantly" implies statistical significance at the 95% level.
Source: *TIMSS-Canada Report*, Robitaille and Taylor (2001).

TABLE 6

PISA Test Results by Jurisdiction, Averages and Confidence Intervals

Reading			Mathematics			Science		
Country or province	Mean	Confid. interval 95%	Country or province	Mean	Confid. Interval 95%	Country or province	Mean	Confid. Interval 95%
Alberta	**550**	**6.5**	Japan	557	10.9	Korea	552	5.4
Finland	546	5.1	**Quebec**	**550**	**5.4**	Japan	550	10.9
British Columbia	**538**	**5.7**	**Alberta**	**547**	**6.6**	**Alberta**	**546**	**6.9**
Quebec	**536**	**6.0**	Korea	547	5.5	**Quebec**	**541**	**6.7**
CANADA	**534**	**3.1**	New Zealand	537	6.3	Finland	538	4.9
Ontario	**533**	**6.5**	Finland	536	4.3	**British Columbia**	**533**	**6.4**
Manitoba	**529**	**7.0**	**British Columbia**	**534**	**5.6**	United Kingdom	532	5.3
Saskatchewan	**529**	**5.3**	Australia	533	6.9	**CANADA**	**529**	**3.1**
New Zealand	529	5.5	**Manitoba**	**533**	**7.3**	New Zealand	528	4.8
Australia	528	7.0	**CANADA**	**533**	**2.8**	Australia	528	6.9
Ireland	527	6.4	Switzerland	529	8.7	**Manitoba**	**527**	**7.1**
Korea	525	4.8	United Kingdom	529	5.0	**Ontario**	**522**	**6.8**
United Kingdom	523	5.1	**Saskatchewan**	**525**	**5.8**	**Saskatchewan**	**522**	**5.9**
Japan	522	10.4	**Ontario**	**524**	**5.8**	Austria	519	5.1
Nova Scotia	**521**	**4.5**	Belgium	520	7.8	**Newfoundland**	**516**	**6.7**
P.E.I.	**517**	**4.8**	France	517	5.4	**Nova Scotia**	**516**	**6.0**
Newfoundland	**517**	**5.6**	Austria	515	5.0	Ireland	513	6.3
Sweden	516	4.4	Denmark	514	4.9	Sweden	512	5.0
Austria	507	4.8	Iceland	514	4.5	Czech Republic	511	4.8
Belgium	507	7.1	Liechtenstein	514	13.9	**P.E.I.**	**508**	**5.4**
Iceland	507	2.9	**Nova Scotia**	**513**	**5.6**	France	500	6.3
Norway	505	5.6	**P.E.I.**	**512**	**7.4**	Norway	500	5.5
France	505	5.4	Sweden	510	4.9	United States	499	14.6
U.S.	504	14.0	**Newfoundland**	**509**	**5.9**	**New Brunswick**	**497**	**4.5**
New Brunswick	**501**	**3.5**	**New Brunswick**	**506**	**4.4**	Hungary	496	8.3
Denmark	497	4.7	Ireland	503	5.4	Iceland	496	4.3
Switzerland	494	8.4	Norway	499	5.5	Belgium	496	8.5
Spain	493	5.4	Czech Republic	498	5.5	Switzerland	496	8.8
Czech Republic	492	4.7	United States	493	15.2	Spain	491	5.9
Italy	487	5.8	Germany	490	5.0	Germany	487	4.8
Germany	484	4.9	Hungary	488	8.0	Poland	483	10.2
Liechtenstein	483	8.2	Russian Federation	478	10.9	Denmark	481	5.6
Hungary	480	7.9	Spain	476	6.2	Italy	478	6.1
Poland	479	8.9	Poland	470	10.9	Liechtenstein	476	14.1
Greece	474	9.9	Latvia	463	8.7	Greece	461	9.7
Portugal	470	9.0	Italy	457	5.8	Russian Federation	460	9.4
Russian Federation	462	8.3	Portugal	454	8.1	Latvia	460	11.0
Latvia	458	10.3	Greece	447	11.1	Portugal	459	8.0
Luxembourg	441	3.2	Luxembourg	446	4.0	Luxembourg	443	4.6
Mexico	422	6.6	Mexico	387	6.7	Mexico	422	6.3
Brazil	396	6.2	Brazil	334	7.4	Brazil	375	6.5

Note: PISA is the Programme for International Student Assessment. 95% confidence intervals provided.
Source: Human Resources Development Canada, Statistics Canada and Council of Ministers of Education, Canada (2001).

needed on curriculum development and other factors that affect the classroom. Despite the size of the education sector, we know relatively little about "best practices" in relation to labour market and other long-term outcomes. More fundamentally, we do not seem to understand the reasons for the substantial differences in outcomes across provinces.

TABLE 7

Prose Literacy Results from the International Adult Literacy Survey (IALS), Selected Countries

Age	26-35	56-65	16-65
Canada	287.3	234.1	278.8
United States	275.4	265.6	273.7
Australia	284.1	241.4	274.2
UK	275.2	235.9	266.7
Germany	284.8	256.8	275.9
Sweden	313.5	275.5	301.3

Note: Score range is 0–500.
Source: Human Resources Development Canada, OECD and Statistics Canada (2000), tables 2.1 and 3.4.

Recent, and controversial, empirical work on secondary school outcomes for some provinces has been conducted by the Fraser Institute. Perhaps the most interesting aspect of these studies is how limited the available data is and the questions that this raises about how much is actually known about the school system. The recent Ontario report (Cowley 2001) ranks 568 schools based on data provided by the province, but omits another 200 or so because the ministry of education simply did not have data on outcomes for those schools. Further, after the report was made public several of the schools complained that their numbers were incorrect. There is enormous scope for future work in understanding best practices in education as they impact on long-run outcomes including productivity, and there is enormous need for basic data collection.

Who Pays? Private and Social Returns on Education

While some work has been done in Canada on who pays for and who benefits from education, the quantity is remarkably small and many questions remain unanswered. Given the evidence on macro- and micro-level returns on education discussed above, and keeping in mind that these returns are financial only and that much of the evidence is not Canada-specific, it appears that there is reason to defend Canada's heavy subsidization of higher education. On the microeconomic side, the main caveat in using the estimates from the causal impact literature is that they all focus on gross wages or earnings and ignore direct costs. The pre-tax return is of interest since it reflects the value of education to firms. However, it does not really address the subsidization issue since it fails to take into account the increase in taxes paid, nor does it address externalities such as those measured by Moretti and discussed above. While it is not clear that taxpayers who have not attended post-secondary institutions receive sufficient indirect benefits to justify their subsidizing others to attend, the spillovers may be sufficiently great to justify an even larger subsidy.[28] We simply do not know.

Among the few attempts to measure the private and public rates of return on university education in Canada are those by Vaillancourt (1995) and Vaillancourt and Bourdeau-Primeau (2002). These authors do not take a causal approach, which, given the evidence presented above, does not appear to be a major problem. Further, they make no attempt to take a wide range of externalities into account, and therefore their estimates are best thought of as private returns and what they call public (government) returns as opposed to a full-blown social return. Their results are quite interesting: for both males and females, and in each of 1985, 1990 and 1995, the private return exceeds the public one at the bachelor's, master's and doctoral levels. Further, all sets of returns decrease as the level of education increases. There are also substantial differences in the rates of return across fields of study. However, as pointed out by Côté and Sweetman (1998), the field of study results

175

from students' choices and a random individual assigned to a field cannot be expected to obtain the same return as those already in the field. Still, it appears that the current distribution of students across fields may not be optimal in an economic sense — that is, it does not maximize the economic return on education for society. Of course, there are also non-financial factors to consider in thinking about the social return to each field. One would be hesitant to pursue policy on this issue in the absence of further study (the current work is a good start, but it is only a start). Clearly, issues such as these regarding the allocation of resources within the education sector have not been addressed sufficiently in Canada.

CONCLUSIONS

The evidence shows that increases in educational attainment continue to have a strong impact on productivity and that education is a worthwhile investment, even considering the high levels existing in Canada. This suggests that the current policy focus on a skills and innovation agenda is appropriate. The evidence is particularly compelling at the individual level. For the nation it appears that high-quality education is an important source of economic growth. It is interesting that measures such as math and science test scores seem to be particularly strongly related to national productivity (as measured by the rate of growth in per capita GDP), while international comparisons using graduation rates or educational spending are apparently much less robustly associated with productivity. What is surprising to many is the magnitude of the (private) return on education in terms of increased productivity, perhaps 10 to 15 percent in pre-

tax terms for individuals. And Barro's rough estimate based on a cross-national average puts the social return at about 7 percent for an "average" nation (it is not clear if a highly developed economy would have a higher or lower number than the average). Though these numbers must be viewed as approximate, anything in this range represents a substantial real rate of return on investment, and suggests a key role for education policy in improving Canada's productivity and standard of living.

Fortunately, convincing evidence regarding elementary and secondary schooling indicates that Canadian youths have remarkably good educational outcomes. Further, these outcomes appear to have improved over time relative to those of other countries. Unfortunately, there has been little comparison of the quality of education at the post-secondary level across countries. There is also some evidence that Canada's education policy has implications for not only average productivity levels, but also income inequality — in fact these two issues may be linked in a fundamental way. Consequently, Canada's approach may serve to both increase mean earnings and decrease earnings variance.

There remain, however, questions about whether the education system is achieving its full potential. Some of the criticisms discussed may be justified in that regard. If the system is not operating efficiently, and if students acquire a less than optimal quality and mix of skills, the impact on their productivity and standard of living will be substantial when cumulated over a lifetime. In particular, there seems to be little correlation between resource use and outcomes across provinces. Also, at the post-secondary level it is unclear whether the distribution of students across fields of study is economically optimal. Of course, there are many other factors to be considered besides economic ones.

Most importantly — especially since ongoing improvements are desirable — there is relatively little information on the school system, and relatively little research has been conducted on the relationship between detailed school inputs and long-term individual outcomes in the Canadian context. There appears to be scope for learning more about, and improving, the system. Policy issues include the appropriate level of subsidization, the distribution of students by field of post-secondary study, and the role of education in the creation and diffusion of innovation.

NOTES

The research underlying this paper was supported by the Social Sciences and Humanities Research Council of Canada. The author is grateful to the editors and a referee for their extremely helpful comments.

1 From a February 12, 2002 fact sheet provided by the Prime Minister's Office, available at http://www.pm.gc.ca. Detailed documentation concerning the federal innovation strategy can be found at http://www.innovationstrategy.gc.ca

2 Concern with these issues at the provincial level is evidenced by the establishment of an Ontario Task Force on Competitiveness, Productivity and Economic Progress, which sees "educators and skill developers" as a key stakeholder group in determining the future growth of the economy. Information on this initiative can be accessed at http://www.competeprosper.ca/institute

3 GDP is a far from ideal measure for what many people intuitively consider to be the rationale for increasing productivity, which is to improve individuals' standards of living. It ignores many items that enter into many persons' utility, and includes others that are not utility-improving. GDP per hour is sometimes thought to be more consistent with people's intuitive understanding of the concept, since measures such as GDP per worker do not take into account the fact that a key item purchased with increased productivity is leisure, which is not included in GDP. Of course, sorting out voluntary leisure from involuntary leisure (e.g., unemployment) is a difficult measurement problem. See the article by Sharpe in this volume for a detailed discussion of the conceptualization and measurement of productivity.

4 I use the term "technology" here as an economist does, not as an engineer might. A production technology includes not only machinery and buildings, but also the procedures and management structure within a firm that influence the way that equipment is used, as well as the legislation and other social structures, including the labour-relations environment, that govern the firm's operation.

5 Most observers would also point to other factors, such as increasing international trade, as key drivers of productivity growth.

6 I use the term "ability" since it is commonly used in this literature. However, it does not adequately capture the concept, which is closer to "pre-existing earnings potential." It might include factors that are not usually thought of as ability such as family wealth (if it causes both education and earnings) and race (if racism impacts on both education and earnings).

7 A standard undergraduate textbook discussion of this issue is Ehrenberg and Smith (1991, pp. 320-322).

8 Though to be fair, he argues for a revolution in the nature of labour-employer relations and for broader changes in society.

9 In contrast, Brink (forthcoming), using auto mechanics as an example, argues that the skill requirements of many jobs are increasing.

10 See also responses by Embleton (2002) and Krahn (2002).

11 The program evaluation literature recently introduced the term "local average treatment effect" (LATE) to describe the causal impact on the marginal group affected by a program change. See Smith and Sweetman (2001) for an introduction to this and related concepts in the context of evaluating social programs.

12 Naturally, non-economic returns need to be taken into account in decision-making, and this principle, though more difficult to apply in non-quantitative environments, remains useful. For example, policy-makers are well aware of the change in public sentiment following an increase in education expenditures compared to the change following an increase in health-care expenditures, which are a foregone opportunity.

13 A few provinces have instituted programs that make small payments to post-secondary institutions based on the outcomes (usually unemployment rates) of their graduates. Whether the payment reflects primarily the causal impact of the institution or the quality of its incoming students remains unclear.

14 For a technical and up-to-date discussion of estimating impacts in the non-medical context see Angrist and Krueger (1999) or Heckman, LaLonde and Smith (1999). More general introductions to the topic can be found in quantitative program evaluation textbooks such as Rossi, Freeman and Lipsey (1999).

177

15　Ignoring such a difference causes the correlation between the observed variable and the outcome of interest to reflect the impact of the observed variable *and* the impact of the omitted variable inasmuch as the two are correlated.

16　This economics literature almost universally ignores the direct costs of education and estimates a "return" where the only cost of schooling is the opportunity cost of not being employed. Also, it is usually observed that if the hourly wage is the outcome measure the rate of return will be smaller than if annual earnings (or some other, similar measure) were used, since increased education is associated with reduced unemployment and a greater number of hours of work per year.

17　Of course, as mentioned, GDP is not an ideal measure of quality of life and related issues, but it is one of the few indicators that is standardized and reported internationally.

18　For a survey of the theoretical and early empirical literature on endogenous growth, see Romer (1990); empirical problems are highlighted by Levine and Renelt (1992) and Levine and Zervos (1993). Krueger and Lindahl (2001) provide an overview of both the micro (individual level) and traditional macro (endogenous growth) literatures and suggest that the macro results are more fragile.

19　See also Decker and Radbill (1999), who use a similar test from 1995 that was administered by 32 countries, and find similar results.

20　I believe that most researchers involved in international literacy testing would agree that early tests in literacy across languages were problematic. But they would also argue that the research underlying efforts such as the international adult literacy survey (IALS) has produced testing procedures that are extremely good and are comparable across countries and languages.

21　Another approach to the measurement-error problem is to painstakingly, and with some guesswork, correct the aggregate country-level education data. De la Fuente and Doménech (2001) pursue this approach for OECD countries and produce sensible estimates of the impact of education on national income in a non-linear model that allows differential growth rates because of "catch-up."

22　When distinguishing between outcomes and impacts, as discussed earlier, it is actually the outcomes that are of concern for the economy. It does not matter if the skills were learned at home, in school or in some other situation. However, if the school system is to have a role to play in generating good outcomes at the national level, it must offer programs with substantial impacts.

23　For a discussion of the brain drain see, for example, Finnie (2002).

24　See Tompa's article in this volume on the relationship between productivity and health.

25　Examples of the debate in the United States include Hanushek and Jorgenson (1996), Hanushek (1994), and the March 1998 issue of the Federal Reserve Bank of New York's *Economic Policy Review*. The latter consists of extremely accessible proceedings of a conference on excellence in education that address these issues in some detail.

26　Statistics Canada and Council of Ministers of Education, Canada (2000) contains all of the school statistics discussed in this section.

27　It is remarkable how little information is available on this topic in Canada, although efforts are underway to collect more, and more comparable, data across jurisdictions, as evidenced by the recent publication *Education Indicators in Canada* (Statistics Canada and Council of Ministers of Education, Canada 2000).

28　For universities, calculating the cost of education is also an ambiguous challenge since it is virtually impossible to separate the institution's teaching and research functions. Gu and Whewell (1999) point out that Canadian universities are important players in creating knowledge and promoting the diffusion of new technologies, apart from their educational role. While overall Canada lags behind other G7 countries in R&D relative to the size of its economy, the share of the nation's R&D that is conducted by universities is among the highest. Universities also play a direct role in the commercialization of technology. Both university functions, teaching and research, have a strong impact on short- and long-term productivity growth.

REFERENCES

Angrist, J.D., and A.B. Krueger. 1991. "Does Compulsory School Attendance Affect Schooling and Earnings?" *Quarterly Journal of Economics* 106(4): 979-1014.

——— 1999. "Empirical Strategies in Labor Economics." In *Handbook of Labour Economics*, Vol. 3A, ed. O.C. Ashenfelter and D. Card. Amsterdam: Elsevier Science B.V.

Barro, R.J. 1991. "Economic Growth in a Cross Section of Countries." *Quarterly Journal of Economics* 106(2):407-443.

——— 2001. "Human Capital and Growth." *American Economic Review* 91(2):12-17.

Barro, R.J., and J. Lee. 1993. "International Comparisons of Educational Attainment." *Journal of Monetary Economics* 32(3):363-394.

Beaudry, P., and D.A. Green. 2001. "Canada-US Integration and Labour Market Outcomes: A Perspective Within the General Context of

Globalization." Industry Canada Conference on North American Integration, Calgary, May.

Bedard, K., and C. Ferrall. Forthcoming. "Wage and Test Score Dispersion: Some International Evidence." *Economics of Education Review.*

Borghans, Lex, and Andries de Grip, eds. 2000. *The Overeducated Worker? The Economics of Skill Utilization.* Cheltenham, UK and Northhampton, MA: Elgar.

Brink, S. 2002. "Comment on the Federal Skills Agenda." In *Towards Evidence-Based Policy for Canadian Education/Vers des politiques canadiennes d'éducation fondées sur la recherche,* ed. P. de Broucker and A. Sweetman. Kingston, ON: John Deutsch Institute for the Study of Economic Policy, Queen's University.

Card, D. 1995. "Earnings, Schooling and Ability Revisited." In *Research in Labor Economics,* ed. S. Polachek. Greenwich, CT: JAI Press.

—— 1999. "The Causal Effect of Education on Earnings." In *Handbook of Labour Economics,* Vol. 3A, ed. O.C. Ashenfelter and D. Card. Amsterdam: Elsevier Science B.V.

Card, D., and T. Lemieux. 2001. "Education, Earnings and the 'Canadian G.I. Bill'." *Canadian Journal of Economics* 34(2):313-344.

Carvel, John. 1997. "Britain to Squeeze Student Numbers." *Guardian Weekly,* February 16.

Charette, M.F., and R. Meng. 1998. "The Determinants of Literacy and Numeracy, and the Effect of Literacy and Numeracy on Labour Market Outcomes." *Canadian Journal of Economics* 31(3):495-517.

Côté, S., and A. Sweetman. 1998. "Does It Matter What I Study? Post-Secondary Field of Study and Labour Market Outcomes in Canada." WRNET Working Paper 00-01. Vancouver: University of British Columbia.

Cowley, Peter. 2001. *Report Card on Ontario's Secondary Schools.* Vancouver: Fraser Institute.

Decker, P.T., and L.M. Radbill. 1999. "Learning to Grow: Educational Quality and Economic Growth in 32 Countries." *Mathematica Policy Research,* mimeo.

De la Fuente, A., and R. Doménech. 2001. "Schooling Data, Technological Diffusion and the Neoclassical Model." *American Economic Review* 91(2):323-327.

Embleton, S. 2002. "Liberal Arts' Value: Response to Kedrosky's January 2nd, 2002, Article." *National Post,* January 21.

Ehrenberg, Ronald G., and Robert S. Smith. 1991. *Modern Labor Economics: Theory and Public Policy.* 4th ed. New York: Addison-Wesley.

Finnie, R. 2002. "The Brain Drain: Myth or Reality— What Is It and What Should be Done?" *Choices* 7(6). Montreal: Institute for Research on Public Policy.

Fogel, R. 1999. "Catching Up With the Economy." *American Economic Review* 89(1):1-21.

Green, D.A., and W.C. Riddell. 2001, March. "Literacy, Numeracy and Labour Market Outcomes in Canada." WRNET Working Paper #01-01. Vancouver: University of British Columbia.

—— 2002. "Literacy Skills, Non-Cognitive Skills and Earnings: An Economist's Perspective." In *Towards Evidence-Based Policy for Canadian Education/Vers des politiques canadiennes d'éducation fondées sur la recherche,* ed. P. de Broucker and A. Sweetman. Kingston, ON: John Deutsch Institute for the Study of Economic Policy, Queen's University.

Gu, W., and L. Whewell. 1999. "University Research and the Commercialization of Intellectual Property in Canada." Industry Canada Occasional Paper 21. Available: http://strategis.ic.gc.ca/sc_ecnmy/mera/engdoc/02c.html

Hall, R.E., and C.I. Jones. 1997. "Levels of Economic Activity Across Countries." *American Economic Review* 87(2):173-177.

Hanushek, E. 1994. *Making Schools Work: Improving Performance and Controlling Costs.* Washington: Brookings Institution.

Hanushek, E.A., and D.W. Jorgenson, eds. 1996. *Improving America's Schools: The Role of Incentives.* Washington: National Academy Press.

Hanushek, E.A., and D.D. Kimko. 2000. "Schooling, Labor-Force Quality, and the Growth of Nations." *American Economic Review* 90(5):1185-1208.

Heckman, J.J., R.J. Lalonde, and J.A. Smith. 1999. "The Economics and Econometrics of Active Labour Market Programs." In *Handbook of Labour Economics,* Vol. 3A, ed. O.C. Ashenfelter and D. Card. Amsterdam: Elsevier Science B.V.

Heckman, J.J., L. Lochner, and C. Taber. 1998*a.* "Tax Policy and Human-Capital Formation." *American Economic Review* 88(2):293-297.

—— 1998*b.* "Gender Equilibrium Treatment Effects: A Study of Tuition Policy." *American Economic Review* 88(2):381-386.

Heckman, J.J., and Y. Rubinstein. 2001. "The Importance of Noncognitive Skills: Lessons from the GED Testing Program." *American Economic Review* 91(2):145-149.

Herrnstein, R.J., and C. Murray. 1994. *The Bell Curve: Intelligence and Class Structure in American Life.* New York and Toronto: Simon & Schuster, Free Press.

Hô, V.H.G. 2002. "Carte socio-économique de la population scolaire." In *Towards Evidence-Based Policy for Canadian*

Education/Vers des politiques canadiennes d'éducation fondées sur la recherche, eds. P. de Broucker and A. Sweetman. Kingston, ON: John Deutsch Institute for the Study of Economic Policy, Queen's University.

Kedrosky, P. 2002. "No Evidence of Arts Funding Problems." *National Post*, January 2.

Krahn, H. 1997. "On the Permanence of Human Capital: Use It or Lose It." *Policy Options* 18(6):17-21.

—— 2002. "Liberal Arts' Value: Response to Kedrosky's January 2nd, 2002, Article." *National Post*, January 21.

Krueger, A.B., and M. Lindahl. 2001. "Education for Growth: Why and for Whom?" *Journal of Economic Literature* 39(4):1101-1136.

Human Resources Development Canada, OECD and Statistics Canada. 2000. *Literacy in the Information Age: Final Report of the International Adult Literacy Survey*. Ottawa: Statistics Canada.

Human Resources Development Canada, Statistics Canada and Council of Ministers of Education, Canada. 2001. *Measuring Up: The Performance of Canada's Youth in Reading, Mathematics and Science: OECD PISA Study – First Results for Canadians Aged 15*. Ottawa: Statistics Canada.

Levine, R., and D. Renelt. 1992. "A Sensitivity Analysis of Cross-Country Growth Regressions." *American Economic Review* 83(2):426-430.

Levine, R., and S.J. Zervos. 1993. "What Have We Learned About Policy and Growth from Cross-Country Regressions?" *American Economic Review* (Papers and Proceedings) 83(2):426-430.

Livingstone, D.W. 1999. *The Education-Jobs Gap: Underemployment or Economic Democracy*. Toronto: Garamond.

Moretti, E. 1998. "Social Returns to Education and Human Capital Externalities: Evidence from Cities." Working Paper #9. Berkeley, CA: Center for Labor Economics, University of California-Berkeley.

Murphy, K.M., C.W. Riddell, and P.M. Romer. 1998. "Wages, Skills, and Technology in the United States and Canada." In *General Purpose Technologies and Economic Growth*, ed. E. Helpman. Cambridge, MA and London: MIT Press.

OECD. 2001. *Education at a Glance: OECD Indicators*. Paris: OECD.

Pritchett, L. 1996, March. "Where Has All the Education Gone?" Working Paper #1581. Washington: Policy Research Department, Poverty and Human Resources Division, World Bank.

Riddell, W.C. 2001. "Education and Skills: An Assessment of Recent Canadian Experience." In *The State of Economics in Canada*, ed. P. Grady and A. Sharpe. Kingston, ON: John Deutsch Institute for the Study of Economic Policy, Queen's University.

Riddell, W.C., and A. Sweetman. 2000. "Human Capital Formation in a Period of Change." In *Adapting Public Policy to a Labour Market in Transition*, ed. W.C. Riddell and F. St-Hilaire. Montreal: Institute for Research on Public Policy.

Riddell, P., and P. Webster. 2002. "Children to Get £40 a Week to Study A Levels." *The Times*. July 2, p. 1.

Robitaille, D.F., and A.R. Taylor. 2001. *TIMSS-Canada Report, Vol. 5: Evidence for a New Century*. Vancouver: Pacific Educational Press, University of British Columbia.

Romer, P. 1990. "Human Capital and Growth: Theory and Evidence." *Carnegie-Rochester Conference Series on Public Policy* 32: 251-286.

Rossi, P.H., H.E. Freeman, and M.W. Lipsey. 1999. *Evaluation: A Systematic Approach*. 6th ed. Thousand Oaks, CA: Sage.

Smith, J.A., and A. Sweetman. 2001, November. "Improving the Evaluation of Employment and Training Programs in Canada." Presented at the HRDC conference From Theory to Practice. Available: http://www11.hrdc-drhc.gc.ca/edd-doc/fttp/conf_paper.shtml

Statistics Canada and Council of Ministers of Education, Canada. 2000. *Education Indicators in Canada: Report of the Pan-Canadian Education Indicators Program 1999*. Ottawa: Canadian Education Statistics Council.

Topel, R. 1999. "Labour Markets and Economic Growth." In *Handbook of Labour Economics*, Vol. 3C, ed. O.C. Ashenfelter and D. Card. Amsterdam: Elsevier Science B.V.

Vaillancourt, F. 1995. "The Private and Total Returns to Education in Canada, 1985." *Canadian Journal of Economics* 28(3):532-554.

Vaillancourt, F., and S. Bourdeau-Primeau. 2002. "The Returns to University Education in Canada, 1990 and 1995." In *Renovating the Ivory Tower: Canadian Universities and the Knowledge Economy*, ed. D. Laidler, Policy Study 37. Toronto: C.D. Howe Institute.

Weiss, A. 1995. "Human Capital vs. Signaling Explanations of Wages." *Journal of Economic Perspectives* 9(4):133-154.

The Impact of Health on Productivity: Empirical Evidence and Policy Implications

Emile Tompa

INTRODUCTION

Improving the living standards of populations is a widespread societal objective. A cornerstone of living standards is the ability of individuals to earn wages and profits in order to purchase goods and services for consumption. In turn, wages and profits reflect the value of the goods and services produced in an economy and the productivity of the factor inputs used to produce them. Though living standards, income and productivity are distinct concepts, the three are very much related. The correlation between labour productivity and real wages both across countries and over time is quite high, indicating the importance of productivity growth rates for the improvement of a country's living standards (Harris 1999). Consequently, economists and historians have focused much attention on better understanding the determinants of productivity growth. There is increasing awareness that human capital is a key factor. Traditionally, human capital has been interpreted as education and skills. Recently, however, increasing attention has been given to health as a form of human capital.

Over the last few years a growing body of literature has developed on the macroeconomic and microeconomic relationship between health and productivity. This chapter reviews the theoretical underpinnings and empirical evidence of this relationship. In particular, it addresses the question: Would an improvement in the health status of working Canadians pay off in terms of higher aggregate productivity? The evidence presented comes from many countries, both developed and developing, and spans a period of over 200 years. The review focuses on implications for public policy and firm-level practices in developed countries, particularly Canada.

Figure 1 provides an organizing framework for this review. It lists a number of strategies that the public and private sectors have employed to promote the health of individuals and populations, as well as several measures of health to assess the effectiveness of these strategies. Some of the strategies are employed with the express intention of improving human capital and, in turn, productivity. Others have improving health as a specific goal. The more traditional strategies of sanitation, nutrition and education are

FIGURE 1

Framework for the Review of Evidence on the Impact of Health on Productivity

Strategies	Health Measures	Labour Productivity Measures	Standard of Living Measures
Sanitation Nutrition Education Health promotion Healthy workplace Occupation, health & safety Population health	Health status Health and function Sickness absence Disability Longevity	Output per hour worked Output per paid labour hour Output per worker Output per labour force participant	Output per capita

public-sector interventions targeted at population health, but they nonetheless have implications for the health and productivity of the labour force. Another traditional public-sector intervention, occupational health and safety, is targeted at the workplace and is focused on the reduction of accidents and chemical exposures and the resultant work-related injuries, illnesses and disabilities. The strategies of health promotion and healthy-workplace promotion are newer, firm-level initiatives developed since the 1970s from the growing awareness that organizational-level interventions can be an effective means of promoting healthy lifestyles, reducing stress, improving employee wellness, and reducing sickness-related absence and health-care costs (Polanyi et al. 2000). Lastly, population health is a new strategy based on the acknowledgement that the determinants of health are multifactorial — biological, social and economic — and that health policy needs to take a broad, multisectoral approach (Frank 1995).

Figure 1 also lists several labour-productivity and standard-of-living measures that can be affected by improvements in the health of the labour force. At the individual level, health can directly increase general output (e.g., through enhanced physical energy and mental acuity), yearly output (e.g., through reduced sickness absence) and career output (e.g., through decreased morbidity or increased longevity, resulting in a longer career). At the aggregate level, these individual increases in output can translate into increases in labour productivity (i.e., output per hour worked, output per worker) and/or standard of living (i.e., GNP per capita) (e.g., by increasing the size of the active labour force relative to the population).

This chapter proceeds as follows: The next section, "Human Capital, Health and Productivity," reviews the theory on the demand for health and its relationship to the accumulation of human capital. "Historical Trends and Current Macroeconomic Evidence" reviews the historical economic evidence concerning the relationship between health and productivity growth as well as current macroeconomic empirical work on measuring this relationship. "Occupational Health and Safety and the Cost of Work Disability" reviews the changing nature of work and the implications for traditional approaches to occupational health and safety regulation — its ability to influence firm and worker behaviours and, through these, health and productivity. "Health, Sickness Absence and Firm-Level Practices" reviews the microeconomic evidence concerning the relationship between health and various productivity markers, with a focus on sickness absence. Lastly, the key implications for policy and future research are summarized.

HUMAN CAPITAL, HEALTH AND PRODUCTIVITY

Grossman's (1972, 2000) model for health demand provides insights into the relationship among health, human capital and consumption at the individual level, as well as a framework for modelling human capital accumulation and its relationship to productivity at the micro and macro levels. The main contribution of this model is that it offers insights into modelling two key aspects of human capital, health and education, and their relationship to labour supply, earnings and productivity. The model is based on Becker's (1965) household-production concept, which in turn is premised on the notion that utility is obtained not directly from market goods and services, but, rather, from final consumption goods produced from market goods and services in conjunction with one's own time. For example, leisure (a final consumption good) may be produced with the purchase of movie tickets and one's own healthy time. Some household production processes provide utility directly (e.g., the production of leisure), whereas others are inputs into other processes such as educational development or labour force participation which provide utility indirectly. A fundamental aspect of the Grossman model is that health or healthy time provides utility not only directly but also indirectly, since it is a critical input into many production processes, as described above. Accordingly, health is both a final consumption good and a capital good.

Human capital theory is premised on the notion that an increase in a person's stock of knowledge and health raises his or her productivity in both market and non-market activities. In the Grossman model, health capital differs from other forms of human capital in its effect on these activities. Health capital determines the total amount of healthy time available for them, whereas knowledge capital affects the productivity of the time spent on them. This approach suggests that health capital provides a flow of healthy time that is uniform in quality, an "all or nothing" state. An alternative formulation would be to have health capital bearing on both the quality and quantity of healthy time. Like all capital, health depreciates over time and is assumed to do so at an increasing rate with age. Consequently, investment is required to restore and/or maintain health stocks through household production activities that include inputs such as exercise, nutrition and health care. The model does not expressly include spillover effects in the production of health and education, which can be an important contributor to the efficiency of their production (e.g., the health of parents can affect child health outcomes, and some of the skills and knowledge acquired by a worker through educational pursuits can be transmitted to colleagues).

There is significant interplay between different types of human capital, specifically between education and health. In the Grossman model, higher levels of education are theorized to improve the efficiency of gross health investment.[1] The empirical literature substantiates the existence of this relationship (Grossman and Kaestner 1997). Whether it is causal — and in which direction — is not clear, though Grossman and Kaestner conclude that the evidence suggests the existence of a pathway from education to health (i.e., individuals with higher education are better at producing health). A third variable,

183

time preference, may also play an intermediate role. Higher education may result in an individual placing more value on the future (i.e., it may lower an individual's time preference, which suggests that time preference is endogenous). Alternatively, a lower discount rate may encourage an individual to seek higher levels of education, which, in turn, bears on the optimal level of health capital investment.[2]

The Grossman model can be used to identify an individual's labour supply as a function of health. The principal implication of the model is that health is determined endogenously (i.e., by the other variables in the model rather than by exogenous/external factors). In principle, education is also determined endogenously, but since most people complete their education early in life it can be treated as an exogenous variable when modelling labour supply, whereas health capital depreciates and requires ongoing investment (Currie and Madrian 1999). As the Grossman model suggests, health is also an important aspect of human capital, and an important input into market and non-market production at the individual level.

At the aggregate level, Bloom and Canning (2000) identify four pathways by which health can affect productivity: a healthy labour force may be more productive because workers have more physical and mental energy and are absent from work less often; individuals with a longer life expectancy may choose to invest more in education and receive greater returns from their investments; with longer life expectancy, individuals may be motivated to save more for retirement, resulting in a greater accumulation of physical capital; and improvement in the survival and health of young children may provide incentives for reduced fertility and may result in

an increase in labour force participation — which may, in turn, result in increased per capita income if these individuals are accommodated by the labour market.

HISTORICAL TRENDS AND CURRENT MACROECONOMIC EVIDENCE

The empirical literature in economic history provides substantive evidence concerning the productivity impact of increased life expectancy and reduced morbidity over the last few centuries in Europe and the United States (e.g., Costa and Steckel 1995; Fogel 1991, 1994; Steckel 2001/2002). Fogel (1991) stresses the importance of long-run dynamics and presents evidence that improvements in health which began some 300 years ago in Europe and North America have not yet fully run their course. This work suggests that an understanding of the key drivers of long-run dynamics may be of value to policy-making in developed countries even today. To this end, evidence from the historical economics literature is reviewed below, followed by empirical evidence based on data from more recent periods that makes use of the growth-accounting framework. Similar measures of health appear in both literatures.

Fogel (1991, 1994) presents historical trends in England, France and Sweden on two anthropomorphic measures associated with nutrition, namely adult height and weight (also known as body mass index). Height and weight provide different information about health. Adult height reflects the adequacy of early-childhood nutrition, whereas adult weight reflects the adequacy of adult nutrition. Using more recent evidence from Norway on the relationship among height, weight and risk of mortality, Fogel estimates the proportion of the decline in mortality in the three countries that can be associated with changes in these anthropomorphic measures since the 18th century. Research on the relationship among height, weight and chronic disease from more recent US data provides further evidence on the detrimental health implications of below-average height and weight (relative to current North American standards). Based on this research, Fogel (1994) concludes that chronic health conditions were significantly more prevalent throughout the life cycle prior to the First World War. Consistent with Fogel's work, Steckel (2001/2002) presents more recent evidence on anthropomorphic measures as proxies of health, supporting the notion that health can influence productivity. He found that the simple correlation between average height and log of GDP per capita ranges from 0.82 to 0.88. Furthermore, he notes that the average height of Americans is falling behind that of Northern Europeans, and that this trend may be reflective of growing income inequality in the United States.

Fogel (1994) presents evidence of the historical impact of population health on labour force productivity drawn from estimates of caloric intake in Britain and France in the 18th and early 19th centuries. He estimates that the daily caloric intake for individuals in the bottom 10 percentile of consumption in France was so low that they did not have enough energy for work, and that those in the next 10 percentile had energy for only three hours of light work (0.52 hours of heavy work). In England the situation was somewhat better. Only individuals in the bottom 3 percentile of consumption lacked enough energy for work, and those in the next 17 percentile had energy for

about six hours of light work (1.09 hours of heavy work). Essentially, those in the bottom 20 percentile had such poor diets that they were excluded from the labour force. As well, many of those in the top 40 percentile were below current North American standards of average height and weight, and hence were likely subject to premature chronic conditions and mortality. Subsequent improvements in nutrition raised the energy levels of individuals in the bottom 20 percentile of consumption such that they were able to enter the labour force. These improvements in nutrition also substantially raised the capabilities of those already in the labour force. Fogel (1991, 1994) estimates that health and nutritional improvements alone can explain some 30 percent of British growth in per capita income since 1790. This value is similar to estimates of the productivity impacts of health found in cross-country studies using data from the last 50 years (World Health Organization 1999).

Recent macroeconomic research on productivity has emphasized the importance of human capital. Like physical capital, human capital in the form of education and health is durable, lasting, and subject to accumulation (Lucas 1988; Romer 1986). One approach to incorporating human capital into the macroeconomic modelling of productivity is to augment the neoclassical growth-accounting equation developed by Solow (1956). Solow's approach to measuring multifactor productivity growth is to associate it with the residual amount of output growth not explained by growth in the key inputs of labour and physical capital. This approach is founded upon several contentious assumptions. First, it assumes that technology (which is associated with the residual) is exogenous, suggesting that labour-productivity growth rates will be the same across economies once they reach a steady state. This runs counter to the trends of sustained differences in growth rates observed across developed countries. Another assumption of this approach is that there is perfect competition such that market prices reflect social costs — that is, there are no information asymmetries, appropriability problems, spillovers or other externalities. Intuitively, these appear to be restrictive assumptions that are likely not met in the real world, suggesting that there is a role for public policy. One can easily imagine spillover effects occurring from higher levels of human capital. They could have a substantial impact not only on an individual's own productivity, but also on the productivity of co-workers and on society as a whole. A number of measurement issues also arise with this paradigm, the most salient of which is how to deal with technological improvements and quality changes embodied in both inputs and outputs.[3] Quality improvements are relevant for both physical and human capital.

In response to the shortcomings of the Solow model, a new approach to growth accounting has evolved, one that attempts to model the key determinants of growth as jointly endogenous (Knowles and Owen 1997). One way to augment the Solow model is to include the accumulation of human capital as well as physical capital, while still treating technology as exogenously determined. This diminishes the importance of exogenous technological growth. The endogenous growth literature attempts to capture two aspects of the impact of health on productivity: its direct impact on the production process — for example, improvements in health can increase productivity due to reduced incapacity, disability and days off sick; and its spillover impact — for example, an improvement in the health of seniors can result in reduced personal-care time required by family caregivers who are members of the labour force.

Human capital in the form of education has received much attention in cross-country empirical growth studies, and researchers have found considerable support for its importance as a productivity driver (Harris 1999). Human capital in the form of health has received less attention, but the relatively few cross-country studies that have included some measure of health have found that it does have a significant and positive association with economic growth.[4] Many of the empirical growth studies that include health have focused on developing countries (e.g., Bhargava et al. 2001; Hicks 1979; Wheeler 1980), though some have included a broader range of countries (Barro and Sala-i-Martin 1995; Bloom et al. 2001; Knowles and Owen 1995, 1997) and some have focused specifically on OECD countries (Knowles and Owen 1995, 1997; Rivera and Currais 1999*a*, 1999*b*).

These studies often use rather crude measures of health, likely due to the lack of data on more refined and comprehensive measures that span both a reasonable time period and a number of countries.[5] Most studies use some measure of life expectancy or mortality (life expectancy at birth, infant mortality rates, adult survival rates), though two recent studies used per capita health-care expenditures (Rivera and Currais 1999*a*, 1999*b*). Life expectancy has increased dramatically over the post-war period in many developed countries (see Chart 1 for Canadian trends). Though mortality and life expectancy are important measures of health status, they may not capture the subtle changes in morbidity, health behaviours, health-related quality-of-life measures, or other measures of health that are particularly salient to developed countries today.

Furthermore, it is likely that the relationship between health and productivity found in these studies is driven by data from developing countries in the sample. Developed countries such as Canada and the United States are virtually indistinguishable across the health measures used (Harris 1999). Chart 2 provides evidence of this fact. As is apparent in the graph, the life-expectancy gradient is much steeper for low levels of gross national income per capita. Indeed, when Knowles and Owen (1997) estimated their specification for 22 high-income countries, they found that the health measure they used, life expectancy, was no longer significant, likely due to the lack of variability for this measure in the sub-sample. Rivera and Currais (1999*a*, 1999*b*) attempt to make a case for their use of health-care expenditures rather than life expectancy as a measure of health, but the meaningfulness of this proxy of health for developed countries is also questionable. Variations in health-care expenditures in developed countries are not highly correlated with health measures such as life expectancy and infant mortality (comparing Japan and the United States highlights this point), and it is not clear whether the marginal dollar spent on medical care reflects morbidity improvements.

A fully specified growth model should include all key inputs into the production process and all drivers of productivity, including measures of all forms of human capital; otherwise one cannot be sure whether a particular variable directly affects growth or is simply a proxy for missing factors. In particular, human capital should include a measure of education and skills, as well as health. All but one study reviewed included some measures of education and/or skills such as average years of schooling, primary/secondary/university enrolment, adult

CHART 1
Canadian Life Expectancy at Birth

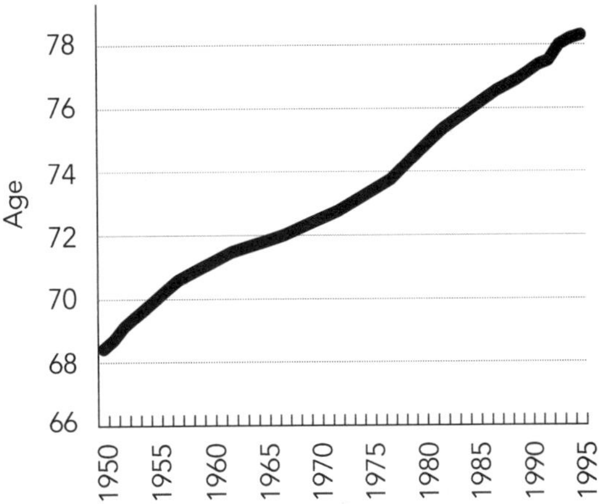

Source: World Bank.

literacy or years of experience. Interestingly, the education and skills variables were not significant in most specifications in the studies, with the exception of Rivera and Currais (1999*a*, 1999*b*) and Barro and Sala-i-Martin (1995), suggesting that health may be a more important determinant of productivity, particularly for developing countries. These results might be driven by other factors, such as the nature of the proxy being used for education or measurement error in the data.

The magnitude of the coefficient for health is difficult to compare across studies, due to a number of differences in the specifications. Some studies used different measures of health, while others used comparable ones with slight variations in their specification. Some studies used the growth of labour productivity as the dependent variable, while others used the growth of total factor productivity; those that used the former generally made use of one of two denominators, an estimate of the size of the labour force or the total population.[6] There were other specification differences as well, making direct comparison impossible.

187

CHART 2

Gross National Income Per Capita (GNIpc) Versus Life Expectancy (LE) at Birth, 1997

188

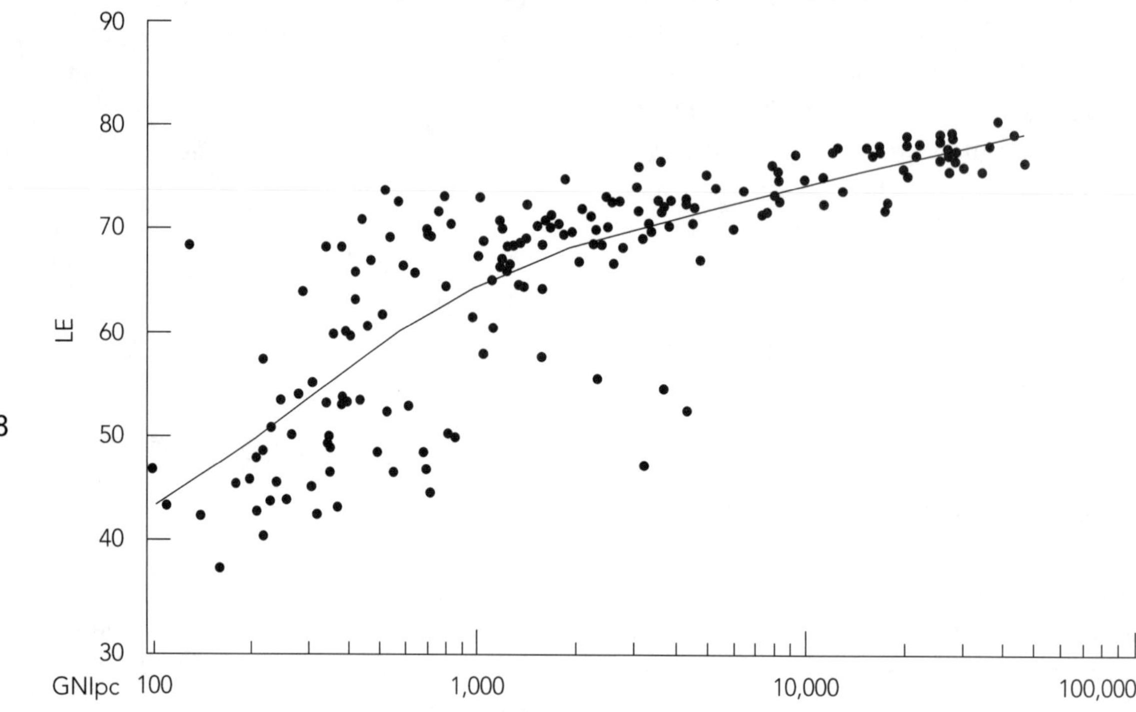

Source: World Bank.

Nonetheless, a comparison of the range of results provides a sense of the impact that health can have on productivity. To this end, Table 1 contains information on the elasticities and percentage effects of health from studies that included developed countries and from which data could be extracted. Studies by Rivera and Currais (1999*a*, 1999*b*) and Knowles and Owen (1995, 1997) suggest that between 21 and 47.5 percent of GDP growth per worker (working-age person) over the last 25 to 30 years can be explained by improvements in the health of populations (defined as health-care expenditures and life expectancy) at the country level. As noted, this range is similar to the value estimated by Fogel in his economic history work. Bloom et al. (2001) also found a significant relationship between health and GDP growth. Each extra year of life expectancy is estimated to increase a country's GDP by 4 percent.

Endogenous growth studies substantiate the importance of health for productivity growth, particularly in developing countries. Health may be equally important for growth in developed countries, but different aspects of health, such as morbidity, vitality, mental health and mental acuity, are likely more critical for these countries than increases in life expectancy. With the shift from manufacturing to services and the increasing importance of new technologies in developed countries, the human-capital needs of the labour force have changed. Intuitively, one can foresee an increasing role for mental health and acuity for knowledge workers providing high-end services. There is evidence of health improvements on this front. Recent research in the field of psychology has found that populations in developed countries experienced steady gains in intellectual ability over the course of the 20th century, and some work suggests that this is attributable to improvements in health and nutrition (World Health Organization 1999). Further decreases in morbidity could also be critical for future productivity gains, given the aging of the labour force in many developed countries. Moreover, according to Mérette (2002) there is no evidence that the performance of older workers is systematically lower than that of younger workers. This may be due in part to improvements in the health of older workers and in part to a decrease in the physical demands of industries in many developed countries (as a result of both the shift towards service industries and technological

TABLE 1

Macroeconomic Growth Studies with Data from Developed Countries that Include Measures of Health

Study	Productivity measures	Health measures	Countries and time period	Elasticities
Rivera and Currais (1999*a*)	log difference of GDP per worker, 1960–90	log percentage of GDP spent on health care	24 OECD countries (1960–90)	0.21–0.22
Rivera and Currais (1999*b*)	log difference of GDP per worker, 1960–90	log percentage of GDP spent on health care	24 OECD countries (1960–90)	0.28–0.33
Bhargava et al.(2001)	log GDP growth rate per capita	log of adult survival rate	125 countries from Pen World Tables 107 countries from World Development Indicators (1965–90)	varies by GDP +ve for low-income countries -ve for high-income countries For the poorest countries, a 1% change in adult survival rate is associated with a 0.05% increase in GDP growth rate.
Knowles and Owen (1995)	log difference of GDP per working age person, 1960–85	log of (80 years less life expectancy at birth)	84 countries 62 developing 22 high-income (1960–85)	0.381 0.382 0.03
Knowles and Owen (1997)	log difference of GDP per working-age person, 1960–85	log of (80 years less life expectancy at birth)	77 countries 55 developing (1960–85)	0.449 0.475
Bloom, Canning and Sevilla (2001)	log GDP growth rate	log of life expectancy at birth	Information not provided	0.04 Each extra year of life expectancy leads to an increase of 4% in GDP.
Barro and Sala-i-Martin (1995)	GDP growth rate per capita	log of life expectancy at birth	134 countries (developing and developed) (1965–85)	0.046-0.082 An estimate of .064 means that a one standard deviation increase in life expectancy (13 years) raises GDP growth rates per capita by 1.4 % per year.

improvements in manufacturing). Nonetheless, there is a need for further research into the impact of health on productivity in developed countries using measures of health that are more salient to these countries.

OCCUPATIONAL HEALTH AND SAFETY AND THE COST OF WORK DISABILITY

If health capital complements firm-specific human capital in that it increases the returns to firm-specific skills and knowledge, one might expect that employers would be willing to bear the cost of investing in the health of workers in order to reap the benefits of productivity gains. But if health capital is generic rather than firm-specific, the fact that workers can take it with them from job to job suggests that firms might be unwilling to bear these costs, even if health capital increases worker productivity (Currie and Madrian 1999). In reality, health capital likely has some degree of complementarity and some generic aspects. If this is the case, firms may voluntarily invest in the health of workers but not necessarily to a socially optimal level. Consistent with this notion, developed countries have recognized the importance of labour market institutions designed to protect the health and safety of workers through financial and regulatory mechanisms. The main policy levers for providing such incentives are occupational health and safety regulation and experience-rated workers' compensation insurance. Occupational health and safety regulation covers a broad range of procedural and equipment standards and is generally enforced through a system of inspections and fines. Experience-rated workers' compensation insurance provides financial incentives for safety consciousness by varying insurance premiums at the sectoral and firm level, in an effort to tie the costs of injury and illness as closely as possible to the employers responsible for them, without unduly penalizing any one firm for costly and unpreventable accidents.

In Canada, the direct cost of work-related injuries and illnesses exceeded $5.7 billion in calendar year 2000 (Institute for Work and Health, 2002). This estimate includes indemnity payments, insurance administration expenses and medical services that are paid by employers through workers' compensation premiums (Chart 3 provides data on the growth of indemnity payments over the 1972-96 period). These direct costs substantially underestimate the true cost of productivity losses attributable to work-related injuries and illnesses. The indirect cost estimate for Canada is $12 billion. This includes costs incurred by employers to accommodate injured workers who return to work, recruitment and training costs incurred for replacing injured workers, earnings lost by workers due to injury and the lost home production of workers. Even these direct and indirect costs likely underestimate the true social cost. For instance, they do not include costs associated with pain and suffering or home care provided by family members, and the number of claims is less than the true number of work-related injuries.[7] Clearly, the financial burden of work-related injuries and illnesses is substantial, but we do not know what proportion of this burden is preventable, the expenditures necessary to reduce the burden, or whether insurance and regulation are the most effective means of reducing the burden.

Over the past 10 to 15 years the number of work-related injury and illness claims has decreased substantially in many jurisdictions in

CHART 3

Total Workers' Compensation Indemnity
Payments in Canada

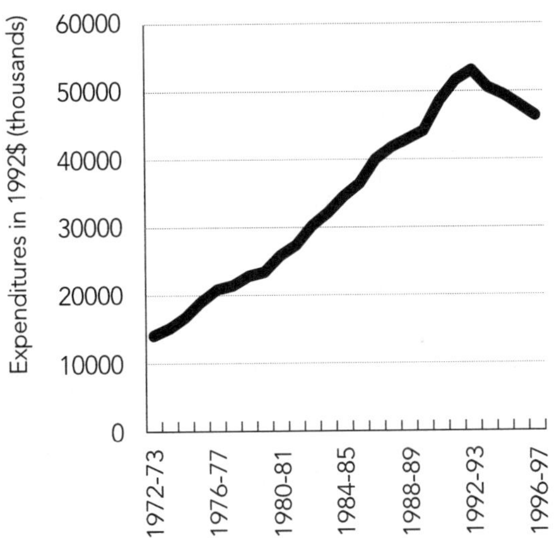

Source: Human Resources and Development Canada
and Statistics Canada

CHART 4

Time Loss/Fatality and No Time Loss
Compensation Claims Per Employee

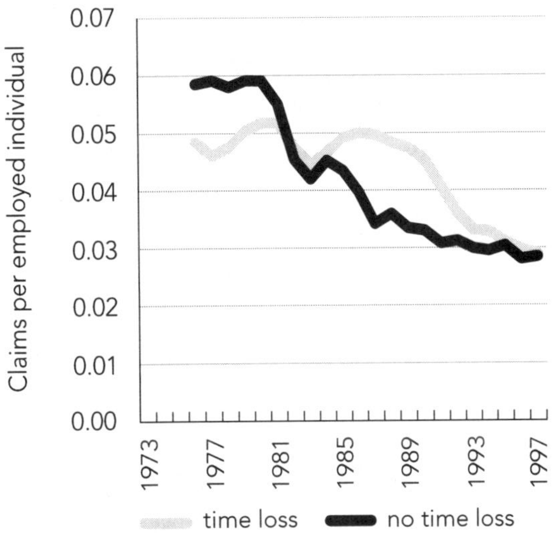

Source: Human Resources and Development Canada
and Statistics Canada.

Canada and other developed countries (see Chart 4 for Canadian trends). In Canada, injury claims decreased by 40 percent between 1990 and 1998, despite the fact that the labour force increased by 10 percent over this period (Mustard et al. 2001). A number of explanations have been put forward for this trend. Though there is evidence to support some of these, it is not clear which factors are the predominant ones.[8] More specifically, it is not clear what fraction of the trend is attributable to the effectiveness of insurance and regulatory mechanisms.

There is a large body of empirical literature on the effectiveness of insurance and regulatory mechanisms using econometric techniques (reviews of this evidence are provided by Curington 1988; Hyatt and Thomason 1998, Kralj 2000; and Smith 1992). Taken as a whole, the empirical evidence on the impact of regulation is mixed. The US evidence suggests that standards can reduce certain types of injuries and that a system of inspections provides, at best, modest general deterrence unless reinforced with penalties. Scholz and Gray (1997) found that regulation facilitating cooperation, such as inspections initiated by workers (regardless of penalty), can be more effective than coercive regulation such as regular inspections, unless penalties are imposed. The effectiveness of facilitative regulation is reinforced by Canadian evidence on the introduction of regulations requiring joint health and safety committees (Lewchuck et al. 1996).[9] The evidence on workers' compensation experience rating suggests that financial incentives can be an effective means of improving occupational health and safety. The appeal of experience rating is that it ties the cost of work-related injuries closer to the firms experiencing them, while allowing firms the flexibility to find the most efficient means of improving health and safety.

One of the challenges of regulatory and insurance mechanisms is that the nature of work and labour market experience have changed profoundly since their introduction in

Canada, yet occupational health and safety regulation and workers' compensation continue to focus on injuries and the impact of physical and chemical exposures characteristic of manufacturing and resource-based industries. The shift away from manufacturing to services, the increasing use of technology, the introduction of new human-resource and management practices, and the growth in demand for knowledge workers have all contributed to a dramatic change in the nature of work-related injuries and illnesses (Sullivan and Frank 2000). For example, mental-stress claims more than doubled in the United States between 1980 and 1987 (Gnam 2000).[10] Furthermore, the growth in non-standard work arrangements has not only made it difficult for workers' compensation boards to assign firm-level responsibility for injuries and illnesses, but has also dramatically changed the nature of labour market experiences. Other factors such as income inequality, job insecurity and unemployment have also been shown to have a bearing on the health of individuals and populations (Deaton 2001; Platt et al. 1999).

HEALTH, SICKNESS ABSENCE AND FIRM-LEVEL PRACTICES

At the microeconomic level, research into the impact of health on productivity focuses on returns to employers and workers. Returns to the accumulation of health capital can be realized by employers in the form of higher profits, by workers in the form of higher wages, or by both. Pauly et al. (forthcoming) provide a theoretical framework (hereinafter the Pauly framework) to identify the principal characteristics of the production process, the market for the good or service being produced, and the labour markets that determine the size and distribution of productivity gains associated with health improvements. The framework focuses on a particular proxy for health-related productivity gains, namely decreases in sickness absence, but the premise of the model can be generalized to all health-related productivity improvements.[11] This framework is examined below, followed by a review of the microeconomic evidence concerning the relationship between health and productivity, and employers' efforts to capture potential health-related productivity gains through health-promotion initiatives. Consistent with this literature, particular attention is given to sickness absence as a proxy for productivity. As background for this discussion, Canadian trends in sickness absence are provided in Chart 5. Rates have been increasing for both men and women over the last few years. This may be due in part to the economic recovery during the period. Similar to work-related accident claim rates, sickness absence rates have a cyclical component (i.e., work-related accident claims tend to increase during periods of economic recovery due to factors such as the increased pace of work). Nonetheless, the rate for women has increased to levels above those of the late 1980s.

Many empirical studies on the cost of sickness absence and the cost-effectiveness of health-promotion initiatives assume that the dollar value of reducing sickness absence is simply the direct cost of wages paid to absent workers (assuming that they are paid for absences). In the Pauly framework, wages are actually the lower bound for losses. In many cases, total costs can be much higher due to indirect costs attributable to sickness absence. If the production process is team-based, or if a penalty is incurred for failure to achieve target output, then the cost of sickness absence

CHART 5

Canadian Absence Rates for Illness and
Disability, Full-Time Paid Workers

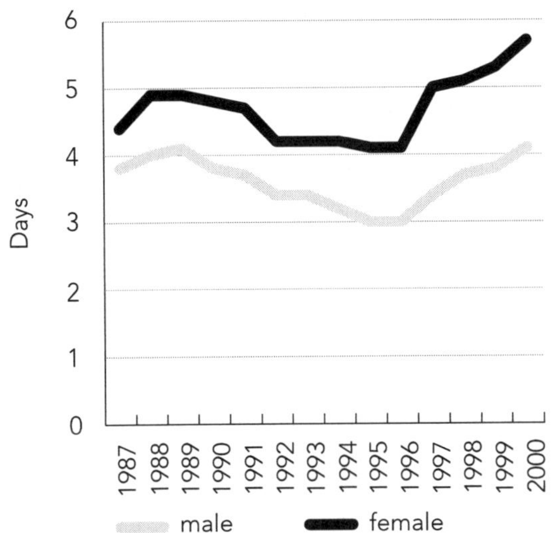

Source: Statistics Canada (data series L91404 & L9140).

can be much higher if a perfect substitute is not available to replace an absent worker (i.e., if there is firm-specific knowledge capital). In the case of team production, sickness absence can also reduce the productivity of co-workers. Penalties associated with failure to achieve target output can also be significant if production is time-sensitive (e.g., perishable goods and travel/transportation services).

The benchmark case used to elaborate the framework is a single homogenous product and a simple production process in which wages reflect the incremental value of production (in which case the cost of absences is the wage rate). If health improvements are observable and transferable to a new employer (e.g., smoking cessation and weight loss), then a worker whose health improves will receive higher wage offers from competing employers. Consequently, in the long run the benefits of health improvements are fully captured by the worker in the form of higher wages.[12] There is a large literature in labour economics investigating the impact of health status on wages, income and labour force participation. A thorough review of this literature is provided by Currie and Madrian (1999). In general, research supports the notion that health is associated with wages and income, though the magnitude of its impact appears to be sensitive to the measure of health used in the particular study. One of the patterns emerging from Currie and Madrian's review is that health has a greater impact on the number of hours worked than on the wages received by workers. Even if workers do capture the benefits of health improvements in the long run, employers may still have an incentive to undertake health-promotion initiatives due to competitive pressures and in order to reap the short-run benefits, particularly if there are complementarities between health capital and firm-specific knowledge capital (Currie and Madrian 1999).

Three factors determine the degree to which the wage rate underestimates the cost of an absence: the extent to which the production process relies on team work, the size of the penalty incurred for failure to achieve target output levels, and the cost of replacing an absent worker with an equally productive one. With full employment, the wage rate is a good measure of lost output for cases in which there is a perfect substitute for a worker at the same wage rate (assuming that, in full employment, the wage rate reflects a convergence of firm, worker and societal values of labour time). The cost of absence exceeds the wage rate if the replacement worker is less productive or costs more *and* if the production process relies on team work or a penalty is incurred for failure to achieve target output levels.[13] If there is less than full employment, the prevailing wage rate may differ from the equilibrium-wage rate, so the firm, worker

193

and societal values of labour time may differ as well. If this difference is small, the gains from reducing sickness absence would be similar to the full-employment case. In general, the benefits from reduced sickness absence are greater than the wage rate. It should be noted that the impact of sickness absence on productivity is greater when measured by output per worker than output per hour, since some of the output not produced due to sickness absence is offset by the reduced number of hours worked.

194

The Pauly framework underscores the potential productivity gains of reducing sickness absence through investments in health capital. Implicit in this line of thinking is the assumption that poor health is the principal reason for sickness absence.[14] But the etiology of sickness absence is quite complex; poor health is but one of many factors that have a bearing on sickness absence. Examples of other factors include personality, job-related attitudes and social context. Two recent literature reviews (Alexanderson 1998; Harrison and Martocchio 1998) identify a broad range of causal factors investigated in the empirical literature on sickness absence and find that few studies have investigated the impact of health on sickness absence.[15] In particular, short-term health conditions are rarely studied. Nicholson and Martocchio (1995) describe this gap in the literature as a "black hole." Alexanderson notes that even though most studies in her review are from the fields of epidemiology and medicine, most do not use a medical model or even consider health status as an explanatory variable. This lack of attention to health is likely due to a focus on sources of variance that are perceived to be avoidable (and thus amenable to change), though the distinction between avoidable and unavoidable is blurry at best. For

example, some people may believe that health status is predetermined and that changes in health status are unavoidable, but an intervention such as an influenza shot can significantly reduce the incidence of colds and flu, and thus may reduce sickness absence more readily than an intervention designed to increase workers' engagement in their work.

Nonetheless, there is evidence to support the notion that health status has a strong influence on sickness absence. Most empirical studies of sickness absence that have included measures of long-term health, chronic conditions or health behaviours have focused on self-reported health status, smoking, illicit-substance use and alcohol consumption. The Whitehall II study provides some of the most compelling evidence for the impact of these factors on sickness absence (Marmot et al. 1995; Marmot et al. 1993; North et al. 1993). Reported "average" or "worse" health over the 12 months preceding the survey was associated with significantly higher levels of sickness absence compared to reported "good" health — a 60 percent increase in short spells (seven days or less) and a twofold increase in long spells (more than seven days). Significantly higher levels of sickness absence were also observed for individuals reporting recurrent health problems, longstanding illnesses or psychiatric symptoms. Mental health factors such as depression, anxiety and emotional stress are a frequently reported cause of sickness absence, particularly among women (Stansfeld et al. 1995), and have been found to be significant predictors of absence and disability (Garrison and Eaton 1992; Kessler et al. 1999; Kouzis and Eaton 1994; Simon et al. 2001; Skodol et al. 1994). Studies of health-related behaviours have found that smokers have higher rates of absence than non-smokers (Bush and Wooden 1995; Leigh

1995; North et al. 1993; Parkes 1987) and that illicit-substance users have high rates of absence (Bass et al. 1996; Normand et al. 1990). The impact of alcohol consumption is more complex. Problem drinking (a level of alcohol consumption that results in social dysfunction) appears to be the point at which sickness absence is affected (Beaumont and Hyman 1987; Casswell et al. 1988), causing long-term absences in particular (Marmot et al. 1993).

Acute conditions related to respiratory and gastrointestinal conditions are the primary reasons for short-term absences (Stansfeld et al. 1995), yet, as noted, few studies have investigated the nature and impact of short-term health conditions on sickness absence. This is surprising given that more immediate inroads into reducing sickness absence might be made by addressing the factors that cause acute conditions. For example, Nichol et al. (1995) found a 43 percent drop in the rate of cold- and flu-related sickness absences among adults receiving an influenza vaccine instead of a placebo.

The evidence regarding the impact of health status on sickness absence, though preliminary, suggests that firm-level initiatives such as health promotion are one means by which employers can reduce absence and increase productivity. Employers have undertaken a variety of initiatives, ranging from targeted to multicomponent programs (fitness/exercise programs are the most widespread). A large empirical literature on the impact of these initiatives on health and productivity has accumulated over the past 30 years. Most of the empirical studies have considered one or more of five outcomes: risk reduction or behavioural change, health/medical-care costs, sickness absence, turnover and other proxies of productivity. One of the motivations for these initiatives in the United States was the growing cost of employee health care in the 1970s and 1980s, which was increasing at a rate of up to 30 percent per year (Conrad 1988). The focus on health-care costs in many US employer initiatives is understandable given that health insurance is generally provided by employers and can make up a substantial component of the benefits provided to workers. In Canada, it is a less salient cost for employers, since health insurance is primarily funded by the public sector, but is nonetheless a factor to consider at the macro level. Canada has also experienced substantial increases in health-care costs since the 1970s, and there is evidence that a growing proportion is paid by the private sector (Polanyi et al. 2000).

Studies of the impact of employer-sponsored health-promotion initiatives generally use quasi-experimental methods (participants self-select into the program) or non-experimental methods (no control group — e.g, before/after comparison) and cost-benefit or cost-effectiveness analysis. The dearth of rigorous research, particularly in the earlier literature in this field, has been commented on in most reviews (Aldana 1998; Baun 1995; Fielding 1990; Heaney and Goetzel 1997; Messer and Stone 1995; O'Donnell 1997; Pelletier 1991, 1993, 1996, 1999, 2001; Shaeffer et al. 1994; Shephard 1992; Warner 1992; Warner et al. 1988).[16] As a whole, these studies show mixed evidence, with non-experimental studies generally demonstrating positive results and more rigorous studies demonstrating less positive results. On average, studies using experimental designs had positive results approximately 25 percent of the time, quasi-experimental designs 50 percent of the time and non-experimental designs 100 percent of the time (Heaney and Goetzel 1997; O'Donnell 1997). In terms of sickness absence, the evidence on the impact of health promotion is mixed (Baun 1995).[17] If the results of a broad

195

range of studies reviewed by Shephard (1992) can be accepted as the true program effects, then the impact on sickness absence is positive but modest; most of the studies found effect sizes in the range of 0.5 to two days per year of improved attendance. In Messer and Stone's (1995) review of cost-benefit studies, those that included the cost of reduced sickness absence as a benefit found that benefits exceeded costs in all cases (benefit-cost ratios ranged from 1.07 to 3.90); for some of the studies, the positive effects may also have been driven by reduced health-care costs.

The quality of research has improved substantially in the most recent generation of studies, providing a rationale for employers to consider such programs as a means of reducing the health and economic costs of illness. The findings provide some support for the hypothesis that health and fitness can have an impact on sickness absence and productivity, though the durability of these effects has not been established. A realistic assumption is that a program will need to engage workers on an ongoing basis if the changes are to be sustained. Though most studies have found only modest reductions in sickness absences as a result of health-promotion programs, the direct costs of these absences represent only a lower bound for the costs attributable to sickness absence, suggesting that productivity gains may be higher.

Polanyi et al. (2000) are less optimistic about the potential for firm-level health-promotion initiatives. They list five reasons why such initiatives may be limited in their ability to improve worker health: (1) this approach does not address the sources of human motivation and behaviour that bear on health, namely the social and economic determinants of health; (2) lifestyle is a less important factor bearing on health than socioeconomic status

(Marmot et al. 1991, 1993), which has health effects that can endure even after retirement (Wolfson et al. 1990); (3) if behavioural and lifestyle changes are to be enduring, the social and cultural context that engendered them must be modified as well; (4) health-promotion initiatives reach only a limited number of workers, since they tend to be implemented in white-collar settings; and (5) unless other job-related and organizational factors are also addressed, workers may perceive such initiatives as a self-serving effort by firms to reduce their health-care and absenteeism costs.

Indeed, it is becoming increasingly evident that general health and functioning are very much affected by work experiences. There is a growing body of evidence showing that psychosocial workplace factors such as job control, psychological demands and social support have an important bearing on workers' health (Shannon et al. 2001). This suggests that broadly based organizational initiatives may be more successful in improving workers' mental and physical health and productivity than focused health-promotion programs. Such broad-based initiatives can include a range of elements such as: redesigning worksites with ergonomic principles in mind; redesigning work flows and communications channels to enhance communication and social support; and providing flexible work hours, leave programs and daycare facilities. Unfortunately, there are few experimental studies in the literature investigating the productivity impact of such initiatives.

SUMMARY AND CONCLUSIONS

Economic well-being in developed countries is growing increasingly dependent on international markets and integrated trade. To maintain a high standard of living in the global marketplace, countries must remain competitive, which in turn depends on the fostering of an innovative, productive labour force. Researchers and policy-makers are becoming increasingly aware that a country's ability to innovate and remain productive depends on the characteristics and quality of its human capital, key elements of which are education, skills and health. Most recently, the links between population health and economic productivity have become a significant policy concern. With the aging of the labour force in Canada and many other developed countries, labour force health will become an even more important issue in the near future. On the positive side, there is evidence that older workers in developed countries are no less productive than their younger counterparts.

Fogel's research in economic history highlights the significance of population health for productivity growth. He provides compelling evidence for the important role of nutrition, particularly in early childhood, on health and functioning throughout the life cycle. Fogel points out that these historic trends still have a bearing on the health of populations in developed countries today. This research provides valuable insights into the critical role that policy can play in supporting population health and ultimately productivity. For example, the enduring effect of childhood experiences is one of the themes in this work, suggesting that financial support for low-income families, parental leave policies and child-care policies can help to ensure healthy child and adult outcomes. The evidence from macroeconomic studies on health and productivity corroborates the evidence from economic history. Health is indeed an important driver of productivity even today. This area of

research focuses on life expectancy as a measure of health, which can be an important productivity driver for developing countries but is less salient for developed countries. In order to better serve the information needs of policy arenas in developed countries, future research in this area should identify more refined measures of health to incorporate into their empirical analyses (e.g., measures of functional status and mental health).

Work-related injuries and illnesses are a major source of productivity losses for society as a whole, suggesting that public policy can play a crucial role in providing incentives for employers to dedicate more resources to occupational health and safety. Most developed countries recognize the importance of labour market institutions designed to protect the health and safety of workers, and have established financial and regulatory mechanisms for this purpose. Different policy levers are available under the umbrella of regulation and insurance, some of which are more effective than others. The evidence suggests that occupational health and safety regulation has had only a modest impact, though preliminary evidence shows that regulation focusing on facilitation rather than coercion may be more promising. The evidence for experience-rating suggests that it is effective, partly because financial incentives allow employers the flexibility to identify the most efficient means by which to improve workplace health and safety. Both insurance and regulation tend to create incentives that focus on acute injuries and the health impacts of physical and chemical exposures characteristic of the industrial sector. Consequently, many of the important factors affecting labour force and population health in developed countries remain outside the purview of traditional insurance and regulatory domains, due to the changing nature of work and labour market experiences in these countries.

Sickness absence is an easily measured proxy for productivity that is often investigated in the organizational practices literature. Yet, surprisingly, the empirical literature on the causes of sickness absence has given little attention to the role of health status as an explanatory variable. The work that has been undertaken in this area suggests that chronic and acute physical and mental conditions, as well as health-related behaviours, explain a significant portion of sickness absence. This evidence provides support for health-promotion initiatives as a means of reducing sickness absence and increasing productivity. Empirical studies evaluating workplace health-promotion programs find that they are effective in reducing absence and health-care costs, though these reductions are modest and the durability of program effects is not known. Nevertheless, the direct costs of absences are only a lower bound for productivity losses attributable to them; the productivity gains to be realized from decreasing sickness absences may be substantially higher. Future research in this area should focus on developing the tools to quantify the various indirect costs associated with sickness absence, as well as improving the methodological rigour of intervention studies. Furthermore, there is evidence to suggest that such initiatives should consider a broader set of organizational factors related to work and the workplace that bear on the health and productivity of workers instead of narrowly focusing on behaviour and lifestyle.

The fact that firm-level initiatives appear to have had a limited impact on productivity suggests that the public sector has a role to play in improving the health of the labour force and population as a whole and, in turn, overall productivity. Identifying priorities in order to achieve the greatest gains from the resources invested is a difficult task at best. Certainly, increasing health-care spending will not necessarily result in higher levels of population health, as evidenced by the differences in per capita health-care expenditures and health profiles across OECD countries. The multifaceted nature of the factors that influence health suggests that policies in a number of areas traditionally considered outside the purview of health policy may be important avenues by which the public sector can have an impact on population health. Key areas are labour market policy, education policy, and child-care and parental leave policy. Furthermore, though improving population health is an important societal objective, there are many other objectives competing for scarce public resources. Achieving an optimal balance when addressing societal objectives requires a sound understanding of the policy options, their impact on the various objectives, and the costs associated with each.

NOTES

1   Muurinen (1982) provides an alternative formulation in which education is theorized to lower the rate of depreciation of health stock.

2   A lower discount rate may also encourage investment in health directly.

3   There are other measurement issues with regard to capturing the full impact of health on welfare. In particular, utility is derived directly from health, as well as indirectly through its role in market and non-market production activities, whereas only market production activities are captured in standard output measures. The direct value of health may be captured to some degree through market goods and services purchased to improve health. The indirect value of health from non-market activities may also be captured to some degree in this way. At the core of this measurement issue is the fact that standard measures of output do not capture non-market resources and activities. Costa and Steckel (1995)

compare alternative methodologies of measuring welfare changes arising from changes in the health of populations as an illustrative exercise to assess the consistency of rankings.

4   Significance does not necessarily imply causality. In fact, the direction of effects might run from productivity growth to health, rather than the reverse. All of the studies address the reverse causality issue by testing for potential endogeneity.

5   Currie and Madrian (1999) classify health measures typically available in the data sets of developed countries into eight categories: self-reported health status, presence of functional limitations on the ability to work, presence of functional limitations on other activities, presence of chronic/acute health conditions, health-care utilization, clinical assessments of health, nutritional status and mortality.

6   GDP per capita growth is highly correlated with GDP per worker growth, with the latter driving the former. None of the studies corrected for the fact that average hours of work can vary substantially from country to country.

7   Leigh et al. (2001) estimate that the total cost of health care and lost productivity due to occupational injuries and illnesses in California is on par with the costs of all cancers combined, and comparable to the costs of heart disease and stroke.

8   These explanations support one of two propositions: that the trend reflects real decreases in work disability, or that the trend is a reporting phenomenon. Following are some of the explanations offered: de-industrialization has resulted in a greater proportion of the labour force being employed in the service sector, which is inherently safer; older capital is being replaced with new capital, which embodies ergonomic and technological improvements that are inherently safer; employers are doing a better job of instituting safety measures in response to insurance and regulatory incentives or because of an increased awareness of the value of health capital; employers are adopting more aggressive claims-management practices; and workers' compensation boards have tightened their eligibility requirements.

9   This study also found that firms that are reluctant to form joint health and safety committees show poorer health and safety performance, suggesting that the climate of the internal-responsibility system is an important element in its success. The authors suggest that, if the internal-responsibility system is to be effective, special measures may be required to educate employers and workers in such cases.

10   Mental-stress claims still represent only a small fraction of workers' compensation claims in North America, though this may be due in part to legislation passed in the early 1990s in many jurisdictions limiting compensability for such claims (Gnam 2000).

11   Decreases in sickness absence are frequently used as a proxy for health-related productivity gains attributable to employer-sponsored initiatives, primarily because sickness absence is readily observable and measurable, and data regularly collected by human-resource departments. Two other proxies considered in the literature are disability and turnover. It should be noted that health improvements can increase not only the amount of time available for work, but also the quality of time spent at work. More comprehensive empirical analyses attempt to assess the entire range of direct and indirect benefits and costs associated with a health improvement.

12   In the case of a salaried worker who is required to make up lost production time, the benefits are in the form of more convenient hours. Note that the value of lost leisure time is not captured by traditional output measures but is nonetheless an important aspect of social welfare.

13   Firms may attempt to insure against losses by hiring extra workers as backups to cover for absences. This imperfect remedy will be relatively less costly for larger firms than for smaller ones.

14   One of the shortcomings of the model is its narrow focus on sickness absence, rather than the impact of worker health on productivity in general. However, the basic tenets of the model can be generalized to this broader perspective.

15   Harrison and Martocchio (1998) review over 500 empirical studies on sickness absence culled from a variety of disciplines conducted from 1977 to 1996.

16   Frequently cited methodological shortcomings are: failure to use a control group or randomization of individuals between program and control groups, failure to adjust for confounders, lack of standardized measures used for exposure and outcome, short time period of studies, small sample sizes, use of self-reported measures, failure to consider all indirect costs and benefits associated with an initiative, bias introduced by evaluations being performed by program advocates, and failure to consider the worksite as the unit of analysis when initiatives are implemented at a selection of worksites.

17   Baun (1995) reviews studies that assess a range of health-promotion initiatives for their impact in terms of reducing sickness absence. He concludes that the evidence for the effectiveness of smoking-cessation programs, health-risk assessment programs and exercise programs is mixed. Only stress-reduction programs appear to have a powerful effect on sickness absence.

REFERENCES

Aldana, S.G. 1998. "Financial Impact of Worksite Health Promotion and Methodological Quality of the Evidence." *The Art of Health Promotion* 2(1):1-8.

Alexanderson, K. 1998. "Sickness Absence: A Review of Performed Studies with (sic) Focused on Levels of Exposures and Theories Utilized." *Scandinavian Journal of Social Medicine* 26(4):241-249.

Barro, R., and X. Sala-i-Martin. 1995. "Empirical Analysis of a Cross Section of Countries." In *Economic Growth*. New York: McGraw-Hill.

Bass, A.R., R. Bharucha-Reid, K. Delaplane-Harris, and M.A. Schork. 1996. "Employee Drug Use, Demographic Characteristics, Work Reactions, and Sickness Absence." *Journal of Occupational Health Psychology* 1(1):92-99.

Baun, W.B. 1995. "The Impact of Health Promotion Programs on Sickness Absence." In *Worksite Health Promotion Economics*, ed. R.L. Kaman. Champaign, IL: Human Kinetics Publishers.

Beaumont, P.B, and J. Hyman. 1987. "The Work Performance Indicators of Problem Drinking: Some British Evidence." *Journal of Occupational Behaviour* 8(1):55-62.

Becker, G.S. 1965. "A Theory of the Allocation of Time." *Economic Journal* 75(299):493-517.

Bhargava, A., D.T. Jamison, L.J. Lau, and C.J.L. Murray. 2001. "Modeling the Effects of Health on Economic Growth." *Journal of Health Economics* 20(3):423-440.

Bloom, D.E., and D. Canning. 2000. "The Health and Wealth of Nations." *Science's Compass* 287:1207-1209.

Bloom, D.E., D. Canning, and J. Sevilla. 2001. "The Effect of Health on Economic Growth: Theory and Evidence." Working Paper #8587. Cambridge, MA: National Bureau of Economic Research.

Bush, R., and M. Wooden. 1995. "Smoking and Absence From Work: Australian Evidence." *Social Science and Medicine* 41(3):437-446.

Casswell, S., L. Gilmore, and T. Ashton. 1988. "Estimating Alcohol-Related Sickness Absence in New Zealand." *British Journal of Addiction* 83(6):677-682.

Conrad, P. 1988. "Worksite Health Promotion: The Social Context." *Social Science and Medicine* 25(5):485-489.

Costa, D.L., and R.H. Steckel. 1995. "Long-Term Trends in Health, Welfare, and Economic Growth in the United States." Historical Paper #76. Cambridge, MA: National Bureau of Economic Research.

Curington W.P. 1988. "Federal versus State Regulation: The Early Years of OSHA." *Social Science Quarterly* 69:341-360.

Currie, J., and B.C. Madrian. 1999. *Health, Health Insurance and the Labor Market*. New York: Elsevier Science.

Deaton, A. 2001. "Health, Inequality, and Economic Development." Working Paper #8318. Washington, D.C.: National Bureau of Economic Research.

Fielding, J.E. 1990. "Worksite Health Promotion Programs in the United States: Progress, Lessons and Challenges." *Health Promotion International* 5(1):75-84.

Fogel, R.W. 1991. "The Conquest of High Mortality and Hunger in Europe and America: Timing and Mechanisms." In *Favorite of Fortunes: Technology, Growth and Economic Development Since the Industrial Revolution*, ed. D. Lander, C. Higgonet and H. Rosovsky. Cambridge, MA: Harvard University Press.

—— 1994. "Economic Growth, Population Theory and Physiology: The Bearing of Long-Term Processes on the Making of Economic Policy." Working Paper #4638. Washington, D.C.: National Bureau of Economic Research.

Frank, J.W. 1995. "The Determinants of Health: A New Synthesis." *Current Issues in Public Health* 1:233-240.

Garrison, R., and W. Eaton 1992. "Secretaries, Depression and Sickness Absence." *Women and Health* 18:53-76.

Gnam, W. 2000. "Psychiatric Disability and Workers' Compensation." In *Injury and the New World of Work*, ed. T. Sullivan. Vancouver: UBC Press.

Grossman, M. 1972. "The Demand for Health: A Theoretical and Empirical Investigation." Occasional Paper #119, Cambridge, MA: National Bureau of Economic Research.

—— 2000. "The Human Capital Model." In *Handbook of Health Economics*, ed. A.J. Culyer and J.P. Newhouse. Amsterdam: Elsevier.

Grossman, M., and R. Kaestner. 1997. "Effects of Education on Health." In *The Social Benefits of Education*, ed. J.R. Behrman and N. Stacey. Ann Arbor: University of Michigan Press.

Harris, R.G. 1999. "Determinants of Canadian Productivity Growth: Issues and Prospects." Discussion Paper #8. Ottawa: Industry Canada.

Harrison, D.A., and J.J. Martocchio. 1998. "Time for Absenteeism: A 20-Year Review of Origins, Offshoots, and Outcomes." *Journal of Management* 24(3):305-350.

Heaney, C.A., and R.Z. Goetzel. 1997. "A Review of Health-Related Outcomes of Multi-Component Worksite Health Promotion Programs." *American Journal of Health Promotion* 11(4):290-308.

Hicks, N.L. 1979. "Growth vs. Basic Needs: Is There a Trade-off?" *World Development* 7:985-994.

Hyatt, D., and T. Thomason. 1998. *Evidence on the Efficacy of Experience Rating in British Columbia: A Report to the Royal Commission on Workers' Compensation in BC*. Vancouver: Royal Commission on Workers' Compensation in BC.

Institute for Work and Health. 2002. Institute for Work and Health Website: www.iwh.on.ca

Kessler, R.C., C. Barber, H.G. Birnbaum, R. Frank, P.E. Greenberg, R.M. Rose, G. Simon, and P.S. Wang. 1999. "Depression in the Workplace: Effects on Short-Term Disability." *Health Affairs* 18(5):163-171.

Knowles, S., and P.D. Owen. 1995. "Health Capital and Cross-Country Variation in Income Per Capita in the Mankiw-Romer-Weil Model." *Economics Letters* 48:99-106.

—— 1997. "Education and Health in an Effective-Labour Empirical Growth Model." *Economic Record* 73(223):314-328.

Kouzis, A.C, and W.W. Eaton. 1994. "Emotional Disability Days: Prevalence and Predictors." *American Journal of Public Health* 84(8):1304-1307.

Kralj, B. 2000. "Occupational Health and Safety: Effectiveness of Economic and Regulatory Mechanisms." In *Workers' Compensation: Foundations for Reform*, ed. M. Gunderson and D. Hyatt. Toronto: University of Toronto Press.

Leigh, P.J. 1995. "Smoking, Self-Selection and Sickness Absence." *Quarterly Review of Economics and Finance* 35(4):365-386.

Leigh, P.J., J.E. Cone, and R. Harrison. 2001. "Costs of Occupational Injuries and Illnesses in California." *Preventive Medicine* 32(5):393-406.

Lewchuck, W., A.L. Robb, and V. Walters. 1996. "The Effectiveness of Bill 70 and Joint Health and Safety Committees in Reducing Injuries in the Workplace: The Case of Ontario." *Canadian Public Policy* 22(3):225-243.

Lucas, R.E. Jr. 1988. "On the Mechanics of Economic Development." *Journal of Monetary Economics* 22:3-42.

Marmot, M.G., A. Feeney, M.J. Shipley, F. North, and S.L. Syme. 1995. "Sickness Absence as a Measure of Health Status and Functioning: From the UK Whitehall II Study." *Journal of Epidemiology and Community Health* 49(2):124-130.

Marmot, M.G., F. North, A. Feeney, and J. Head. 1993. "Alcohol Consumption and Sickness Absence: From the Whitehall II Study." *Addiction* 88:369-382.

Marmot, M.G., G.D. Smith, S. Stansfield, C. Patel, F. North, J. Head, I. White, E Brunner, and A. Feeney. 1991. "Health Inequalities Among British Civil Servants: The Whitehall II Study." *The Lancet* 337:1387-1398.

Mérette, M. 2002. "The Bright Side: A Positive View on the Economics of Aging." *Choices* 8(1):1-28. Montreal: Institute for Research on Public Policy.

Messer, J., and W. Stone. 1995. "Worksite Fitness and Health Promotion Benefit-Cost Analysis: A Tutorial Review of Literature, and Assessment of the State of the Art." *AWHP's Worksite Health* 2:34-43.

Mustard, C.A., D. Cole, H. Shannon, J. Pole, T. Sullivan, R. Allingham, and S. Sinclair. 2001. "Does the Decline in Workers' Compensation Claims 1990–1999 in Ontario Correspond to a Decline in Workplace Injuries?" Working Paper #168. Toronto: Institute for Work & Health.

Muurinen, J.M. 1982. "Demand for Health: A Generalised Grossman Model." *Journal of Health Economics* 1:5-28.

Nichol, K.L, A. Lind, K.L. Margolis, M. Murdoch, R. McFadden, M. Hauge, S. Magran, and M. Drake. 1995. "The Effectiveness of Vaccination Against Influenza in Healthy Working Adults." *New England Journal of Medicine* 335(4):889-893.

Nicholson, N., and J.J. Martocchio. 1995. "The Management of Absence: What Do We Know? What Can We Do?" In *Handbook of Human Resources Management*, ed. G.R. Ferris, S.E. Rosen and D.T. Barnum. Oxford: Blackwell.

Normand, J., S.D. Salyards, and J.J. Mahoney. 1990. "An Evaluation of Preemployment Drug Testing." *Journal of Applied Psychology* 75(6):629-639.

North, F., S.L. Syme, A. Feeney, J. Head, M.J. Shipley, and M.G. Marmot. 1993. "Explaining Socioeconomic Differences in Sickness Absence: The Whitehall II Study." *British Medical Journal* 306:361-366.

O'Donnell, M. 1997. "Health Impact of Workplace Health Promotion Programs and Methodological Quality of the Research Literature." *The Art of Health Promotion* 1(3):1-7.

Parkes, K.R. 1987. "Relative Weight, Smoking, and Mental Health as Predictors of Sickness and Absence from Work." *Journal of Applied Psychology* 72:275-286.

Pauly, M.V., S. Nicholson, J. Xu, D. Polsky, P.M. Danzon, J.F. Murray, and M.L. Berger. Forthcoming. "A General Model of the Impact of Sickness Absence on Employees." *Health Economics*.

Pelletier, K. 1991. "A Review and Analysis of the Health and Cost-Effective Outcome Studies of Comprehensive Health Promotion and Disease Prevention Programs." *American Journal of Health Promotion* 5(4):311-313.

—— 1993. "A Review and Analysis of the Health and Cost-Effectiveness Studies of Comprehensive Health Promotion and Disease Prevention Programs at the Worksite: 1991-1993 Update." *American Journal of Health Promotion* 8(1):50-62.

—— 1996. "A Review and Analysis of the Health and Cost-Effectiveness Studies of Comprehensive Health Promotion and Disease Prevention Programs at the Worksite: 1991-1993 Update." *American Journal of Health Promotion* 10(5):380-388.

—— 1999. "A Review and Analysis of the Clinical and Cost-Effectiveness Studies of Comprehensive Health Promotion and Disease Management Programs at the Worksite: 1995-1998 Update (IV)." *American Journal of Health Promotion* 13(6):333-345.

—— 2001. "A Review and Analysis of the Clinical and Cost-Effectiveness Studies of Comprehensive Health Promotion and Disease Management Programs at the Worksite: 1998-2000 Update." *American Journal of Health Promotion* 16(2): 107-116.

Platt, S., S. Pavis, and A. Gazala. 1999. *Changing Labour Market Conditions and Health: A Systematic Literature Review (1993-98)*. Dublin: European Foundation for the Improvement of Living and Working Conditions.

Polanyi, M.F.D., J.W. Frank, H.S. Shannon, T.J. Sullivan, and J.N. Lavis. 2000. "Promoting the Determinants of Good Health in the Workplace." In *Settings for Health Promotion: Linking Theory and Practice*, ed. B.D. Poland, L.W. Green and I. Rootman. Thousand Oaks, CA: Sage.

Rivera, and L. Currais. 1999a. "Economic Growth and Health: Direct Impact or Reverse Causation?" *Applied Economics Letters* 6:761-764.

—— 1999b. "Income Variation and Health Expenditure: Evidence for OECD Countries." *Review of Development Economics* 3(3):258-267.

Romer, P.M. 1986. "Increasing Returns and Long-Run Growth." *Journal of Political Economy* 94(5): 1002-1037.

Schaeffer, M.A., A.M. Snelling, M.O. Stevenson, and R.C. Karch. 1994. "Worksite Health Promotion Evaluation." In *Economic Impact of Worksite Promotion*, ed. J.P. Opatz. Champaign, IL: Human Kinetics Publishers.

Scholz, J.T., and W.B. Gray. 1990. "OSHA Enforcement and Workplace Injuries: A Behavioral Approach to Risk Assessment." *Journal of Risk and Uncertainty* 3(3):283-305.

—— 1997. "Can Government Facilitate Cooperation? An Informational Model of OSHA." *American Journal of Political Science* 41(3):693-717.

Shannon, H., C.A. Mustard, and G. Hepburn. 2001. "Opportunities to Enhance Measurement of Workplace Health in Workplace and Employee Survey." Discussion Paper. Toronto: Institute for Work & Health.

Shephard, R.J. 1992. "A Critical Analysis of Work-Site Fitness Programs and Their Postulated Economic Benefits." *Medicine and Science in Sports and Exercise* 24(3):354-370.

Simon, G., C. Barber, H.G. Birnbaum, R. Frank, P.E. Greenberg, R.M. Rose, P.S. Wang, and R.C. Kessler. 2001. "Depression and Work Productivity: The Comparative Costs of Treatment Versus Nontreatment." *Journal of Occupational and Environmental Medicine* 43(1):2-9.

Skodol, A.E., S. Schwartz, B.P. Dohrenwend, I. Levav, and P.E. Shrout. 1994. "Minor Depression in a Cohort of Young Adults in Israel." *Archives of General Psychiatry* 51:542-551.

Smith, R.S. 1992. "Have OSHA and Workers' Compensation Made the Workplace Safer?" In *Research Frontiers in Industrial Relations and Human Resources*, ed. D. Lewin, O.S. Mitchell, and P.D. Sherer. Madison, WI: Industrial Relations Research Association.

Solow, R. 1956. "A Contribution to the Theory of Economic Growth." *Quarterly Journal of Economics* 70(1):65-94.

Stansfeld, S.A., A. Feeney, J. Head, R. Canner, F. North, and M.G. Marmot. 1995. "Sickness Absence for Psychiatric Illness: The Whitehall II Study." *Social Science and Medicine* 40(2):189-197.

Steckel R.H. 2001/2002. "Health Indicators of the Standard of Living." *Indicators: The Journal of Social Health* 1(1):139-159.

Sullivan, T., and J. Frank. 2000. "Restating Disability or Disabling the State: Four Challenges." In *Injury and the New World of Work*, ed. T. Sullivan. Vancouver: UBC Press.

Warner, K.E. 1992. "Effects of Workplace Health Promotion Not Demonstrated." *American Journal of Public Health* 82(1):126.

Warner, K.E., T.M. Wickizer, R.A. Wolfe, J.E. Schildroth, and M.H. Samuelson. 1988. "Economic Implications of Workplace Health Promotion Programs: Review of the Literature." *Journal of Occupational Medicine* 30(2):106-112.

Wheeler, D. 1980. "Basic Needs Fulfillment and Economic Growth: A Simultaneous Model." *Journal of Development Economics* 7:435-451.

Wolfson, M., G. Rowe, J.F. Gentleman, and M. Tomiak. 1990. "Career Earnings and Death: A Longitudinal Analysis of Older Canadian Men." *Journal of Gerontology* 48(4):S167-S179.

World Health Organization. 1999. "WHO on Health and Economic Productivity." *Population and Development Review* 25(2):396-402.

Social Divergence and Productivity: Making a Connection

R. Quentin Grafton, Stephen Knowles and P. Dorian Owen

INTRODUCTION

The purpose of this chapter is to explain how social divergence affects labour productivity and total factor productivity (TFP).[1] We define social divergence as the social barriers to communication among social groups and hypothesize that social divergence inhibits the growth and diffusion of knowledge, which, in turn, lowers TFP and labour productivity. Social divergence may be proxied by the number of social groups and the "distance" between them in an economy. In practice, proxies may include inequality measures of income, wealth and education, and societal differences in terms of religion, language and ethnicity. These differences across groupings, all other things being equal, increase the social barriers to communication that, in turn, prevent the exchange of ideas that enhance productivity and contribute to economic performance.

Despite difficulties in measuring TFP over time and across countries (Diewert 2000), analyses of the factors that cause (or are associated with) productivity changes are becoming increasingly important, and conclusions based on such evaluations are used to justify a range of economic and social policy initiatives. In Canada, various explanations have been offered to explain domestic TFP performance, particularly in comparison with its southern neighbour.[2] Harris (2002) lists 13 variables possibly associated with TFP, including marginal tax rates, the rate of inflation, income inequality, labour mobility and the size of the public sector. We broaden this debate to focus on social divergence and "make a connection" that may help to explain some of the cross-country differences in TFP and other stylized facts.

This chapter is a first step in examining the extent to which social barriers to communication across groups determine productivity differences. The objectives of the study are twofold: to place the notion of social divergence in the context of the existing literature, and to provide some preliminary empirical evidence on the effects of different aspects of social divergence on TFP and labour productivity. First, we define the concept of social divergence and outline hypotheses as to why it may negatively affect TFP. Then, we move on to contrast social divergence with existing concepts

R. Quentin Grafton, Stephen Knowles
and P. Dorian Owen

such as social cohesion, social diversity and, in particular, social capital. A key aim of this comparison is to emphasize the distinct and sharp focus of social divergence compared to broad, encompassing concepts like social capital. The study also provides a review of the social capital literature related to economic performance to highlight the differences between social capital and social divergence and their expected impacts on TFP. The review of past work provides a point of departure to the presentation of new empirical results on the statistical relationships between social divergence and TFP and labour productivity. The preliminary nature of these results provides an opportunity to discuss the need for further research and the policy implications of the study, especially for Canada. The concept of social divergence, the preliminary evidence of its impact on TFP and labour productivity, and its policy implications are reviewed in the concluding remarks.

SOCIAL DIVERGENCE AND TOTAL FACTOR PRODUCTIVITY

The first step in appreciating the importance of social divergence is to observe that humans (and other primates) have a tendency to associate and communicate with others with whom they can identify. Group identification of "like with like" occurs on multiple levels and on both a social and a professional basis. In traditional and pre-literate societies, bonds between members of groups are often based on kinship (Dunbar 1996). In modern societies, however, the bonds within groups may arise from various commonalities. For example, people often associate with others in the same age group and of similar income or levels of wealth, cultural background, education and marital status.

From our observation of the like-with-like association in human behaviour, we hypothesize that the greater the similarity of social characteristics between individuals, the lower the social barriers to communication. We further hypothesize that the lower the social barriers to communication in terms of costs or effort, time and dissonance associated with social interactions, for a given level of potential gain from specialization, the higher the incidence of mutually beneficial knowledge exchange. In other words, social barriers to communication across groups — social divergence — may prevent individuals from transcending their knowledge set and hinder "cooperation among highly specialized workers that enables advanced economies to utilize a vast amount of knowledge" (Becker and Murphy 1992, 1144). If religious, ethnic, educational, wealth or other social characteristics hinder communication across groups, the economic impact is likely to be greater on long-term TFP than on factor accumulation. This is partly because spillovers of technological knowledge between agents are likely to be more important than spillovers from factor accumulation, given that "technological knowledge is inherently more nonrival and nonexcludable than factor accumulation" (Easterly and Levine 2001, 208). Thus communication barriers that arise from social divergence, and that hinder disembodied technical change, are likely to be significant impediments to technological progress.

Barriers to communication can be characterized in terms of the configuration of networks linking individuals in a society. This view is consistent with recent work in network sociology showing that the structure of networks has a significant effect on the distribution of resources, including information, that flow through them (e.g., Burt 2000; Moody and White 2000).[3] In particular, social networks are more important in the transfer of "tacit knowledge/know how" than "explicit knowledge/know what" (Brown and Duguid 2000). Figures 1 and 2 illustrate the potential effects of social divergence. In Figure 1, social divergence prevents communication between individuals in group A and individuals in group B. We assume no social barriers to communication between individuals within a group and, in this extreme example, suppose that social barriers to communication are so prohibitive that no communication links exist between the two groups. Thus, with social divergence there are only two productivity-enhancing exchanges or communication links in the whole society. Figure 2, by contrast, shows that in the absence of social divergence there are six communication links.[4]

The figures illustrate the potential "increasing returns" in the number of exchanges from a decline in social barriers and social communication costs across groups. For example, for an economy with N individuals, there exist $N(N-1)/2$ possible pair-wise communication links. If the economy were divided into M social groups, each containing the same number of individuals, with no communication links across groups, then the maximum possible number of pair-wise communication links within each group would be only $N(N-M)/2M^2$ and for the society as a whole $N(N-M)/2M$, which is strictly less than $N(N-1)/2$, if M is greater than one. Thus, the larger the economy (defined by N) and the number of social groups (M), the greater the potential benefits from a lowering of social barriers to communication, all other things being equal.[5] An ideal economy is one with large complementarities in knowledge across individuals but with low social barriers to communication, so as to maximize both the number and the quality of exchanges between individuals and across social groups.

The social divergence view has commonalities to Lazear (1999), who argues that a common culture increases the pool of potential trading partners; the lack of a common culture inhibits the circle of contacts, which may leave economies of scale unexploited. Lazear focuses specifically on a common language, with an emphasis on opportunities to trade. The social divergence hypothesis, by contrast, emphasizes that the lack of a common culture will create communication barriers, inhibiting the diffusion

FIGURE 1

Communication Links with Social Barriers that Prevent Any Communication Across Groups (Communication Links = 2).

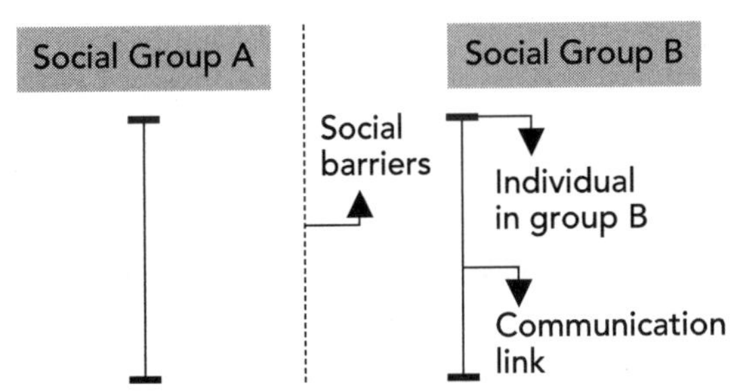

FIGURE 2

Communication Links in Absence of Social Barriers to Communication (Communication Links = 6)

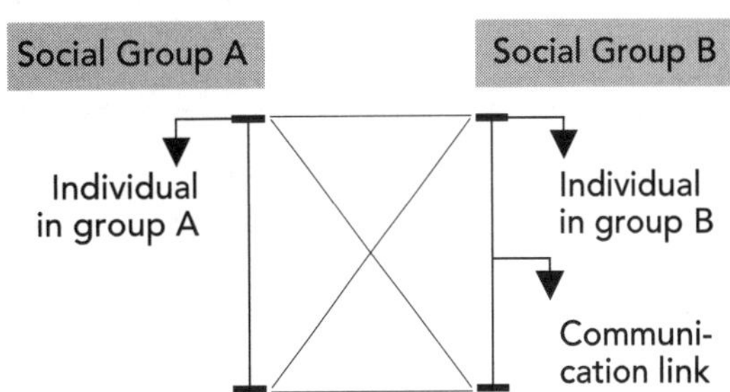

R. Quentin Grafton, Stephen Knowles
and P. Dorian Owen

of ideas and knowledge and reducing productivity. The notion of social divergence is also consistent with the empirical work of McCallum (1995) and Helliwell (1999), who show that border effects reduce trade flows by up to a factor of 20 for the United States and Canada, despite a free-trade agreement. Similar results have been found for the European Union (Nitsch 2000) and are consistent with the finding that a common language significantly increases trade densities between countries (Wei 1996). These studies do not focus on social divergence, but it seems likely that if differences in culture reduce trade, they will also create communication barriers.

Closer to our interpretation of social divergence are aspects of a theoretical model developed by Gradstein and Justman (2000) to examine the role of state schooling, as a source of common socialization, in reducing the social distance between individuals. They assume that the social distance between agents affects the productivity of human capital in transactions, citing Lazear's arguments but also referring in general terms to empirical work on social capital and the effects of ethnic heterogeneity. However, apart from a passing comment that their focus is "the negative impact of economic performance of people lacking the means to communicate effectively with each other" (fn. 4), they do not consider the broader implications in any detail.

Social barriers can also affect the rate of technological progress through the misallocation of skills across occupations. Galor and Tsiddon (1997) examine the relationship between technical progress and wage inequality. In their model, the rate of technological progress and growth is determined by intergenerational earnings mobility, while technical progress, in turn, plays a part in determining the evolution of earnings inequality and inter-

generational earnings mobility. Although not explicitly modelled, their analysis suggests that social barriers to mobility may distort the allocation of skills across occupations, hence reducing the rate of technological innovation and growth. From a social divergence viewpoint, a lack of social mobility will also reduce technological progress because it reinforces barriers to communication, hindering the implementation of best-practice techniques.

Social divergence does not imply that it is desirable for every individual to be identical. Some degree of diversity is likely to be beneficial; indeed, the value of communication between people of different backgrounds has long been recognized.[6] However, our contention is that the extent of communication barriers is an increasing function of the social distance between individuals, and that — other than, possibly, at relatively low levels of social distance — the negative effects of diversity on TFP will dominate any potential gains from diversity.[7] A key point is that social divergence tends to impede the exchange of information, regardless of the extent and distribution of potential productivity payoffs, partly because such payoffs are unknown due to the lack of communication between groups. Thus social divergence, by increasing the social barriers to communication, prevents productivity-enhancing exchanges between social groups, *even if* such potential benefits are greater for across-group interactions than within-group interactions.

SOCIAL DIVERGENCE AND SOCIAL CAPITAL

To fully understand the concept of social divergence we must review a number of related concepts (e.g., social cohesion, social exclusion, social capital, social capability, social diversity/heterogeneity, social polarization). These related concepts, associated with societal features of interactions between individuals and groups, have become widely used in theoretical and empirical work in the social sciences in recent years and have also become central to public policy discussions. Given the range of existing labels, the introduction of yet another — social divergence — requires some justification. Our view is that social divergence is both different from and more focused than existing concepts. A particular concern with several of these is their vagueness, as reflected in a worryingly long list of alternative definitions for the same entity, leading some to wonder whether we can "trust" such concepts (Sobel 2002).[8]

The term "social cohesion," for example, has been variously applied — with different meanings — in the social sciences. In sociology, it has been defined as outcomes of processes whereby individuals become linked to social systems (Barchas and Mendoza 1984). It has also been defined in terms of network connectivity, as "the minimum number of actors who, if removed from a group, would disconnect the group" (Moody and White 2000, ii); cohesive groups are those that are well-connected and difficult to break apart. Ritzen et al. (2000) define social cohesion as "a state of affairs in which a group of people…demonstrate an aptitude for collaboration that produces a climate for change" (6). In other words, it occurs when individuals and groups have the means, willingness and opportunity to collectively participate in improving society. According to Ritzen et al., "social exclusion" and social cohesion can be viewed as "two sides of a coin," with the main causes of social exclusion ascribed to poverty, unemployment, lack of access to rights, and development that com-

promises future generations. Any attempt to reconcile the differences in and linkages between definitions for the various concepts is beyond the scope of this paper. However, it should be noted that none of these interpretations of social cohesion or social exclusion highlights the barriers to communication, and the consequent implications for TFP, that result from social divergence.

Most views of social cohesion (Berger-Schmitt 2000) and other broadly defined concepts such as "social capability" (Temple and Johnson 1998) explicitly or implicitly embrace social capital as an important dimension. We therefore concentrate, in the rest of this section, on social capital as an example of a concept with a broad (and malleable) definition and compare it with the more focused notion of social divergence.

Trust and Ease of Cooperation

Paldam (2000) identifies three "families" of definitions of social capital, those based on "trust," "ease of cooperation" and "networks." Putnam (1993) emphasizes ease of cooperation in his earlier definition of social capital as the "features of social organization…that facilitate coordination and cooperation for mutual benefit" (35-36); this is reflected in his choice of the density of voluntary organizations and the extent of associational activity as proxies for social capital. Others (e.g., Fukuyama 1995; Knack 2001) stress the importance of trust, particularly "generalized" or "wide-radius" trust, for national economic performance; this is mirrored in the widespread use of survey measures of trust in empirical work (e.g., Zak and Knack 2001). Paldam (2000) argues that, together trust, which he views as constituting the "deepest definition of social capital," (629) and cooperative behaviour form "a solid basis for social capital" (636).

R. Quentin Grafton, Stephen Knowles
and P. Dorian Owen

Even if we focus solely on trust, important distinctions can be drawn within the concept. James (2002), for example, distinguishes between trust that is fostered through incentives and trust whereby "players retain a vulnerability to the actions and choices of others" (293). The former is the type of trust that can be engendered through reward and/or enforcement mechanisms, as represented in prisoner's dilemma games by changing preferences, by introducing explicit or implicit contracts, or through repetition. The latter is closer to what is popularly regarded as trust. Durlauf (1997) argues that trustworthiness is "cooperative behavior that occurs in the absence of either an enforcement mechanism or the prospect of future reward, and is perhaps better thought of as an internalized ethical norm," but "[e]xplaining ethical behavior is very different than explaining adherence to socially-enforced norms" (262). The point is that broadly defined labels may obscure subtle but important differences among various mechanisms. If the aim is to analyze the implications of or to promote the notion of different types of trust, then a more focused approach is desirable.

Zak and Knack's (2001) model, which examines the role of social distance, or "social heterogeneity," in building generalized trust, illustrates an important difference between trust-based social capital and social divergence. In their principal (investor)-agent (broker) model, the greater the social distance between randomly matched investors and brokers, the greater the likelihood that cheating will occur. Investors can forego resources to monitor their investments and hence check on the honesty of brokers. Zak and Knack's approach is based on the existence of transactions costs in monitoring and enforcing contracts, but it does not capture the barriers to communication that result from social divergence, nor does it address the importance of these barriers in hindering disembodied technical change. The economic importance of social divergence lies in the reduced exchange of ideas and knowledge, rather than in the increased transactions costs associated with the exchange and enforcement of property rights.

Networks

More recently, there has been an emphasis on the "networks" interpretation of social capital, as epitomized by Putnam's (2000) more encompassing definition of social capital as "connections among individuals — social networks, and the norms of reciprocity and trustworthiness that arise from them" (19). Paldam (2000) takes a positive view: "The network definition fits rather well into the trust-cooperation definitions. Everything might be shades of and approaches to the very same basic phenomenon" (641). By contrast, Woolcock (2001) argues that definitions of social capital should emphasize its sources ("norms and networks that facilitate collective action") rather than its consequences (e.g., trust).[9] A disadvantage of any all-encompassing definition of social capital is that it encourages researchers to regard beliefs, behavioural norms and networks as capable of being lumped together, which obscures different potential mechanisms and effects (Dasgupta 2000).

Unpacking the different elements contained in encompassing concepts such as social capital or social cohesion requires a sharper focus on the various mechanisms involved in economic performance. This is one of the motivations for the specific focus, in the social divergence approach, on social impediments to interaction among individuals and the exchange of the ideas and knowledge that lead to innovation and diffusion of productivity-enhancing methods.[10] Social divergence is more closely associated with the "networks" view than the trust, norms or cooperation aspects of social capital, but its focus is information flows and the impediments that arise due to "fractures" in the network structure resulting from different dimensions of social distance.

Social divergence can also have direct effects on economic performance, unrelated to the trust-civic engagement axis included in most definitions of social capital (a point seen by Knack [2001] as a criticism of using measures of ethnic diversity, inequality, etc., as proxies for social capital). For example, Temple and Johnson (1998) argue that a robust correlation between their index of mass communications and growth could exist because the former is a good proxy for the level of civic engagement, as measured by the World Values Survey data on trust and membership in associations. From the viewpoint of the concept of social divergence, however, no indirect effect is required. Mass communications reduce the physical barriers to communications that partly mitigate social divergence and thus can promote the exchange of ideas and knowledge that lead to TFP gains.

Bonding, Bridging and Linking Social Capital

Although they are different concepts, social divergence and social capital are nonetheless related. For example, different dimensions of social divergence (ethnic diversity, income inequality, etc.) will affect levels of trust and civic engagement (Zak and Knack 2001). Further, a networks perspective of social capital, including the distinction between "bonding," "bridging" and "linking" social capital (Woolcock 2001; Narayan 1999; Putnam 2000), complements the focus of social divergence.

Bonding social capital involves linkages (usually "strong ties") within groups of like-minded individuals (e.g., families, clans, gangs), corresponding to denser, more localized networks. In this sense, bonding social capital is similar to the idea, first formulated by Davis (1967), that a society can be divided into clusters whereby within-group cooperation does occur but group-to-group cooperation does not. Bridging social capital involves linkages, usually somewhat "weaker," among heterogeneous groups. Linking social capital refers to "vertical" connections among different strata in a hierarchical structure, with respect to, for example, wealth or power. Social divergence focuses on dimensions of social distance that act as impediments to linkages among groups; these are likely to be reflected in lower levels of bridging and linking social capital among groups distributed along the relevant dimensions of social distance. Knack (2001) notes that such factors affect not only overall trust levels but also the radius of trust; for example, in ethnically diverse societies there may be high levels of trust within ethnic groups but low levels of generalized (wide-radius) trust. Impediments to like-with-like interactions, while suggesting a lack of bridging and linking social capital, are not necessarily associated with high levels of bonding social capital. For example, groups with low income or educational levels are less likely to have strong within-group identification than, say, minority ethnic groups.

The fact that social distance with regard to dimensions such as ethnolinguistic or religious background can have an adverse effect on productivity does not imply — it should be emphasized — that social homogeneity is optimal. Diversity is a source of potential gain from specialization and exchange. The essence of the social divergence argument is that social

R. Quentin Grafton, Stephen Knowles
and P. Dorian Owen

barriers to the flow of information across trans-actors or groups of transactors will, to some degree, prevent the benefits of diversity from being realized. The challenge for Canada and other socially diverse countries is to overcome, through institutional improvements, the impediments to communication among groups with different ethnic, religious, educational or resource characteristics, in order to achieve the full social and economic benefits of diversity.

210 INDICATORS OF SOCIAL DIVERGENCE

We hypothesize that social barriers to communication can result from differences in ethnolinguistic background, religion, income or asset holdings, educational attainment and national boundaries. Each of these variables has been featured, usually in a piecemeal fashion, in theoretical and empirical studies of economic growth. For most of the variables, different mechanisms have been hypothesized to explain the connection with growth. These indicators are briefly discussed below, together with some details of relevant empirical work and the specific measures used to proxy the different aspects of social divergence.

Ethnic and Religious Diversity

The economic effects of polarization of societies along ethnic lines have received considerable attention in the development literature, and many of the issues are also applicable to developed economies. The main mechanism by which ethnic diversity affects output growth is usually argued to be an excessive rent-seeking focus on the distribution of output among competing interest groups, determined by ethnic background, at the expense of policies that are growth-promoting.[11]

Fractionalized interests are reflected in incentives by local and national governments that lead to sub-optimal outcomes such as a lower quality and quantity of public goods (Alesina et al. 1999), lower educational levels (Goldin and Katz 1999), political instability (Mauro 1995), vulnerability to external terms-of-trade shocks (Rodrik 1999) and lower levels of trust (Zak and Knack 2001; Alesina and La Ferrara 2000). Barro (1997, 72) also observes that such diversity may reduce the likelihood of a society becoming or remaining a democracy. Where democracy does not exist, development-impeding institutions may form a "trap" whereby exploitive institutions and severe inequities are mutually reinforced (Grafton and Rowlands 1996). More generally, social polarization (usually characterized by the existence of a small number of similarly sized groups that differ markedly on a range of attributes) may reduce the stability of government decision-making (Keefer and Knack 2000), leading to increased uncertainty. This in turn is compensated for by investors investing in less risky enterprises.

Easterly (2001*a*) observes that the impact of ethnic diversity on economic growth hinges on a society's institutions: the poorer the quality of those institutions, the more adverse the impact. Unfortunately, "good" institutions are less likely to exist in a society characterized by ethnic diversity. Even where institutional structures are relatively well developed, the expected productivity of rent-seeking activity is a key determinant; for example, Osborne (2000) notes that a well-established and accessible legal system (usually regarded as useful in protecting property rights) may encourage rent-seeking activity through litigation, so that redistributional tendencies, while less obvious, may still be present.

In addition to the studies cited above (some of which use US data), cross-country empirical evidence supports the view that ethnolinguistic diversity is a predictor of conflict, political instability, and growth-retarding institutions and policies (Easterly and Levine 1997). Nettle (2000) finds a significant negative association between linguistic diversity and the level of per capita GDP.[12] Easterly and Levine's work is representative of most cross-country studies of the effects of ethnic diversity in using an index of ethnolinguistic fractionalization (ELF), developed by Soviet researchers and first used in the growth literature by Mauro (1995). The ELF index measures the probability that two randomly selected individuals in a country belong to different ethnolinguistic groups.[13] From the perspective of social divergence, ethnolinguistic differences should affect TFP and disembodied technical progress rather than investments of physical inputs into the production process, although these mechanisms are not mutually exclusive.

The argument that religion affects economic performance dates back to Max Weber's arguments concerning the "Protestant ethic." In this vein, proportions of the population that belong to major religious groups are sometimes included in estimated models explaining growth and related variables; for example, Barro (1997) provides evidence of an association between religious affiliation and democracy. He observes that Protestant countries are almost exclusively democratic while Islamic nations are not. Zak and Knack (2001) observe that "[t]wo of the three hierarchical religion variables — percent Catholic and percent Muslim — are negatively and significantly associated with trust" (310). Religious diversity is conventionally measured using a Herfindahl-style index by summing the squared proportions of the population accounted for by each religious group (Grafton et al. 2001; Paldam 2001). The effects of religious diversity are often considered together with ethnolinguistic differences — for example, with respect to the potential for political and social instability and the other effects noted above. By contrast, there is some evidence that religious diversity may reduce corruption, with positive consequences for economic performance (Paldam 2001).

211

Income and Asset Inequality

A large literature emphasizes the relevance of income inequality as a causal factor in the growth process. High levels of income inequality are hypothesized to reduce growth by influencing the level of savings and investment; by increasing rent-seeking activities and policies, such as high marginal tax rates, that may hinder growth (Persson and Tabellini 1994); by reducing human capital accumulation due to borrowing constraints and indivisibilites in investment (Galor and Zeira 1993); by reducing the size of markets and the ability to capture increasing returns (Murphy et al. 1989); by leading to a lack of political consensus and a breakdown of democratic institutions, resulting in reduced investment and hence growth (Benhabib and Rustichini 1996); and by reducing the security of property rights (Keefer and Knack 2000). Some of the earliest work on income inequality and growth, however, stresses that rising income levels can affect income inequality. For example, Kuznets (1955) hypothesized and observed that income inequality may rise, along with income levels, as migration from rural to urban areas initially widens the rural-urban income divide, but that income inequality will eventually reach a turning point and then decline as income increases further. Aghion et al. (1999), who review and evaluate some of the growth-inequality theoretical mechanisms, also emphasize the two-way relationship. However, they focus on the issue of technical progress and inequality, noting in particular that technological progress that differentially affects productivity of different types of labour is a key source of income inequality.

The empirical evidence on inequality and growth is mixed. Persson and Tabellini (1994, 607) find that a one-standard-deviation increase in the income share of the top quintile lowers average annual growth rates by just under half a percentage point. Alesina and Rodrik (1994), using different data, find a negative correlation between income inequality and subsequent economic growth. Perotti (1996) and Clarke (1995) also find evidence of a negative relationship between growth and inequality. By contrast, Forbes (2000) finds a positive relationship between inequality and growth using panel data for a cross-section of countries.

Most empirical testing has focused on the effect on growth of income inequality rather than asset inequality, even though the theoretical models are mostly concerned with asset inequality. However, some recent empirical studies — for example, Birdsall and Londoño (1997), Deininger and Squire (1998) and Deininger and Olinto (2000) — examine the role of asset inequality in growth equations. Deininger and Olinto, using a Gini coefficient for land distribution as a measure of asset inequality in a cross-country analysis, find that asset inequality has a statistically significant and relatively large negative effect on growth but that income inequality does not. As with the measure of ethnolinguistic diversity, the empir-

ical studies tend to focus on the effects of inequality measures on overall economic growth rather than on TFP, which is emphasized in social divergence arguments.

Educational Inequality

Building on the relevance of human capital for growth and productivity (see Temple 2000 for a recent survey), there is a growing literature on the potential effects of educational inequality on levels or growth rates of output per capita. The usual argument (e.g., López et al. 1998) is that non-market mechanisms, and factors such as parental income, supply constraints and location, determine the allocation of education. As a result, there are likely to be significant differences in marginal products of education across individuals that are not explainable in terms of variation in ability. This implies that the distribution of education will affect the level of output per capita. A complementary explanation, suggested by the social divergence approach, is that educational inequality, a proxy for social divergence, hampers the transfer of information and ideas.

Birdsall and Londoño (1997) find that initial levels of educational inequality, measured by the standard deviation of schooling, are significantly correlated with subsequent economic growth. More recently, Gini coefficients for education have been constructed using different vintages of the Barro and Lee (1993, 1996, 2001) data on educational attainment. López et al. (1998) estimate educational Gini coefficients for 12 countries, expanded to 20 countries in the work reported in Thomas, Dailami, et al. (2000). Thomas, Wang, et al. (2000) calculate educational Gini coefficients for 85 countries, covering a wide range of developing and developed economies, for the period 1960-90. The (preliminary) empirical work presented in these papers suggests that growth in income per capita is negatively associated with educational inequality. This finding is supported by the results of Castelló and Doménech (2001), who calculate educational Gini coefficients and the distribution of education by quintiles, from the Barro and Lee (2001) data, for 108 countries at five-year intervals from 1960 to 2000 and report a tendency for educational inequality to decline in most countries. For the full sample, which includes wide diversity in levels of development, there is a strong negative (though seemingly non-linear) association between average years of schooling and educational Gini values.

While countries with lower levels of human capital can have markedly different distributions of education with comparable average years of schooling, economies with higher levels of human capital (average years of schooling) have relatively equal distributions. In OECD economies, therefore, compared to developing economies, educational inequality may have less effect on growth, independent of the level of human capital. By contrast, issues of quality and type of education and training, which are not captured in the average years of schooling measures, are likely to be more important in developed economies.

National Boundaries

National boundaries are a defining feature of national identity and hence a potential impediment to communication, particularly when reinforced by language differences. This may be one reason why trade densities are so much greater within countries than across countries and why distance effects are many times larger than can be explained by trans-portation costs (Hazledine 2000; Helliwell and Verdier 2001).

Many authors have assessed the effects of trade orientation on economic performance. Most of the empirical studies have used cross-sectional data and analysed the effect in terms of economic growth (Dollar 1992; Harrison 1996; Edwards 1998). Miller and Upadhyay (2000) specifically address the effect on TFP of human capital and openness to trade in a pooled cross-section of countries using time-series data. They find that the greater the openness, the higher the level of TFP — a result that holds for low-, middle- and high-income countries.

Connections Between Indicators

The different indicators of social divergence are clearly not independent. Ethnic, linguistic and religious differences will sometimes be correlated, although, surprisingly, there is only a small positive correlation between measures of income and human capital inequality (Castelló and Doménech 2001). Further, in situations where, for example, income inequality and ethnic diversity coexist, their negative effects on economic performance can be mutually reinforcing.

Easterly (2001*b*) presents evidence of a "middle-class consensus." In a cross-country context, consensus is defined as a high share of income for the middle of the income distribution (quantiles 2 to 4) and a low level of ethnic division (measured by an ELF index). Easterly finds that such a measure is positively associated with the level and growth rate of income per capita, levels of educational and health components of human capital, infrastructure, a range of indicators of favourable economic policy, democracy, political stability, urbanization and proxies for a more "modern" economy.

R. Quentin Grafton, Stephen Knowles
and P. Dorian Owen

Subjective and Objective Measures

In summing up the empirical literature, we should acknowledge that the chosen proxies for social divergence in empirical work measure "objective divergence" rather than "subjective divergence." Objective divergence could be thought of as the number and size of gaps between individuals, or social distance. For example, educational diversity is a function of both the number of educational groups and the objective distance (in terms of years of schooling) between groups. The subjective component of social divergence refers to how large a gap this creates between individuals in terms of barriers to communication, which can differ across time and space. It is possible that in some societies university graduates do not interact with the unschooled and in some societies they do. To give a different example, the Catholic-Protestant distinction is more likely to create barriers to communication in Ulster than in Ontario.[14] Although subjective divergence is not unimportant, it is not clear how it could be measured in an aggregate cross-country context. In the following section, we address the issue of measurement and the significance of objective measures of social divergence for both labour and TFP.

TOTAL FACTOR PRODUCTIVITY, LABOUR PRODUCTIVITY AND SOCIAL DIVERGENCE

Despite the huge literature relating social factors to various measures of productivity, only one study has empirically tested for the significance of social divergence on TFP. This study, Grafton et al. (2001), regresses the Hall and Jones (1999) estimates of TFP on proxy measures for social divergence using data for a cross-section of 31 developing countries,[15] and tests whether the broad objective measures of social divergence have a significant and negative effect on TFP. The chosen measures of social divergence used in the study include an ELF index, an index of religious homogeneity, a measure of educational distance and a Gini coefficient for personal expenditure.[16] The results suggest, separate from any effects due to factor accumulation, that higher levels of social divergence are associated with lower levels of TFP and that these effects are quantitatively significant.

Using a much larger cross section of countries than in Grafton et al. (2001), we investigate here the association between estimates of output per worker (or labour productivity) and TFP (Hall and Jones 1999) and various indicators of social divergence.[17] The chosen indicators are a measure of religious homogeneity, an educational Gini, a land-ownership Gini and an ELF index. The religious homogeneity measure (RH) is constructed for 1980 from data presented in Barrett (1982). This index measures the probability that two randomly selected individuals will have the same religious affiliation. The educational Gini is for 1990 and the data are obtained from Castelló and Doménech (2001). The land-ownership Gini data are from the period 1960-70 and come from Deininger and Olinto (2000). The ELF index is for 1960 and uses data from Mauro (1995) measuring the probability that two randomly selected individuals in a country belong to different ethnolinguistic groups. With the exception of religious homogeneity, increases in the measures correspond to increases in social divergence. Thus, we would expect a positive correlation for TFP and labour

CHART 1

Scatter Plot of Religious Homogeneity (RH) and TFP

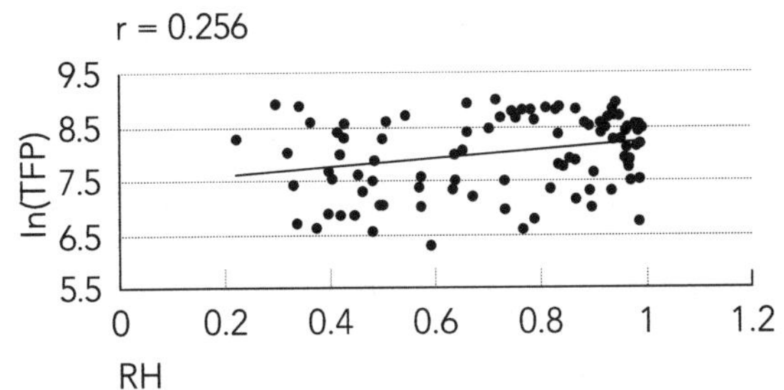

CHART 2

Scatter Plot of Educational Gini and TFP

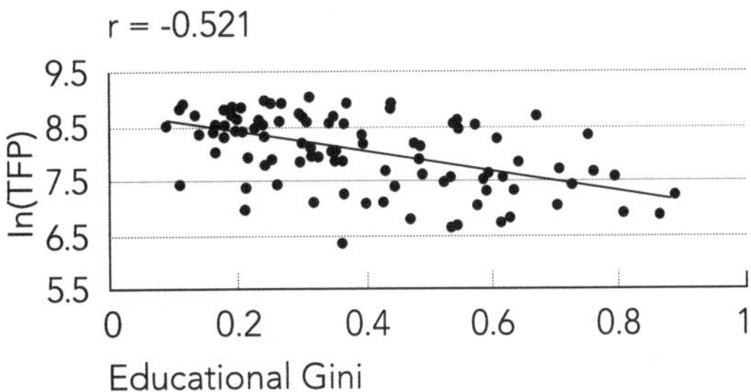

215

CHART 3

Scatter Plot of Ethnolinguistic
Fractionalization (ELF) Index and TFP

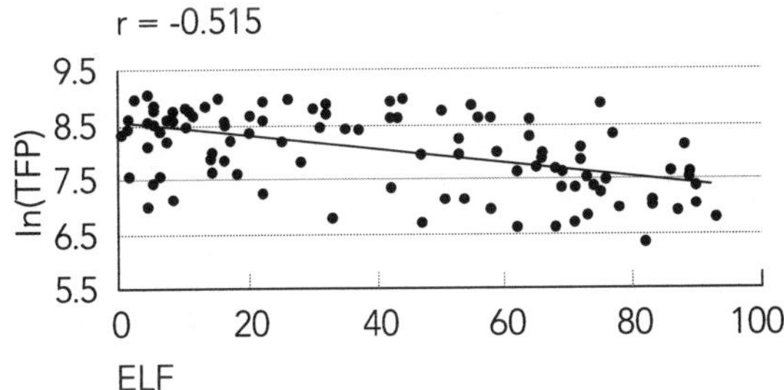

CHART 4

Scatter Plot of Land-Ownership (LO) Gini
and TFP

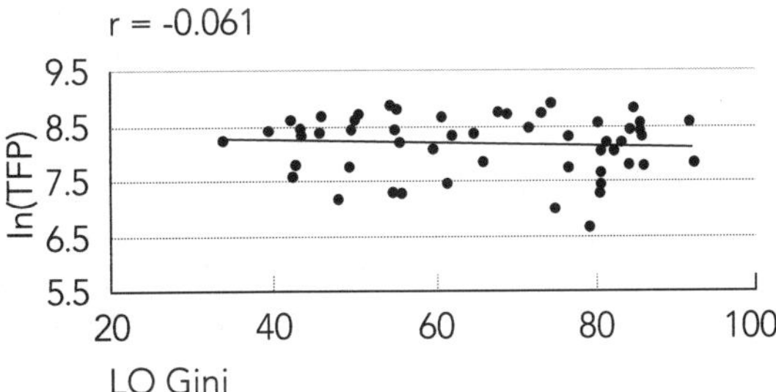

productivity with the variable religious homogeneity and a negative correlation with all the other variables. The number of countries with data available to test the association between TFP and the measures of social divergence are: 96 (religious homogeneity), 95 (educational Gini), 52 (land-ownership Gini) and 100 (ELF index).

Total Factor Productivity

We present simple correlations and bivariate scatter plots between the chosen measures of social divergence and the (natural log of) estimates of TFP for 1988 from Hall and Jones (1999).[18] At best, such an exercise can be only suggestive; the existence of a statistically significant negative correlation between ln(TFP) and a measure of social divergence does not necessarily imply a causal relationship. The correlations between ln(TFP) and the measures of social divergence are 0.256 (religious homogeneity), -0.521 (educational Gini), -0.515 (ELF index) and -0.061 (land-ownership Gini). Scatter plots of the relationships are presented in Charts 1 to 4. With the exception of the land-ownership Gini, there appears to be a substantial association between TFP and the measures of social divergence.

Labour Productivity

Estimates of output per worker, herein defined as labour productivity, for 1990 come from the Penn World Tables v5.6. Correlations between labour productivity and the measures of social divergence are 0.160 (religious homogeneity), -0.715 (educational Gini), -0.130 (land-ownership Gini) and -0.452 (ELF index). Scatter plots of the

CHART 5

Scatter Plot of Religious Homogeneity (RH)
and Output Per Worker

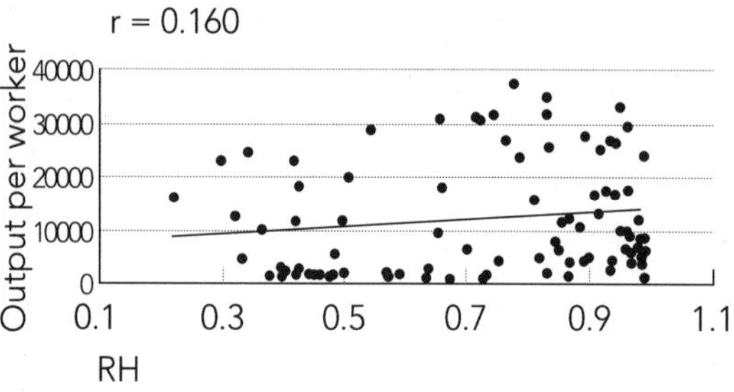

CHART 6

Scatter Plot of Educational Gini and Output
Per Worker

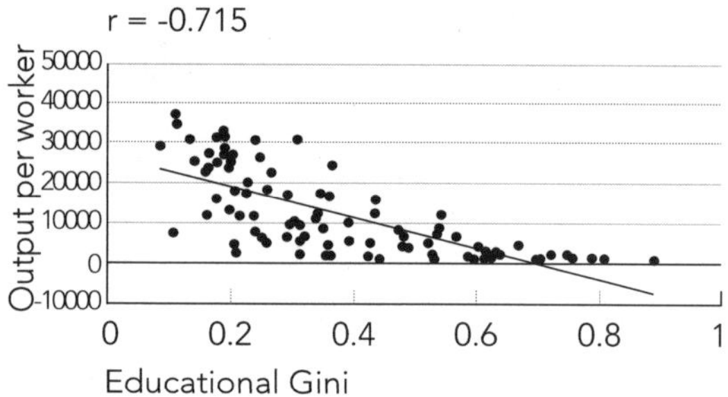

CHART 7

Scatter Plot of Ethnolinguistic Fractionalization
(ELF) Index and Output Per Worker

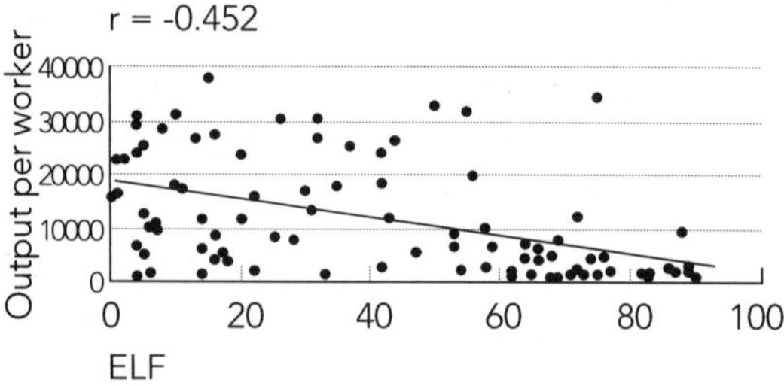

CHART 8

Scatter Plot of Land-Ownership (LO) Gini and
Output Per Worker

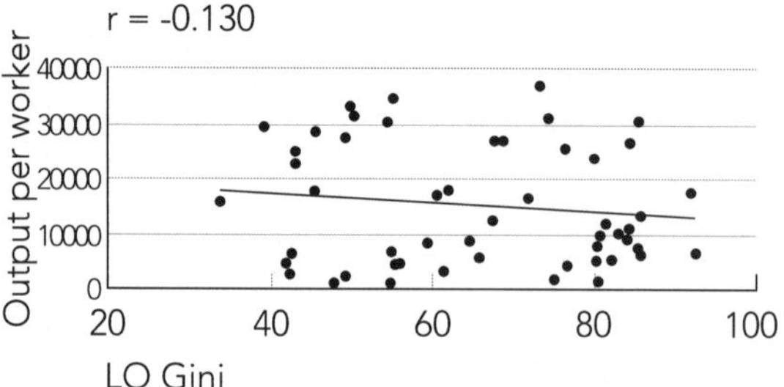

associations are provided in Charts 5 to 8. The correlations suggest that the measures of social divergence are associated with labour productivity.

Empirical Relationships

To quantify the importance of measures of social divergence for TFP and labour productivity, a model of the empirical relationship should be estimated. In such a model, Grafton et al. (2001) compare the predicted mean TFP levels of countries in the highest and lowest quartile of countries sorted in ascending order for their measures of social divergence. For each of their explanatory variables (religious homogeneity, ELF index and a personal expenditure Gini), they found that the mean TFP levels of those countries in the lowest quartile in terms of social divergence were, on average, more than twice those of countries in the highest quartile. Their simulation results imply that, for the countries in their sample, those with the highest levels of social divergence could double their levels of TFP (and hence labour productivity) if they could reduce their levels of social divergence to those of the low-social-divergence countries.

The associations between social divergence and TFP (and labour productivity) and the empirical work of Grafton et al. (2001) are consistent with the hypothesized productivity-social divergence relationships. Nevertheless, there are alternative explanations for the results, especially in terms of the association between social divergence and output per worker. For example, the social capital literature indicates that high ethnic diversity is associated with lower levels of trust, which, in turn, is correlated with lower growth rates (Zak and Knack 2001). In addition, Hall and Jones (1999) have developed the concept of social infrastructure, which combines an index of government antidiversion policies and the level of openness to international trade. Antidiversion policies are defined as those which divert resources from their most productive use (e.g., distortionary taxes, trade barriers and corrupt practices).[19] They find that their measure of social infrastructure is the primary determinant of total output per worker in a sample of 79 countries. Whatever the explanation or mix of factors, the empirical evidence suggests that measures of social divergence, civic social capital (especially trust) and public social capital (especially corruption) have a significant effect on economic performance.

Further work is, however, needed to provide more robust evidence for a causal relationship[20] between social divergence and economic performance using a sample of both rich and poor nations. Such a study could test for differences between rich and poor nations and determine whether, for example, the higher levels of education overall and mass communications in richer nations mitigate the negative effects of social divergence.

IMPLICATIONS FOR POLICY AND FUTURE RESEARCH

The hypothesis that social barriers to communication across social groups can affect productivity requires further study. In particular, our chosen indicators of social divergence are proxies for the number of groups (religious homogeneity, ELF index) and distance between social groups (educational Gini, land-ownership Gini); they do not distinguish between subjective and objective divergence because they are *not* direct measures of the number or quality of links or exchanges across individuals. For example, impediments to knowledge spillovers at the micro level would include those that separate scholars in different disciplines. Such differences would not be identified with broad societal measures of social divergence, but could be important because of the potentially significant synergies and cross-fertilization of ideas from interdisciplinary activities and communication.

Ideally, physical measures of the quantity and quality of exchanges within and across social groups would more directly indicate the impact of social divergence, enhancing our ability to discriminate between a social divergence explanation of the associations reported and other explanations. On a micro level, physical measures of exchange could include the number, direction and connectivity of electronic mail within organizations. Such measures could reveal the existence of clusters of communications and provide evidence of like-with-like groups within the organizational network that may be similar to the notion of self-forming neighbourhoods (Schelling 1978). Where such measures exist, they could provide evidence of social barriers to communication that may affect micro-level productivity. For example, *The Economist* (2001) reports on work at CERN (the European particle-physics laboratory) indicating that communications links established for past research projects persist and may hinder the development of links required for new research projects.

Further work on social divergence might include its relationship to the emergence of complex social systems. For instance, in the world of

R. Quentin Grafton, Stephen Knowles
and P. Dorian Owen

social insects the organization and coordination of building activities depend upon the nest structure itself, in a process called *stigmergy* (Bonabeau et al. 1999). To the extent that social groups are self-organized, in the sense that complex behaviour can arise from simple individual interactions, the interplay of the physical structures of communication and individual interactions may help determine the level and quality of inter- and intra-group interactions on a societal level. For example, the number and diversity of languages in the highlands of Papua New Guinea are a result of high and steep mountains that have hindered trade and communication between settlements for thousands of years. Even in a modern economy with a well-developed infrastructure, geographical features may result in differential access to modes of communication, thus reinforcing existing like-with-like social interactions on a regional level or accentuating a rural-urban divide. Physical and human geography also determine population density, which may, in turn, influence the number and quality of interactions between individuals and thus the social barriers to communication.

Another issue worthy of further research is whether social divergence can explain the self-organization of social networks with clusters of like-with-like interactions. For instance, geographically localized knowledge about domestic patents and patent citations (Jaffe et al. 1993) is economically important and provides evidence for the importance of localized networks. Further, agglomeration economies that explain why firms of a similar type locate near each other may simply be manifestations of spillovers that arise when social barriers to communication are lowered due to proximity and increased social exchange. In this sense, social divergence provides a social analogue to the self-organizing behaviour found in large networks with a complex topology. In such networks, as when firms preferentially locate with like firms or when innovations are localized and clustered, new connections are preferentially linked to vertices/points/agents that already have a large number of connections (Barabási and Albert 1999).

If further work supports our hypothesis, especially concerning the existence of a significant relationship between social divergence and TFP in both rich and poor countries, our study could have important policy implications, in particular for how policy-makers might increase productivity for a given level of social divergence. Easterly (2001*a*) observes that improvements in the quality of institutions can mitigate the potentially negative effects of ethnic diversity on economic performance. In reference to social divergence, we might argue that economies with well-developed mass communications and physical infrastructure can increase communication and exchange across social groups for a given level of social divergence. Similarly, comprehensive schooling and inclusive and outward-focused curricula, cross-cultural and cross-religious exchanges, and support for common national languages may also reduce social barriers to communication.[21] Thus, there are social and economic policies that can increase exchange across social groups. Indeed, to some extent such policies have been pursued in Canada and other countries, but for social rather than economic reasons. For example, Canada's policy of multiculturalism is intended to promote cross-cultural understanding, while one of the aims of bilingualism is to overcome the communication barriers of the English-French divide. The postulated social divergence-productivity relationship would suggest that such policies could also help raise Canada's long-term level of TFP.

CONCLUDING REMARKS

This chapter presents preliminary evidence on the hypothesis that social divergence, the social barriers to communication across social groups, inhibits the exchange of productivity-enhancing ideas in an economy. Using cross-country data we find an association between three proxies of social divergence and TFP and labour productivity. This finding is supported by regressions in a smaller sample of poor countries that indicate a statistically and economically significant negative relationship between measures of social divergence and TFP (Grafton et al. 2001).

If the productivity-social divergence hypothesis is supported in further empirical work, especially in rich and poor countries, it provides a number of important policy implications. First and foremost is the implication that policies to lower social barriers to communication may have a substantial economic payoff in terms of higher TFP and labour productivity. Such policies could include raising the level of mass communications and improving physical infrastructure to mitigate social barriers to communication, developing school curricula that foster an open and outward-oriented approach to learning, cross-cultural and cross-religious exchanges, and language training for recent immigrants. To some extent, Canada has implemented such policies, but to achieve social rather than economic objectives. Our study suggests that, if bilingualism has helped to overcome linguistic divisions and if multiculturalism has promoted cross-cultural understanding, these cornerstones of Canada's cultural policies may have important economic benefits by raising the long-term level of TFP.

NOTES

We are grateful for financial support from the Marsden Fund, administered by the Royal Society of New Zealand. We thank Keith Banting, Tue Gorgens, Andrew Sharpe, France St-Hilaire and an anonymous reviewer for helpful comments on earlier versions of the paper. Authorship is alphabetical.

1   TFP is an index of how efficiently inputs (such as labour, human capital and physical capital) are transformed into final goods and services. For example, if country A requires twice as many inputs to produce a given level of output as country B, then country A's level of TFP is only half that of country B's.

2   A recent and detailed review of Canadian productivity performance is provided by Baldwin et al. (2001). Sharpe (2001) provides a useful comparison of the economic and productivity trends in Canada and the United States over the 1990s.

3   Dasgupta (2000) notes that networks that act as "economic enclaves" can retard economic development by constraining the flow of resources (labour, financial capital, knowledge, ideas, etc.) across groups, creating inefficiency.

4   In the terminology of social network analysis (Scott 2000), Figure 2 may be described as a 1-clique of size 4 in that all points (individuals) in the graph are directly connected with each other.

5   For instance, in an economy with 100 individuals and zero social communication costs, the maximum number of pair-wise communication links is 4,950. If the same economy had just two social groups (and no communication links across groups) the maximum number of pair-wise links is 2,450, with 10 groups the maximum number of links is 450 and with 100 groups the number of links is zero. As M increases, other things may not remain equal; as $M \Rightarrow N$, barriers between groups may be lessened as the situation starts to approximate that of M heterogeneous individuals rather than M "groups."

6   For instance, J.S. Mill (1848) shrewdly observed that "it is hardly possible to overrate the value…of placing human beings in contact with persons dissimilar to themselves, and with modes of thought and action unlike those with which they are familiar" (594).

7   Gradstein and Justman (2000) adopt a similar stance. In their model, the productivity of a transaction reflects the balance between the probability of a "successful" transaction, which decreases with social (or "cultural") distance, and the conditional productivity of the transaction, which may increase with social distance. Like us, they assume that, beyond some relatively low level of social distance, productivity is a decreasing function of social distance.

8   Jenson (1998) points out that a concept such as "social cohesion" is a "contested concept," the interpretation of which can depend on different underlying theoretical traditions. Given the breadth of interest from different disciplines, and from policy-makers as well as academics, the lack of consensus is not altogether surprising.

9   In Woolcock's (2001) view, "there is an emerging consensus on the definition of social capital… social capital refers to the norms and networks that facilitate collective action" (70).

10   An alternative, broader view of social divergence would be as an umbrella concept that emphasizes the effects of different dimensions of social distance on productivity and growth. However, as discussed below, there are several hypothesized mechanisms by which each of the different dimensions of social distance affect economic performance, so an encompassing view would be subject to the same criticisms applied above to social capital and social cohesion.

11   Easterly (2001c) succinctly summarizes this view: "divided societies' governments face incentives to redistribute existing income. In more cohesive societies, governments face incentives to promote development" (256).

12   By contrast, Lian and Oneal (1997) construct their own index of diversity, which includes (equally weighted and standardized) components for ethnic, linguistic and religious diversity, and find that it is not statistically significant in an otherwise conventional growth regression.

13   There is some debate over whether fragmentation or inequality (as measured by the ELF index), polarization (which is maximized with only two different groups) or dominance (measured by the proportion of the population in the largest ethnic group) is the most relevant aspect in assessing the effects of ethnic division on economic performance (Collier 2001).

14   We are grateful to an anonymous reviewer for this point.

15   To reduce the potential overlap with mechanisms that affect factor accumulation (labour, physical capital and human capital), Grafton et al. (2001) focus specifically on the effects of proxies for social divergence on TFP.

16   The exclusion of developed countries and the small sample are a consequence of the decision to use only consistently measured data for expenditure inequality that are also labelled "reliable."

17   Sargent and Rodriguez (2000) observe that both TFP and labour productivity are appropriate productivity measures. Where the interest is over long periods of time (greater than 10 years), TFP may be a better choice provided that capital stock data are comparable across countries.

18   Note that the associations summarized are based on variation across countries, not over time. Such correlations should be relatively robust to the different dates at which the indicators of divergence are measured as these vary relatively little over time compared to their variation across countries.

19   Hall and Jone's index of government antidiversion policies is, for each country, an equally weighted average of five ratings related to law and order, bureaucratic quality, corruption, risk of appropriation and government repudiation of contracts, compiled by Political Risk Services.

20   See, for example, Durlauf's (2002) critique of Putnam's (2000) empirical evidence.

21   These policies are complementary to those reviewed by Helliwell (2001) for Canada from a social capital perspective.

REFERENCES

Aghion, P., E. Caroli, and C. García-Peñalosa. 1999. "Inequality and Economic Growth: The Perspective of the New Growth Theories." *Journal of Economic Literature* 37(4):1615-1660.

Alesina, A., R. Baqir, and W. Easterly. 1999. "Public Goods and Ethnic Divisions." *Quarterly Journal of Economics* 114(4):1243-1284.

Alesina, A., and E. La Ferrara. 2000. "The Determinants of Trust." Working paper #7621. Cambridge, MA: National Bureau of Economic Research.

Alesina, A., and D. Rodrik. 1994. "Distributive Politics and Economic Growth." *Quarterly Journal of Economics* 109(2):465-490.

Baldwin, J.R., D. Beckstead, N. Dhaliwal, R. Durand, V. Gaudreault, T.M. Harchaoui, J. Hosein, M. Kaci, and J.-P. Maynard. 2001. *Productivity Growth in Canada*. Ottawa: Statistics Canada.

Barabási, A.-L., and R. Albert. 1999. "Emergence of Scaling in Random Networks." *Science* 286:509-512.

Barchas, P.R., and S.P. Mendoza. 1984. "Preface." In *Social Cohesion: Essays Toward a Sociophysiological Perspective*, ed. P.R. Barchas, and S.P. Mendoza. Westport, CT: Greenwood Press.

Barrett, D.B. 1982. *World Christian Encyclopedia: A Comparative Study of Churches and Religions in the Modern World, AD 1900-2000*. Nairobi: Oxford University Press.

Barro, R.J. 1997. *Determinants of Economic Growth: A Cross-Country Empirical Study.* Cambridge, MA: MIT Press.

Barro, R.J., and J.-W. Lee. 1993. "International Comparisons of Educational Attainment." *Journal of Monetary Economics* 32(3):363-394.

—— 1996. "International Measures of Schooling Years and Schooling Quality." *American Economic Review* 86(2):218-223.

—— 2001. "International Data on Educational Attainment: Updates and Implications." *Oxford Economic Papers* 53:541-563.

Becker, G.S., and K.M. Murphy. 1992. "The Division of Labor, Coordination Costs, and Knowledge." *Quarterly Journal of Economics* 107(4):1137-1160.

Benhabib, J., and A. Rustichini. 1996. "Social Conflict and Growth." *Journal of Economic Growth* 1:125-142.

Berger-Schmitt, R. 2000. "Social Cohesion as an Aspect of the Quality of Societies: Concept and Measurement." EuReporting working paper #14. Mannheim: Centre for Survey Research and Methodology (ZUMA).

Birdsall, N., and J.L. Londoño. 1997. "Asset Inequality Matters: An Assessment of the World Bank's Approach to Poverty Reduction." *American Economic Review* (Papers and Proceedings) 87:32-37.

Bonabeau, E., M. Dorigo, and G. Theraulaz. 1999. *Swarm Intelligence: From Natural to Artificial Systems.* Oxford: Oxford University Press.

Brown, J.S., and P. Duguid. 2000. *The Social Life of Information.* Boston, MA: Harvard Business School Press.

Burt, R.S. 2000. "The Network Structure of Social Capital." In *Research in Organizational Behavior*, Vol. 22, ed. R.I. Sutton, and B.M. Staw. Greenwich, CT: JAI Press.

Castelló, A., and R. Doménech. 2001. "Human Capital Inequality and Economic Growth: Some New Evidence." *Economic Journal* 112(478):C187-C200.

Clarke, G.R.G. 1995. "More Evidence on Income Distribution and Growth." *Journal of Development Economics* 47(2):403-427.

Collier, P. 2001. "Ethnic Diversity: An Economic Analysis for its Implications." *Economic Policy* 16(32):128-166.

Dasgupta, P. 2000. "Economic Progress and the Idea of Social Capital." In *Social Capital: A Multifaceted Perspective*, ed. P. Dasgupta, and I. Serageldin. Washington, D.C.: World Bank, pp. 325-424.

Davis, J.A. 1967. "Clustering and Structural Balance in Graphs." *Human Relations* 20:181-187.

Deininger, K., and P. Olinto. 2000. "Asset Distribution, Inequality and Growth." World Bank Policy Research working paper #2375. Washington, D.C.: World Bank.

Deininger, K., and L. Squire. 1998. "New Ways of Looking at Old Issues: Inequality and Growth." *Journal of Development Economics* 57(2):259-287.

Diewert, E. 2000. "The Challenge of Total Factor Productivity Measurement." *International Productivity Monitor* 1:45-51.

Dollar, D. 1992. "Outward-Oriented Developing Economies Really Do Grow More Rapidly: Evidence from 95 LDCs, 1976-1985." *Economic Development and Cultural Change* 40(3):523-544.

Dunbar, R. 1996. *Grooming, Gossip and the Evolution of Language.* London: Faber & Faber.

Durlauf, S.N. 1997. "The Memberships Theory of Inequality: Ideas and Implications." Working paper #97-05-047. Santa Fe, NM: Santa Fe Institute.

—— 2002. "Bowling Alone: A Review Essay." *Journal of Economic Behavior and Organization* 47:259-273.

Easterly, W. 2001*a*. "Can Institutions Resolve Ethnic Conflict?" *Economic Development and Cultural Change* 49(4):687-706.

—— 2001*b*. "The Middle Class Consensus and Economic Development." *Journal of Economic Growth* 6(4):317-335.

—— 2001*c*. *The Elusive Quest for Growth: Economists' Adventures and Misadventures in the Tropics.* Cambridge, MA: MIT Press.

Easterly, W., and R. Levine. 1997. "Africa's Growth Tragedy: Policies and Ethnic Divisions." *Quarterly Journal of Economics* 112(4):1203-1250.

—— 2001. "It's Not Factor Accumulation: Stylized Facts and Growth Models." *World Bank Economic Review* 15(2):177-219.

The Economist. 2001. "Network Collaborations: The Big Picture." *The Economist,* January 6, p. 75.

Edwards, S. 1998. "Openness, Trade Liberalization, and Growth in Developing Countries." *Journal of Economic Literature* 31(3):383-398.

Forbes, K.J. 2000. "A Reassessment of the Relationship between Inequality and Growth." *American Economic Review* 90(4):869-887.

Fukuyama, F. 1995. *Trust: The Social Virtues and the Creation of Prosperity.* New York: Free Press.

—— 1999. *The Great Disruption: Human Nature and the Reconstitution of Social Order.* New York: Free Press.

Galor, O., and D. Tsiddon. 1997. "Technological Progress, Mobility, and Economic Growth." *American Economic Review* 87(3):363-382.

Galor, O., and J. Zeira. 1993. "Income Distribution and Macroeconomics." *Review of Economic Studies* 60(1): 35-52.

Goldin, C., and L. Katz. 1999. "The Shaping of Higher Education: The Formative Years in the United

R. Quentin Grafton, Stephen Knowles
and P. Dorian Owen

States, 1890 to 1940." *Journal of Economic Perspectives* 13(1):37-62.

Gradstein, M., and M. Justman. 2000. "Education, Social Cohesion and Economic Growth." Mimeo. Beer-Sheva, Israel: Monaster Center for Economics Research, Ben-Gurion University.

Grafton, R.Q., S. Knowles, and P.D. Owen. 2001. "Social Divergence and Economic Performance." Working Paper 0103E. Ottawa: University of Ottawa.

Grafton, R.Q., and D. Rowlands. 1996. "Development Impeding Institutions: The Political Economy of Haiti." *Canadian Journal of Development Studies* 27(2):261-277.

Hall, R.E., and C.I. Jones. 1999. "Why Do Some Countries Produce So Much More Output Per Worker Than Others?" *Quarterly Journal of Economics* 114(1):83-116.

Harris, R.G. 2002. "Determinants of Canadian Productivity Growth: Issues and Prospects." In *Productivity Issues in Canada*, ed. S. Rao, and A. Sharpe. Industry Canada Research Volume. Calgary: University of Calgary Press.

Harrison, A. 1996. "Openness and Growth: A Time-Series, Cross-Section Analysis for Developing Countries." *Journal of Development Economics* 48(2):419-447.

Hazledine. T. 2000. "Review of 'How Much Do National Borders Matter?'" *Canadian Journal of Economics* 33(1):288-292.

Helliwell, J.F. 1999. "Canada's National Economy: There's More to It Than You Thought." In *Canada: The State of the Federation 1998/99*, ed. H. Lazar, and T. McIntosh. Kingston and Montreal: Institute of Intergovernmental Relations and McGill-Queen's University Press.

——— 2001. "Social Capital, the Economy and Well-Being." In *The Review of Economic Performance and Social Progress 2001: The Longest Decade: Canada in the 1990s*, ed. K. Banting, A. Sharpe, and F. St-Hilaire. Montreal and Ottawa: Institute for Research on Public Policy and Centre for the Study of Living Standards.

Helliwell, J.F., and G. Verdier. 2001. "Measuring Internal Trade Distance: A New Method Applied to Estimate Provincial Border Effects in Canada." *Canadian Journal of Economics* 34(4):1024-1041.

Jaffe, A.B., M. Trajtenberg, and R. Henderson. 1993. "Geographic Localization of Knowledge Spillovers as Evidenced by Patent Citations." *Quarterly Journal of Economics* 108(3):577-598.

James, H.S. Jr. 2002. "The Trust Paradox: A Survey of Economic Inquiries into the Nature of Trust and Trustworthiness." *Journal of Economic Behavior and Organization* 47(3):291-307.

Jenson, J. 1998. "Mapping Social Cohesion: The State of Canadian Research." Study #F03. Ottawa: Canadian Policy Research Networks.

Keefer, P., and S. Knack. 2000. "Polarization, Politics and Property Rights: Links Between Inequality and Growth." Working paper #2418. Washington, D.C.: World Bank, Development Research Group.

Knack, S. 2001. "Trust, Associational Life and Economic Performance." In *The Contribution of Human and Social Capital to Sustained Economic Growth and Well Being, International Symposium Report*, HRDC-OECD. Ottawa: HRDC.

Kuznets, S. 1955. "Economic Growth and Income Inequality." *American Economic Review* 45(1):1-28.

Lazear, E.P. 1999. "Culture and Language." *Journal of Political Economy* 107(6):S95-S126.

Lian, B., and J.R. Oneal. 1997. "Cultural Diversity and Economic Development: A Cross-National Study of 98 Countries, 1960–1985." *Economic Development and Cultural Change* 46(1):61-77.

López, R., V. Thomas, and Y. Wang. 1998. "Addressing the Education Puzzle: The Distribution of Education and Economic Reforms." World Bank Policy Research working paper #2031. Washington, D.C.: World Bank.

Mauro, P. 1995. "Corruption and Growth." *Quarterly Journal of Economics* 110(4):681-712.

McCallum, J. 1995. "National Borders Matter: Canada-US Regional Trade Patterns." *American Economic Review* 85(3):615-623.

Mill, J.S. 1848. *Principles of Political Economy with Some of Their Applications to Social Philosophy* (1965 edition with an introduction by V.W. Bladen). Toronto: University of Toronto Press, Routledge & Kegan Paul.

Miller, S.M., and M.P. Upadhyay. 2000. "The Effects of Openness, Trade Orientation, and Human Capital on Total Factor Productivity." *Journal of Development Economics* 63(2):399-423.

Moody, J., and D.R. White. 2000. "Social Cohesion and Embeddedness: A Hierarchical Conception of Social Groups." Working paper #00-08-049. Santa Fe, NM: Santa Fe Institute.

Murphy, K., A. Schleifer, and R.W. Vishny. 1989. "Income Distribution, Market Size, and Industrialization." *Quarterly Journal of Economics* 104(3):537-564.

Narayan, D. 1999. "Bonds and Bridges: Social Capital and Poverty." World Bank Policy Research working paper #2167. Washington, D.C.: World Bank.

Nettle, D. 2000. "Linguistic Fragmentation and the Wealth of Nations: The Fishman-Pool Hypothesis Reexamined." *Economic Development and Cultural Change* 49:335-348.

222

Nitsch, V. 2000. "National Borders and International Trade: Evidence from the European Union." *Canadian Journal of Economics* 33(4):1091-1105.

Osborne, E. 2000. "Diversity, Multiculturalism, and Ethnic Conflict: A Rent-Seeking Perspective." *Kyklos* 53(4):509-526.

Paldam, M. 2000. "Social Capital: One or Many? Definition and Measurement." *Journal of Economic Surveys* 14(5):629-653.

—— 2001. "Corruption and Religion: Adding to the Economic Model." *Kyklos* 54(3):383-413.

Perotti, R. 1996. "Growth, Income Distribution, and Democracy: What the Data Say." *Journal of Economic Growth* 1:149-187.

Persson, T., and G. Tabellini. 1994. "Is Inequality Harmful for Growth?" *American Economic Review* 84(3):600-621.

Putnam, R. 1993. "The Prosperous Community – Social Capital and Public Life." *American Prospect* 4(13):35-42.

Putnam, R.D. 2000. *Bowling Alone: The Collapse and Revival of American Community.* New York: Simon & Schuster.

Ritzen, J., W. Easterly, and M. Woolcock. 2000. "On 'Good' Politicians and "Bad" Policies: Social Cohesion, Institutions, and Growth." World Bank Policy Research working paper #2448. Washington, D.C.: World Bank.

Rodrik, D. 1999. "Where Did All the Growth Go?" *Journal of Economic Growth* 4(4):385-412.

Sargent, T.C., and E.R. Rodriguez. 2000. "Labour or Total Factor Productivity: Do We Need to Choose?" *International Productivity Monitor* 1:41-44.

Schelling, T.C. 1978. *Micromotives and Macrobehavior.* New York: W.W. Norton.

Scott, J. 2000. *Social Network Analysis: A Handbook.* Thousand Oaks, CA: Sage.

Sharpe, A. 2001. "Determinants of Trends in Living Standards in Canada and the United States, 1989–2000." *International Productivity Monitor* 2:3-10.

Sobel, J. 2002. "Can We Trust Social Capital?" *Journal of Economic Literature* 40(1):139-154.

Temple, J. 1999. "The New Growth Evidence." *Journal of Economic Literature* 37(1):112-156.

—— 2000. "Growth Effects of Education and Social Capital in the OECD Countries." Working paper #263. Paris: Economic Department, OECD.

Temple, J., and P.A. Johnson. 1998. "Social Capability and Economic Growth." *Quarterly Journal of Economics* 113:965-990.

Thomas, V., M. Dailami, A. Dhareshwar, D. Kaufmann, N. Kishor, R. López, and Y. Wang. 2000. *The Quality of Growth.* New York: Oxford University Press (for the World Bank).

Thomas, V., Y. Wang, and X. Fan. 2000. "Measuring Education Inequality: Gini Coefficients of Education." World Bank Policy Research working paper #2525. Washington, D.C.: World Bank.

Wei, S.-J. 1996. "Intra-National Versus International Trade: How Stubborn Are Nations in Global Integration?" Working paper #5531. Cambridge, MA: National Bureau of Economic Research.

Woolcock, M. 2001. "The Place of Social Capital in Understanding Social and Economic Outcomes." In *The Contribution of Human and Social Capital to Sustained Economic Growth and Well Being. International Symposium Report,* HRDC-OECD. Ottawa: HRDC.

Zak, P.J., and S. Knack. 2001. "Trust and Growth." *Economic Journal* 111(470):295-321.

Should Productivity Growth Be a Social Priority?

Should Productivity Growth Be a Social Priority?

Joseph Heath

THE REVIEW OF ECONOMIC PERFORMANCE AND SOCIAL PROGRESS | 2002

INTRODUCTION

Perhaps the most fundamental axiom of modern economic science is that there is no such thing as a free lunch. It is this axiom that gives us the concept of opportunity cost, an idea that has led to enormous gains in the clarity of our understanding of individual and societal choice. But while continuing to endorse this fundamental axiom, many economists have also been extremely attracted by the appeal of increased economic efficiency. Efficiency gains are often treated, if not exactly as a free lunch, certainly about as close to a free lunch as one can get in this sublunar realm. As a result, economists often react with a certain incredulity when someone questions the need for such gains. It is tempting to suppose that the critic simply misunderstands the relevant concepts, or else fails to grasp the full set of constraints under which economic activity occurs.

Productivity growth is widely regarded as a subset of the efficiency gains that can be realized in our economy. Thus to question the need for increased productivity seems initially to fall under the same category of suspicion.

Yet this is precisely what I intend to do. As a way of conferring some initial legitimacy upon this enterprise, I would like to start out simply by appealing to the "no free lunch" principle. To adopt productivity growth as a social priority is to set aside other objectives that we might like to pursue. Therefore, one cannot maintain rational adherence to a program of increased productivity without a clear sense of what the benefits of such a program are likely to be, compared to the other things that we might choose to do. The bulk of this paper consists of an attempt to evaluate the size and scope of these benefits. More controversially, I will try to show that these benefits are often exaggerated.

The conclusion that I draw on the basis of this survey will strike many as complacent. But it is a principled complacency. I argue that we have good reason, as a society, to strive for productivity gains, but that there is nothing *urgent* about this objective. Furthermore, we should not strive to *maximize* productivity gains, nor should we be overly concerned about our *relative* productivity levels. The note of urgency that is struck in much of the popular discussion is, I will argue, based on a widespread tendency to overestimate the contribution that economic growth will make to the welfare of individual Canadians. The underlying problem, I will argue, is that even though we live in an extremely rich society, we continue to think and act as though we lived in a poor one. Correcting this bias allows us to put the issue of productivity growth into perspective.

WHY PRODUCTIVITY GROWTH?

When evaluating the merits of increased productivity, it is helpful to begin by examining the benefits that have traditionally been thought to flow from productivity growth — or, more accurately, the benefits that were promised in much of the popular and academic writing on the subject. Needless to say, productivity is not an intrinsic value. It is a technical efficiency concept, stating in effect the ratio of useful economic output to some specified bundle of inputs.[1] Thus increased productivity, roughly put, allows us to do more with less, but it does not specify what it is that we intend to do. In order to evaluate the merits of increased productivity, therefore, we need to look at what these increases were supposed to allow us to do. Here are some of the benefits that have often been thought to flow from productivity growth:

Increased Leisure. This is the big payoff that has always been the expected outcome of increased labour productivity. It is certainly the payoff that has most widely captured the popular imagination. Between the late 19th century and the second half of the 20th, there was a steady decline in the length of the average workweek. It was assumed that productivity growth would allow this trend

to continue. After all, if it takes us less time to produce all of the things that we need to lead happy and fulfilling lives, then it seems natural that we should have to work less. And even if the aggregate number of hours worked remains constant or increases, productivity growth should give individuals much greater freedom when it comes to choosing the number of hours that they themselves want to work.

Increased Consumer Satisfaction. Increased productivity essentially gives us a "bonus" that we can choose to spend in one of two ways, by cutting back on work hours or by producing more. It is natural that individuals will differ in their choice between these two options, and that a significant number will opt to increase their consumption of market goods rather than their leisure. As a result, productivity growth should generate economic growth, permitting increased consumption, which in turn should increase consumer satisfaction.

Elimination of Poverty. These first two points are not really that dissimilar — in both cases productivity growth is touted as a way of increasing welfare. Increases in productive efficiency are regarded here as a way to generate gains in Pareto-efficiency. (The fact that increased leisure needs to be treated in its own category is merely an artifact of the way that the system of national accounts is compiled.) However, the Pareto-efficiency standard is neutral with respect to questions of distribution. Thus it is quite possible for the benefits of productivity gains to be entirely "captured" by one stratum of society — and this would still count as an improvement according to the first two criteria. Nevertheless, it was often suggested that the benefits of productivity growth would be enjoyed by all classes of society. The rising tide would lift all boats. Thus absolute poverty would be eliminated.

Decreased Social Inequality. While many proponents of productivity growth suggested that the problem of poverty could be eliminated through economic growth alone, without the need for redistribution, there was also, for a long time, the expectation that growth would make it easier to implement redistributive social policies. Society could therefore diminish not only absolute poverty but also relative poverty. This idea found expression in the ideal, widely shared in the 1950s, of a society in which everyone was essentially middle class. The thought, simply put, was that affluence would make people less possessive, that an excess of riches would make them less hostile to the prospect of sharing with others. This thought was of course not universally shared, nor was the underlying egalitarian project endorsed in all corners, but it did nevertheless serve as an important source of hope for many.

So, did productivity growth deliver on these promises? I think we must concede that, in the past 25 years, results have fallen significantly short of expectations. In some cases, productivity gains have provided necessary but not sufficient conditions for the realization of these objectives. In other cases, increased productivity seems to have contributed nothing at all.

As far as increased leisure is concerned, the last three decades of the 20th century were singularly unimpressive. Most significantly, the trend towards a reduced workweek, which dominated the first half of the century, seems to have come to a halt in North America.[2] Between 1981 and 1992, for instance, average working hours among employed Canadians increased by over 15 percent (Zuzanek and Smale 1997, 78).

Furthermore, there has been a dramatic increase in the number of two-career households, corresponding to the widely shared perception that it is no longer possible to maintain a middle-class family lifestyle on the basis of only one salary. Thus achieving "work-family balance" has become increasingly difficult for many Canadians.

I think it is easy to lose track of how unexpected and puzzling this development (or rather this lack of development) is. If one had done a survey of Canadian economists in 1975, asking them to predict the length of the standard workweek in the year 2000, I wonder how many would have guessed that it would be unchanged? In fact, the goal of increasing leisure has come to seem so remote that it has almost completely fallen off the public agenda. The case for increased productivity is almost always made as a way of increasing per capita GDP. (Thus in the discussion that follows I will simplify the presentation somewhat by assuming that productivity is valued for the sake of increasing output, not decreasing input.)

As for increased satisfaction, there is also something of a puzzle here. While the standard of living has risen quite steadily, there is no evidence that this has led to any lasting gains in welfare. The issue here is not simply one of diminishing marginal returns to increases in consumption of market goods. Beyond a certain basic consumption level, there is simply no correlation between higher consumption and increased happiness (Frey and Stutzer 2001, 76-91; see also Easterlin 1974). Of course, there are important measurement problems when it comes to talking about people's level of happiness. Nevertheless, given the instruments we have, study after study has shown that in poor countries increased wealth is strongly correlated with increased subjective happiness, but that once the threshold of about US$10,000 GDP per capita is passed, happiness levels have no further tendency to rise in response to economic growth. As a case in point, average happiness in the United States fell by about 9 percent between 1946 and 1991, according to one measure (Frey and Stutzer 2001, 76).

With respect to poverty, it was widely assumed that capitalism would generate such a preposterous excess of wealth that nothing even vaguely resembling poverty could persist. Joseph Schumpeter (1950, 66), for example, in *Capitalism, Socialism and Democracy*, predicted that

> *If capitalism repeated its past performance for another half century starting with 1928, this would do away with anything that according to present standards could be called poverty, even in the lowest strata of the population, pathological cases alone excepted.*

Of course, capitalism did much more than repeat its past performance between 1928 and 1978, but this did not lead to the eradication of poverty.

Where there have been significant improvements in the welfare of the poor, it has largely been due to redistributive government programs, such as socialized medicine, or old age pensions. Thus significant reductions in the level of poverty were recorded in Canada after the Second World War, with the growth of the welfare state, but there has been no decrease in the rate of "basic needs" poverty since the late 1970s (see Sarlo 2001).

Finally, there has been a disturbing trend towards increased social inequality in the last 30 years in North America. This has been mitigated to some extent in Canada through progressive taxation and redistributive policies of the welfare state (see Wolfson and Murphy 2000). Nevertheless, popular wisdom suggests that resistance to such redistribution has been increasing. Certainly, tax resistance among the middle class has been growing, although it is not clear how much of this reflects a free-rider incentive and how much reflects genuine opposition to redistribution. In any case, it is difficult to imagine that the North American population has become more receptive to egalitarianism in the past 30 years.

This having been said, I think it would be entirely unreasonable to question the massive contribution that productivity gains in general have made to our overall quality of life. It is of course because of these gains that we now live in a rich society and not a poor one. But the fact that past productivity gains have given us so many of the things that we now enjoy does not guarantee that future gains will continue to deliver the same results. The track record on this score has become quite mixed in the last 25 years.

SOLVING THE MYSTERY

If there is one trend that I think should be most disturbing to proponents of productivity growth, it is the failure of economic growth to increase happiness. After all, what is the point of producing more if the result is no net gain in consumer satisfaction? Productivity growth was supposed to create something of a "bonus," to create some slack in the average consumer's budget. It was assumed that society would react to growth in much the same way that individuals react to getting a raise or a tax refund. It should have allowed us to relax a bit, not work as hard, indulge some tastes that previously could not be satisfied, and perhaps even share a bit more with those less fortunate than ourselves. Unfortunately, even the prosperous middle classes continue to feel "squeezed" economically. Despite decades of growth, people continue to act and feel as through they were under a severe budget constraint.

What could possibly explain this? The most obvious explanation is simply that consumption standards have increased at approximately the same pace as economic growth. This will be pretty obvious to anyone who has seen a recently constructed suburban home. Not only has the average size of new single-family dwellings increased, from 1,100 square feet in the 1950s to over 2,000 square feet today, but even base models now include amenities that were once available only to the very rich (Frank 1999, 21). Most new homes, for example, contain at least one bathroom *per bedroom*. Yet are people any happier once they move into these houses? All available evidence suggests that the answer is no. Yet they still buy them. And not only do they buy them, they pay more for them. Hence the puzzle — why no increase in satisfaction?

The issue acquires greater urgency when we realize that, if expanding production is not the route to increased happiness, perhaps there is something else we might be doing with our time and energy that would be more effective. Thus it will pay to explore some of the hypotheses that have been advanced to explain the "gap" between wealth and happiness, in order to map out these possibilities more perspicuously.

One way of approaching the issue is to note that the no-happiness outcome would not occur if markets and welfare were tied together in the way that the first fundamental theorem of welfare economics presuppos-es. Thus a promising strategy is to look at the assumptions needed for this result to hold, and consider which ones may not be satisfied. The first theorem, for instance, assumes that consumers are never satiated, that their preferences are fixed and that their consumption does not generate any externalities. These assumptions are tolerably close to reality in cases where people are extremely poor, but it is not at all obvious that they remain plausible in more affluent societies. It is possible that one or more of these effects has become large enough that it has begun to negate the welfare gains achieved through increased satisfaction of consumer demand.

There is, however, considerable disagreement over the source of these effects. We can discern roughly three currents of thought in the literature.

Proliferation of Desire

The most common diagnosis of the problem can be referred to, following John Kenneth Galbraith (1976), as the "squirrel-wheel hypothesis." According to this view, increased consumption does not generate lasting increments in welfare because the process of production itself generates new wants and needs.[3] The standard pro-growth picture imagines that humans have a relatively fixed set of desires, and that, as time passes, we acquire the capacity to satisfy more and more of them. If welfare is a function of how many of our desires get satisfied, or to what extent, then increased production should lead to greater welfare. However, if the process through which we satisfy our desires generates new ones, then consumption will not necessarily increase welfare. This is the hypothesis that Galbraith entertained.

Such a process could occur through an entirely internal psychological mechanism.

The idea that attempts to satisfy our desires might have a self-defeating character is one of the oldest, and more recurrent, ideas in the history of philosophical reflection on the nature of the good life. According to most Greek philosophers of the classical period, for instance, the problem with hedonism was that it could not generate satisfaction or happiness. As soon as you satisfy one desire, another one springs up to take its place. Furthermore, this second desire is likely to be more extravagant and difficult to satisfy. As a result, we are much better off in the long run if we try to moderate our desires, and control their proliferation. This is what makes self-mastery such an important moral idea in classical Greek philosophy.

Put in more contemporary terms, one can summarize this theory as the view that consumption in general has the structure of an addiction. For example, Tibor Scitovsky (1992) argues that the feeling of subjective well-being is generated not by the state of having one's desires satisfied, but rather by the stimulus associated with the process of satisfying them. As a result, acquiring some new good generates an initial burst of pleasure, but this feeling tapers off quite quickly as the individual adapts. In the same way that individuals can "feel" only acceleration, not velocity, we experience pleasure only from changes in our consumption, and not from its absolute level. Thus just as individuals get "velocetized" when travelling at high speeds, they get "consumerized" when living with high levels of absolute consumption.

Other theorists have advanced somewhat "thinner" psychological theories to explain the phenomenon. Richard Easterlin (1996), for instance, argues that the level of satisfaction an individual derives from his consumption will be relative to his expectations. As a result, when the general consumption level rises, expectations rise along with it, leaving satisfaction constant. More generally, there is an influential current of popular social criticism that blames advertising for the "manufacture of desire." According to this view, advertising creates demand for products by stimulating dissatisfaction, continuously reminding us of what we don't have and the pleasures that we are missing out on.

Competitive Consumption

While there is clearly some truth in the squirrel-wheel hypothesis, there are some aspects of the no-satisfaction puzzle that it seems unable to explain. In particular, there is an unmistakable correlation between income level and experienced happiness *within* every society (Frey and Stutzer 2001, 83). In other words, while the *absolute* income level seems not to be that important beyond a certain point, the *relative* income level remains quite central (Frank 1999, 111-115; also Scitovsky 1992, 134-136). If consumption just generates a further proliferation of desire, it is unclear why such a pattern should obtain.

The most obvious explanation for the relationship between happiness and income level can be referred to as the "neo-Veblenian" analysis. In *The Theory of the Leisure Class*, Thorstein Veblen (1979) observes that goods have both material and "honorific" properties. Consumption of a good not only satisfies a given individual need, but also communicates important information to others about the consumer's status, class, upbringing, taste and aspirations. These messages help to position the consumer within a variety of different social hierarchies. The problem with this second dimension of consumption is that the relevant set of hierarchies has a zero-sum structure. The intrinsic logic of a status, for example, is that for one person to acquire more, another person must have less. Similarly, beauty is entirely relative — when one very beautiful person shows up, everyone else starts to look somewhat less beautiful.

In Veblen's terms, the value of such goods depends upon some aspect of "invidious comparison." As a result, consumption of these goods creates what we would now refer to as a prisoner's dilemma, or a collective action problem, because everyone's consumption generates negative externalities for others. If one person works a bit harder in order to purchase an exotic imported automobile, everyone else's car begins to look somewhat inferior. This may prompt the neighbours to follow suit. Once they are all driving exotic automobiles, this cancels out whatever gain in status may have accrued to the first person who got one. Thus escalating material consumption can easily coincide with an absence of gains in satisfaction, simply because the goods are being purchased primarily for their social properties rather than their intrinsic ones. Under such circumstances, the absolute consumption level will be poorly correlated with welfare, whereas relative consumption will be more determinative, simply because it is relative consumption that determines the position that one is able to achieve in the various social hierarchies.

Robert Frank, perhaps the most influential contemporary neo-Veblenian, has emphasized that individuals need not be superficial or status-obsessed in order to fall into this sort of competitive consumption. The central issue is whether the goods consumed derive some significant fraction of their value from a comparison with others. For example, the adjective "nice" is often used to flag the comparative value of goods. One can go out for dinner to a restaurant, or one can go to a "nice" restaurant; one can buy a simple corkscrew for a friend, or one can buy a "nice" corkscrew, and so on. What makes the good in question "nice" is its superiority to the plain one. Thus wanting to live in a house with nice things implicitly commits one to the logic of competitive consumption, because as others acquire nice things as well, what was once nice becomes increasingly plain.

Frank points out that the concept of a "spacious" home has the same structure. What counts as spacious is very much dependent upon the size of everyone else's home. Extremely rich people in New York city live quite happily in apartments that would seem impossibly cramped by the standards of Palo Alto. These apartments actually feel quite spacious when one is in New York, simply because they are large relative to what other people have. But because of this comparison, the only way to satisfy such a preference is to buy a home that is of above-average size. When everyone does this, the average size creeps upwards. Thus more resources are invested in home construction and maintenance, while the increase in satisfaction associated with the feeling of spaciousness is quickly eroded.

People are often forced to engage in this sort of competition even if they have no desire to surpass others, but simply a desire to keep up. This can be thought of as "defensive consumption." Such consumption generates no welfare gain; it just forestalls a loss induced by negative externalities from other consumers. For example, a candidate for a job may increase his or her chances of success by purchasing a very expensive suit. As a result, the other job candidates may be forced to do the same, even though it does not increase their chances beyond the prior probability — it simply prevents them from falling behind. This process goes on in many different areas (the amount that one must spend in order to purchase a respectable wedding present, to take a date to a nice restaurant, etc.), creating a general tendency for standards of consumption to "ratchet up" over time.

Positional Goods

The neo-Veblenian critique focuses on the social character of certain goods as a source of unproductive competition. There is a closely related strand of discussion in the literature, stemming from the work of Fred Hirsch, that focuses simply on the fact that the supply of some goods is necessarily fixed, and so not subject to expansion with the rest of the economy. Insofar as these goods are coveted, this means that one's access to them will be determined not by one's overall level of wealth, but rather by one's relative ability to pay. Hirsch refers to these as positional goods.

There is significant overlap between this analysis and the neo-Veblenian one. In both cases the supply of a given good is governed by a zero-sum logic, and so consumers can get caught up in unproductive competition when they try to acquire them. In the case of positional goods, however, there is not necessarily an element of comparison involved in their valuation. For example, the amount of waterfront property in a given region is fixed. As a result, one's access to this good is always going to be determined by one's relative level of wealth. Economic growth is, in general, not going to increase any particular individual's chances of acquiring it.

The second major component of Hirsch's analysis is the view that, in our society, the pri-mary differences between the consumption habits of the rich and the poor all involve access to positional goods. In a poor country, absolute deprivation often means that the rich have material goods that the poor do not: food, shelter, clothing, clean water and so on. This makes it possible to narrow the gap between rich and poor through increased production. After a while, however, the poor wind up with approximately the same material goods as the rich. At this point, the only outstanding differences are ones that involve access to positional goods — that is, goods that the rich have access to precisely by virtue of their relative, rather than absolute, level of wealth.

According to Hirsch, this is why economic growth in our society, rather than reducing the frustration of the broad middle classes, has tended to exacerbate it. "What the wealthy have today can no longer be delivered to the rest of us tomorrow, yet as we individually grow richer, this is what we expect" (Hirsch 1976, 67). It is easy to imagine, for instance, the nice house that one could buy with a 10 percent increase in salary. But if this 10 percent increase is achieved through economic growth, one will be in no better position to purchase that house than before, simply because all the people that one is competing against to get the house will have more to spend as well. The fallacy here is one of composition. "To see total economic advance as individual advance writ large is to set up expectations that cannot be fulfilled, ever" (Hirsch 1976, 9).

This affects welfare in several ways. Hirsch argues that the national accounts inevitably generate false expectations because they treat all household purchases as final consumption. Many of the purchases made within the household, though, have a purely instrumental character.

Individuals derive no satisfaction from the good itself; they simply use it to acquire access to some other good that they want. Almost all of the money spent on transportation, for example, has a purely instrumental character. The problem, then, is that as competition for positional goods intensifies, households may be forced to make greater investments in instrumental consumption goods.

As an example, many people move to the suburbs seeking a positional good — easy access to both city and countryside. Because of this, they are forced to make certain investments in transportation. But suburban development is notoriously unstable, since it just encourages the next generation of suburban migrants to "leapfrog" existing developments and build up the nearest countryside. Suppose, then, that in order to retain access to the positional good in question, a family is forced to move to a more outlying district, and thus to purchase a second car. This consumption has a purely instrumental, defensive character, and thus generates no increase in welfare. Yet it shows up as an increase in their wealth.

When we talk about productivity gains and economic growth, what we are really talking about is an expansion of the *material economy*. The process of expansion does not increase the quantity of positional goods available; it increases their relative prices only. Thus, as individuals get richer some goods become easier to acquire while others continue to recede over the horizon. The material goods that they can acquire, however, are subject to diminishing returns in general. Thus the unsatisfied demand for positional goods acquires greater relative urgency. As a result, individuals may even neglect outstanding material needs in order to purchase goods that are instrumental in achieving positional

goods, only to find themselves frustrated as others make the same investments.

Thus we have a tendency to greatly overestimate the contribution that further economic growth will make to our quality of life, because we fail to "factor out" all of the positional goods, which economic growth will not make us any more likely to obtain.

WHY NOT PRODUCTIVITY?

These three strains of critical inquiry each identify a mechanism through which consumption can fail to generate satisfaction. Put very crudely, we can imagine consumers engaging in three different types of "non-productive" consumption: compulsive, defensive and instrumental. If all economic growth is absorbed into one or another form — and there is no reason why people cannot engage in all three simultaneously — then a situation can arise in which no increase in satisfaction is observed, either in the aggregate or at the individual level.

However, this does not show that we should not strive to achieve productivity gains. Suppose that we have available to us a more cost-effective industrial process, which allows us to boost output with no increase in either capital stock or labour intensity. Even if we are sceptical about the possibility that an increase in the supply of goods will generate any lasting satisfaction, there is still no reason *not* to implement the improved process. It is a pure efficiency gain, and as such would seem to generate no losers. Similarly, Galbraith's diagnosis of the modern economy as a giant squirrel-wheel does not present a compelling case against increasing production. All it says is that as far as overall satisfaction is concerned, we are standing still when we try to move forward. This may not be such a problem. Perhaps the voyage is more important than the destination.

The case becomes more difficult to make, however, when we talk about dedicating significant resources to the pursuit of increased productivity. There have been calls, for instance, for the government of Canada to make significant investments in research and development in order to further a productivity agenda. There have also been calls for various types of tax reductions, with the same end in view. Of course, if we had nothing else to do with these resources, there would be nothing wrong with funnelling them into such projects. But given that alternative uses are available, we need to consider the possibility that they could be better employed elsewhere. In particular, given that economic growth is not likely to generate much further increase in satisfaction, we must consider the possibility that other forms of investment will be more effective at enhancing the welfare of Canadians.

When it comes to considering what these other uses might be, one way of organizing the conceptual space is to think of the individual as a consumer of a variety of different types of goods. It has become conventional to divide these up into private goods (bought and sold through the market), public goods (provided by the state, paid for through taxation) and club goods (provided collectively within an organization) (Cornes and Sandler 1996).[4] We can then bisect this categorization with the distinction between material goods and positional goods (with "material" as a somewhat crude term for the set of goods whose supply can be expanded). Economic growth essentially tracks increases in the output of material private goods, along with some material club goods.

Now, as Galbraith has pointed out, just as increased consumption of any single good will tend to generate less and less of a gain in satisfaction, the entire set of private material goods will also be subject to diminishing returns. People will satisfy their most important desires first, then move on to less important ones. As a result, we get less "bang for the buck" out of economic growth as the country becomes wealthier. However, because economic growth directly increases only the set of private material goods available, we can easily find ourselves in a situation in which we have satisfied all of our urgent needs for private goods, but in which we still have serious, unresolved needs for goods that private markets fail to supply. But because of unresolved collective-action problems in the non-market sector, we may continue to consume more private goods, even though we would all prefer to spend our money on goods that markets are failing to supply.

Reasonable people may disagree as to whether we currently suffer from an imbalance in private and public spending. Galbraith thought that the United States did, hence his characterization of American society as having a peculiar combination of "private opulence" and "public squalor." Certainly the expressed preference of many Canadians for increased spending on health and education suggests that Canada suffers from such an imbalance. But regardless of where one stands on this empirical question, the analytic framework is important because it shows that in order to make the case for increased productivity, we need to show that this point has not been reached. In other words, the value of a straightforward expansion of the private material economy is not self-evident. Thus when it comes to committing public resources to a "productivity agenda," it is not clear that the money would not be better spent on the direct provision of public goods.

The same analytical framework is quite helpful when we consider the fact that all production and consumption creates externalities, both positive and negative. This is in fact a monumental consideration when we keep in mind that all measures of productivity growth ignore externalities. It is quite possible for the negative externalities associated with a particular production process to completely outweigh the value of the goods produced. There is good reason, for instance, to think that the negative externality associated with the use of leaded fuel represented a much larger total cost to society than the positive economic value associated with improved valve lubrication. Thus to ask whether productivity growth is, in general, a good thing is to propose a cost-benefit analysis that takes into account only some of the costs and benefits. It is of course impossible to provide an assessment of such a proposal without finding out what the missing costs and benefits are.

The problem, of course, with externalities is that their magnitude is very difficult to measure. This is in fact why they remain externalities — if we could quantify them, it would be much easier to internalize them. Thus it is not obvious that one can say anything at a general level about the relative size of these "external" costs and benefits. But in this context again, Galbraith's analysis provides us with some helpful ideas. Analytically, we can divide the problem into two questions: How large are the positive and negative externalities relative to one another?, and How large is the net value of these externalities relative to the economic value of the good?

Positive Versus Negative Externalities. Economists sometimes speak of externalities as if they were an isolated occurrence. This is deeply misleading. Externalities are ubiquitous, a necessary consequence of every production and consumption process. If I enjoy watching the patrons in a café having a drink, then their consumption generates a positive externality. But if they have taken up all the seats, so that I am forced to have my drink standing, then their crowding creates a negative externality for me. Because of this, the set of externalities produced by every good is extremely complex. This would seem to make it difficult to say anything general about their relative level. If most goods generated positive externalities on balance, we would have nothing to worry about. Unfortunately, we have reason to believe that such will not be the case. It is a structural feature of the market that firms have an incentive to "externalize" costs whenever possible, along with an incentive to "internalize" benefits as much as they can. Thus if a regulatory regime remains unchanged, we can expect the balance of positive and negative externalities to shift toward the negative. Firms will find ways to "monetize" portions of the value they create that has traditionally escaped in the form of positive externalities, just as they will find ways to shift costs around in such a way as to displace them onto those who cannot demand financial compensation for the loss.

Value of Externalities Versus Economic Value. Just as we can expect the relative size of negative externalities to grow relative to the positive ones, we can also expect them to grow relative to the economic value of the goods produced. This is again due to the diminished urgency of our need for more private material goods. This means that under a static regulatory regime, it is inevitable that social cost will eventually come to exceed private economic benefit. At this point, the welfare-maximizing course of action is to adopt a zero-growth policy — even though opportunities for expansion of the sphere of private material goods are available. Of course, the regulatory regime is never static, since government does tend to respond to new problems as they arise. The point is more a conceptual one. It is that there is no reason *a priori* to prefer increased growth over increased regulation as a strategy for improving the welfare of Canadians. The case must be made on empirical grounds.

Both of these arguments suggest that focusing on productivity growth may mean ignoring potential Pareto-improvements — and thus would be inefficient in the welfare economist's sense of the term. Thus the argument here is not a disagreement over values. The question is simply whether productivity growth is able to deliver what its own proponents have promised. The first consideration — that there may be an imbalance in the relative satisfaction levels of consumers of private and public goods — suggests that the resources consumed in expanding the private material economy may be misallocated, and hence wasted. The second consideration — which focuses on externalities — suggests that such an expansion may mean not only that certain other opportunities are foregone, but also that the expansion itself may directly generate harms that negate any welfare gains associated with the goods produced. Furthermore, there is no reason why these two considerations may not come into play simultaneously. Thus, the case for increased growth is a lot harder to make than it may initially have seemed.

ALTERNATIVE PRIORITIES

You can't beat something with nothing. So if not productivity growth, what? What other broadly "economic" objective might we establish as a social priority? Here are a few suggestions, in no particular order. It is worth noting that none of these proposals is *necessarily* antagonistic to a policy of increased productivity, although in each case one can easily imagine situations in which the two might conflict. My goal is simply to identify some other policy agendas that would be, in my view, as likely to improve social welfare as a commitment to increased productivity.

Internalize Externalities. We might choose to pursue the ideal of a society in which all externalities are fully internalized. Call it the "pay as you play" society. The goal would simply be to have each individual pay the full cost that his or her choices impose upon others. At the moment, we make only a half-hearted effort in this direction, and we have not dedicated nearly enough creative energy to the task of designing appropriate incentive mechanisms. There is clearly enormous room for improvement, most obviously when it comes to the environment. Even if one does not believe that catastrophic environmental collapse is imminent, the mere risk of inducing such a collapse is difficult to justify when these risks are being run in the service of a growth policy whose welfare gains have become either negligible or non-existent.

Reduce Crowding. One of the most significant structural transformations taking place in Canadian consumption patterns involves the erosion of suburban lifestyles. This is largely caused by intense competition for positional goods. The result has been a significant increase in crowding and congestion, which in turn has generated significant quality dilution of the goods sought. It is this phenomenon that, in my opinion, has generated the widespread feeling of being economically "squeezed" among the middle classes. Part of the problem stems from public complacency on the issue of crowding, simply because Canada has such a low overall population density. But these statistics are very misleading. Canada is currently one of the most highly urbanized societies in the world. Thus crowding is likely to become an increasingly important quality of life issue for many Canadians. Designing and implementing systems to manage access to positional goods therefore has enormous potential welfare benefits.

Increase the Supply of Public Goods. Public opinion surveys of Canadians consistently show a very low level of concern for increased consumption of private goods, combined with a strong desire for increased consumption of public goods, including health, education, communication and even transportation (Bricker and Greenspon 2001). This generates a strong presumption in favour of the hypothesis that there is currently an imbalance between spending on private and on public goods. The root cause of this imbalance is tax resistance — which is rational at the level of the individual citizen and consumer, insofar as it reflects a free-rider incentive, but is often irrational at the level of public policy.

Promote Leisure. Implicit in the discussion of productivity growth is often the assumption that increased productivity should be used to increase economic output. This has certainly been the trend in the past 25 years. However, given the increase in complaints about time pressure and work-family balance, we might consider taking more assertive measures aimed at reducing the workweek. Regulatory intervention, along the lines recently undertaken in France, might be welfare-enhancing.

Increase Security. Studies have shown that unemployment has a serious negative impact on subjective well-being (Frey and Stutzer 2001, 95-102). Furthermore, the risks that individuals face in the marketplace generally, and the labour market in particular, represent a source of disutility that, like leisure, is largely invisible from the standpoint of the national accounts. Policies aimed at reducing labour market volatility could lead to significant welfare gains (even though they might also produce overemployment, and hence reduced productivity).

Again, it is worth stating that none of these objectives is necessarily in tension with productivity growth. For example, if it is true that "work expands to fill the time available for its completion," then legislatively imposed limitations on the workweek could lead to important productivity gains. However, increased leisure could also be promoted through the introduction of a more progressive income tax. It is widely believed that such a tax regime would dampen productivity growth. The choice of how to prioritize the various objectives is therefore political, in the broadest sense of the term. The claim here is simply that a negative impact on productivity growth should by no means be sufficient to take any of the options off the table.

Finally, it should be noted that each of these proposals is motivated by a desire to improve the efficiency of our economic institutions (understood in terms of welfare, not wealth).[5] The underlying intuition is that since economic growth seems to have been generating no payoff in terms of individual satisfaction, any one of these policies seems more likely to improve welfare as a policy of productivity growth. I have not even ventured to consider some of the other values that we might like to promote, beyond mere efficiency. It could easily be argued, for instance, that as a society we have been willing to accept considerable inequality in the distribution of wealth in order to promote economic growth, but now that economic growth has ceased to provide significant social benefits, these outstanding inequalities have become increasingly unjustifiable. Such an argument would be much more controversial than anything advanced here, which is why I have chosen to limit myself to efficiency concerns.

CONCLUSION

Consider the following, surprising fact: the average speed of traffic in the city of London is the same now as it was 100 years ago — 11 miles per hour. How can this situation be improved? In the first half of the 20th century, the solution might have seemed obvious: "faster cars." But can anyone still believe this?

Believing that productivity growth is the key to resolving our problems is essentially the same as believing that faster cars will speed up the traffic in London. If the proposed solution hasn't worked so far, it is not likely to start working any time soon. This doesn't mean that we shouldn't build faster cars, if we have the means and opportunity to do so. Similarly, there is nothing wrong with productivity growth. But we shouldn't delude ourselves into thinking that it is going to accomplish very much.

The commitment to productivity growth becomes somewhat pernicious, however, when we assign it lexical priority, or when we try to maximize it. Furthermore, there is no particular reason to be concerned about our relative productivity levels.[6] After all, what do we lose by falling behind? Unless one misunderstands the logic of comparative advantage in international trade, it is difficult to see where the downside lies. When we talk about the relative "standard of living" of Canadians, it is important to remember that this, for the most part, means relative "consumption of private material goods." Since preferences over this bundle of consumption goods may vary, there is no reason why a decline in relative "standard of living" should entail a decline in relative "quality of life." In fact, if over-investment in the production of private goods in another country stems from unresolved collective action problems in its public sector, there is no reason why our "quality of life" could not increase relative to theirs, even as our relative "standard of living" drops.

Furthermore, it is worth noting that the vast majority of Canadians compete only with other Canadians for positional and status goods. As a result, lower productivity here is unlikely to affect their relative position when it comes to this competition. And in cases where it does, there are often relatively simple legislative remedies available. Thus the welfare of the average Canadian is unlikely to be affected by the superior purchasing power of foreigners. The same cannot be said for the small "international set" of privileged Canadians who fancy purchasing real estate in New York or Paris. For them, slow productivity growth leads to an erosion of their relative position. But it should be recognized that their interests are those of a very small, albeit vocal, minority.

One of the great conceptual revolutions of the 19th century was the discovery that the production and consumption of wealth is not a zero-sum game, and thus that growth can be much more powerful than redistribution when it comes to improving the welfare of the lower and working classes. But with the growth of riches comes a steady erosion of the positive-sum character of our economy. Increasingly, the difference between social classes in our society is not that one class has a lot of stuff and the other does not. More often, they both simply have different *versions* (often, different *brands*) of the same stuff. No increase in general prosperity will ever narrow this gap. As a result, we are now in danger of overestimating the amount that can be achieved through growth, and underestimating the power of redistribution.[7]

NOTES

1 I distinguish a "technical" efficiency concept from a "welfare" efficiency concept, such as the Pareto principle.

2 For an overview of developments, see Wong and Picot (2001).

3 I lump wants and needs together because any distinction between the two relies upon an extremely controversial and problematic normative judgement.

4 Note that I am not using the more restrictive definition of a public good popular among some economists — a good that is "non-rival and non-excludable." I take a good to be public in cases where an underlying market failure makes it more efficient to organize the transactions through taxation. Thus I treat government health insurance as a public good, for example, even though it is easy to exclude individuals from enjoying the benefits.

5 For a more general discussion of this distinction, see Heath (2001).

6 It is also important to note that concern over relative productivity, in an international context in which at least one nation is trying to maximize productivity, implicitly commits one to a policy of maximization.

7 Here I am rephrasing suggestive remarks by Hirsch (1976, 67).

REFERENCES

Bricker, D., and E. Greenspon. 2001. *Searching for Certainty*. Toronto: Doubleday.

Cornes, R., and T. Sandler. 1996. *The Theory of Externalities, Public Goods and Club Goods*. 2nd ed. Cambridge: Cambridge University Press.

Easterlin, R.A. 1974. "Does Economic Growth Improve the Human Lot? Some Empirical Evidence." In *Nations and Households in Economic Growth*, ed. P.A. David and M.W. Reder. New York: Academic Press.

——— 1996. *Growth Triumphant*. Ann Arbor: University of Michigan Press.

Frank, R.H. 1999. *Luxury Fever*. New York: Free Press.

Frey, B.S., and A. Stutzer. 2001. *Happiness and Economics*. Princeton, NJ: Princeton University Press.

Galbraith, J.K. 1976. *The Affluent Society*. Boston: Houghton Mifflin.

Heath, J. 2001. *The Efficient Society*. Toronto: Penguin.

Hirsch, F. 1976. *The Social Limits to Growth*. Cambridge, MA: Harvard University Press.

Sarlo, C.A. 2001. *Measuring Poverty in Canada*. Vancouver: Fraser Institute.

Schumpeter, J. 1950. *Capitalism, Socialism and Democracy*. 3rd ed. New York: Harper.

Scitovsky, T. 1992. *The Joyless Economy*. 2nd ed. New York: Oxford University Press.

Veblen, T. 1979. *The Theory of the Leisure Class*. New York: Penguin.

Wolfson, M., and B. Murphy. 2000. "Income Inequality in North America: Does the 49th Parallel Still Matter?" *Canadian Economic Observer* 13(8). Statistics Canada catalogue no.: 11-010-XPB.

Wong, G., and G. Picot, eds. 2001. *Working Time in Comparative Perspective, Vol. 1: Patterns, Trends and the Policy Implications of Earnings, Inequality and Unemployment*. Kalamazoo, MI: Upjohn Institute.

Zuzanek, J., and B.J.A. Smale. 1997. "More Work – Less Leisure? Changing Allocations of Time in Canada, 1981 to 1992." *Society and Leisure* 20(1):73-106.

Canadian Attitudes Towards Productivity: Balancing Standard of Living and Quality of Life

Frank L. Graves and Richard W. Jenkins

INTRODUCTION

During the late 1990s much was made in Canada, especially in elite and media circles, about the slow pace of productivity growth, especially relative to the United States, and this concern and focus are still evident. In government terms the debate about productivity has recently shifted to talk about innovation. A somewhat cynical view might see the shift from productivity to innovation as largely a linguistic manoeuvre on the part of government, since both are part of the government's plans for expanding the economy and ensuring prosperity for Canadians. Ironically the new lexicon of innovation is premised on the empirically suspect assumption that the public was leery of the "*p* word." In fact the terms innovation and productivity produce roughly comparable levels of public interest. It is important to recognize at the outset that the public is a far different citizenry from what it was just a decade ago when a previous government tried, in vain, to rally public support around another *p* word — prosperity.

The policy debate about Canada's economic performance and productivity has obviously implications for the public, not only because the public will face any costs, in terms of lower standard of living, of the failure to address productivity but also because addressing the productivity gap will necessitate some form of state action. Those who bemoan Canada's current levels of productivity do so with an agenda for government in mind. In simplistic terms, the state has two options: to be active in terms of spending (either more or differently) in ways that might improve productivity, or to scale back the state. In the latter case, tax cuts are expected to stimulate investment in new, innovative ways of producing goods and services. In the former case, government spending is expected to address the underlying fundamentals of economic activity through infrastructure development, incentives for innovation and improvements in human capital. The allocation of resources across these different areas raises important questions for government in terms of both its expected return on investment — a largely economic and social calculus — and the public support for this allocation.

The other contributors to this volume have more to say than we do about the nature of productivity in Canada and the relative impact of various alternative strategies on the level of productivity. While we do not propose to weigh in on these debates since our attention is focused on the attitudes of Canadians, it is worth setting out some of the key elements of the debate so as to place our survey findings in context. Concern is most often raised that Canada lags behind the United States in terms of productivity growth (the take-up of new technology/innovation and consequently the output per worker). Clearly, productivity is directly linked to the standard of living that the public enjoys. According to Richard Harris, "over long periods of time, productivity is the single most important determinant of a nation's living standard or its level of real income" (1999, 3). Sharpe (2001) makes the link between Canada's lagging productivity growth relative to the US performance and the relative decline in Canadian standard of living over the same period.[1] Though many understand productivity in narrow economic terms, it is clear in much of the debate that productivity is intrinsically linked to social as well as economic progress. In fact, as we argue, one cannot understand Canadian attitudes without acknowledging the link between the components of the debate and social well-being.

There are a number of reasons why it will be crucial to understand the public perspective on economic growth and the role of the state, not the least being that one of the key failures of the earlier prosperity agenda was that it did not ignite a sense of enthusiasm or ownership amongst the Canadian public. Citizens are no longer deferential bystanders to the economic policy process. They are far more sophisticated, cynical and interested in issues of economic policy. Both general education and economic literacy are

rising dramatically in Canadian society, and public attitudes to the economy, globalization, technology and public finances are profoundly different from what they were only 10 years ago. The public will want "in" on the debate about their economic future, which they increasingly see as intricately tied to the ultimate question of their quality of life. Finally, it is the behaviour of the public as consumers, investors and taxpayers that will determine whether we see productivity gains. The policy process, therefore, ignores public attitudes at its peril.

In 1999, EKOS undertook a public opinion study of Canadians' understanding of productivity and public receptivity to a government response. The survey, conducted between May 20 and June 10, 1999, involved a random sample of 2,500 respondents. In this paper we report on some of the findings from this survey along with more recent data drawn from Rethinking Government[2] and an Innovation survey (2001).[3] Together, these multiple data sources provide a picture of how Canadians approach the debate. The public response to the productivity challenge over the past four years reveals much about how Canadians link social and economic outcomes and how they understand the role of the state in delivering public goods. For a majority, any approach to improving productivity must be aimed not just at economic efficiency and economic benefits but also at other social goods.

A variety of forces have produced a very different public orientation to the economy and public policy. These forces include broad culture shifts in advanced Western societies (Inglehart 1990; Nevitte 1996), burgeoning levels of post-secondary education, unprecedented levels of public participation in the economy (e.g., over half of the public own equities either inside or outside an RRSP, and labour market participation remains high relative to earlier decades[4]), focused public attention on the relationship between the economy and public finances during the fiscal crisis, and mass media (including new media) which provide more intense public exposure to finance, markets and economic policy issues. Not surprisingly, this set of forces has produced a very different economic citizen — one more capable of and interested in playing a role, while at the same time more pragmatic and less ideological. Nowhere is this more evident than in the shifting attitudes to technology and globalization, which were seen as threatening a decade ago and are now seen as presenting more opportunity than risk.

PUBLIC ATTITUDES TOWARDS THE ECONOMY AND THE ROLE OF THE STATE

Perhaps the best starting point for considering public attitudes toward productivity is the state of the economy. Perceptions of poor economic performance should be an indicator of concern about the underlying fundamentals of the economy and may in fact result from a decline in relative productivity in Canada. It would be hard to imagine continued Canadian satisfaction with economic performance in the context of stagnation in the "real" incomes of Canadians. In addition, the economy is perhaps one area where public perceptions are often particularly in tune with the current economic environment, even if there are occasional lags between how the public sees the economy and its true state (Graves 2001).[5] Since the late 1990s, perceptions of the economy have largely been improv-

ing. Despite considerable talk throughout 2001 about a significant downturn, most Canadians held on to a relatively optimistic view of the economy. Many experienced a decline in their short-term financial situation and outlook but viewed their situation as better now than it was five years ago.

At fairly regular intervals over the past three years, we have asked Canadians to indicate whether they think their standard of living *and* quality of life have improved or declined over the preceding 10 years (we have asked half about quality of life and half about standard of living). Chart 1 shows the results of three readings for both indicators. Given that one of the consequences of declining or stagnant productivity is a decline or stagnation in real incomes, it is worth noting that across all three readings we find that a plurality, and a majority in some cases, believe their standard of living and quality of life have improved. The lack of movement in this indicator is a further indication that if productivity is adversely affecting Canadians' standard of living, then the net effect is being offset by other factors.

Canadians may think that their financial situation and their quality of life/standard of living have generally improved relative to five years ago, but they are keenly aware of their position in income terms relative to the United States. A plurality (48 percent) — a majority when one sets aside the "don't knows" — say that Canadian workers and households have lower incomes than their US counterparts (Chart 2). Without comparable data for another time period, we cannot clearly establish whether this perception of lagging income is growing, but it is an indication that the terms of the productivity debate are widely understood.

CHART 1

Tracking Personal Quality of Life/Standard of Living

"Thinking about your ..., do you think it has gotten better or worse in the past 10 years?"

(a) Overall Quality of Life

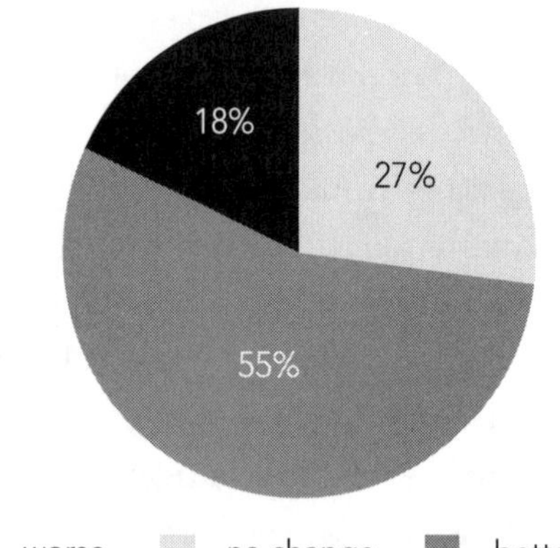

	Jan. 01 (n=818)	Dec. 99 (n=1522)	June 99 (n=2500)
Worse	18	23	23
No change	27	24	28
Better	55	53	49

(b) Material Standard of Living

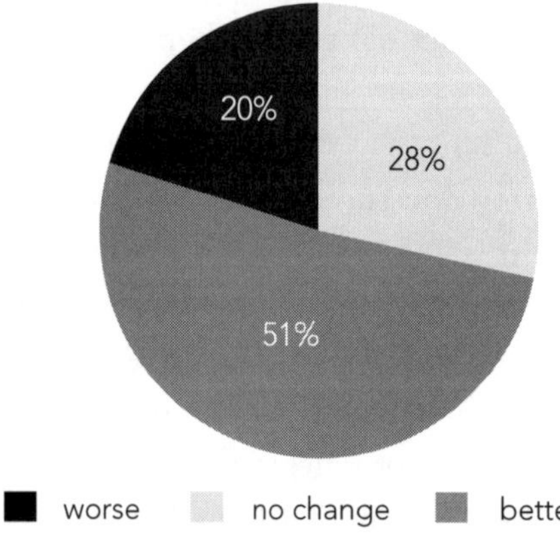

	Jan. 01 (n=818)	Dec. 99 (n=1522)	June 99 (n=2500)
Worse	20	28	23
No change	28	25	28
Better	51	47	49

Source: Rethinking Government and Productivity Study, June 1999.

That said, Canadians overwhelmingly believe that their quality of life is better than that of Americans. This finding may reflect an optimistic rationalization of the current situation, but it should be kept in mind that the public perceives there are more opportunities to achieve a high standard of living in the United States. The distinction between Canada's advantage on quality of life and disadvantage on income is a central aspect of the productivity debate. While Canadians are positive about their current standard of living and quality of life, they place considerably greater emphasis on quality of life as a goal as compared with a high standard of living when these are traded off. They may, therefore, be willing to sacrifice some standard of living in return for a better quality of life.

THE PRODUCTIVITY DEBATE

One might have predicted that the productivity debate would go over the heads of a public more concerned about highly salient issues like health care and more concrete issues like the state of their pocketbook. Yet the productivity debate, with its connections to savings, investment, technology and change, provides a test of the degree to which the public is capable of weighing complex public policy matters. How, then, would we expect average Canadians to understand and conceptualize the debate about productivity? As EKOS and others have argued, public assessments of economic performance are fairly closely tied to the macroeconomic indicators of economic performance. This might, then, provide the basis for a reasoned approach, for many members of the public, to assessing the debate.

CHART 2

International Comparison

(a) "How do you think the average personal income for a Canadian worker compares to that in the United States?"

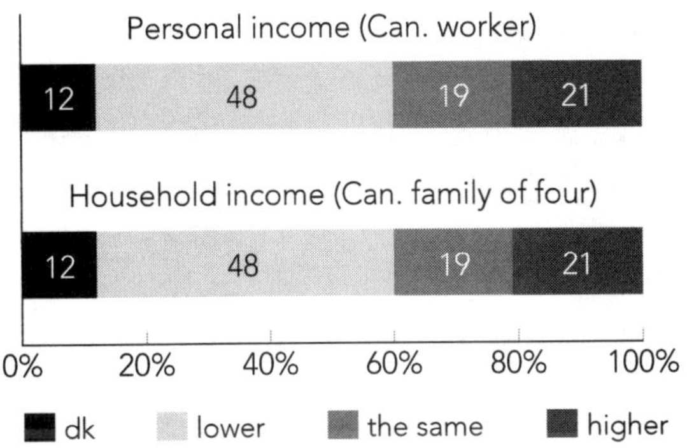

Note: Each question asked of 1/2 sample. n=1250.
Source: Productivity Study, June 19.

(b) "How do you think Canada compares with the US in each of the following areas...?"

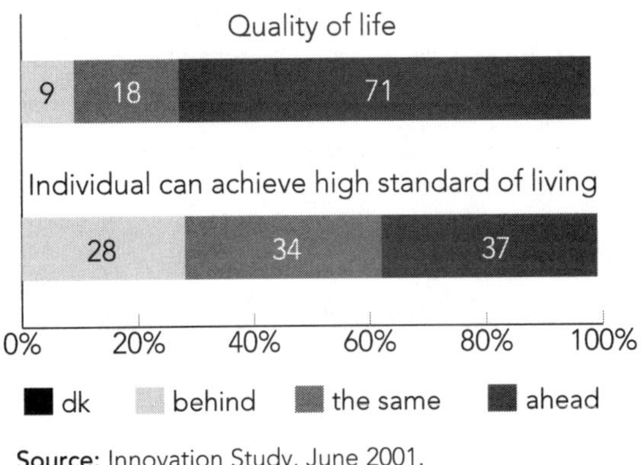

Source: Innovation Study, June 2001.

We offer two hypotheses about how Canadians may come to terms with the productivity challenge:

> Productivity may be understood as an element of the macroeconomy. Those who understand economic realities may be more engaged in the debate, leaving those who lack such an understanding unable to fully participate. We would also expect that those who are worried or concerned about either current or future economic performance would identify productivity as a critical issue.

> Productivity may be understood in ideological terms. In particular, those who see an active role for the state may be more likely to want government to act but are also more suspicious of the motivations underlying the debate and unwilling to see the solution in terms of less government.

It is possible, then, to consider these two different perspectives — productivity as an element of a strong economy and productivity as a political project with winners and losers — as lenses through which to examine the public's understanding of the meaning and nature of productivity in Canada and the arguments surrounding it. As we shall see, there are elements of both these perspectives in the views of Canadians.

The evidence from the 1999 EKOS survey indicates that many features of the productivity debate resonate with the public — with most Canadians able to offer a top-of-the-mind image of what it means for them (Chart 3), while about 26 percent were unable or unwilling to respond. In addition, the general public defines productivity in terms that resemble those used by economists. The most frequent response terms were grouped under the label "production, effort and efficiency," followed by general references to work and employment.[6] These and other data indicate that, for most people, productivity does not engender fear but rather a connection to, or a sense of, hard work, effort, results and security.[7]

Improving economic productivity is also a priority for the public. It is a lower priority than health, education, environment and crime, but a higher priority than taxation, immigra-

CHART 3

Top-of-Mind Images

"What is the first thing that comes to mind when you hear the term 'productivity'?"

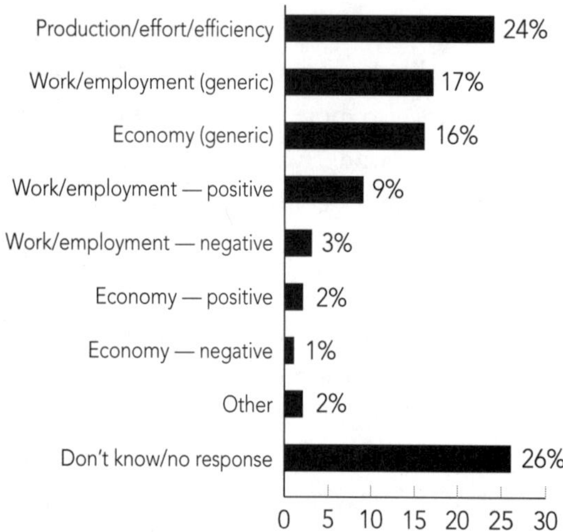

Note: n=2500
Source: Productivity Study, June 1999.

tion and social assistance (not shown). An overwhelming majority (82 percent) believe that improving productivity is *essential* to improving our standard of living (Table 1). Substantial majorities, 70 and 67 percent respectively, also claim to be worried that if we don't improve our productivity there will be a decline in both our quality of life and standard of living. This is an initial indication that for the public productivity is linked not only to economic concerns (standard of living) but also to broader, quality-of-life issues. Concern with productivity is, however, fairly universally shared among Canadians. For example, 67 percent of university-educated people are concerned about the impact on standard of living, compared with 66 percent of those with high school or less education. Concern is also unrelated to individuals' perceptions of future economic performance.

However, the public is not without some scepticism about the motivation underlying some of the debate about productivity and some of the potential costs. A slim majority (53 percent) agree with the statement that large business and wealthy Canadians have manufactured recent concern about productivity.[8] Chart 4 shows that scepticism is highest among lower-income, less-educated Canadians, and is also high among people who do not recall hearing about productivity[9] and people who rate Canada's level of productivity as good. As we will show, most Canadians do think that productivity is good in Canada but this is an indication that thinking things are good produces a resistance to the arguments about the need for a productivity agenda.

In an earlier survey we also found the public divided about whether talk of productivity was code for job losses and longer hours for the same pay. While increasing productivity would affect jobs — especially for those in less productive sectors — as fewer people produce a larger amount of product, both of these indicators suggest that talk of productivity,

TABLE 1

Perceptions of Productivity/Innovation

	Agree	Neither	Disagree
Increasing Canada's economic productivity is essential to improving our standard of living.[1]	82	11	6
I really worry that if we don't improve the productivity of the economy, the QUALITY OF LIFE will suffer.[2]	70	16	13
I really worry that if we don't improve the productivity of the economy, the STANDARD OF LIVING will suffer.[2]	67	19	14
Much of the recent concern about our level of productivity has been manufactured by large business and wealthy Canadians.[1]	53	10	23
Talk of economic productivity is just code for job losses and longer hours for the same pay.[2]	36	27	33

[1] Rethinking Government, Nov-Dec. 1998.
[2] Productivity Study, June 1999.

CHART 4

Skepticism by Key Demographic and Attitudinal Groups

"Much of the recent concern about our level of productivity has been manufactured by large business and wealthy Canadians."

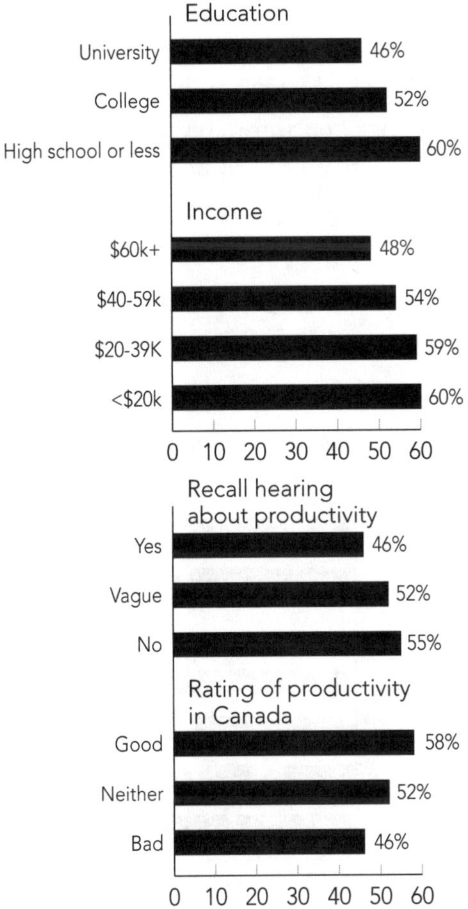

despite its importance on the agenda, is partially an ideological signal for some Canadians.

Nevertheless, when forced to make a choice between productivity as a job destroyer and productivity as a job creator, three in four respondents choose the latter (Chart 5). So, although a minority sees improving productivity as a job destroyer, a focus on productivity is one of the few areas that most people do not see

as a zero-sum game but as a source of improvement in the overall number of jobs. Similarly, when probed further about what kinds of jobs they expected to be produced, three in four thought high-skill jobs were more likely to emerge. Thus, productivity is seen as an important goal, but the pursuit of a productivity agenda is not seen in purely optimistic terms. Although the public leans toward the positive, it has a healthy dose of scepticism about the motivations behind and the consequences of an emphasis on productivity.

How, then, does the public see Canada measuring up in terms of the level of productivity? Does the scepticism indicate a naïve belief that Canada has a high level of productivity? Or, alternatively, does the high priority accorded to productivity indicate a belief that Canada is in a troublesome position? As

CHART 5

Net Impact on Jobs

"Which of the following two statements is closest to your point of view?"

Improving productivity will improve efficiency in the economy and LEAD TO JOB LOSSES as fewer people are needed to do the work required

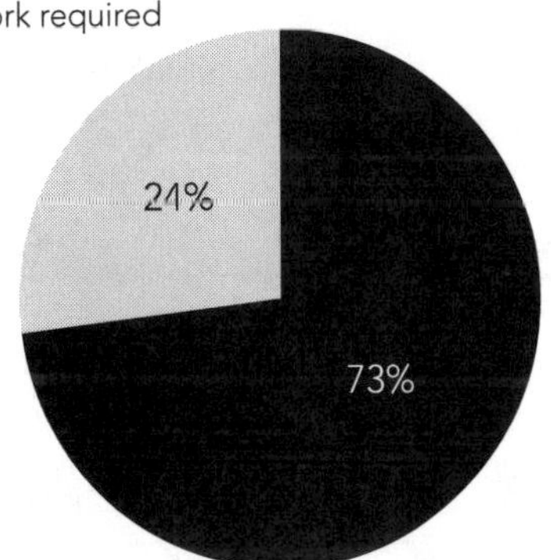

Improving productivity will stimulate the economy and CREATE MORE JOBS for Canadians

Note: n=2500
Source: Productivity Study, June 1999.

Chart 6 indicates, the public does lean toward the positive in assessing Canadian productivity in the abstract but tends to be more negative when comparing our level of productivity to that in the United States. Few people (18 percent) rate Canadian productivity as poor, and a plurality (44 percent) rate it as good overall. The distribution leans in the positive direction, but few give Canada high marks. On the seven-point scale, 32 percent give a five, the weakest positive assessment, and only 3 percent give a seven, the strongest positive assessment. No wonder there is concern about the quality-of-life and standard-of-living ramifications of failing to address productivity.

Ratings of Canada's level of productivity are generally unrelated to general socio-demographic indicators (Chart 7). Men are marginally more positive, but there are no substantive differences across education and income. The only age group to differ significantly is youth, those under 25 who tend on average to express greater levels of optimism on many indicators despite their tendency to be less engaged in

250

CHART 6
Rating Productivity
(a) "How would you rate Canada's current level of productivity?"

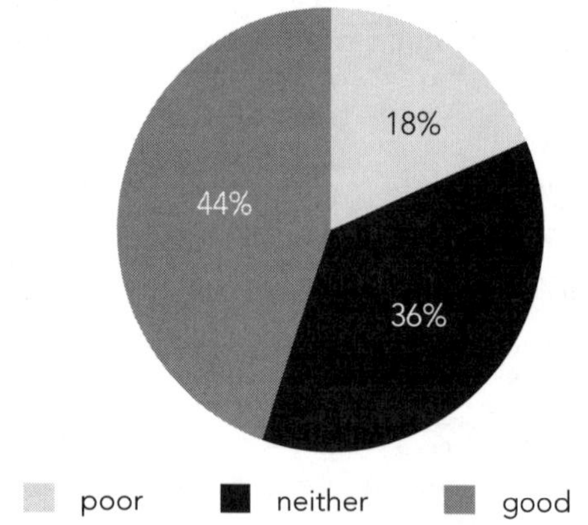

(b) "And how do you think Canada's level of productivity compares to that of ...?"

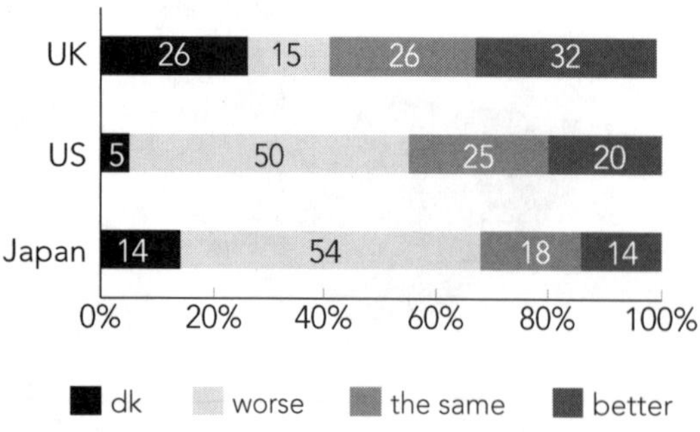

Note: Each option asked of 1/3 sample. n=2500
Source: Productivity Study, June 1999.

CHART 7
Rating Productivity by Key Groups
"How would you rate Canada's current level of productivity?"

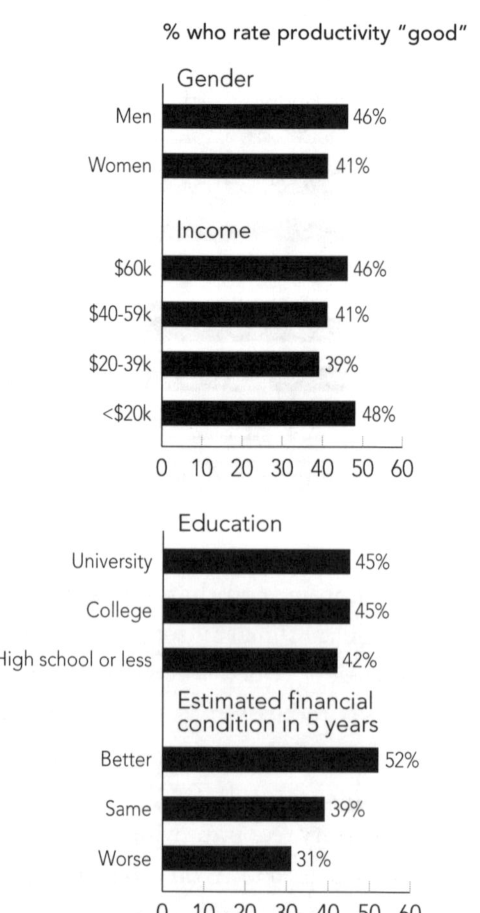

day-to-day politics. This is a broad indication that productivity is understood to be an element of the macroeconomy in the same way, perhaps, as unemployment or inflation.

Those who are cynical about the motivations underlying a productivity agenda, as indicated by their agreement with the statement that the recent concern has been manufactured, are considerably more likely to rate Canada's productivity as good. However, when we consider attitudes about the likely impact of improving productivity on jobs, those who think there will be job improvements and those who think there will be job losses rate productivity the same. There is, therefore, only modest evidence that attitudes toward productivity are symbolic of ideological positioning. The most important drivers are expected economic performance and perceived changes in quality of life and standard of living in Canada. Chart 7 shows that those who are pessimistic about their financial situation (expect it to get worse) are more likely to rate Canada's level of productivity as poor. Though only a minority in 1999 thought things were getting worse, those who said things were getting worse for either quality of life or standard of living were twice as likely to rate Canada's productivity as poor (Table 2).

While the overall evaluation may be positive, Canadians are aware of Canada's comparative disadvantage on this measure vis-à-vis the United States (Chart 6b). Each respondent was asked to compare Canada to one of three possible countries (the United States, Japan and the United Kingdom).[10] The only country they perceive Canada as having a productivity advantage over is the United Kingdom (though one in four are unable to say how Canada would fare in such a comparison). Roughly one in two believe that Canada's level of productivity is worse than that of the United States[11] and Japan, while few believe that it is higher (20 and 14 percent respectively). Recall that the public also believes that Canada has an income gap with the United States. Though not shown, those who believe Canada's quality of life or standard of living have deteriorated are more likely to say that Canada has a productivity deficit with the United States.

When we asked senior Canadian decision-makers and elites[12] to compare Canada's productivity to that of the United States in the 2000 iteration of Rethinking Government, a majority gave Canada a lower rating (Chart 8). Assessments of the future are somewhat more optimistic, but negative expectations continue to outweigh positive ones by a margin of almost two to one. The public appears to be more positive than elites but not so much more as to be out of touch with the debate or to be unlikely to support a policy response. In fact, the Canadian

251

TABLE 2

Impact of Quality-of-Life/Standard-of-Living Assessment on Rating Productivity

	Quality of Life			Standard of Living		
Rating of Canada's productivity	Worse	Same	Better	Worse	Same	Better
Poor	31	21	12	29	17	14
Neither	41	42	33	40	42	32
Good	**28**	**38**	**54**	**31**	**41**	**54**

Source: Productivity Study, June 1999.

CHART 8
Elite Views of Canadian/US Economy

"How would you rate Canada's economic productivity compared to that of the United States? Do you think Canada's economic productivity is comparatively ...?"

"Thinking ten years in the future, do you think Canada's economic productivity will be ... compared to that of the United States?"

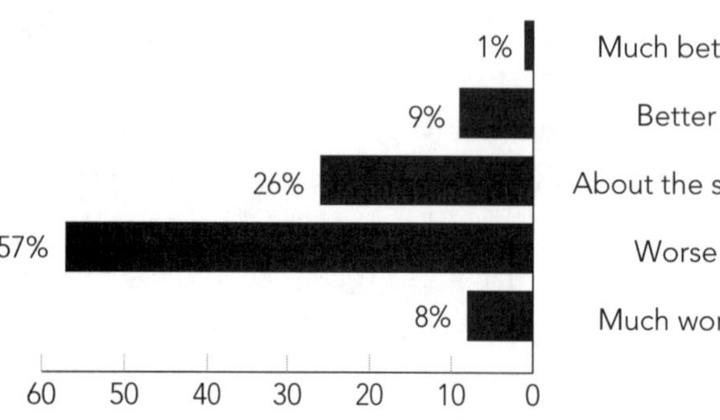

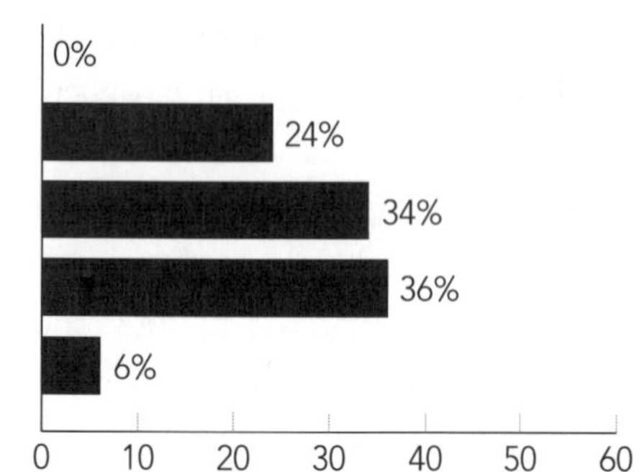

Note: n=488
Source: Rethinking Government, Elite Survey 2000.

public appears to favour a policy response, as evidenced by its concern about the potential cost, to quality of life and standard of living, of failing to improve productivity.

In general the public has an appetite for improving productivity, the consequence of both a general view that Canada is under-performing relative to the United States and a lukewarm overall rating of Canadian productivity. Perceptions of Canada's level of productivity are also firmly rooted in current assessments of our standard of living and quality of life and expectations of future economic prosperity. This is not to say that there are not points of dispute. Elites in particular are more likely to rate Canada poorly, and some reject the need for a productivity agenda.

THE ROLE OF GOVERNMENT

It is clear that the public has a reasonable understanding of the essential components of the productivity debate and appreciates the benefits of a productivity agenda. But does the public see the need for a state-driven productivity agenda? The answer is clearly yes, but the preferred toolkit is mixed and at odds with some of the main prescriptions (e.g., tax cuts, R&D investment) offered by key voices in the debate.

Few Canadians see the federal government as taking a leadership role in improving productivity (Chart 9). A majority would prefer that the government act as an equal partner with the provinces, the private sector and the public. A similar role is envisioned for government when it comes to improving quality of life, which suggests that there is nothing unique, when it comes to productivity, in the leadership role attributed to the federal government.[13] It also suggests that the public would prefer that government be strategic about things so as to ensure that the public gets the collective goods it wants.

The public toolkit for addressing productivity through state action is heavily

CHART 9

Preferred Federal Role

"Overall, thinking about a national goal of improving ..., which of the following is the most appropriate role for the Government of Canada?"

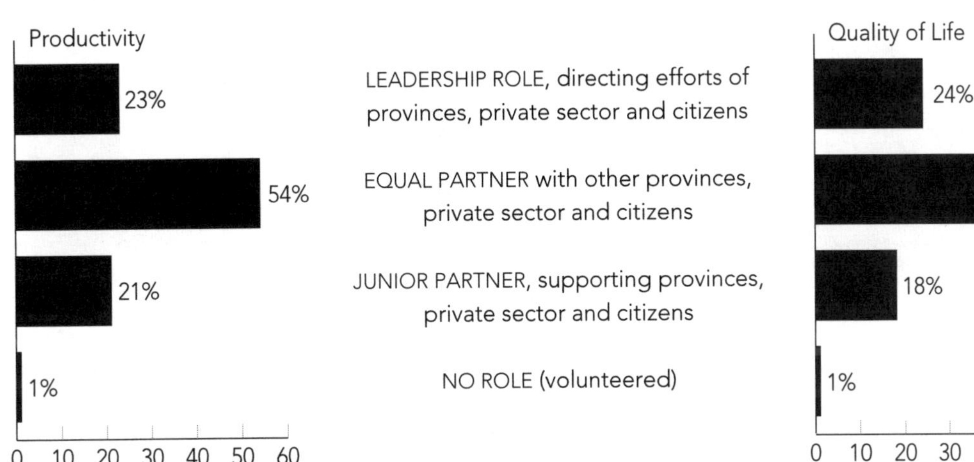

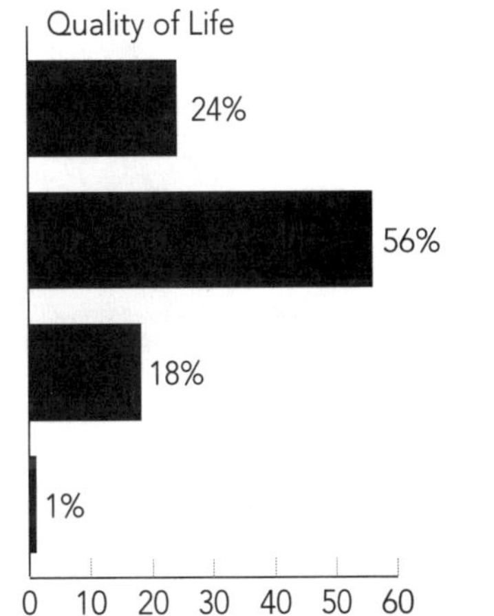

Note: n=2500. Each question asked of 1/2 sample.
Source: Productivity Study, June 1999.

weighted toward human and social investment priorities. Chart 10 shows the results of a trade-off analysis in which the reported score is the percentage of time that each option is selected over another randomly drawn option.[14] Health care is seen as the best allocation of money aimed at improving productivity, followed by a fund to help workers improve their skills and incentives to steer students toward science and technology. An early childhood development initiative also scores high. All of these options address productivity by improving human capital. These types of government investment are part of an agenda aimed at improving the standard of living of Canadians (Sulzenko and Kalwarowsky 2000).

Corporate tax cuts as an option fares the worst, with personal income tax cuts and debt reduction faring better in the tradeoffs. The public appears to reject the idea that cutting corporate tax would lead to increased investments in new, innovative and more productive approaches. Both tax-reduction options are more strongly supported by those at the top of the income scale and by those who rate Canada's current level of productivity as low. An infrastructure, "roads and potholes" approach is also rejected compared with the other options.

A range of more specific policy approaches to productivity has a reasonable level of support. These include supporting innovation in natural resources, incentives for business R&D and updating of machinery, and tax relief to attract high-tech investment. In forced tradeoffs with other options, these options are chosen one time out of two.

In a separate study, Rethinking Government, conducted at roughly the same time, we posed a number of questions to both members of the general public and a sample of senior decision-makers and elites in Canada

CHART 10
Productivity Tradeoffs

"If you were Prime Minister for one day and you had to choose how to allocate $1 billion to improve Canada's productivity, which of the following two would you choose in the best public interest?"

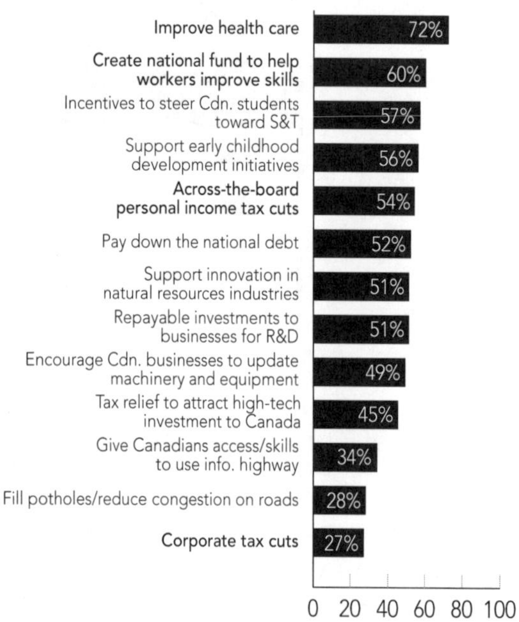

Note: Presented in series of random paired choices Percent indicates average number of times option is selected over all others. n=2500
Source: Productivity Study, June 1999.

CHART 11
Best Way to Improve Productivity

"On the issue of productivity, which one of the following three choices would be the best way for governments to help improve Canada's overall economic productivity?"

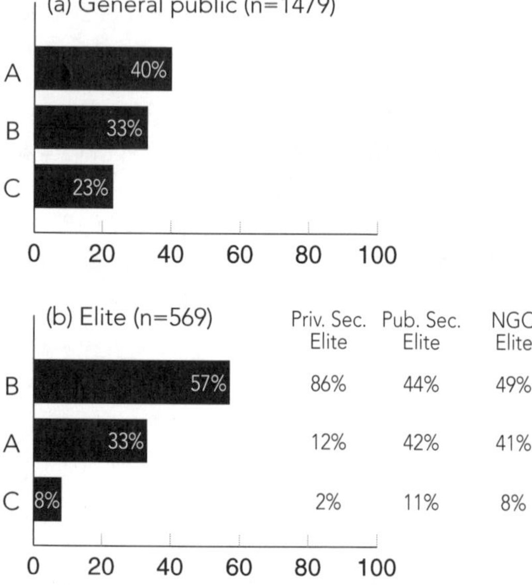

A - A national learning strategy to help Canadian workers.
B - A corporate and personal tax-cut strategy to reduce costs and stimulate the economy.
C - A national technology and "connectiveness" strategy to help business and citizens access the latest high-tech processes and equipment.
Source: Productivity Study, June 1999.

(Chart 11). To both groups, we offered three alternative ways that the government could improve the level of Canada's overall economic productivity: a national learning strategy, a corporate and personal tax-cut strategy, and a technology strategy. The alternatives are not exhaustive, but they cover the three basic elements of what productivity is often understood to be about: highly skilled workers, a positive investment climate, and a focus on innovation and technology.

Although people generally reject single-focus approaches in favour of mixed strategies, forcing them to choose one of the three does pro-duce significant findings. Among the general public, all three approaches receive some support, with the least preferred approach — a technology strategy — favoured by 23 percent. The most favoured option is the national learning strategy to help Canadian workers (human investment strategy). These results are consistent with the tradeoff analysis. Among the decision-makers and elites, the pattern is strikingly different. A majority of decision-makers (57 percent) choose a strategy of cutting corporate and income taxes as the preferred option followed by a national learning strategy. Surprisingly, elites tend to reject a technology strategy, perhaps because of an ideological perspective on the role of government. However, there are important differences among the elite groups. The tax-cut strategy is the almost unanimous preference (86 percent) of private-sector elites, while public-sector and NGO elites are closer to the general public, although they are even less interested in a technology strategy.

Another way to demonstrate the importance of human investment as a role of government is to look at how Canadians would measure a successful innovation agenda (Chart 12). Again using the tradeoff approach, drawn this time from the Innovation study in 2001, the two options most frequently chosen were both related to human benefits: more skilled workers staying in Canada and a higher quality of life. The next set of options chosen was related to economic performance: a stronger

CHART 12

Measuring a Successful Innovation Agenda
"What would be the best test of the success of a focus on innovation?"

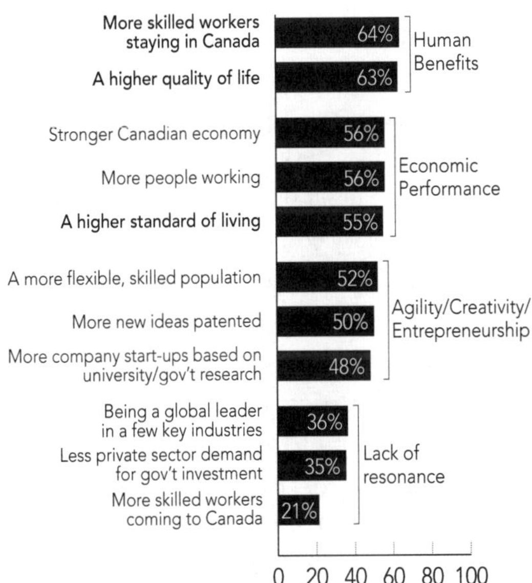

Note: Randomly selected paired tradeoffs. Percentages represent aggregate wins.
Source: Innovation Study, June 2001.

CHART 13

Social Programs/Productivity Linkage
"Which of the following two statements is closest to your point of view? (a) Social programs DETRACT FROM CANADA'S PRODUCTIVITY because they cost so much and keep taxes higher (b) Social programs are important human investments which INCREASE CANADA'S PRODUCTIVITY by ensuring a healthy, secure population"

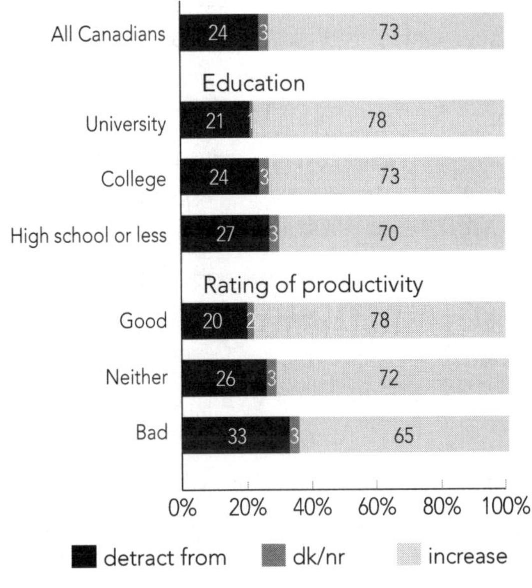

Note: Base: All Canadians

economy, more people working and a higher standard of living.

Further evidence comes from public rejection of the idea that the current level of social spending is an impediment to improving Canada's current level of productivity (Chart 13). When asked to choose between the view that "social programs detract from Canada's productivity because they cost so much and keep taxes higher" and the view that "social programs are important forms of investment which increase Canada's productivity by ensuring a healthy, secure population," Canadians agree with the pro-productivity proposition by a margin of 75 to 25 percent.

Is the support for the benefits of social programs merely wishful thinking? Chart 13 also breaks down the results by the respondent's level of education and perception of current Canadian productivity. Not surprisingly, those who rate Canada's productivity as poor are more likely to say that social programs detract.[15] Indeed, those who think that Canada is faring poorly are more likely to see our social programs as the culprit, though even here 65 percent support the view of social programs as providing important benefits. Significantly, those with higher levels of education, and presumably more knowledge and considered views about the debate, are actually less likely to say that social programs detract. The idea of social spending as an investment does resonate with Canadians.

There is clearly a significant gap in the understanding of how productivity should be dealt with between the residents of Canada's family rooms and the residents of its boardrooms: the fairly balanced approach of the general public with its accent first on lifelong learning skills and knowledge compared with the strong preference toward a tax-cut strategy among the elites. There are competing explanations for these different opinions on policy. On the one hand, despite understanding many of the fundamentals of the productivity debate, the policy options favoured by the public may simply reflect the kinds of activities that they prefer to have government undertaking irrespective of their impact on productivity. Certainly the policy options that come out on top are firmly rooted in the priorities and values that the public expresses in general about the role of government. On the other hand, those who rate Canada's productivity as poor are more likely to support the tax-cut strategy and less likely to emphasize human investment. This suggests that a more negative attitude concerning the current level of productivity might produce a different policy toolkit. It is just that a seriously negative outlook has not emerged.

CONCLUSIONS

Many features of the debate on the need to improve productivity had filtered down to the public as early as 1999, even though at that time a majority could not recall hearing much about it and those who could were divided about whether they were hearing positive or negative things. That said, most people believe that Canada is in a relatively weaker position than our major trading partner in terms of both productivity and income. The perceived gap is partially related to the view that improving productivity is central to the long-term economic well-being (standard of living) and social well-being (quality of life) of Canadians. Importantly, those who think that Canada's situation has worsened in terms of either quality of life or standard of living are more pessimistic about Canadian productivity.

Ultimately, the degree to which Canadians are able to consider the key elements of the debate is symptomatic of a public that is more in tune with contemporary economic developments and more capable of taking part than might be expected. Certainly the argument can be made that discussions about productivity, innovation and other aspects of economic performance should not be left solely to the purview of the private sector, economists, politicians and other experts. The Canadian public today, like that in most other advanced Western countries, is much less deferential than in the past — much less willing to see such decisions made on their behalf by others, behind closed doors. Many members of the public recognize the key components of the debate and have a position on the kinds of responses government should undertake.

In part, public attitudes derive from the fact that the public understands the issues and looks to the state to provide public goods, and a strong vibrant, productive economy is clearly one such good. The desire to establish a link between economic and social progress is clear in the public mind and could be identified under the rubric of *humanomics* (Graves 2000). People want to understand productivity as something associated with having a healthy economy, which requires human investment, and which is ultimately sought for the purpose of having a higher quality of life. Productivity for a higher *standard of living* might be characterized as a Bay Street model focused primarily on tax cuts and minimal government. This model does have a constituency — about one in four Canadians — who, not surprisingly, tend to be male, affluent and economically secure. The Bay Street model, however, does not resonate with most Canadians who want more of a Main Street productivity agenda. An agenda focused primarily on achieving a higher quality of life. The choice of policy instruments and approaches is related to perceptions about the state of the productivity problem, with those whose assessment is most negative being most supportive of the Bay Street model.

In moving forward, the public believes there are some clear winners and losers among the various strategies. Some elements are seen as more important than others. For example, the clear winners were human capital and innovation. The clear losers, relatively speaking, were corporate tax cuts, minimal government

and the old passive redistribution tools for dealing with inequality. Governments and others interested in advancing a productivity agenda would do best to frame it as a means for achieving a higher quality of life. There is a growing desire to explicitly link and coordinate social and economic policy, and not to see them as tradeoffs. Canadians are evidently not in the dark about the current state of the economy, so it is not simply a matter of overcoming an information deficiency. In fact, the Canadian public preference for a human investment approach to productivity is consistent with Heath's argument, in this volume, that an emphasis on productivity should not come at the expense of other priorities, many of which are not inconsistent with productivity growth.

257

NOTES

The authors would like to thank Keith Banting, Andrew Sharpe and the anonymous reviewer for their helpful comments on earlier versions of this paper. All errors remain, of course, those of the authors.

1   There is some debate about these conclusions. Trefler (1999) cautions that productivity levels vary considerably by type of output, with low-end manufacturing performing well.

2   *Rethinking Government* is a syndicated research program that began in 1994 and is continued on an annual basis. Each year approximately 6,000 Canadians are interviewed as part of a three-wave survey program that tracks Canadian attitudes on a range of government issues.

3   The Innovation survey was conducted between June 13 and 22, 2001 with a nationally representative random sample of 1,955 Canadians.

4   Between 1976 and 1989, aggregate labour market participation rose rapidly to an all-time high in 1989 fuelled largely by the entry of women into the labour force (Ip 1998).

5   By lags we mean that the public may be slow to fully appreciate an improvement in the economy or slow to recognize the depth of a downturn. The lags are, of course, evident at the macro level and should not

be read as indicating irrationality in public assessments of the economy.

6   All responses were transcribed by the interviewers and then grouped by common theme by trained coders.

7   We also presented respondents with a set of paired terms (damaging vs. rewarding for Canada; pessimistic vs. optimistic; insecure vs. secure) and asked them to select the one that best described their attitude to productivity. Majorities for all pairs chose the positive response.

8   Of course, this is a reflection of the broader resonance for the public of the idea that big business has too much influence on government policy.

9   The wording of the question was, "Do you recall reading, hearing or seeing anything recently about the state of Canada's productivity?" Whereas 67 percent said no, 19 percent said, "yes, vaguely" and 13 percent said, "yes, clearly."

10   Perceptions of a productivity gap are highly related to educational attainment, with more education associated with a greater likelihood of seeing Canada as behind.

11   Beliefs about Canada's productivity are highly related to assessments of its position relative to the United States. Those who are positive about Canada's productivity are considerably less negative about the comparison with the United States. A respondent who thinks Canada is doing poorly is twice as likely to think that the United States has a higher level, which suggests that the comparison with the United States is factored into the overall assessment of our own level.

12   These elites are drawn from among the CEOs of the largest companies, the deputy minister cadre in senior governments, elected officials and the largest NGOs.

13   This is a critical element of the public's current understanding of the role of government in the process of achieving collective goods. The public wants the government to extend its role across many policy areas and adopt a long-term vision, but it also sees government in a less paternalistic light.

14   Each respondent was given four sets of pairs, randomly assigned, so the results here aggregate across all respondents and all pair selections.

15   Though not shown, one would find similar results if one looked at ratings of Canada in comparison with the United States.

REFERENCES

Graves, F. L. 2000. "Rethinking Government as If People Mattered: From Reaganomics to 'Humanomics'." In *How Ottawa Spends, 1999-2000, Shape-Shifting: Canadian Governance Toward the 21st Century*, ed. L. Pal. Toronto: Oxford University Press.

——— 2001. "The Economy Through a Public Lens: Shifting Canadian Views of the Economy." In *The Review of Economic Performance and Social Progress 2001. The Longest Decade: Canada in the 1990s*, ed. K. Banting, A. Sharpe, and F. St-Hilaire. Montreal and Ottawa: Institute for Research on Public Policy and Centre for the Study of Living Standards.

Harris, R. 1999. "Determinants of Canadian Productivity Growth: Issues and Prospects." Discussion paper #8. Ottawa: Industry Canada

Inglehart, R. 1990. *Culture Shift in Advanced Industrial Societies*. Princeton, NJ: Princeton University Press.

Ip, I. 1998. "Labour Force Participation in Canada: Trends and Shifts." *Bank of Canada Review* Summer:28-52.

Nevitte, N. 1996. *The Decline of Deference*. Peterborough, ON: Broadview.

Sharpe, A. 2001. "Determinants of Trends in Living Standards in Canada and the United States, 1989-2000." *International Productivity Monitor* 1(2): 3-10.

Sulzenko, A., and J. Kalwarowsky. 2000. "A Policy Challenge for a Higher Standard of Living." *ISUMA* 1(1): 125-129.

Trefler, D. 1999. "Does Canada Need a Productivity Budget?" *Policy Options* 20(6): 66-71.

Bad Translation or Double Standard? Productivity and Accountability Across the Private, Public and Voluntary Sectors

Janice Gross Stein

INTRODUCTION

Conventional wisdom in public policy dictates that public services should be delivered as efficiently as possible. Who would want to "waste" public money, especially when resources are always scarce? This maxim is so obvious that we often slide right by it and move on to more interesting challenges. When we begin to unpack the phrase "efficiently as possible," however, we quickly run into difficulties. It soon becomes apparent that the transfer of the concept of efficiency, understood as productivity, to public service delivery creates problems that are not obvious when private goods and services are produced and delivered through markets. What are these problems?

In the relentless drive for increased productivity in the public and voluntary sectors, a drive often fuelled by the need to secure private funding and to build public-private partnerships, these two sectors have adopted, at times unwillingly, a rhetoric and a language of productivity that is considerably narrower than that of the private sector. They are consequently far less able to provide for unex-pected contingency, to invest seriously in the research and development (R&D) that they need to be productive, and to deal with the challenges of accountability. I argue that the language of efficiency, translated narrowly as productivity and taken to extremes in the public and voluntary sectors, can compromise social trust, our sense of social responsibility, as well as our capacity to be accountable in meaningful ways, to produce new knowledge and innovate, and even to prosper.

Efficiency, as I have argued elsewhere, is not easily applied as an organizing concept outside the context of markets (Stein 2001). In the broad public sector, it is often unclear what we want to be efficient at providing and how cost-effective services are defined. The most serious challenge comes, surprisingly, on the effectiveness side of the cost-effective equation. There is often widespread disagreement, reinforced by gaps in knowledge and feedback, about what constitutes an effective education, or effective health care, or effective environmental policies. Public-sector outputs are often multi-dimensional and the quality of public services is often very difficult to establish. They are also much more difficult to measure without the timely, corrective feedback that markets provide to the private sector. It is within the context of this general argument that I examine three specific challenges to the delivery of public services where the public and voluntary sectors suffer particularly badly from the unreflexive translation of private-sector language.

The first, one that generally receives relatively little attention, is redundancy. When we are providing public services, we need to build in some redundancy to cope with unexpected contingencies. The unexpected contingency, the shock, the "wild card" can have far graver consequences when the services are public rather than private, essential rather than optional, especially when timelines are short. We have some knowledge, but not enough, about appropriate timelines needed to gear up and deliver public services. And for reasons that I will make clear, there is far less tolerance for redundancy in the public and voluntary sectors than in the private sector.

The second challenge to increased productivity is the need for a strong base of research and innovation to improve the effectiveness, as well as the delivery, of public services. We know that significant investment in R&D is a critical requirement for improving productivity, particularly in that part of the private sector that produces capital goods. In a global "knowledge-based" economy, where knowledge has become among the most important resources, leading firms in the telecommunications sector and in computer hardware and software, for example, attach even greater significance than they did two decades ago to investment in R&D. It is not only firms that produce capital goods, however, that are significant investors. Throughout the private sector, firms invest in research to stimulate

innovation and increase productivity in their delivery of goods and services. When we look at the public sector and the voluntary sector, we find significant constraints on their capacity to invest in the production of knowledge they need to improve their cost-effectiveness. Ironically, these constraints often come from the private-sector demand for cost-containment in the other two sectors.

The third challenge is the absence of the easily available corrective feedback that markets generally provide to producers of private goods. Without feedback, it is difficult to determine how productive the public and voluntary sectors are. Public services at times seem to fall into a "black hole." To deal with this problem, policy-makers are turning increasingly to accountability as a surrogate for market feedback. But accountability includes far more than the feedback markets generally provide. We are not clear what we mean by accountability: do we include only "upward" accountability, or "outward" accountability as well? Is accountability system-wide or individual? Some argue that personal accountability rests on a useful myth: the "social convention and construction by which political actors affirm the preeminence of intentional human control over history" (March and Olsen 1995, 157-158, 161).[1] To make matters even more complicated, constructing systems of accountability is also "expensive." This should come as no surprise to economists who understand the costs of the structures we have built to regulate markets. It is a (relatively) straightforward matter, however, to offset the costs of market regulation against the anticipated costs of widespread cheating and destabilization of markets for private goods and services. Alas, the problem becomes far more complicated in the public and voluntary sectors.

THE MEANING OF "EFFICIENCY"

Before considering these three challenges, I want to briefly situate productivity within the different meanings of efficiency. These differences, as we shall see, are not trivial, for they have quite different implications for the delivery of public services. We usually understand efficiency as the best possible use of scarce resources to achieve a valued end. Efficiency generally means productivity, or cost-effectiveness, where the maximum amount of output is produced from a given set of resources, or a given output is produced with fewer resources.[2] Productivity increases, for example, when people make better use of the resources they have, including their time, to increase the quantity of work that they can accomplish while maintaining the quality.

Embedded in the concept of productivity is an assessment of quality and effectiveness as well as quantity. As I have argued elsewhere, judgements about effectiveness — extraordinarily difficult to make and always subject to political contestation and debate — must logically precede any calculation of productivity (Stein 2001). It is no accident that productivity is often defined as cost-effectiveness. It relates cost to effectiveness.

The concept of productivity, when it is applied to the delivery of public services, is not without its contradictions. Consider for a moment the example of hospitals that, in the last decade, have significantly increased their productivity. Their cost per weighted patient has dropped as acutely ill patients cycle through more quickly, usually without adverse consequences. Hospitals, in other words, are treating patients more efficiently than they did a decade ago and, consequently, can handle larger numbers of patients.

But absolute costs are rising, since most of the costs of treating acute illness occur at the beginning of the hospital stay. The most efficient hospitals, those with the lowest costs per weighted patients, therefore tend to run the largest deficits. The government funding formula rewards efficient hospitals only at the margin and, consequently, hospitals find themselves trapped in the "efficiency squeeze." Within current constraints, the logic is clear: hospitals that want to increase their productivity should admit fewer patients and close beds.

We could argue that if productivity were applied to the health-care system as a whole, rather than to just one silo, and if government funding genuinely rewarded productivity, some of these contradictions would disappear. Meeting these conditions, however, would require a widespread transformation of the health-care system; the removal of existing silos among hospitals, physicians, chronic care and home care; the creation of an integrated system; and a fundamental change in government funding formulae. One would not have to be a cynic to conclude that these kinds of fundamental changes are not yet visible on the policy horizon. In their absence, hospitals will continue to struggle with the perverse consequences of the efficiency squeeze created by the use of productivity measures in their sector.

It is not only that productivity creates unintended contradictions and negative externalities when it is used within segments of public-service sectors as a measure of efficiency. As Joseph Heath argues convincingly in his chapter in this volume, productivity does not necessarily equate to welfare. On the contrary, he insists, the costs of productivity are often understated and its benefits exaggerated. This apparent paradox is less puzzling when we consider efficiency not as productivity but within the broader utilitarian tradition that speaks of maximizing satisfaction rather than the number of outputs for a given input. Using microeconomic models, we think of individuals as "rational" when they make choices that increase their welfare. Welfare is defined not only in material terms, but also includes the moral, psychological and spiritual satisfaction people get from the consequences of the choices they make. What matters is whether people have made the choice that best satisfies their needs, whatever their needs may be. Here, efficiency, rationality and satisfaction are all conflated.

Efficiency as the maximization of utility or satisfaction is quite different from efficiency used to describe increased productivity. The two are frequently confused. Productivity requires some external standard — how many doctoral students does a university graduate, and at what cost — while utilitarian arguments depend on internal standards like satisfaction and utility. We may increase our productivity but significantly reduce our utility. The familiar contradiction between the increased productivity of coal-burning furnaces and environmental damage is only one among a host of such examples. If the reduced quality of the air matters more to us than the gain in productivity, then we have diminished our utility. An increase in productivity would consequently be inefficient. This is precisely the compelling argument that Heath makes. The concept of efficiency defined as the pursuit of self-interest is much broader than the concept of productivity that economists use to explain economic growth. The two are not at all equivalent.

When we discuss "efficiency" in connection with public rather than private services, we need to be especially clear. We need to be clear not only because markets generally do not provide feedback, but, even more to the point, because the collective stakes are so high. Are we discussing the productivity of the public sector, or do we mean satisfaction with public services? Is satisfaction — an inherently subjective concept — conceptually and technically equivalent to welfare? And if we mean satisfaction, is it individual satisfaction with schools, health care, public transportation and policing, or collective satisfaction? And if it is collective satisfaction — a hotly contested issue — is it satisfaction of only "citizen-consumers," or providers as well? How do we think about those individuals and groups within the collectivity who are dissatisfied? Do the reasons for dissatisfaction matter? Should those who are dissatisfied with some public services be permitted to opt out and purchase them privately if they can afford to do so? What is the appropriate balance, to use economists' language, between the negative and positive externalities of this kind of policy? Do those who are dissatisfied because they do not have full access to public services deserve special consideration and additional help?

Often, we are not clear in our thinking about efficiency. As we begin to peel away the layers of the concept, it becomes more and more difficult to remain strictly within the confines of economic analysis. Deciding which is the appropriate concept and criterion of efficiency when public services are at stake is often a deeply political decision. How we balance the at times contradictory imperatives of productivity and satisfaction (or welfare) is a political choice. And how we think — as citizens as well as scholars — about opportunity costs is only partly informed by economic analysis, since externalities extend far into the future. The longer our collective time horizon, the more difficult these externalities are to estimate, especially since we rarely have the kind of baseline probability distributions that such estimates assume. As societies, in other words, we often gamble, without the probability distributions that gamblers can use in games of chance. How we calculate the odds and make our bets is as much a function of our politics and of our concept of citizenship as it is of economic analysis.

To make matters simpler, for purposes of this chapter I use efficiency to mean only productivity. And, in examining the transfer of language from the private sector to public services, I look not only at the public sector — the traditional provider — but also at not-for-profit organizations in the voluntary sector that increasingly deliver public services that were once provided by the state.[3] "To a large measure," Chris Miller observes, "they are engaged in the delivery of state-defined public services, not as a supplement to state provision but as a main provider" (1998, 414). How the voluntary sector is defined, and whether it exists as a sector, is the subject of considerable controversy.[4] Most definitions exclude unmediated acts of volunteering and focus on organizations that are not-for-profit, significantly engage volunteers and are independent of other organizations (Dreessen and Reed 2000).[5] These criteria would include charitable organizations and other not-for-profit organizations in the voluntary sector that deliver public services and exclude hospitals, universities and schools that are heavily funded by government and have statutory status (Sharpe 1994). Conventionally, these are included in the "broader public sector."[6]

I argue that we use the same language

across the three sectors, but the language often has very different meanings. The problem is not simply one of poor translation from the private to the other two sectors. The inconsistencies in the meaning of productivity mask a deeper problem: leaders in the private sector have exported the concept of productivity to the public and voluntary sectors, but, in their simultaneous insistence on cost-containment in the sectors that provide public services, they are generally critical of increases in spending, even when spending on R&D, for example, is an important component of improved productivity. The problem is not simply one of poor translation of concepts as they travel across sectors. It is a far deeper problem of double standards.

REDUNDANCY, PRODUCTIVITY AND SATISFACTION

On September 11, most of the firms housed in the World Trade Center were operational again within a few hours. With only a few exceptions, data were not lost, key personnel were in place and firms were able to transmit from makeshift headquarters. That there was so little disruption is largely a function of the "redundancy" that many of the large firms had built into their operations. It was not only that they had backed up their data systems; most institutions in all three sectors do so routinely. They also backed up their most fundamental resource, their people (Coffey 2002). Essential personnel were identified, and in some cases replacement personnel were assigned in the event of an emergency. After the attack on the World Trade Center in 1993, many of the firms moved emergency command-and-control centres off-site as a protection against a second attack. These kinds of capacities existed not only among firms in the World Trade Center, who understandably might have taken such precautions, but more broadly throughout the financial sector. The large banks in downtown Toronto, for example, had built in similar kinds of safeguards.

Redundancy is usually understood as excess — unproductive — capacity. Capacity may be redundant because it has no present or foreseeable productive use. When we speak of a redundant capacity to deal with contingency, however, this kind of capacity is expressly designed to duplicate in case of breakdown or to meet unanticipated needs. The first kind of redundancy is clearly a drag on productivity, with few imaginable benefits. The second kind of redundancy reflects familiar precautionary or insurance logic, where we incur costs to protect against an improbable but highly damaging contingency. Unlike other insurance problems, when "redundant" headquarters were constructed away from the World Trade Center it was impossible to estimate the likelihood that a second attack would occur, since there were no reliable baseline probabilities. It would have been impossible to calculate the costs and benefits *ex ante* of the decision to establish and maintain off-site headquarters, since the probabilities of future attacks were unknown. The costs of doing so were known, but the benefits were hypothetical. Before the fact, we could make no determination that establishing emergency headquarters off-site was efficient. We could not even conclude that the policy was instrumentally rational: if, for example, no attack had occurred for 50 years, would we think that the costs incurred were justified?

If this seems to be a frivolous question in the wake of the subsequent attack on the World Trade Center, consider our retrospective evaluation of Y2K-related expenditure in early 2001. Billions of dollars were spent, in both the private and the public sector, to fix the anticipated problem. When significant disruption did not occur, commentators began to complain about the unnecessary expenditure and the drag of those expenditures on productivity that became apparent the following year. Some attributed malevolent motives to the computer sector; it had overblown the problem and artificially stimulated demand and unnecessary expenditure.[7] Yet it was the elaborate preparations for Y2K and the built-in redundancy that enabled most of the large firms across the financial sector to resume operations as quickly as they did in September 2001. Even financial firms that were not physically disrupted immediately went into "Y2K mode" to protect against further disruption. As a CEO of a large financial services firm in Toronto put it to me, "As we dispersed our personnel on the morning of September 11th, Y2K saved us. We all knew exactly where to go and what to do, and had all the backup personnel and procedures in place."

Firms in the private sector have shown little compunction in the last five years in building in redundancy to back up both their essential operating systems and human resources so that they could continue to deliver basic goods and services in the event of an unexpected contingency. In this case, they were relatively unconstrained by short-term considerations of productivity. It was this redundancy that proved extraordinarily valuable in a contingency that few could have imagined, much less predicted. Firms made these decisions to protect the part of their operations that they considered essential. Building in redundancy consequently becomes an indicator of importance and priority.

Before September 11, few in the public sector could justify a similar kind of investment in redundancy. On the contrary, redundancy was almost always synonymous with "inefficiency." In Canada, hospitals with "redundant" emergency and trauma capacity were considered inefficient. Public-health facilities built in almost no redundancy to cope with large-scale emergencies, as political leaders discovered to their chagrin in the wake of September 11 and accelerated fears of biological warfare.[8] A decade ago, "surplus" nurses were dismissed wholesale; today, the shortage of nurses is one of the most severe constraints on the productivity of the health-care system. Public personnel with expertise in water safety were reduced, even though the public generally considers safe water an essential public good. Much of this was done to increase short-term productivity.[9]

One can make the argument that similar practices occurred in the private sector. Large-scale dismissal of personnel in the technology sector, for example, has followed the downturn in technology stocks over the last few years. Henry Mintzberg and his colleagues, in a trenchant analysis of the "culture of selfishness" that enables these kinds of dismissals, argues that in the last decade corporations have lost their capacity to balance the legitimate claims of all their stakeholders and now respond first and foremost to shareholders (Mintzberg 2002; Mintzberg et al. 2002). A short-term focus on market valuation of shares interferes with the capacity to invest over the long term to increase productivity and reduces the capacity of senior executives to manage effectively. The negative consequences of widespread dismissal are real, but they are only part of the story, for few large corporations engaged in widespread dismissal of core personnel in what they considered to be their essential services. Not so in the public sector.

There are exceptions. Arguments for redundancy are, of course, widely accepted when it comes to security and defence. We generally invest in the armed forces, intelligence agencies and policing even when perceived threats to security are low. Here, arguments for productivity do not trump all other arguments, but are balanced against others. We make these "unproductive" investments over time for several reasons. First, the state has been defined for the last three centuries by its capacity to provide security from attack. It is the priority, the "core business" of the state. We recognize the large consequences of failures of readiness in a contingency that we cannot currently predict or imagine. We also recognize the long lead time needed to develop capabilities and acknowledge that we cannot put the required capabilities in place once an emergency is upon us. Even when we anticipate a "peace dividend," we no longer reduce our investment in these kinds of capabilities below what we consider a critical threshold.

We seem to be highly selective in our thinking about public services. We do not, for example, insure against environmental catastrophe by building in "backup" capacity the way we do against military attack, even though arguably the consequences could be as catastrophic. Globally, we do not build redundant capacity to treat multi-bacteria-resistant diseases or viral epidemics, even though the fatalities from AIDS are now anticipated to exceed those of all the wars of the last century. In other words, with the exception of the priority status we give to security and defence, we generally pay less attention to the possibility that public services will be severely disrupted than do leading private-sector firms responding to market imperatives.

I find this pattern deeply puzzling. It is especially surprising given the long lead time required to build up essential services in the public sector. We understand that we need trained militaries with appropriate capabilities even if they are not being currently used. Yet we do not extend this kind of thinking to nurses, for example, an essential building block of the health-care system.[10]

It is no small irony that attention to contingency and tolerance for backup is far greater in the private sector than in the public sector, which provides the private sector as well as the public with services that are essential and that the market is unlikely to provide. It is remarkable, when we stop to think about it, that "insurance-like thinking" is more acceptable in the private sector, despite its commitment to productivity. The analogy of insurance-like thinking is illuminating, for we generally insure what is most important to us and what we cannot afford to replace if it is destroyed, even if the probability of loss is low. Large firms in the private sector identify core capacities and personnel, what is essential, what they cannot afford to lose, even if the probability of loss is low, and build in redundancy without close attention to productivity measured along short-time horizons.

When the services are public, we do far less well in identifying core capacities, and succumb to thinking about short-term productivity as if it were the only criterion. In this respect, we are more extreme in the "culture of selfishness" than the private sector. The public and voluntary sectors cannot and should not back up all their programs and all the staff that deliver public services. They too need a precautionary principle that identifies public services that are essential in an environment of uncertainty where risk cannot, by definition, be calculated with confidence. They can and should make decisions about what are essential public

services and build in the critical backup they need to deal with unforeseen contingency. The criteria for these decisions need public discussion and debate, for inevitably some difficult choices will have to be made. Here, the trade-off between efficiency and welfare is clear: devoting increased resources to these kinds of public services will inevitably reduce productivity, but may well increase welfare.

Most importantly, we should not hold these two sectors to a stricter standard in terms of efficiency, a standard urged on governments by the private sector over the last decade even while it budgeted for important contingencies. Decisions about where we build in redundancy are clearly deeper signals about what we as a society consider basic and what we consider expendable. They should be read that way.

PRODUCTIVITY AND RESEARCH AND DEVELOPMENT

Research and development is one of the keys to gains in productivity. Traditionally, it has been through the innovation that grows out of R&D that the private sector improves the effectiveness of the goods and services it delivers, brings new and better products on line, and improves the cost-effectiveness of management, production and delivery systems. Leading-edge corporations have often captured market share as a result of significant investment in R&D. It would be inconceivable today for any globally competitive firm to make no serious investment of this kind. Generally, a norm of at least 5 percent of total expenditure prevails, but many of the leading firms surpass this level.

Within large firms, there is no expectation that R&D divisions be productively efficient within short horizon terms. Rather, they are expected to generate benefits that diffuse throughout the firm and improve performance across the organization. They are evaluated not through an "internal" measure of productivity but through their contribution to the productivity of the firm as a whole. It is well acknowledged, moreover, that investment in R&D may increase productivity only in the long term, with negative implications for short-term productivity.

In the last decade the public sector has begun to learn this lesson, but in a very limited and skewed way. Political leaders have acknowledged the lagging performance in R&D in the private sector in many countries and acted to stimulate better performance. In Canada, for example, governments have recognized the importance of innovation to economic performance and have begun to invest to promote partnerships among the corporate sector, research institutes and universities to enhance R&D. Most of this investment, however, focuses on the development from basic research of spin-off goods and services that can be taken to market. The private sector has often been a willing member of the new partnerships created and partially funded by government. Here, it has not called for a reduction in government spending.

Even though governments now accept the importance of investment in R&D for the economy as a whole, they have invested alarmingly little themselves in in-house research on how public services can be improved and in centres of excellence that work on innovation in the public sector. If anything, over the last two decades political leaders have reduced the capacity for policy analysis, the analogue in the public sector to R&D, in order to reduce costs.

There are, of course, important exceptions, largely within the "broader public sec-

tor." New institutes to gather information on the performance of the health-care sector have been established, and consequently we do have much better information than we had a decade ago.[11] We can at least map the field of health care with some confidence. There has been relatively little public investment in innovation in health care, however, despite its centrality as a public good and as a component of government spending. A parallel in the private sector would be difficult to find. It is almost inconceivable that firms would make no serious investment in innovation in an area that constituted 40 percent of the goods and services they supplied to the market.

Inside government, the reduction in capacity for research and policy analysis in the last fifteen years is striking. The most visible examples were the closing of some of the most important centres of research and analysis by provincial and federal governments; the Economic Council of Canada, the Science Council of Canada, the Law Reform Commission and the Ontario Economic Council are among the best known. Inside almost every major department of the federal government, the size of policy units was frozen or reduced, significantly reducing the capacity of government to do research and serious program evaluation. This reduction in analytical capacity occurred at the same time as governments were contracting out and downloading service delivery, leaving as their principal responsibility policy analysis and development. In short, governments strangled their capacity for policy research and development even as that became their "core business." Senior officials in central agencies now bemoan the serious erosion of R&D capacity.

If governments have reduced their capacity to generate the knowledge they need to improve the cost-effectiveness of public services, the voluntary sector is even more constrained. The "third" sector has become an essential component in the delivery of public services as the state has retreated from the field over the last decade (Miller 1998; Panet and Trebilcock 1996).[12] Yet it has been severely limited in its capacity to invest in the knowledge it needs to improve its performance and to assess the cost-effectiveness of the public services that it provides.

Responding to pressures for productivity from its funders, the voluntary sector has moved to reduce its administrative costs as a proportion of the funds it raises and spends. Agencies often compete to achieve the lowest proportion of administrative costs per dollar spent on the delivery of goods and services and then proudly claim to be the most efficient.

This kind of calculation ignores the effectiveness component of the cost-effectiveness equation that constitutes productivity. As agencies race to reduce costs — and therefore staff — in response to pressure, they are less and less able to evaluate the effectiveness of the programs they deliver. They cannot learn systematically from their failures or their successes and develop a code of best practices that is constantly updated as new research becomes available. Individual agencies delivering services, especially the smaller agencies that serve local communities by now have almost no capacity to do this kind of work, but there has been almost no central coordination of investment in research and knowledge generation. Nor is there sustained capacity to share knowledge across the sector.[13] Research that is commissioned is currently charged as an administrative cost and treated as overhead, a drag on productivity, rather than as an investment in improving productivity. Somehow, the formula of the private sector has been turned on its head when funders think about the voluntary sector.

The voluntary sector is largely unable to make the kind of investment in R&D that is taken for granted in the private sector. As firms within the private sector move to become "learning organizations," leaders of many of these same firms have pressed hard for greater efficiency — translated as lower overhead — in the voluntary sector. Efficiency is translated as cost-containment rather than as improved performance in the work of agencies in the community. Consequently, the lag in the voluntary sector in R&D is stunning. It is no surprise that the pace of innovation is consequently slower and a significant impediment to improved productivity.[14] It is no exaggeration to suggest that as long as investment in R&D is considered a cost, a drag on productivity, rather than a spur to innovation and cost-effectiveness, the voluntary sector will be imprisoned within a hollowed-out concept of efficiency.

ACCOUNTABILITY AND RESPONSIBILITY

Accountability in the private sector seems relatively straightforward in comparison to that in the public and voluntary sectors. The word *accountability* derives from the old French term *comptes à rendre*, or the rendering of accounts (Dubnik 1998, 68; Keohane 2002). The private sector renders accounts to markets, and markets in turn depend in large part on the release of accurate information by corporations. Markets need accurate information to know only whether firms are profitable. They do not need to know whether the goods and services that firms supply are as effective as they can be for the cost. Individual firms do. They need to satisfy their customers or they will go out of business, so they are constantly trying to improve the quality and value of the goods and services that they sell. The challenge is to improve quality while remaining profitable.

In the wake of the scandals surrounding Enron, Arthur Andersen and WorldCom, serious challenges to corporate concepts of accountability have begun to capture widespread public attention. Concern among scholarly observers of corporate accountability, however, has been growing for over a decade. The issue is not only the accuracy of information that firms release, but the larger problem of the increasingly narrow criteria of accountability. A culture of selfishness, Mintzberg argues, has created a narrow view of society as an aggregation of "homo economicus," and a distorted concept of accountability, where firms are principally accountable to shareholders. No longer are customers central, except as purchasers of goods and services, nor are employees critical, again except as contributors directly to the profitability of the corporation and indirectly to the value of the shares. A decade ago, Mintzberg argues, shareholders were traditionally residual claimants on the corporation, after obligations to customers and employees had been met. Now, the shareholder has become the immediate and, at times, the only locus of corporate accountability (Mintzberg 2002).

Not only has the locus of corporate accountability shifted and narrowed, but time horizons have shrunk. Investors respond increasingly to quarterly reports, and as shareholders become the most important focus of accountability, corporate decisions respond to shrinking horizons, with less and less capacity to invest to increase productiv-ity over the long term at the cost of short-term losses. Ironically, the hollowed-out concept of efficiency exported by the private sector to the other two sectors has now cycled back to haunt many corporate leaders and their employees. These narrowed concepts of efficiency and accountability have translated into cost-reduction when profits fall and drastic reduction of non-essential staff. It is not surprising that employees feel less and less loyal to their employers. The long-term results may well be troubling: less commitment, lower productivity over the long term and a reduced capacity to innovate, as even valuable employees have every incentive to move on when new opportunities arise.

The evolution of concepts of corporate accountability is more complex than analysis of firms alone would suggest. Even as accountability has narrowed to respond largely to investors and markets, there has been a growing emphasis on corporate "social responsibility," the responsibilities of corporations to society as a whole (Forcese 1997; Held et al. 1999; Project on Canadian Democracy and Corporate Accountability 2002). It is no accident that the language is one of social "responsibility" rather than accountability, for responsibility is both a more demanding and a less explicit concept than accountability. Responsibility derives at times from authorization by others to act, at times from representation, but more often from internalized values, which motivate people to act according to these norms and values, whether or not they are held specifically accountable.

Locally and globally, sometimes willingly and sometimes under considerable pressure, corporate leaders have begun to acknowledge their responsibility to contribute to the protection of the environment, to fairer labour practices, to the elimination of child labour in factories around the world and to the improvement of communities where they operate (Rovere 2000). Corporate leaders have moved beyond the traditional pattern of charitable investment in culture and the arts to play important roles — for example, in sponsoring educational opportunities for disadvantaged youth and in rebuilding decaying cities. More and more, they are coming to the table with the other sectors to negotiate agreements on norms and shared practices that are "responsible." Outside the corporate sector, there is a growing demand for the "social audit" of firms.

I term this kind of accountability "outward," in contrast to the more traditional model of "upward" accountability.[15] Upward or vertical accountability encompasses traditional principal-agent relationships in which one has superior authority to the other: governments to publics, corporate executives to boards, subordinates to superiors. Outward or horizontal accountability, which is much closer to concepts of responsibility, occurs among relative equals with no formal reporting relationships: different sectors of society coming together to solve shared problems, networks that link multiple nodes together in lateral relationships. It is this kind of accountability, at times animated by shared norms, at times motivated by the prospect of sanctions, that is beginning to enter corporate discourse.

How sectors integrate and balance the at times complementary and at times competing demands of upward and outward accountability gives meaning and content to the broader concept of responsibility. Leaders in the corporate sector, for example, are often caught between demands of shareholders for constantly increasing value and their accountability to other sectors and society as a whole.

I skip over the challenges of political accountability, in large part because these challenges have been the subject of serious and sustained public and scholarly investigation. The problems are well mapped. Accountability in the public sector at first glance seems to be straightforward, at least in democratic political systems. Through representation and delegation of authority, political leaders are empowered to act, but they are responsible to those who elect them. It hardly needs saying, however, that citizens are increasingly dissatisfied with their capacity to hold their governments accountable in meaningful ways. The "democratic deficit" has been the subject of an enormous amount of investigation and discussion, and proposals for enhancing political accountability are rife. In the last two decades, as governments have moved to private-public partnerships to deliver public services, in part to become more productive, the problem of accountability has become even more acute. Governments and citizens are struggling with new kinds of outward accountability even as the traditional forms of upward accountability remain inadequate.

The challenges of accountability in the voluntary sector have received much less scholarly and public attention. Governments have devolved the delivery of public services not only to the private sector, but also to the voluntary sector, and in the process have layered new problems of accountability over already existing difficulties. In Canada, the federal government funded and created the Voluntary Sector Initiative (VSI), a partnership between the government and voluntary-sector leaders to improve service delivery, to increase the capacity of the sector and to reform its regulation. The focus is on fairer and more transparent registration of charities so that they are more accountable, and the reform of regulatory institutions and current restrictions on advocacy (Brock 2001; Institute for Media, Policy and Civil Society 2001, 2002; Panel on Accountability and Governance in the Voluntary Sector, 1999). Voluntary organizations are expected to be productive in the way they deliver goods and services as well as transparent and accountable.

The demand from donors, funders and government for accountability on the part of the voluntary sector is reasonable and appropriate. It is inconceivable that the voluntary sector, alone among the three sectors, would not meet the demands for productivity and upward accountability that the other sectors are required to meet. As we unpack the language of accountability in the voluntary sector and decode its meaning, however, we gradually come to see its dark side.

Accountability requires, at a minimum, performance set against a standard. The first issue is how the standard is determined. We have seen that the voluntary sector has not been able, as it has struggled to reduce its administrative costs, to make the investment in R&D proportionate to those of the other two sectors. The knowledge base for standards of performance is much thinner in this sector than it is in the other two. The loop between outcomes and performance has not received the same kind of careful investigation and research.[16] This sector, moreover, has generally not had the resources to share best practices as well as the private and public sectors. Determination of an appropriate standard consequently becomes much more problematic.

In the absence of a strong knowledge base, the relevant question then becomes who sets the standard — is it the funder, the organization or agency, or the client? Internationally,

global financial institutions have moved aggressively to set uniform standards of performance to increase productivity, and often have established criteria of accountability, with little attention to the knowledge and experience of the non-governmental organizations that deliver the programs. The World Bank, for example, aggressively urged the marketization of health-care services in many poorer countries in the mid-1990s. Local NGOs were held to strict measures of outputs, despite their warnings that much of what they would accomplish was unsustainable because the necessary local infrastructure was lacking, especially in the countryside. NGOs often found themselves trapped between the standards of large institutional funders and the needs of the communities they served. In this sense, they were caught, and at times caught deeply, between upward accountability for productivity and outward responsibility. The former is in direct tension with the latter.

The same kinds of dilemmas arise within Canada, although not as acutely. As governments have stepped back from service delivery, it is the voluntary sector that has largely filled the gap, sometimes with and sometimes without government funding. When governments do fund, they set standards of performance and, sometimes in consultation with agencies and sometimes not, set the benchmarks for performance. Local agencies, with deep knowledge of their communities, find themselves caught between funder-imposed standards and their sense of responsibility to the communities they serve.

The creation of standards of accountability is complicated further by the issue of appropriate time horizons for evaluation. For programs that deliver very specific services to identifiable communities, timelines are not a significant issue. When programs are designed to address complex social problems and to build capacity, appropriate timelines become problematic in any scheme of accountability. If timelines are too short for a proper assessment, then upward accountability again competes directly with outward responsibility. Local agencies are forced to abandon programs and the people they serve, despite their engagement with the community and their deep knowledge of local needs.[17]

In considering accountability, there are intriguing parallels between the private and voluntary sectors. The private sector exported its language of productivity to the voluntary sector, but in the translation the concept was so narrowed that it came to mean the lowest administrative cost. The push to cut administrative costs reduces the capacity to invest in the research that is required not only to innovate but also to evaluate and to be held accountable. It also reduces the capacity to engage over longer time horizons and puts at risk community trust when agencies are forced to withdraw. In other words, responsibility is compromised by the demands of accountability. One of the pernicious consequences of a sense of compromised responsibility is an appreciable decline in satisfaction (or welfare), both within the agency and within the community. The push for accountability, using narrowly defined standards of productivity, is inefficient.

Ironically, these problems are not dissimilar to the challenges faced by corporations operating in a "culture of selfishness," where they are accountable principally to shareholders. Here too, short-term accountability to shareholders reduces the capacity to engage over longer time horizons and destroys commitment and trust among employees. Here too, corporate leaders face an increasingly intensified conflict between accountability and responsibility. The significant difference is their capacity to invest in R&D and protect their knowledge base for subsequent rebuilding and innovation.

CONCLUSION

When we look at the organizing language of the private sector, productivity looms large. The language of the private sector was exported to the public and voluntary sectors, but it did not travel well. Joseph Heath argues in this volume that a single-minded focus on productivity does not necessarily contribute to increased welfare. To make matters worse, as it travelled to the other two sectors, the concept of productivity was narrowed even further.

The other two sectors are constrained from making investments to deal with contingencies that may threaten or overwhelm their capacity to deliver public services, the voluntary sector even more than the public sector. They are also constrained in their capacity to invest in R&D, to build the knowledge they need and to innovate. Again, the voluntary sector is far more limited than the public sector. This knowledge gap compromises the capacity for program evaluation and for meaningful participation in the development of appropriate standards of accountability. Upwardly dictated accountability, aggravated by significant knowledge gaps, compromises responsibility.

It is not without irony that the private sector, after a decade of excess, is now beginning to confront some of the same challenges. Here too, productivity has been distorted and accountability so narrowly defined that it has been hollowed out. And here too, the sense of responsibility has been compromised, as have trust and commitment.

We know that trust and commitment are the social glue that holds our societies together (Putnam 1993). Those societies that have high levels of trust and commitment tend to prosper, while those that face deficits in social trust do not. The moral of this story may be that the language of productivity, narrowed and taken to extremes, can compromise social trust, our sense of social responsibility, our capacity to be accountable, our capacity to produce new knowledge, and even our capacity to prosper.

NOTES

1   March and Olsen (1995) conclude that the myth is useful largely as a motivator for individuals to do their best. The arguments that individual accountability is a myth and that it is useful only as a motivator are both open to challenge.

2   Economists usually distinguish further between allocative efficiency, or movement towards the productivity possibilities curve, and dynamic efficiency, the outward movement of the production possibilities curve.

3   There are an estimated 175,000 not-for-profit organizations in Canada, and estimates of their contribution to GDP range from 4 to over 12 percent, depending on how the sector is defined (Day and Devlin 1997; Sharpe 1994). The sector employs at least 9 percent of the workforce, accounting for more employment, salaries and benefits than sectors such as construction, real estate, finance and insurance (Canadian Policy Research Networks and Canadian Centre for Philanthropy [CPRN and CCP] 1998; Sharpe 1994). These data underestimate due to the way Statistics Canada has traditionally collected information. Approximately 100,000 not-for-profits are not captured by existing data (Quarter 1992).

4   There is little consensus on what constitutes the voluntary sector and whether indeed there is a single sector. It has been variously described as "charitable," "non-profit," "not-for-profit" and "voluntary." Generally, the voluntary sector encompasses those organizations that are neither part of the state nor private market-based organizations.

5   Salamon and Anheier (1997) consider not-for-profit organizations to be: (1) organized; (2) private, or institutionally separate from government; (3) self-governing; (4) non-profit-distributing — that is, they do not return profits to owners or directors; (5) voluntary — that is, their management or operation involves some degree of voluntary participation. See also CPRN and CCP (1998) and Febbraro et al. (1999).

6   The line between the public and voluntary sectors tends to blur at the edges, and the classification of individual organizations is controversial. Some, for example, include hospitals and schools within the voluntary sector, while others classify these within what has come to be called the "broader public sector." Canadian studies have generally separated out the large "statutory" not-for-profit institutions such as hospitals and universities from the rest (Sharpe 1994). For our purposes, what matters is that both sectors deliver public services.

7   One of the anonymous reviewers made exactly this kind of comment.

8   It is interesting to note, in this context, that the increase in the fear of biowarfare was not based on any change in probabilities, since the probabilities could not be calculated. Rather, experts updated in response to a single salient event. This is a common cognitive error in judgement among experts.

9   The reduction in public-sector capacity in the mid-1990s in Canada was driven by an acute fiscal crisis. Irrespective of the motivation, the cuts severely reduced the capacity of the public sector to deal with unexpected contingencies. The scope of the problem became apparent in the wake of September 11 as governments assessed their capacity to respond.

10   Arguably, it was not productivity arguments but cost-cutting which ignored productivity issues that led to the reduction of nurses in the health-care system across Canada.

11   Analysts of health care, for example, are increasingly dependent on the valuable information provided by the Canadian Institute for Health Information (CIHI).

12   From the financial data provided by Revenue Canada, it is not possible to separate out the revenues that not-for-profits earn in relation to government contracts from their other sources of government revenue. The not-for-profits have become the government's preferred supplier for many social services where outputs are difficult to define (CPRN and CCP 1998, 24). Total federal grants to national organizations and provincial grants to not-for-profits grew 4.5 percent annually from 1994 to 1997. In Ontario, in 2000-2001, approximately $9 billion was transferred to 10,000 not-for-profits that provided over 200 programs in 19

273

ministries. These data exclude hospitals, schools and universities. In Ontario, there has been an increase of 227 percent in the past decade in the contracting of not-for-profits to deliver public services. (Interview, Ontario Public Services, 27 June 2002.)

13   There are, of course, important exceptions. In Canada, the Centre for Voluntary Sector Research and Development is a partnership of the voluntary sector, the University of Ottawa and Carleton University to undertake collaborative research on governance, policy and management. The Peter F. Drucker Canadian Foundation seeks to recognize innovative work in the not-for-profit sector. The Masters of Management for National Voluntary Sector Leaders is delivered through a partnership between McGill University and the J.W. McConnell Family Foundation; it has played a leadership role in educating leaders and building capacity across the sector to share knowledge.

14   The American United Way Movement is now exploring the creation of a National Center of Excellence through a strategic partnership with a major university in the United States. Its mandate would be to develop new strategies, practices and products in partnership with local United Ways, conduct focused research, and publish relevant studies and reports. Such a Center, with a projected annual budget of $15 million, would begin to speak directly to the gap in investment in R&D. Currently, the United Way of Toronto is beginning to explore the creation of a Centre for Excellence in Innovation and Knowledge (United Way of Greater Toronto 2002).

15   I use these concepts somewhat differently from others who write about vertical and horizontal accountability. See O'Donnell (1999), Schmitter (1999) and Keohane (2002).

16   The title of a recent article reviewing the sector, "What We Should Know About the Voluntary Sector but Don't," is illuminating (Dreessen 2001). Dreessen argues that the gaps in knowledge about the voluntary sector in Canada are so large that the sector cannot effectively be mapped.

17   A third challenge is the seemingly trivial issue of the reporting requirements established by funders. As government and other donors move increasingly to fund programs, it becomes more difficult to finance expert staff and other overhead. The reporting demands in parts of the voluntary sector have become so onerous in the last decade that many agencies do not have adequate staff to meet the demand. This is especially true for agencies that are engaged directly in service delivery. One small agency in Toronto revealed that it had to complete more than 140 reports to funders last year. The agency could not afford the professional staff required to meet the complex reporting requirements. There is a serious shortage of capacity in the voluntary sector that delivers public services to local communities, in terms of both available staff and levels of knowledge and skills.

REFERENCES

Brock, K.L. 2001. "Promoting Voluntary Action and Civil Society Through the State." *ISUMA* 2(2): 53-61.

Canadian Policy Research Networks and Canadian Centre for Philanthropy. 1998. *The Voluntary Sector in Canada: Literature Review and Strategic Considerations for a Human Resources Sector Study*. Ottawa: CPRN and CCP.

Coffey, C. 2002. Discussion with the author. June 4.

Day, K.M., and R.A. Devlin. 1997. *The Canadian Nonprofit Sector*. Ottawa: Canadian Policy Research Networks.

Dreessen, E.A.J. 2001. "What We Should Know About the Voluntary Sector But Don't." *ISUMA*. Vol. 2, no. 2.

Dreessen, E.A.J., and P.B. Reed. 2000. "Treatment of the Voluntary Domain in Canadian Official Statistics." *Nonprofit Sector Knowledge Base Project*. Ottawa: Statistics Canada.

Dubnik, M.J. 1998. "Clarifying Accountability: An Ethical Theory Framework." In *Public Sector Ethics: Finding and Implementing Values*, ed. C. Sampford, and N. Preston, with C.-A. Bois. London: Routledge.

Febbraro, A.R., M.H. Hall, and M. Parmegiani. 1999. "Developing a Typology of the Voluntary Health Sector in Canada: Definition and Classification Issues." Prepared for the Voluntary Health Sector Project. Ottawa: Canadian Policy Research Networks.

Forcese, C. 1997. *Commerce with Conscience?* Montreal: International Centre for Human Rights and Democratic Development.

Held, D., A. McGrew, D. Goldblatt, and J. Perraton. 1999. *Global Transformations*. Stanford, CA: Stanford University Press.

Institute for Media, Policy and Civil Society. 2001. *The Law of Advocacy for Charitable Organizations — the Case for Change, Options for Change*. Vancouver: Institute for Media, Policy and Civil Society.

——— 2002. *Let Charities Speak: Report of the Charities and Advocacy Dialogue*. Vancouver: Institute for Media, Policy and Civil Society.

Keohane, R.O. 2002. "Political Accountability." Paper prepared for the Conference on Delegation to International Organizations, Park City, Utah, May 3-4.

March, J., and J. Olsen. 1995. *Democratic Governance*. New York: Free Press.

Miller, C. 1998. "Canadian Non-Profits in Crisis: The Need for Reform." *Social Policy and Administration* 32(4):401-419.

Mintzberg, H. 2002. "Beyond Selfishness." Available: www.henrymintzberg.com

Mintzberg, H., R. Simons, and K. Basu. 2002. "Memo to CEOs." *Fast Company* (June).

O'Donnell, G. 1999. "Horizontal Accountability in New Democracies." In *The Self-Restraining State: Power and Accountability in New Democracies*, ed. A. Schedler, L. Diamond, and M.F. Platter. Boulder, CO: Lynne Rienner.

Panel on Accountability and Governance in the Voluntary Sector. 1999. *Building on Strength: Improving Governance and Accountability in Canada's Voluntary Sector*. Ottawa: Panel on Accountability and Governance in the Voluntary Sector.

Panet, P., and M. Trebilcock. 1996. "Contracting Out Social Services." WPS 20. Toronto: Centre for the Study of State and Market, University of Toronto.

Project on Canadian Democracy and Corporate Accountability. 2002. "Report of the Project on Canadian Democracy and Corporate Accountability." Available: www.corporate-accountability.ca

Putnam, R. 1993. *Making Democracy Work: Civic Traditions in Modern Italy*. Princeton, NJ: Princeton University Press.

Quarter, J. 1992. *Canada's Social Economy*. Toronto: James Lorimer.

Rovere, D. 2000, 26 September. *Canadian Corporate Contributions to Democratic Development and Citizen Participation in Developing Countries: Recommendations on Identifying and Supporting Corporate Efforts through Canadian Foreign Policy*. Ottawa: Centre for Innovation in Corporate Responsibility.

Salamon, L.M., and H.K. Anheier. 1997. *Defining the Nonprofit Sector: A Cross Sectional Analysis*. Manchester and New York: Manchester University Press and St. Martin's Press.

Schmitter, P. 1999. "The Limits of Horizontal Accountability." In *The Self-Restraining State: Power and Accountability in New Democracies*, ed. A. Schedler, L. Diamond, and M.F. Platter. Boulder, CO: Lynne Rienner.

Sharpe, D. 1994. *A Portrait of Canada's Charities: The Size, Scope, and Financing of Registered Charities*. Ottawa: Canadian Centre for Philanthropy.

Stein, J.G. 2001. *The Cult of Efficiency*. Toronto: Anansi.

United Way of Greater Toronto. 2002, May. "Community Building." Discussion document. Toronto: United Way of Greater Toronto.

Social Policy, Inequality and Productivity

Social Policy and Productivity Growth: What Are the Linkages?

Richard G. Harris

INTRODUCTION

The equity versus efficiency argument has been the bread and butter of economic policy and social policy discussions since the emergence of the modern welfare state in the post-Second World War period. In virtually all aspects of policy, the twin goal of promoting economic progress and promoting social justice stands as a hallmark of the modern industrial democracy. By the late 1960s the general view was that a conflict existed between the efficiency objective and the equity objective, nicely summarized in Okun's famous 1975 book, *Equality and Efficiency: The Big Tradeoff.*[1] In the 1990s a new debate has emerged covering similar, although conceptually different, ground. Productivity growth is widely regarded as the major long-run determinant of per capita income growth in industrial countries. Over the last two decades, economists have been preoccupied with understanding the sources of productivity growth, and slow productivity growth in Canada has been a major policy concern for several years. Prior to the mid-1980s, traditional economic analysis

focused on the static effects of economic policy — the so-called size-of-the-pie effects. For example, when looking at the impact of taxes on labour supply, the analysis was concerned with the one-time effect an increase in wage taxes could have on the labour supply, rather than its effect on long-run economic growth. However, it is evident that, in the longer term, how fast the pie grows is more important. The reason is simple: a small change in long-term growth rates — on the order of 1.0 percent, or even less — has dramatically larger consequences than a similar percentage change in GDP. This explains the emphasis put, in both research and policy, on understanding the factors leading to higher, or lower, productivity growth, as opposed to other factors that do not have permanent consequences on growth. Social policy might well be one factor that has an impact on growth. The expansion of the welfare state was heavily dependent on strong economic growth in the 1950s and 1960s. The fiscal repercussions of slow productivity growth, which had set in by the mid-1970s and were evident in a debt and deficit build-up by the mid-1980s, raised concerns about the sustainability of heavy social spending. For both of these reasons, the dynamics of social policy became inevitably linked with the issue of economic growth.

That growth depends on productivity is not a fact in serious dispute; but the long-run sources, or ultimate determinants, of productivity growth are not completely understood. At the most general level, this is Adam Smith's question: What are the sources of the wealth of nations? At a more restricted level, there is agreement on the proximate sources of productivity growth — new investment, human capital formation, new technology and product innovation. What drives these factors in an economy has been accounted for largely by economic determinants — that is, those impinging directly on investment, innovation, education and trade, which appear to have a direct and medium-term impact on productivity growth. However, recent research has put forward the hypothesis that social factors may also be a major determinant of productivity growth. Social factors would include the distribution of income and wealth in an economy, the range of social policy interventions including health, education, labour market regulation and a variety of income support programs. These social policies may be defined to include the tax-transfer system, which finances the social budget. The implications of this change of perspective are potentially quite powerful in making a case for social policy. If it could be established that social determinants are a quantitatively major factor in productivity growth, then the traditional efficiency-equity tradeoff may not exist. Social policies to promote equity could also be defended on grounds that they simultaneously increase economic growth. The tradeoff is replaced by a virtuous circle in which equity-enhancing policies also promote economic growth. This paper provides a critical evaluation of these arguments.

The paper present a survey of the evidence and debate on the social determinants of productivity in the context of the Canadian productivity debate. It examines both the basic theoretical arguments and the evidence advanced by economists, and their relationship to what might be called modern social policy. Not all social policy is directly motivated by equity considerations. In particular, modern social policies in the area of education and health focused on promoting the growth of human capital represent one category where both the evidence and debate on the growth effects are qualitatively different from those in other areas of social policy.

It is instructive to consider the context in which this often heated, and at times politically loaded, debate surrounding the impact of social policy on economic growth has taken place. Three trends have been driving the wider debate in industrial countries — all of which are noticeable in Canada. First, the slow growth in Europe, particularly of employment, had led many to put the blame on the welfare state.[2] "Eurosclerosis" became the term employed to describe the slow growth and poor employment record of a number of European countries through the 1980s and early 1990s. A parallel debate in the Scandinavian countries has led many to the conclusion that the Scandinavian welfare state had similar consequences. Assar Lindbeck's critique is one of the most well-known (see Lindbeck 1975, 1995). Part of the European record was the perception that generous social programs were a major factor responsible for the poor growth record. This debate was fuelled in part by the famous *OECD Jobs Study* (1994) and an attack by all OECD governments on the growth of debt and deficits in the mid-1990s. It may well be that the factors behind the slow employment growth in Europe ultimately have little to do with long-term productivity growth; but in the popular debate, the impacts of the European welfare state on productivity, employment and fiscal policy tend to get lumped together. Canada is typically viewed as somewhere between the United States and Europe on the welfare state spectrum, so that these arguments have likewise played out here.

A second major element, of more recent origin, is the debate on the "new economy" in the United States in contrast with the slow growth in Europe. The long and extraordinary economic expansion in the United States throughout the 1990s was accompanied by high employment and strong productivity growth. While the sources of this growth remain a matter of discussion, the new economy hypothesis claims that it is driven by the impact of innovations in the information, communications and telecommunications fields, giving rise to an entirely new phase of economic development — the so-called Third Industrial Revolution. Prior to the recent surge in growth, beginning in the mid- to late-1970s but continuing into the 1980s, there was a significant rise in market income inequality in the United States and the United Kingdom. These trends have subsequently shown up in most OECD countries, including Canada, but in Europe particularly it appeared that inequality was not increasing to the same degree. The acceleration of growth in the United States during the 1990s led some to infer that inequality contributed to growth. The divergent US and European growth patterns in the 1990s have brought

the charge that the redistributive and labour-market policies responsible for Eurosclerosis have also prevented Europe from experiencing the growth benefits of the new economy. Economic growth and the preservation of equality as seen through this debate appear to be conflicting goals, reinforcing the old view that equity and growth are in opposition with one another.

Thirdly, an intellectual challenge to the existence of an equity-efficiency tradeoff emerged at about the time that the Eurosclerosis debate began. In the mid-1980s economists began to seriously rethink the sources of economic growth, which led to both the New Growth Theory[3] and a large empirical literature on the determinants of growth and productivity. The development of new data sets for a large number of developing and developed countries allowed researchers to pose new and interesting questions about the sources of growth. Much if not all of the intellectual impetus to discover links between social factors and growth is found in this literature on cross-country growth comparisons. In the early 1990s a number of researchers identified a robust negative empirical correlation between measures of inequality and economic growth — lower inequality would be associated with higher growth. Other researchers began to look for other policy determinants of growth, many of which bear directly or indirectly on the issue of social policy, such as education and fiscal policy. Lastly, a voluminous literature has emerged on the rising wage inequality in advanced industrial countries over the last two decades. While not directly about productivity and social policy, the wage inequality issue figures prominently in the productivity-social policy debate, for a simple reason. Much of this literature adopts the opposite perspective — what is driving inequality is economic growth, which in turn is driven by technological change. From this perspective, understanding the consequences of any policy intervention on inequality and growth requires an understanding of the complex interaction between technological change and productivity growth, and its implications for wages and employment.

My purpose in this paper is to try to make sense of these often seemingly contradictory pieces of theory and evidence linking social policy to economic growth. Essentially the paper looks at two areas of research: the growth and inequality debate, and the small but growing literature on the policy determinants of economic growth. To provide the context for this discussion, the paper also includes some background material on economic growth, productivity and social policy in OECD countries.[4]

By way of a caveat, the paper is focused specifically on issues that are pertinent to Canada, or at least to countries like Canada — those with a democratic, high-income, small, open OECD economy. Nothing in what follows is meant to prescribe what development strategies are, or are not, appropriate for the developing world. The paper does not discuss the other main objectives of social policy that are not directly related to growth. Lastly, the paper does not discuss two areas of social policy that do have growth effects but are not directly related to the productivity issue. These are: the effects of social security reform on savings — a very active debate driven by the aging population issue; and the effects of labourmarket regulation on employment, which have been extensively discussed since the release of the *OECD Jobs Study*.[5]

My main conclusion is in the form of a non-conclusion. This is one case where strong policy conclusions are well ahead of both the-

ory and evidence. Neither provides conclusive support for the proposition that either (a) policies directed at reducing inequality will increase productivity growth, or (b) increased social spending will raise productivity growth. Both advocates and opponents of such policies will find little comfort in these conclusions: advocates, for the obvious reason that they are left in the position of dealing with the charge that equity and efficiency are often conflicting goals; opponents, because the evidence is often sufficiently indecisive to leave ample room for a priori reasoned arguments to the contrary. Lastly, it should be stressed that most of the research is relatively recent. It is entirely possible that the balance of evidence will shift one way or the other as new studies are published.

SOME BACKGROUND: PRODUCTIVITY GROWTH AND SOCIAL POLICY

Productivity Growth: Concepts and Framework[6]

Economic growth is measured as an increase in real economic output per person at the national level and is generally regarded as reflecting four factors:

> capital accumulation

> employment growth relative to population growth

> external market factors

> productivity growth

Of these four factors, productivity growth has generally been found the most important for industrial countries. However, all the other factors can play an important role at various times. For example, a sudden increase in the fraction of the population that is employed would have substantive effects on growth for a few years. Moreover, a strict additive decomposition of these four factors could easily lead to incorrect inferences as to what is driving growth. For example, an increase in productivity growth caused by the availability of new technologies can lead to greater investment, which has an additional knock-on effect on the growth rate. Causality can also run the other way — investment can carry spillover effects through improved knowledge flows, leading to higher productivity.

The *productivity* of an economic activity is defined by economists as the ratio of an index of outputs to an index of inputs. It can be defined at the level of an individual performing a certain task, a plant producing a particular good, a firm carrying out a diverse set of economic activities, an industry, or an entire country. Productivity goes up when you can get more output with the same inputs. The definition of productivity hinges critically upon how one measures the inputs and the outputs. In the economic literature, the starting point is a production function depicting a microeconomic relationship at a point in time and mapping input to outputs. So we write, for example:

$$Y = AF(K,L)$$

where Y is output, K and L are measures of capital and labour, $F(K,L)$ is a time-invariant functional relationship between capital and labour, and A is a time-varying parameter, referred to as an efficiency parameter or total factor productivity (TFP) parameter. The productivity level is defined as the output per unit of labour input — the average labour productivity — either per worker or per hour worked, defined as Y/L. In this framework, productivity growth is the sum of two effects: the increase in the TFP parameter A, and the

increase in capital per worker K/L. This approach is extremely well-known and is used at both the individual micro-unit level and the level of the entire economy.[7] In the latter case, output is measured as real GDP and L is either the working population or the total number of hours worked. At the macro level, A is also referred to as the *stock of knowledge*, in line with the recent emphasis on knowledge as the truly ultimate determinant of technological feasibility. In practice, growth in A is invariably done by attributing to it what other factors cannot explain. In macroeconomics, this is often referred to as the Solow residual. For most industrial countries, growth in labour productivity is accounted for by changes in A, while relatively little growth is accounted for by changes in capital per unit of labour. However, the range of estimates varies considerably.[8]

While this framework is conceptually simple and widely used because productivity growth can be identified by the residual method (i.e., the change in A calculated by subtracting from the growth in Y a weighted average of the growth in K and L), it has long been recognized that this approach presents some serious shortcomings. In particular, there is no institutional context describing how economic incentives are determined, where new technology comes from, or what factors determine investment. The major accounts of the Industrial Revolution or of economic development offered by economic historians place great emphasis on these last factors.[9]

A more general diagram depicting the determinants of productivity growth is given in Figure 1, which distinguishes between three interrelated categories — the economic determinants of productivity, the social determinants of productivity, and the policy and

FIGURE 1
A Conceptual Framework for the Analysis of Productivity

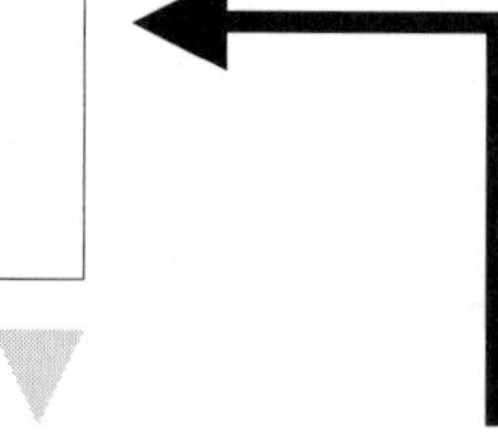

Economic Determinants of Productivity
- Investment
- New Technology and Innovation
- Human Capital
- Market Structure / Openness
- Business Cycle Factors

284

Social Determinants of Productivity
- Wealth Inequality
- Income Inequality
- Social Cohesion
- Trust and Association
- Political Stability

Policy and Institutional Framework
- Macroeconomic Policy
- Microeconomic Policy
- Social Policy
- Financial Market Structure
- Education System
- Political Structure
- Legal System

A direct or medium- to short-term causal linkage

A foreign or long-term indirect linkage

institutional framework in which these factors interact. The arrows indicate the possible directions of causality running between the three sets of interrelated factors. It is conventional to distinguish between the direct effect and the indirect or feedback effect each of these variables has on each other. It is generally agreed that investment, particularly in machinery and equipment, has the most direct measured impact on business sector productivity. This shows up in both country microstudies and cross-country studies. Many social determinants could have an impact on productivity growth through their effect on investment. For example, greater political stability contributes to investment growth by reducing uncertainty; this greater investment in turn raises productivity growth, which leads to high economic growth. More generally, government policies — economic and social — probably have some medium-term effect on productivity growth via their impact on the economic determinants of productivity growth, such as investment. However, both economic and social policy also impact on the social determinants of productivity growth. For example, education policy affects both the average level of human capital in the economy and the longer-run wage distribution between skilled and unskilled workers, which in turn affects future investments in human capital. There are also linkages running between the economic and social determinants to the list of institutional and policy factors. Greater income inequality can influence political decisions on social policy, for example, which would have second-round effects on growth and inequality, and so on. For the purposes of this paper, these highly indirect factors will be mentioned only occasionally, largely because there is not a lot of evidence in the literature. However, they certainly figure prominently in the larger debate on the sources of differences in national economic performance.[10]

One of the major problems affecting research on the deeper causal pathways running from policy to growth is the time frame involved. Tax policy changes are likely to affect investment next year; education policy reforms may not change the stock of human capital in the economy for years to come. This time-horizon problem has forced researchers to use empirical data and methods that are capable of identifying medium-term measurable linkages between particular inputs and economic growth. Much of the cross-country research, for example, tries to identify the long-term effect of policy on growth by using averages of long-term growth rates over long periods, often two or more decades, and samples of countries with vastly different levels of economic development. The difficulty with this approach is that one is forced to assume that the effect of a given variable on growth is the same for all countries, thus ignoring potentially significant differences between countries in the way a given policy or social factor might impinge on growth.

As discussed in a companion paper to this (Harris 1999), the bulk of the micro evidence on productivity is primarily about the so-called economic determinants. This reflects both data availability and the fact that eco-

nomic theories linking these factors to productivity growth have received a lot more attention from economists than potential social determinants. We now turn to a description of where this evidence stands, and a review of recent trends in social policy.

Economic Determinants of Productivity

The bulk of the productivity literature is concerned with either (a) measuring productivity, or (b) attempting to assess the quantitative importance of a set of limited economic determinants, largely at the microeconomic level but also at the macroeconomic level. The determinants that have received the most attention are investment, human capital, innovation and diffusion of technology, effects of international and domestic competition, various forms of knowledge spillovers, and most recently geographic agglomeration of economic activity. The success of these explanations has varied. Beyond the first four explanations, the measured effects are highly variable and in many cases difficult to detect statistically.

The social policy-inequality-growth debate has been partially motivated by and conducted almost entirely within a macroeconomic framework focused on national comparisons. This is not surprising since differences in social determinants are generally regarded as having systemic economy-wide effects that would tend to impact on all sectors of the economy. The search for empirical regularities has therefore largely focused on differences between economies, averaged over a number of years. Attributing differences in productivity growth across time within a national economy to a single policy is fraught with difficulty. In particular, the

285

fact that so many economic variables tend to trend together makes it impossible to prove the importance of one particular factor relative to any number of others. The most prevalent form of evidence that has been offered in the modern debate, therefore, is either reduced-form or structural growth equations in which the explanatory variable is the average growth of GDP per worker, or per hour, across a number of countries. Researchers in this area are well aware of the possible complex causal relations linking these variables at the aggregate level. Success may thus be judged by the standard scientific criteria of demonstrating that a few variables explain the data fairly well, or that particular variables show up repeatedly as quantitatively significant, despite variations in the data or statistical methods used. So far, it has been difficult to show that the economic determinants do a fairly good job in explaining the growth experience of countries at all levels of economic development.

Using a full sample of countries at all stages of development and only a limited set of economic variables leaves a lot to be explained. In discussing this issue, Hall and Jones (1999) point out that vast differences in income levels cannot be explained by savings behaviour or even measured human capital levels:

> *Output per worker in the five countries with the highest levels of output per worker in 1988 was 31.7 times higher than output per worker in the five lowest countries (based on a geometric average). Relatively little of this difference was due to physical and human capital: differences in capital intensity and human capital per worker contributed factors of 1.8 and 2.2, respectively, to the difference in output per worker. Productivity, however, contributed a factor of 8.3 to this difference:*

> *with no difference in productivity, output per worker in the five richest countries would have been only about four times larger than in the five poorest countries. In this sense, differences in physical capital and educational attainment explain only a modest amount of the difference in output per worker across countries.* (92)

International productivity differences (in levels) are enormous and any coherent explanation will have to rely on institutional and social infrastructure factors. The relevance of this to the OECD countries — many have very similar levels of economic development and quite similar institutional structures — is questionable. For these countries, similarities in institutions and developmental stages imply that the sources of growth are more likely to be found in a common set of factors. Most economic theories simply assume the problem away. Contemporary growth theory largely assumes a well-functioning market system with efficient financial markets, and markets that clear (most of the time) for labour and capital. Are these theories — now textbook material for most graduate students — capable of describing the modern economic growth experience of advanced countries? The answer is not a decisive yes or no, but, as we will see below, the support for these models in the case of industrial countries is fairly good. In general, however, the task they face is considerably less daunting than it is for models attempting to explain what Hall and Jones describe, given that the maximum difference in income levels can be expressed as factors of 2 to 3.

Growth theory and empirical work have made some progress in the last decade toward reducing the uncertainty surrounding the determinants of growth in industrial countries. Temple (1999), for example, is cautious but optimistic in his assessment of the literature. I would summarize the evidence on modern empirical growth models as involving three stages — the reduced-form literature, and then the structural models of growth without and with explicit transitional dynamics.

First, in the cross-sectional reduced-form literature, there is a consensus that relatively few variables are statistically robust in a growth equation (see Levine and Renelt 1992; Sala-i-Martin 1997). In a growth equation, average labour-productivity growth is the dependent variable with a set of potential explanatory variables on the right-hand side. The *successful* variables include:

> the initial income level at the beginning of the period

> investment-to-GDP ratios

> schooling levels

> population growth

> indicators of openness in trade and/or foreign direct investment (FDI)

Temple (2000) surveys this literature and notes that, given the lack of an explicit theoretical structure, a large number of variables have been tried and the whole literature suffers heavily from data mining. That said, the growth regression literature has been very influential, although more so with respect to developing country issues than advanced country issues. The early work also revealed a number of variables that, to some, were not good explainers of growth. These included fiscal policy, R&D measures, and various political and legal variables.

Second, an important structural model of growth is the Mankiw-Romer-Weil (1992) augmented Solow model. This is the basic neoclassical growth model of Robert Solow with exogenous savings in physical capital, to

which is added a third factor input — human capital. This is all done within a constant returns to scale aggregate production framework. The model is empirically implemented by imposing a steady-state restriction which implies that countries are on a steady-state long-run growth path for the period examined. Under this assumption, growth rates (the dependent variable) can be expressed without reference to the stocks of physical or human capital, but as functions of the savings rate, a schooling variable, and an initial productivity level assumed to be randomly distributed across countries. Attempts to make this model fit OECD cross-sectional data have not met with much success. This can be regarded as either a failure of the theory or a reflection of the fact that the steady-state restriction is too constraining.[11]

Third, the 1990s have brought a variety of structural growth models that incorporate human capital and drop the assumption that observed growth is of the steady-state kind. By incorporating dynamic transition effects to allow theoretical growth rates to vary over time, the models have met with somewhat more success. Barro (1991) was an early pioneer in this area, but numerous methodological, measurement and econometric improvements have been made over the last decade. A good technical survey of this literature is provided by Durlauf and Quah (1999), and it is covered in part in the Barro and Sala-i-Martin (1995) textbook. More significantly, the most recent versions of these models use panel data that exploit both cross-sectional and time series variation and are estimated using a variety of what are referred to as *dynamic panel methods*. Initially, there was some debate about the way in which the human capital variables should enter the model and some of the early results on human capital were quite odd. However, this human capital paradox has recently been largely resolved. Many of these estimates support the view of close to non-diminishing returns to a broad measure of human and non-human capital. Non-diminishing returns imply that increases in broad capital per worker yield incremental output increases that do not diminish as more capital is added. This comes very close to supporting what is known as *endogenous* long-run growth. Endogenous growth, as developed by Romer (1990) and Lucas (1988), occurs when a policy variable, such as the savings rate, can have a permanent effect on the *growth rate* as opposed to the long-term level of income. Non-diminishing returns to capital are a sufficient condition for a growth model to generate endogenous growth. A model exhibits exogenous growth when policy variables have only transitional effects on growth rates, although they can impact on steady-state levels of income. The Mankiw-Romer-Weil model is an example of an exogenous growth model.

Measurement and data issues have turned out to be quite important in this literature. Changes in data on capital stocks, human capital and specific economic policy variables have tended to have a substantial effect on estimated parameter values (see Temple 1999).

Policy enters these models either as an additional explanatory variable or as a structural characteristic of the model. While in principle one can distinguish between endogenous and exogenous growth models, empirically identifying the effect of a policy variable on the steady-state income level *versus* the medium-term growth rate has proven to be very difficult with data sets covering 20 to 30 years. This is simply because convergence in these models is relatively slow, and when the

share of profit and returns to human capital becomes large (on the order of 2/3 or greater for most high-income countries), endogenous and exogenous growth models begin to behave qualitatively in a very similar fashion. A lot of the most recent literature works largely within an augmented Solow framework, in which policy impacts on the transitional growth rate, although the effects can last for a couple of decades. Policy is often discussed in terms of its impact on the *rate of convergence*. This refers to the fact that holding policy constant, these theories predict income levels that tend to converge to the steady-state income level. The rate of convergence is defined by reference to how long the process takes. Typical estimates are in the range of 15 to 30 years. When an economy is out of steady-state growth, which is usually assumed to be the case of interest, changes in policy impact on the rate of convergence as well as on the long-run level of income. Other things being equal, a policy that raises long-run income and has a shorter period of convergence is preferable to one that has a longer period of convergence.[12]

A recent paper by Bassanini et al. (2001) provides a good example of the use of this type of econometric model for a cross-country analysis of growth in OECD countries over the 1971-98 period with a specific emphasis on economic determinants. The basic growth model is a dynamic version of the augmented Solow model discussed in chapter 5 of Barro and Sala-i-Martin (1995) with human capital and R&D. Policy variables interact with accumulation variables and also have a potential impact on long-run steady-state levels of productivity. The model does not impose similar dynamics on all countries — rates of convergence are allowed to vary among countries — but it does assume that in the long run all countries are governed by similar parameter values up to a constant level of difference between countries. The model does quite well at tracking the data, and the authors provide an illustrative decomposition of the factors that determine aggregate productivity growth. The set of variables that explain growth includes a group of baseline variables (those derived from the basic theory) and a group of economic policy variables that shift the growth path:

Baseline variables:

> the initial productivity level
> the share of investment in GDP
> population growth
> human capital

Policy variables:

> trade intensity
> R&D expenditures
> inflation variability
> government investment
> government consumption

In the estimation of the model, government investment turned out to be insignificant, while the R&D variable had to be dropped due to limited country coverage, although both were significant on a more limited data set. Table 1 reports the decomposition of the growth rate for each country expressed as a deviation from the OECD average. Looking at the row for Canada, we see that the country's annual growth rate of

TABLE 1
Economic Determinants of Economic Growth in OECD Countries, 1971–98

Country	Annual Average Growth Rate	Growth Differential	Initial Condition GDP/Pop.	Investment Share	Human Capital	Population Growth	Variability of Inflation	Government Consump.	Trade Exposure	Residual Country-specific Effect
Australia	1.68	0.13	-0.37	0.20	0.52	-0.25	0.03	0.01	-0.41	0.40
Austria	1.57	0.02	-0.41	0.07	0.26	0.01	0.05	0.00	0.03	0.01
Belgium	1.66	0.11	-0.53	0.02	-0.15	0.20	0.03	-0.05	0.53	0.06
Canada	1.32	0.23	-0.90	-0.21	0.62	-0.18	0.04	-0.07	0.14	0.32
Denmark	1.69	0.14	-0.57	0.28	0.21	0.12	0.02	-0.14	-0.05	0.27
Finland	1.82	0.27	0.51	0.05	0.02	0.15	0.00	-0.06	-0.26	-0.14
France	1.35	0.20	-0.59	-0.09	-0.10	0.07	0.07	-0.08	0.05	0.48
Greece	1.15	-0.40	2.00	0.19	-0.56	-0.07	-0.16	0.17	-0.51	-1.48
Ireland	3.02	1.47	1.54	-0.18	-0.32	-0.18	0.01	0.09	0.17	0.34
Italy	1.73	0.18	0.22	-0.13	-0.69	0.13	0.02	0.01	0.14	0.48
Netherlands	1.26	-0.29	-0.47	-0.03	0.25	0.01	0.06	-0.13	0.52	-0.50
New Zealand	0.53	-1.02	0.34	-0.17	0.31	-0.29	-0.07	0.10	-0.36	-0.87
Norway	1.72	0.17	-0.12	-0.05	0.35	0.07	0.03	-0.06	-0.04	-0.01
Portugal	2.15	0.60	2.56	0.58	-1.20	0.07	-0.10	0.10	0.11	-1.52
Spain	1.28	-0.27	0.73	0.04	-1.12	0.00	0.03	0.07	-0.14	0.11
Sweden	1.20	-0.35	-0.60	-0.10	0.21	0.11	-0.10	-0.17	0.01	0.30
Switzerland	0.81	-0.74	-1.75	0.08	0.59	-0.04	0.00	0.15	0.02	0.21
United Kingdom	1.63	0.08	0.05	-0.21	0.17	0.15	-0.03	-0.02	0.31	-0.34
United States	1.93	0.38	-1.62	-0.34	0.63	-0.09	0.07	0.09	-0.25	1.89

Source: Bassanini et al. (2001), Table 9.

labour productivity was 0.23 percentage points above the OECD average for the period. The last column reports the country-specific residual effect, which is that part of the growth differential unexplained by the model. For Canada, it turns out that 0.32 percentage points of growth are unexplained. Factors that impact on Canada's growth relative to the OECD average include:

> a high initial income, which tended to reduce Canada's growth relative to other OECD countries, which started the period at much lower productivity levels;

> a share of investment in GDP that was lower than in other countries;

> human capital levels that account for a large positive effect on the Canadian growth differential (0.62 percentage points per year);

> openness to trade, which accounts for a positive 0.14-percentage-point growth differential; and

> population growth, government consumption levels and inflation variability, which account for very little of the growth differential.

The model performs well except for two countries, Greece and the United States. The authors note that Greece is an unusual case, which also raises some data issues. However, the US results are quite interesting. The large positive unexplained residual for the United States reflects the inability of the model to explain the acceleration of labour-productivity growth in the 1990s. To that extent, it is clear that the explanation of growth being offered by this model is less than complete. Nevertheless, the model provides an impressive example of how far modern theory and econometric methods can go in terms of explaining the growth performance of industrial countries. Providing explanations for the country-specific effects remains an important issue. There could be either social determinants or other unaccounted-for economic determinants at work. It is important to emphasize that it would appear that a large portion of economic growth can be accounted for by a relatively small set of determinants.

Social Policy

The basic policy question to be addressed is the extent to which social policy might have consequences for productivity. As most of the empirical work in the area hinges on differences among countries in social policies, this subsection provides a brief review of some indicators of social policy. In Canada, social government expenditure covers a range of public-sector activities. A typical classification scheme based on public finance theory would be as follows:

> Public goods and services — *pure* public goods such as national defence and general public services such as administration, legislation and regulation.

> Merit goods and services — quasi-public goods provided on grounds of market failure, externalities or economic justice principles. For example, government provision of education is common because citizens may ignore the social returns of human capital investment or may have limited access to capital markets. Health care is another example.

> Economic services — private goods or services prone to natural monopoly or strong externalities. Examples include public utilities and financial support for specific activities such as research and development.

> Social transfers — transfers providing support for income and living standards that have declined sharply or to individuals who face exceptional expenses due to old age, disability, sickness, unemployment or family circumstances.

Under this classification, social policy would tend to be defined in terms of spending under the *merit goods and services* and *social transfers* categories. An alternative perspective would be focused not on the classification of spending, but more directly on the goals of social policy. Social policy pursues a number of goals, including:

> increasing self-reliance
> readjusting intergenerational burdens
> improving flexibility and economic growth
> reducing the incidence of low income and child poverty
> improving the efficiency and quality of service delivery
> improving public finances
> improving social cohesion
> ensuring that basic social needs are met

Clearly, economic growth is one goal, but only one of many, and almost certainly not the most important. The recent social policy debate in many OECD countries tended to emphasize the cost side of the ledger. The *incentive cost* argument emphasizes that social protection can generate long-term welfare dependency and the capacity for flexible adjustment to shocks. The funding of social security contributions in the form of payroll taxes or general tax revenues increases the *distortionary welfare cost* of taxation. High social security and health-care contribution liabilities for employers and other non-wage labour costs can lead to lower employment, especially for low-wage unskilled workers. All of these factors might contribute to lower productivity growth.

However, in principle, social programs can facilitate economic adjustment and thus economic growth. For example, unemployment benefits can provide replacement income while people search for a job. Social protection provides collective insurance to cover risks that may occur during a person's life (such as unemployment, sickness, disability, maternity), usually at a much lower cost than if such risks were insured privately, leading to increased investments in human capital and greater mobility. Active measures to encourage and facilitate labour force participation contribute to economic growth by enhancing the flexibility of the labour force. Policies to improve the health and safety of the workforce can increase labour productivity.[13]

Assessing the productivity effects of social policy is inherently difficult. Aside from the direct human capital effects, a lot of the impact is likely to be indirect, working through changes in incentives to invest, save or work or through the induced fiscal effects on similar variables. The search for empirical regularities linking growth to social policy is almost non-existent. OECD comparisons are inevitably going to be the data most discussed in this respect. To make matters worse, these comparative data are almost all related to expenditures — that is, they measure inputs to social programs but not their outputs, which would be preferable in a productivity study. The growth literature has investigated quite extensively two categories of public spending — public investment and government consumption. Generally, the results are mildly favourable toward the productivity or growth effects of public-sector investment, and distinctly negative with respect to public-sector consumption, as is illustrated by the results reported in the last subsection. However, neither of these captures what would be called various forms of social expenditure. Differences between countries in social spending is the only form of evidence available thus far to estimate the growth effects of social policy.

Under the public finance classification of spending, Canada tends to spend relatively little on what might be called public goods or economic services. Of total public spending, a great deal is accounted for by social spending. In 1995, public goods accounted for 2.6 percent of GDP, merit goods (health, education and other social services) 12.3 percent, income transfers 11.5 percent, economic services 2.4 percent and interest on the public debt 9.6 percent. However, comparative numbers are more interesting. Table 2 compares Canada to two other countries perceived to be at opposite ends of the social policy spectrum with respect to spending on education, health and transfers — Sweden and the United States.

TABLE 2

Selected Social Expenditures as a Percentage of GDP, Canada, Sweden and the United States

	1980	1990	1995
Health			
Canada	5.0	5.4	5.8
Sweden	8.4	7.6	5.7
United States	4.0	5.2	6.5
Education			
Canada	5.4	6.7	6.5
Sweden	7.6	6.8	6.6
United States	5.3	5.3	5.0
Transfers			
Canada	8.1	10.8	11.5
Sweden	16.5	19.2	21.2
United States	9.3	8.5	9.4

Source: OECD (2000).

While there were substantial differences among the three countries in 1980, some convergence has occurred between Canada and the United States while Sweden continues to stand out in its spending on social transfers.

Here are some other characteristics of OECD social spending patterns worth noting:

> A well-established empirical regularity in public finance is what is known as Wagner's Law. The demand for certain types of social protection rises more than proportionately with the level of per capita income. While this relationship is not observed in a cross-section of countries, it holds very strongly in almost every national time series on public expenditure. This fact, usually explained by using simple arguments about voter preferences, implies that economic growth is likely to have a positive impact on social spending, confounding the detection of causal channels running in the other direction — from social spending to economic growth.

> Much of what government does is redistributive (Boadway, 1998), but the interesting fact is that the bulk of the redistribution is not from the rich to the poor. During the 1980s and 1990s the reforms to the personal tax system in nearly all OECD countries and the pressure on public budgets meant that the generosity of benefit schemes was reduced. While benefit systems redistribute income, they redistribute primarily not from the rich to the poor but, rather, from the young to the old, from those who work to those who do not, and from childless families to families with children. Social policy, therefore, is

not primarily directed at equity per se, and its growth effects are dependent on the details of specific programs.

> There has been a general and persistent upward trend in total government spending within OECD countries. From 1970 to 2000, the OECD average went from 29.2 percent to 36.5 percent of GDP. Canada went from 33.8 percent in 1970 to 46 percent in 1990, and then down to 37.8 percent in 2000 with the successive Martin budgets. The major factor to which most analysts attribute this growth is the creation and expansion of programs and the provision of services in the social policy area. The income support element of these entitlements is reflected in a persistent rise in income transfer payments until the mid-1990s.

The common social policy experience of so many countries points to the difficulty inherent in attempting to use these variables to explain differences in the growth experiences within OECD countries. However, there are some notable differences, as noted above, and these will prove important in the identification of the effects of social expenditures on productivity.

INEQUALITY, SOCIAL POLICY AND PRODUCTIVITY

In this section we review the theoretical and empirical literature that points to a causal linkage running from inequality and social policy to productivity growth. It is instructive first to assess what has been a key driving force behind the policy dimension of this debate — the recent changes in income inequality. Looking at the total income of the working population, the changes have not been as dramatic as one might imagine from the popular debate on this topic. In Table 3, the levels and changes of two standard inequality indexes, the Gini coefficient and the ratio of income of the 90th decile to the 10th decile are recorded.[14] It is well-known that total income inequality rose in the United States and the United Kingdom from the mid-1970s through the mid-1980s. These trends were never as evident in other countries. However,

TABLE 3
Inequality Levels and Changes, Working-age Population, Mid-1970s to Mid-1990s

	Levels		Absolute Changes Between Periods			
	Gini Coefficient	P90/P10 Decile Ratio	Gini Coefficient	Gini Coefficient	P90/P10 Decile Ratio	P90/P10 Decile Ratio
	mid-90s	mid-90s	mid-70s / mid-80s	mid-80s / mid-90s	mid-70s / mid-80s	mid-80s / mid-90s
Canada	28.7	3.9	0.1	0.1	-0.1	0.0
Sweden	24.7	3.1	-0.6	2.3	0.0	0.2
United Kingdom	30.4	4.1	3.7	2.7	0.7	0.4
United States	33.3	5.3	2.9	0.6	1.0	-0.1

Source: Förster and Pellizzari (2000).

from 1985 to 1995 the trends slowed somewhat. The effects on the distribution of income for the working-age population are shown for four countries: Canada, the United Kingdom, the United States and Sweden. While the level of inequality of income within the working-age population would be considered higher in Canada than in Sweden, there has been virtually no change from the mid-1970s to the mid-1990s. However, with respect to market income, the underlying trend has been similar in most countries. A recent OECD summary of the trends with respect to Canada is provided in Box 1.

What has happened in Canada is typical of a number of OECD countries: from the 1980s to the mid-1990s there was a fairly significant change in the distribution of market income towards the upper end of the distribution despite the relatively mild changes in total inequality, which measures income after taxes and transfers.[15] Specifically for Canada, from 1988 to 1995, changes recorded in the market income share of different deciles are presented in Table 4.

There is little doubt that these data have been a major factor behind the renewed interest in growth and inequality. Specifically, it is being argued that there is a causal chain running in the following sequence:

TABLE 4

Market Income Share Levels and Changes, Canada

	Share in 1995 (percent)	Change over 1988-95 (percentage points)
Three Bottom Deciles	9.6	-0.9
Four Middle Deciles	35.5	-0.5
Top Three Deciles	54.9	1.4

Social policy ⇒ Income inequality ⇒ Economic growth

with the presumption that increased income inequality lowers growth. The debate was given a great deal of impetus by two related developments in the field of economic growth: first, an empirical finding that claimed to show a positive link between lower inequality and higher growth, based on cross-sectional growth regressions; second, some theoretical work in the *new growth theory* tradition that provided a rationale for this link. In this section, we look at both developments. Finally, it should be pointed out that it has long been recognized that causal links could also run the other way — from growth to inequality — although the sign of the effect is largely viewed as ambiguous. In the broad sweep of evidence on the Industrial Revolution and economic development, the received wisdom was summarized by a concept known as the Kuznets (1955) curve, which showed that as income levels rise inequality first increases and then decreases. However, the existence of an inverted U-shaped Kuznets curve says nothing directly about growth and inequality, other than to argue that as income levels get sufficiently large, inequality will fall.

Growth-Inequality Regressions

Evidence on the positive link running from inequality to growth was first provided by Persson and Tabellini (1994), who looked at cross-sectional and time-series data for both developing and OECD countries. They found a significant *order of magnitude* effect of inequality on growth. The equations were a reduced-form growth regression with per capita GDP growth as the dependent variable and controlled for the initial GDP level (per capita)

BOX 1

Inequality Trends in Canada: An OECD Summary

In Canada, the distribution of disposable incomes remained broadly stable over the last two decades, and some summary measures point to a slight decrease in inequality. This holds for both the working-age and the elderly population. During the first period, mid-1970s to mid-1980s, there was some "hollowing out" of the middle incomes, as both the bottom and the top incomes gained income shares at the expense of the middle incomes. This trend did not continue into the second period, from the mid-1980s to the mid-1990s. Real incomes, on average, did not improve in Canada over the last 10 years; they fell for the upper incomes while the real value was maintained for those at the bottom. There was redistribution across age groups in the last ten years: relative incomes of the elderly, in particular older senior citizens, increased more than in all other OECD countries (Austria excepted), namely by 3 percent for those aged 55 to 64, by 8 percent for those aged 65 to 74 and by 10 percent for those aged 75 and over. All other age groups lost ground.

As in most other countries, the share of market income, in particular capital and self-employment income, going to the bottom deciles among those of working-age decreased, and related to that, tax shares fell, too. At the same time, Canada is one of the few countries in which the transfer share of bottom incomes did not increase during the past ten years. Nevertheless, a decomposition of levels and trends in inequality among the working-age population shows that both taxes and transfers contributed to equalize the distribution of disposable incomes over time. As in a majority of countries, a process of "employment polarisation" took place in Canada in the last ten years. However, both fully employed and workless households increased their relative incomes while those of multi-adult households with only one worker fell. The contributions of these three groups to the slight decrease in overall inequality were different: while inequality within and between those groups contributed largely to the decrease, structural changes drove overall inequality up but did not outweigh the other decreasing effects.

Source: Förster and Pellizzari (2000, pp. 36-37).

295

and schooling. They estimated that a 0.07-increase in the income share held by the top 20 percent of the population lowered the growth rate of per capita income by just under 0.5 percent — a very large effect. They argued that this result also holds for OECD historical data. Using a 70-country post-war data set, Alesina and Rodrik (1994) found that a one-standard-deviation increase in the Gini coefficient of land distribution affects growth rates by 0.8 percentage points per year. A number of studies came to similar conclusions, although it is important to note that the majority of these studies were done with samples dominated by developing countries.[16]

Very few empirical variables that have been asserted to *explain* growth have not gone unchallenged. The same can be said for inequality within samples of both OECD and developing countries. Here are some of the issues that have been raised in the growth-inequality context:

> Empirical growth regressions are very sensitive to the set of explanatory variables used. The significance and magnitude of coefficients often change when the set of explanatory variables changes. For example, most theory suggests that both investment levels and human capital should be important conditioning vari-

ables. Barro (1999) noted this sensitivity and specifically found that when fertility rates are included in the full sample (developed and developing countries), the inequality variable becomes insignificant.

> One of the major problems in this debate relates to the inclusion of both developing and high-income countries in the data sets. These countries differ not only in income per capita but also for a wide range of political and institutional factors. The convergence literature on developing countries has come to the conclusion that there appears to be evidence of non-convergence, suggesting that these differences are very persistent. How this should be dealt with statistically is a major issue. Purely cross-sectional methods have the disadvantage of imposing common parameters on a number of effects that might be expected to differ between countries at different levels of development. One way around this issue is to use dynamic panel methods of estimation that attempt to use both time-series and cross-sectional variation as a way of identifying the determinants of growth while controlling for country-specific effects.[17] One of the first to use this methodology with respect to the inequality issue was Forbes (2000), who found that once country-specific fixed effects were included, changes in inequality either had the opposite effect on growth rates or were insignificant.

> Arjona et al. (2001) adopt a panel approach to look specifically at this issue and at the level-of-development issue in a sample of OECD countries. They use the transitional version of the Mankiw-Romer-Weil model, in which growth depends on population growth, investment, initial income and human capital. They find virtually no evidence that inequality affects growth.

> Another major issue is causality. A standard criticism of much of the cross-sectional growth literature is that one can never be certain that correlation is causation. Usually, there is an attempt to control for this by using data covering long periods of growth as well as conditioning variables measured at the beginning of the period. More sophisticated studies will often try to estimate a structural model in which the causal linkages are more precise. There are a number of different theories linking inequality to growth, and the transmission channel is quite different in each case. It is unfortunate that there have been few attempts to identify the underlying structural link. For example, if increased inequality is assumed to lower human capital investment it would be useful to check whether this structural relationship exists. Perhaps future work will take this into account, but at the moment it is a major weakness of the underlying methodology.[18]

Should any of this be very surprising? Hardly, for two reasons. First, it has long been known that relatively few variables are robust in growth regressions (see Levine and Renelt 1992; Sala-i-Martin 1997). Second, there are the basic data one has to work with. With a few exceptions, there is not much variation in inequality across OECD countries relative to developing countries. The United States and the United Kingdom tend to have higher levels of inequality, but their long-term growth performance was not very different from that of most other industrialized countries until very recently. The recent surge in US growth has, if anything, added to the perception that the causality runs in the other direction. Chart 1 presents a simple plot of growth versus average income inequality.

The chart is plotted for the subset of older OECD countries (it excludes the recent joiners: Mexico, South Korea, Greece, Spain, Portugal and Turkey). Not surprisingly, there is not much to be detected here using ocular statistical methods. The search for a more complicated correlation in these data is largely what the empirical debate has been about.

On balance, the empirical case for a link running from growth to inequality for the high-income countries is at best statistically fragile and at worst insignificant. Note that none of this points to the opposite conclusion — that increases in inequality cause higher economic growth.

The Theoretical Linkages

Often in economics, in the absence of decisive evidence for or against a hypothesis, economic theory plays an important role in determining the priors of economists both as social scientists and as policy advisers. Part of the renewed interest in this debate is the new theoretical literature that shows that increases in inequality can hurt growth. Most of this theory is rooted in endogenous growth theory,[19] in which productivity growth is an endogenous characteristic of the economic system. Recent surveys that focus on inequality include Aghion et al. (1999) and Lloyd-Ellis (2000). As it turns out, however, these theoretical developments, while insightful, do not establish a strong case. They provide interesting examples of models

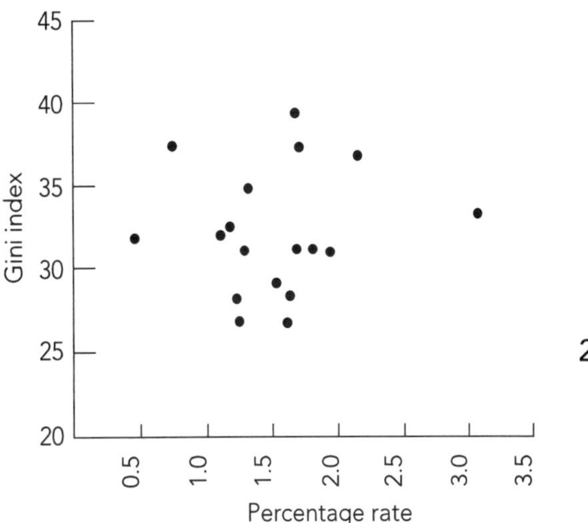

CHART 1

Growth and Inequality Scatter Plot, Average Annual Productivity Growth, OECD, 1971–98

where changes in inequality can lead to lower growth under highly specialized assumptions. To obtain these results, one must dramatically simplify the models themselves. Now, this is not a criticism. It merely serves to point out that often, in economics, theory does not suggest a one-sided causal pathway between two variables. In this particular case, there is also an older literature that suggests the opposite effect — higher inequality can raise growth. There is also a political economy literature that emphasizes the endogenous nature of policy and growth consequences.

A brief summary of the theoretical arguments is provided below.

Traditional Theory

> Kaldor (1957): With savings-driven accumulation, and assuming the rich have a greater propensity to save than the poor, more inequality leads to greater savings, which can lead to higher transitional growth rates.

> Large investment indivisibilities: Assuming that capital markets are very imperfect, significant individual wealth accumulation may be necessary to make an investment. More inequality could help growth in these circumstances by facilitating the concentration of large pools of investment funds.

> Incentive or Mirrlees-type theories (Mirrlees 1971): With imperfect monitoring of contracts due to transaction costs, moral hazard is to be expected. Borrowers using traditional debt contracts are quite likely to behave opportunistically and not always in the lenders' interest. In such cases, optimal contracts should reward output, and with heterogeneity among borrowers the successful would be rewarded, not the unsuccessful. This implies a need for *ex post* inequality in rewards to maintain incentives. Similar arguments carry through to the taxation of savings in endogenous growth models driven by capital accumulation. Taxing savings results in lowered growth (Rebelo 1991). Both classes of arguments suggest that increased income inequality, as opposed to more equality supported by a highly progressive tax system, leads to higher growth.

Political Economy Models (Persson and Tabellini 1994)

> Inequality affects taxation through the political process: In unequal societies, more voters prefer redistribution assuming the median voter determines policy outcomes. They consequently vote for redistribution, which reduces the incentives to invest and hence lowers the growth rate. Note that this argument assumes that: more inequality ⇒ more redistribution ⇒ less growth.[20]

> Social protection reduces growth through rent-seeking: This argument was made by Lindbeck (1975, 1995), who looked at the link between growth and social protection. He suggested that the universality of Scandinavian welfare states *politicized* the returns to economic activity and thus encouraged people to seek material gain through the political process, by passing redistributive legislation, rather than through entrepreneurial and innovative activity.

> A variant on the first set of theories, but with reverse implications, assumes that interest groups determine policies and that a strong social safety net exists: In the presence of a free-rider problem, interest groups work hard at preventing policies that hurt them but that otherwise may have positive, widely diffused growth effects (e.g., trade liberalization, labour market reforms). With social protection, these losses are partially insured against, thus reducing the opposition of interest groups to growth-promoting policies and increasing the likelihood that they will vote in favour of such measures.

New Growth Theory

> Imperfect markets and diminishing returns to investment: Aghion et al. (1999) refer to this as the opportunity-enhancing effect of redistribution with imperfect capital markets. Given the diminishing returns on individual investments and restrictions on the ability of individuals to pool funds, people with

large endowments have low marginal returns on investment, and conversely for the poor. Redistribution from the rich to the poor raises the average return and thus enhances growth.

> Reversal of the traditional incentive argument: This argument stresses the Mirrlees case, but with the added assumptions that the effort of borrowers is related to initial income and that limited liability effects are important. Let us assume that the probability of success of an investment project depends on the effort of the borrower, but that moral hazard exists for the usual reasons. With limited liability, individual borrowers do not bear the risk of failure (the lenders lose), and this affects their effort. If the effort increases the borrowers' own wealth, then redistribution towards poor borrowers will have a positive effect on their effort, thus promoting growth. Aghion et al. argue that redistribution will increase the effort because it reduces borrowing by the poor, who now get a larger share of residual output; with a larger share, they have an incentive to work harder.

As is evident, there are a variety of theories suggesting alternative linkages between inequality and growth. Note that most economic theories hinge on one market failure argument or another, and particularly on imperfect capital markets. In the case of a developed country, this would seem to make sense only in the context of human capital, given well-developed capital markets for other forms of investment in physical capital. If redistribution is to occur, it would have to be financed by distortionary taxes on wages and savings. This would have the traditional negative-incentive effects on growth,

which are offset or perhaps overcome by the opportunity-enhancement effect. However, it is far from evident that the appropriate policy to stimulate growth is passive redistribution of income. With inequality of access to investment across individuals, a more suitable policy response would be to either (a) reform financial institutions and markets such that able individuals could invest in education, or (b) provide more direct support for public education.

The political economy theories point to the fact that one must distinguish carefully between three related factors: inequality, which can be measured before the tax and transfer system apply; redistribution, which is income-based; and social insurance, which is situation-specific. Depending upon the assumptions made, more market income inequality before taxes and transfers may lead to greater or less redistribution *ex post*. Lindbeck views social protection as inducing greater political rent-seeking, whose opportunity cost is growth; the other view of social policy is that it provides insurance in a world with insufficient private markets for insuring risk against sickness, unemployment and so forth.

Thus, social safety nets (a) promote individual investments in human capital, and (b) reduce political opposition to growth-promoting adjustments and policies. Which of these effects is more important?

In this instance, economic theory points to interesting hypotheses and provides the empirical economist, or policy-maker, with some insight on what road marks to look for in determining the set of interactions amongst variables. Beyond that, however, the theories themselves are too diverse and too malleable to changes in assumptions or parameter choice to form a basis for reliable policy formulation without empirical validation.

Social Policy and Growth Evidence

It is entirely possible, and theoretically reasonable, that social policy might affect growth without greatly affecting income distribution. For example, many of the theoretical arguments about the consequences of active-labour market policies suggest that these could, in principle, be growth-enhancing. These same policies might also reduce the degree of market-income inequality, but one cannot be certain of this without carefully specifying the dynamic feedback effects from growth to income distribution. It is, however, reasonable to ask whether one can empirically identify the linkage between social policy and growth without reference to an intervening effect on inequality. Unfortunately, very few studies have been published on this issue, and it is one that requires further research. There is a fairly well-developed body of evidence on the effects of government spending on growth, but it generally does not distinguish government spending directed at a social policy objective from spending directed towards other objectives.[21] A large number of studies on the growth consequences of fiscal policy have documented a significant and negative effect of government consumption on growth.[22]

One innovative study that attempts to look specifically at social policy for OECD countries is Arjona et al. (2001, 2002). The authors use a framework similar to that discussed in the second section of the present paper to infer the impact of social expenditures on growth in OECD countries. The growth equation is a Mankiw-Romer-Weil transitional one that controls for investment and human capital intensity across countries, and is estimated using an annual sample of 21 OECD countries over the period 1970-88. The authors find virtually no evidence that post-tax-transfer inequality affects growth rates in OECD countries. There is some evidence that total government spending on social programs reduces growth. The magnitude of the effects is consequential. In the basic model, with aggregate social expenditure as a fraction of GDP, the coefficient is -0.134. This compares with a coefficient on the investment share of 0.345. Both are significant at the 95-percent level.[23] Quantitatively, the implication is that if one were to decrease social spending by 1.0 percent of GDP and increase investment by 1.0 percent of GDP, the impact on aggregate labour-productivity growth would be on the order of 0.5 percent per year. Not a large impact, but over a number of years it would begin to have a significant effect on income levels. Recall that until recently annual labour-productivity growth was in the area of 1.5 percent.

The authors do find, however, that when social spending is disaggregated by function the results are cleaner in terms of both significance and magnitude. Passive social spending is prejudicial to growth, while active social spending promotes growth. Interestingly, they also find that when the definition of active social spending is expanded to include health expenditures, the coefficient estimates on social spending become insignificant. When they include both passive and active social spending as explanatory variables the coefficient on passive social spending is significant and negative, while the coefficient on active social spending is significant and positive. The orders of magnitude are interesting. The coefficient estimates imply that a shift of 1.0 percent of GDP from passive to active spending produces a positive effect on growth of about 0.5 percent. Overall, the results suggest that social expenditures that promote adjustment and labour market participation tend to increase labour-productivity growth, while other forms of social expenditures do not contribute to growth and in fact may reduce it.

Obviously, one should interpret these results with caution, given the limited time-series variation in the data and other potentially omitted variables in the growth equation such as R&D and openness. Nevertheless, this is a good start on an important research and policy issue.

An alternative and in many ways unrelated body of evidence links social capital to economic growth. Social capital as defined by Putnam (1993) and Woolcock (1998) refers to the nature of trust in societies engendered by various forms of community association. One of the best known and most representative definitions can be found in the highly influential work of Putnam (1993):

> *Social capital…refers to features of social organisation, such as trust, norms, and networks, that can improve the efficiency of society by facilitating co-ordinated actions.* (167)

To an economist, as Arrow pointed out long ago, trust is an important substitute for markets and contracts. *A priori*, one would imagine that more trust would imply higher growth. The issue is pertinent to the debate on social policy because there is a strong presumption that social cohesion and social capital are closely related, as argued by Ritzen et al. (2000). A major objective of social policy is the creation of social cohesion. These authors argue that social cohesion creates an environment in which good policy is possible if policy-makers are given room to manoeuvre. The latter is created by reducing societal conflict over distributional objectives, in part through common institutions such as social policy.

However, the empirical evidence on social trust and growth is simply non-existent, so there seems to be little point in continuing in this vein. What evidence exists from cross-country comparisons based on the World Values Survey seems to show that a higher index of *trust* actually leads to lower growth rates (see, e.g., Knack and Keefer 1997). When Knack and Keefer exclude socialist countries and focus on a more recent period (1980-92), they get stronger results. Controlling for initial income per head, human capital and the relative price of investment goods, an increase of 10 percentage points in the level of their *trust* index (slightly less than one standard deviation) is associated with an annual growth rate higher by 0.8 percentage points. Typically, the results are weaker when attention is restricted to a sample of OECD countries. Also using World Values Survey data, Helliwell (1996) found that trust has a negative effect on growth in a sample of 17 OECD countries. Knack (2000) reports that in a sample of 25 OECD countries the impact of trust is imprecisely measured, and the hypothesis that it has no effect cannot be rejected at conventional significance levels. This literature may prove to be influential at a future date, but thus far there is little in it that could be used as a major justification for policy.

CONCLUSION

The linkages between economic growth and productivity are both complex and subject to a variety of potential causal mechanisms. This paper has reviewed the evidence and theory linking the social determinants of productivity growth, which include such factors as the distribution of income and wealth in society; the set of social policies existing in a country, including social insurance and redistributive programs and the education and health systems; and the degree of social cohesion. The complexity in uncovering a link running from social factors to productivity growth is compounded by the fact that these broad institutional arrangements, including the social determinants but also the political and legal systems, may have indirect effects in the long run that are difficult if not impossible to detect in conventional economic data. In spite of these problems, there is a new body of research, both theoretical and empirical, that attempts to identify the relationship among social policies, economic inequalities and productivity growth.

The traditional economic debate on these matters was usually framed in terms of the equity-efficiency tradeoff, in which more economic growth could be achieved only at the expense of increased economic inequality. The newer literature suggests that, in fact, growth and social objectives may be complements rather than substitutes. This certainly provides a more optimistic view of the choices facing governments than has been the case based on the existence of a growth-equity tradeoff.

While these recent empirical and theoretical contributions are interesting and suggest some important new areas for research, it is premature to assume that this literature proves the existence of a robust linkage running from social policy and inequality to productivity growth. One cannot conclude that reduced income inequality leads to increased productivity growth or that more social spending leads to increased productivity growth. The empirical evidence establishing such a linkage, which at this point is largely based on macroeconomic cross-country comparisons, either is simply not in the data or is statistically fragile. Moreover, much of what has been offered as evidence in favour of this hypothesis rests on developing-country data, which are of questionable relevance to an advanced industrialized country like Canada. It is important to emphasize the recent origins of this research. Virtually all of it has been done in the last 10 years, and the total number of studies is still quite limited. It is possible, therefore, that our views based on the weight of evidence will change in the next few years. The one major exception to these observations concerns education. There is a very large body of evidence showing that increasing education has a substantial effect on productivity. The role of human capital in Canada's economic growth has been an enduring theme of both social policy and economic policy. The evidence surveyed in Harris (2002) provides a strong endorsement of this view. The evidence on health expenditures is less convincing, but in general the productivity case for improving human capital is compelling and warrants further research.

In summary, the major conclusion of this paper is as follows:

> The general case linking social policies or inequality to productivity growth remains unproven. Justification for any particular social policy innovation must rest on its cost-effectiveness in reaching its stated social goals. What little evidence we have suggests that social policies promoting labour market participation, rather than passive cash-transfer programs, are most likely to generate productivity benefits, although the magnitude of the effects remains uncertain. A great deal more research is necessary to link social policies to productivity, particularly at the micro level, before a productivity

argument can to be used to promote a particular social policy.

To this can be added the further conclusions of Harris (2002):

> Policies that have been proven to most likely increase productivity are those focused on the proximate economic levers to productivity growth — those that stimulate investment, innovation and competition, and facilitate the international diffusion of knowledge.

> The one social policy for which there is ample evidence of positive productivity effects is education. A substantial portion of Canada's economic growth appears to be attributable to the country's high levels of educational attainment.

> The "new economy" perspective provides a coherent explanation of both recent growth and inequality trends as endogenous reactions to a common cause — the acceleration of technological change. The growing evidence linking both recent and past productivity data, together with evidence on wage inequality trends in industrial countries, provides a more coherent perspective from which to assess policies linking productivity and inequality. A growth-oriented policy must both promote technological adaptation through investment and skills acquisition, and facilitate the required structural change across regions, industries, firms and workers. Social policy can facilitate these adjustments by providing the least well-off with the resources to make the required investments in human capital both for themselves and for their children.

The major rationale underlying social policies in the modern mixed economy has never been higher productivity growth. The general concerns for social justice and the political demands of an increasingly wealthy society for improved education, health and social insurance have long been the major reasons why voters have requested these policies in Canada. This will undoubtedly continue to be true provided economic growth is sustained. Failure to increase or keep pace with living standards in other advanced countries is ultimately the greatest threat to Canada's social programs. In that sense, productivity issues and social policy will always be linked.

303

NOTES

This article is an abridged version of Harris (2002), published with the permission of Industry Canada.

1   For a recent review of these arguments from a Canadian perspective, see Osberg (1995).

2   Krugman (1994) provides a very readable statement of this argument.

3   Also referred to as endogenous growth theory. Surveys of this field are presented in Aghion and Howitt (1998) and Jones (1999).

4   Harris (2002) contrasts the social determinants of productivity with more conventional economic determinants, such as investment and innovation, by examining two specific social policies — education and health — and the literature on major technological change, wage inequality and the new economy.

5   On aging and social security reform, see OECD (1998). The literature subsequent to the *OECD Jobs Study* is voluminous. A review is provided by Disney (2000).

6   This section draws on material in Harris (1999).

7   For a brief and non-technical review of productivity measurement, see Harris (1999). For an extensive review of the literature and a history of the subject, see Hulten (2000).

8   In the Canadian data, the majority of productivity growth is accounted for by TFP growth or multifactor productivity (MFP) growth. MFP growth data are published regularly by Statistics Canada.

9   A good example is Mokyr (1990).

10   For a recent survey, see Ritzen et al. (2000).

11 For the non-OECD sample, the model was actually somewhat more successful, although this result has been criticized on a number of fronts.

12 These models almost always ignore adjustment costs, which is a serious problem in using them for welfare evaluations. With high adjustment costs, fast convergence is not always a good thing.

13 These are covered in greater detail in the section "The Human Capital Dimension of Growth" in Harris (2002).

14 An increase in the Gini coefficient corresponds to an increase in inequality.

15 Beach and Slotsve (1996) document these trends for Canada.

16 A survey of this literature is provided in Benabou (1996).

17 Contributions to the analysis of growth using panel data sets and fixed-effects estimation include Barro and Lee (1994) and Barro and Sala-i-Martin (1995).

18 An exception is Perotti (1996), who looks at the effect of inequality on female education and fertility for developing countries and finds a significant effect. This suggests that it may be the important causal channel in developing country data.

19 For a comprehensive survey, see Aghion and Howitt (1998).

20 Aghion et al. (1999) claim that this is inconsistent with evidence showing that redistribution has a positive effect on growth and that measures of redistribution are uncorrelated with inequality — they cite Perotti (1994), whose Tables 4 and 8 report regression results. The measure of redistribution is the marginal tax rate.

21 There are a few older studies that claim to focus on the links between social expenditure and growth. Unfortunately, they rely on the cross-sectional approach and most suffer from data deficiencies. Results have generally been mixed, but most come to the conclusion that social expenditure is bad for growth. See, for example, Landau (1985), Gwartney et al. (1998), Hansson and Henrekson (1994), Lindert (1996) and Weede (1986, 1991).

22 This is the literature on fiscal policy and growth. A modern example is Easterly and Rebelo (1993). Temple (1999) covers the evidence in his survey.

23 Results reported in Table 6.4, column 2, of Arjona et al. (2001).

REFERENCES

Aghion, P., E. Caroli, and C. Garcia-Penalosa. 1999. "Inequality and Growth: The Perspective of the New Growth Theories." *Journal of Economic Literature* 37(4): 1615-1660.

Aghion, P., and P. Howitt. 1998. *Endogenous Growth Theory*. Cambridge, MA: MIT Press.

Alesina, A., and D. Rodrik. 1994. "Distributive Politics and Economic Growth." *Quarterly Journal of Economics* 109(2): 465-490.

Arjona, R., M. Ladaique, and M. Pearson. 2001. "Growth, Inequality and Social Protection." Labour Market and Social Policy Occasional Paper #51. Paris: OECD Directorate for Education, Employment, Labour, and Social Affairs.

Arjona, R., M. Ladaique, and M. Pearson, 2002. "Growth, Inequality and Social Protection.'" *Canadian Public Policy* 28(2).

Barro, R.J. 1991. "Economic Growth in a Cross-Section of Countries." *Quarterly Journal of Economics* 106(2): 407-443.

———. 1999. "Inequality, Growth and Investment." NBER Working Paper #7038. Cambridge, MA: National Bureau of Economic Research.

Barro, R.J., and J.W. Lee. 1994. *Sources of Economic Growth*. Carnegie-Rochester Conference Series on Public Policy #40, pp. 1-46.

Barro, R.J., and X. Sala-i-Martin. 1995. *Economic Growth*. New York: McGraw-Hill.

Bassanini, A., S. Scarpetta, and P. Hemmings. 2001. "Economic Growth: The Role of Policies and Institutions. Panel Data Evidence from OECD Countries." Working Paper #283. Paris: OECD Economics Department.

Beach, C.M., and G.A. Slotsve. 1996. "Are We Becoming Two Societies? Income Polarization and the Myth of the Declining Middle Class in Canada." In *The Social Policy Challenge*, 12. Toronto: C.D. Howe Institute.

Benabou, R. 1996. *Inequality and Growth*. NBER Macroeconomics Annual #11. Cambridge, MA: National Bureau of Economic Research.

Boadway, R. 1998. "Redistributing Smarter: Self-Selection, Targeting and Non-Conventional Policy Instruments." *Canadian Public Policy* 24(3): 363-369.

Disney, R. 2000. "The Impact of Tax and Welfare Policies on Employment and Unemployment in OECD Countries." Working Paper #WP/00/164. Washington, D.C.: Fiscal Affairs Department, International Monetary Fund.

Durlauf, S.N., and D.T. Quah. 1999. "The New Empirics of Economic Growth." In *Handbook of Macroeconomics*, ed. J. Taylor and M. Woodford. Amsterdam: North-Holland.

Easterly, W., and S. Rebelo. 1993. "Fiscal Policy and Economic Growth: An Empirical Investigation." *Journal of Monetary Economics* 32(3): 417-458.

Forbes, K. 2000. "A Re-assessment of the Relationship Between Inequality and Growth." *American Economic Review* 90(4): 869-887.

Förster, M.F., and M. Pellizzari. 2000. "Trends and Driving Factors in Income Distribution and Poverty in the OECD Area." Labour Market and Social Policy Occasional Paper #42. Paris: OECD.

Gwartney, J., R. Lawson, and R. Holcombe. 1998. "The Size and Functions of Government and Economic Growth." Joint Economic Committee Paper. Washington, D.C.

Hall, R.E., and C.I. Jones. 1999. "Why Do Some Countries Produce So Much More Output per Worker Than Others?" *Quarterly Journal of Economics* 114: 83-116.

Hansson, P., and M. Henrekson. 1994. "A New Framework for Testing the Effect of Growth." *Public Choice* 81(3-4): 381-402.

Harris, R.G. 1999. "The Determinants of Productivity Growth: Issues and Prospects." Discussion Paper #8. Ottawa: Industry Canada. Also published in *Productivity Issues in Canada, Industry Canada Research Volume*, ed. S. Rao and A. Sharpe. Calgary: University of Calgary Press, 2002.

———. 2002. "Social Policy and Productivity Growth: What Are the Linkages?" In *Productivity Issues in Canada, Industry Canada Research Volume*, ed. S. Rao and A. Sharpe. Calgary: University of Calgary Press.

Helliwell, J. 1996. "Economic Growth and Social Capital in Asia." NBER Working Paper #5470. Cambridge, MA: National Bureau of Economic Research.

Hulten, C. 2000. "Total Factor Productivity: A Short Biography." NBER Working Paper #7471. Cambridge, MA: National Bureau of Economic Research.

Jones, C.I. 1999. *Introduction to Economic Growth*. New York: W.W. Norton.

Kaldor, N. 1957. "A Model of Economic Growth." *Economic Journal* 67, 91-624.

Knack, S. 2000. "Associational Life and Economic Performance in the OECD." Manuscript. Washington, D.C.: World Bank.

Knack, S., and P. Keefer. 1997. "Does Social Capital Have an Economic Payoff? A Cross-Country Investigation." *Quarterly Journal of Economics* 112(4): 1251-1288.

Krugman, P. 1994. "Part and Prospective Causes of High Unemployment." In *Reducing Unemployment: Current Issues and Policy Options*. Kansas City, MO: Federal Reserve Bank of Kansas City.

Kuznets, S. 1955. "Economic Growth and Income Inequality." *American Economic Review* 45(1): 1-28.

Landau, D.L. 1985. "Government Expenditure and Economic Growth in the Developed Countries: 1952–1976." *Public Choice* 47(1): 459-477.

Levine, R., and D. Renelt. 1992. "A Sensitivity Analysis of Cross-Country Growth Regressions." *American Economic Review* 82(4): 942-963.

Lindbeck, A. 1975. "Inequality and Redistribution Policy Issues (Principles and Swedish Experience)." In *Education, Inequality and Life Chances 2*. Paris: OECD, 229-385.

———. 1995. "Hazardous Welfare State Dynamics." *American Economic Review* 85(2): 9-15.

Lindert, P. 1996. "What Limits Social Spending?" *Explorations in Economic History*, 33:1-34.

Lloyd-Ellis, H. 2000, May. "The Impacts of Inequality on Productivity Growth: A Primer." Strategic Policy Research Paper #R-00-3E. Ottawa: Human Resources Development Canada, Applied Research Branch.

Lucas, R.E. 1988. "On the Mechanics of Economic Development." *Journal of Monetary Economics* 22: 3-42.

Mankiw, N.G., D. Romer and D. Weil. 1992. "A Contribution to the Empirics of Economic Growth." *Quarterly Journal of Economics* 107(2):407-437.

Mirrlees, J.A. 1971. "An Exploration into the Theory of Optimum Income Taxation." *Review of Economic Studies* 38: 175-208.

Mokyr, J. 1990. *The Levers of Riches: Technological Creativity and Economic Progress*. New York: Oxford University Press.

OECD. 1994. *OECD Jobs Study: Evidence and Explanations*. Paris: OECD.

———. 1998. *Maintaining Prosperity in an Ageing Society*. Paris: OECD.

———. 2000. *OECD Social Expenditure Database, 1980-1997*. Paris: OECD.

Okun, A. 1975. *Equality and Efficiency: The Big Tradeoff*. Washington: Brookings Institution.

Osberg, L. 1995. "The Equity-Efficiency Tradeoff in Retrospect." *Canadian Business Economics* 3(3): 5-19.

Perotti, R. 1994. "Income Distribution and Investment." *European Economic Review* 38: 827-835.

———. 1996. "Growth, Income Distribution and Democracy: What the Data Say." *Journal of Economic Growth* 1(2): 149-187.

Persson, T., and G. Tabellini. 1994. "Is Inequality Harmful for Growth?" *American Economic Review* 84(3): 600-621.

Putnam, R. 1993. *Making Democracy Work*. Princeton, NJ: Princeton University Press.

Rebelo, S. 1991. "Long-Run Policy Analysis and Long-Run Growth." *Journal of Political Economy* 99(3): 500-521.

Ritzen, J., W. Easterly, and M. Woolcock. 2000. "On "Good" Politicians and "Bad" Policies: Social Cohesion, Institutions, and Growth." Working Paper. Washington: World Bank.

Romer, P.M. 1990. "Endogenous Technological Change." *Journal of Political Economy* 98(5):S71-S102.

Sala-i-Martin, X. 1997. "I Just Ran Two Million Regressions." *American Economic Review* 87(2): 178-183.

Temple, J. 1999. "The New Growth Evidence." *Journal of Economic Literature* 37: 112-156.

—— 2000. "Growth Effects of Education and Social Capital." Working Paper #263. Paris: Economics Department, OECD.

Weede, E. 1986. "Sectoral Reallocation, Distributional Coalitions and the Welfare State as Determinants of Economic Growth Rates in OECD Countries." *European Journal of Political Research* 14: 501-519.

——. 1991. "The Impact of State Power on Economic Growth Rates in OECD Countries." *Quality and Quantity* 25: 421-438.

Woolcock, M. 1998. "Social Capital and Economic Development: Toward a Theoretical Synthesis and Policy Framework." *Theory and Society* 27: 151-208.

Social Policy and Productivity: Anybody Here See Any Levers?

William Watson

If you give a man a fish, you feed him for a day. If you teach a man to fish, he'll destroy the cod stock.

Old policy saying

INTRODUCTION

The topic I have been assigned is "social policy and productivity." After a detour that takes on the prior task of trying to establish the usefulness of productivity growth, the conclusion I draw is that the connections between social policy and productivity are not yet (and may never be) clear enough to provide policy-ready estimates of the payoffs from the many different social policies that today are often thought to encourage productivity growth. For the time being, therefore, it may be better to base decisions about social policy on considerations other than its presumed ability to boost economic performance. Such a conclusion may disappoint those who see growth effects as a persuasive new rationale for greater spending on social policy, but even in a post-Reagan, post-Thatcher era, older rationales having to do with fairness and equality still have political and intellectual purchase, even if they may not justify spending at the levels to which we have become accustomed in the last few decades.

PRODUCTIVITY DEFINED

Most Canadians think about productivity the way most children think about spinach: they have often been told that it will be good for them in the long run but they suspect it's not going to be fun. When it's their employers asking them to increase their productivity, they generally assume that means they're going to have to work harder. When it's the government asking them, they probably have little idea of what's intended — and neither, in fairness, may the government. In fact, most Canadians apparently don't spend much time thinking about productivity: a Pollara poll taken in 1998 revealed that only 21 percent of respondents felt they had a good understanding of what the word meant. (This is only slightly less than the number — 36 percent — who were able to correctly define the number "one billion.") Among those with university degrees, 37 percent felt they understood the productivity issue, though among those with a high school education or less only 14 percent did. Pollara's president, Michael Marzolini, said, "A 14 percent awareness level is the lowest that I have ever seen for an issue this important, an issue being called a national priority" (Marzolini 1999). It was because of poll numbers like these, presumably, that the federal government reportedly abandoned the idea of a productivity budget.[1]

The gut feeling of many Canadians that raising their productivity is going to require them to work harder is only partly correct. Improving effort per worker hour *is* one way to increase output per worker hour (a standard definition of productivity). But in fact economists usually focus on other methods, such as giving workers more and/or better capital to work with, or making workers themselves "better" by increasing their "human capital" (economists' jargon for knowledge, skills and experience). Finally, there's also the possibility of increasing the efficiency with which all these "factors of production" are combined, so that more output can be produced with a given set of inputs. If, for instance, a firm can figure out how to get people to move around the factory floor without bumping into each other so much, things will run more smoothly and more output will be produced without anyone in particular working harder.

Increasing productivity without increasing the number or quality of inputs used sounds dangerously like the free lunch economists are not supposed to believe in. In the real world, figuring out how to use existing resources more efficiently probably takes

money: you may have to hire time-and-motion experts, or spend paid downtime with your employees, who are often their own best time-and-motion experts, asking them how a given set of tasks could be done smarter. Raising productivity in this way is therefore an investment. Effort and expense are incurred now in anticipation of a reward later — a reward measured in terms of reduced effort and expense for a given output, or increased output for given effort and expense. The other obvious way of increasing productivity — by making machines and/or workers smarter — also involves investment: it takes time, effort and expense to figure out how to do that; new machines have to be designed and developed and workers have to be trained in how to use them. And even if it's just a question of increasing the number of old-style machines that workers work with, buying more machines costs money.

HOW POLICY FITS IN

Casting the productivity problem in these terms allows us to borrow some tried-and-true rules from investment theory. For example, if an investment in increased productivity is to make sense economically, its cost should be less than its benefit. That may sound obvious, but in some circles "productivity" is a motherhood phenomenon: you supposedly can't have too much of it. On the contrary, a basic rule of economics is that you *can* have too much of a good thing. If the effort required to increase productivity is greater than the value of the extra output gained, then the game isn't worth the candle, and society should do without the extra productivity. The American cartoonist Rube Goldberg made a career drawing infinitely complex machines that accomplished trivial tasks. Society wouldn't want the Rube Goldberg version of a productivity agenda: a massive investment that brings forth only trivial returns. In theory, at least, there may be better places to put the money.

An obvious investment strategy is therefore to go for the productivity improvements whose benefits most exceed their costs and to stop when the rate of return of the next investment considered is less than the going rate of interest. Going beyond that and investing in any project that cannot pay back the money it requires is a misallocation of resources. The advantage of a market economy is that lots of people throughout society will have every incentive to follow this strategy in pursuing productivity investments, the reason being that they stand to profit — either financially or otherwise — by doing so. Workers can increase their productivity, and therefore their wages, by investing in their own human capital. Firms can cut their costs or increase their revenues by investing in physical capital. Researchers can make money inventing new intellectual capital. And so on. From this perspective, the role of the policy-maker is secondary: to seek out high-return investments in productivity that, because of one form or another of "market failure," are not being undertaken. Are workers unable to find financing for their educational self-improvement because the capital market won't lend them money they would have every likelihood of being able to pay back if only they could get the education? Are researchers unable to appropriate the benefits of their research — and are they therefore discouraged from undertaking it — because new ideas are easily commandeered by competitors? Are

firms not investing in enough machinery or equipment because tax policy has been designed with insufficient attention to its effects on the incentive to make such productivity-raising acquisitions?

Stated this way, the job of the policy-maker is simple: look around the society, canvass all the possible productivity-improving investments, and use taxes, subsidies and any other policy instruments you can think of to encourage those that aren't being done. Of course, lots of apparently simple things are hard to do well. High jumping, for instance. What could be simpler? "Jump high!" But very few people excel at it. Designing policies, in this case social policies, to improve productivity is similarly difficult. The main problem is that costs and benefits do not reveal themselves spontaneously. And in those cases where "externalities" or "non-pecuniary benefits" are involved, they may not reveal themselves at all.

THE VALUE OF "OUTPUT," THE MEANING OF "EFFICIENCY"

Before going on to consider the assigned topic — the relationship between social policy and productivity — it may be useful to consider an objection to this overall framework that has been raised by Joseph Heath, both in his contribution to this volume and in his remarkable book *The Efficient Society: Why Canada Is as Close to Utopia as It Gets* (Heath 2001).

Heath's main objection, to paraphrase very baldly, is that productivity increases may not have the payoff we seem to expect from them. He is, of course, at least partly right. As already argued, even in traditional economics productivity isn't everything. The blind pursuit of productivity increases may well turn out to be wasteful: they may not offer, even *ex ante*, benefits greater than their costs. But Heath argues, more provocatively, that some improvements that do pass the economist's customary cost-benefit test may not be worthwhile from a broader perspective. In particular, he complains that productivity growth has not (1) brought increased leisure, as was widely expected; (2) increased consumer satisfaction; (3) eliminated poverty; or (4) decreased social inequality. I want to consider each of these points very briefly and in reverse order.

Inequality

Why increasing productivity, all on its own, should be expected to reduce social inequality is not immediately obvious. If productivity gains were systematically greater among society's least productive members than among its most productive, then productivity growth *would* reduce social inequality. The well-known "convergence hypothesis" holds that this is exactly what happens among nations: growth rates do tend to be higher in countries that start out behind. But there is no obvious reason to presume it should also happen among individuals. And if the ability to become more productive really is greater among those who already have acquired human capital, as both the conceit of academics and the folklore of the new economy suggest, then productivity growth may well *increase* inequality, as a good deal of literature suggests has happened in the United States in the last two decades.

Heath has a more complicated process in mind, however. If a taste for income redistribution is income-elastic — that is, if people want to share more as their incomes grow — then increased productivity eventually will lead to increased redistribution. But there is at least some evidence to suggest that this is exactly what has happened in Canada. Over the last five decades, increases in the rate of income redistribution in Canada have effectively offset increases in inequality in "market incomes," with the effect that the post-tax and -transfer distribution of income has remained almost eerily constant. A dramatic illustration of that is provided by a graph of the ratio of the incomes of the top fifth and bottom fifth of families as ranked by income (Statistics Canada 1999). In terms of pre-tax and pre-government-transfer income, the top fifth earns more than 20 times as much as the bottom fifth. In terms of post-tax and post-government-transfer income, however, the top fifth earns only a little more than five times as much as the bottom fifth. This difference between what might loosely[2] be called "pre-government" and "post-government" ratios is, of course, the result of income redistribution. While the post-tax and -transfer ratio has been quite constant over time, the pre-government ratio has fluctuated considerably and in recent years has risen (it was between 10 and 15 in the early 1990s and rose almost to 25 in the early 1990s). That the post-government ratio nevertheless has not changed appreciably means that the amount of income redistribution has in fact increased, as the hypothesis Heath disputes would suggest. The only complication in this story is that the evident increase in redistribution has not coincided with any great productivity boom.[3]

Poverty

Inequality may or may not be a problem. Poverty clearly is a problem. But if absolute measures of poverty are used, there is simply no question that productivity increases have dramatically reduced poverty in Canada and throughout the Western world. As Nathan Rosenberg and L.E. Birdzell, Jr., put it: "If we take the long view of human history and judge the economic lives of our ancestors by modern standards, it is a story of almost unrelieved wretchedness... Only during the last two hundred years has there come to Western Europe, the United States, Canada, Australia, Japan, and a few other places one of history's infrequent periods when progress and prosperity have touched the lives of somewhat more than the upper tenth of the population" (Rosenberg and Birdzell 1986, 3). And even the favoured upper decile often lived in conditions that would be widely unacceptable today. A recent biography of Queen Elizabeth I informs us that one reason the royal household moved frequently during the summer months was that "the smells of a household occupied for several days by many people, and of stables and courtyards crowded with horses, could not be tolerated for long... There were no water closets in any of the royal palaces until 1597 (Hibbert 1992, 130–131). Moving further forward in time: my McGill colleague, economic historian Mary Mackinnon, tells of how, during the Great Depression, in some Canadian jurisdictions welfare recipients could be cut off by the authorities if they were discovered to have indulged themselves in the luxury of owning a toothbrush. In the 21st century, the debate over what welfare recipients should be entitled to involves such things as colour televisions and personal computers. It is hard to imagine the fury that would be unleashed on any politician who dared suggest they should be deprived of toothbrushes.

If, on the other hand, relative standards of poverty are the metric of choice, then, in the absence of any presumption that productivity improvements should disproportionately increase the incomes of lower-income workers, it shouldn't surprise anyone that productivity increases may not have reduced poverty. If that is what people expected, they were simply wrong to expect it.

Happiness

Whether higher productivity has led to greater consumer satisfaction or, to use the technical philosophical term, "happiness," is a more difficult question. At any given time, income does seem to be associated with people's declared estimate of how happy they are. On the other hand, through the decades there apparently has been no persistent increase in people's characterization of their lives as happy or not happy. Again, this may not be surprising. Rosenberg and Birdzell's observation on the possibility that societies can "move from poverty to wealth without producing a people serenely satisfied with itself" is that "in fact it may be doubted that self-satisfied people could move from poverty to wealth in the first place" (1986, 5). Another possibility, favoured by Heath, is that happiness is a relative thing and that humans, in their characteristically misanthropic way (my judgement, not his), feel best off when they are doing better then their fellows.

Of course, if rankings really are what counts, it might seem that we could all save ourselves a good deal of trouble by agreeing to strive less. If everyone did cut back on striving by, say, 10 percent, then happiness rankings would be preserved and absolute happiness levels would be higher, since striving presumably consumes energy. (If striving is itself satisfying in some way that does not show up in standard audits of happiness, then the policy obviously would have to be reconsidered.) One problem with this policy strategy, however, is that laws to reduce unproductive striving are unlikely to preserve rankings. The analogy is often used of a crowd at a football game. If everyone stands up, it is argued, everyone expends more energy but no one sees any better. We would be better off if we all sat down. To someone such as myself, who is six foot six inches tall, that argument has never made sense. My height is in my legs. If everyone stands up, I see much better. If a regulation is passed requiring everyone to sit down, I will be relatively disadvantaged; the ranking will not be preserved. On balance, the law may increase aggregate welfare (everyone will sit) but it will also redistribute welfare (the tall will see less well than formerly).

There is also the problem that regulation forcibly restricts people's choices. Although a majority may feel the restriction is justified, a substantial minority may not. Applying the Pareto principle, which is so beautifully elaborated in Heath's book, the majority might be able to compensate the minority. (In this case the grounds for compensation — how long a person's legs were — would not be easily subject to dissimulation.) But in practice compensation is seldom paid, and there is therefore good reason for the potential victims of any such regulation to resist it.

Heath's discussion of the contemporary addiction to consumption does have the ring of truth — though as applied to other people, of course, never oneself. Addiction is probably always harmful, but at least many of the good things in life — books, travel, music, restaurant meals, abundant insurance, hyperfast computers, single-malt Scotch, to enumerate the standard professorial compulsions — are not generally "positional goods," and

can therefore be enjoyed by increasing numbers of people as productivity increases. Beyond that there is the question of whether addictions are best overcome by state action. Will anti-consumption laws — or anti-work laws, as in France — do a better job of changing behaviour than other means by which mores change, as they clearly do from era to era? Governments do not have a sterling record when it comes to discouraging addiction. As is often observed, they are themselves addicted to gambling revenues.

Leisure

Finally, there is the question of leisure. In the immediate post-war years, it probably was expected that increasing affluence would lead people to consume more leisure. That this has not happened, however, does not necessarily mean the impressive productivity improvements that have occurred since then either were for naught or should be reversed. It may simply be that people's preferences turned out to be different from what they had thought they would be. Or other things may have occurred that frustrated their desire to consume more leisure — steep increases in taxes, for instance. It is also true that rising affluence has increased the price of "positional goods," such as desirably located houses, with the result that the benefits of productivity increases have been transferred from those who have brought about the productivity gains to the original owners of such assets. (Baby boomers who have seen their parents sell the family home for many times what they paid for it in real terms will understand this argument well.) If some way could be found to limit the transfer, then such assets could be purchased at a lower cost in time and effort, though also at a lower gain to owners. This is an argument not so much about productivity, however, as about production. If the goal is to limit incomes to a certain level, that level can be achieved with less effort if productivity is higher.

PRIVATE AFFLUENCE, PUBLIC SQUALOR?

The other major part of Heath's critique of our normal assumptions about productivity is the Galbraithian one that the public sector is stunted. Or at least, to put a contemporary spin on Galbraith, that the dramatic late-20th-century growth in the size of the public sector — its remarkable de-stunting in most jurisdictions since 1958, when *The Affluent Society* appeared — has been entirely justified, and in fact was and is "efficient" in the economist's sense of that word (Galbraith 1958).

In the definition of productivity provided above, the economist's generic term *output* was used. But surely it matters what the output in question is. If productivity increases serve merely to increase the size and garishness of automobile tail fins, as seemed to be the case when *The Affluent Society* was written, not just philosophers will wonder whether the effort has been worth it.

Two qualifications are necessary here, however. The first is *de gustibus non disputandum*. There may be greater willingness these days than 20 years ago to hold to absolute standards of taste — and indeed Galbraith himself was perfectly happy to look down his (very long) nose at some people's preferences. But elite opinion is still careful in dismissing the pleasure other people derive from what may seem to be bizarre consumption choices. Heath is

aware of and accepts this point. As he writes in *The Efficient Society*, "Bad taste is not a crime, nor should it be. We can use the critique of consumerism as grounds to harangue our fellow citizens and try to get them to improve their consumption choices, but we cannot use it as a basis for public policy. The problem, ultimately, is that the standard critique of consumerism is a disguised form of perfectionism" — by which he means "the idea that the purpose of political association is to achieve 'the perfection of man'," and to organize "all of society to assist individuals in the pursuit of [the]...ideal of the best human life" (Heath 2001, 254, 28). We generally don't do that any more. Within limits, we let people make their own consumption choices for themselves.

Even in a purely Galbraithian perspective, however, productivity improvements may be useful. If productivity increases mean that any given number of tail fins of a standard size and vulgarity can be produced with less effort, then that presumably is a gain to society. At least in principle, the resources freed up by the productivity gains could be put to "better" use, even if in practice there is the danger that tail-fin designers will move on to making video games or body jewellery, with no resulting betterment and possibly a depreciation in the human condition as a result.

Although Heath parts company with Galbraith on perfectionism, his key policy recommendation is decidedly Galbraithian. But it derives from the more mainstream economic view that because markets fail many public expenditures are likely to be efficient. (Hence the title of his book.) That is certainly true for goods that suffer from the traditional market failures of externalities or "publicness," and few economists will disagree with this possibility. But Heath goes on to

313

argue that a more general form of market failure causes consumers of private goods to play negative-sum games with one another. "Prisoners' dilemmas" and other forms of "collective action problem" are, he believes, endemic in modern society. For example, drivers persist in passing one another on the road even though both logic and empirics suggest that traffic moves more quickly when people stay in their own lanes. Or, still on the subject of driving, in a world in which no one drives a sport utility vehicle, buying an SUV will improve the purchaser's chances of surviving a highway collision; but if everyone drives an SUV, no one's chances are improved. Or, to switch to professional sports, the first user of steroids may obtain a significant competitive advantage, but once steroid use is widespread users no longer achieve any competitive advantage and yet still suffer the dangerous side-effects of steroids.

If market failure of this sort is endemic, then, Heath argues, corrective government intervention may also have to be endemic. To my mind, this ignores two serious difficulties. The first is that although game theory of the sort Heath exploits so adeptly may well result in a longer list of potential market failures, it also introduces a whole new category of potential *government* failures. The "tragedy of the House of Commons," to use a phrase coined by Ken McKenzie of the University of Calgary (McKenzie 2001), is that politicians will spend much of their time in prisoner's dilemmas from which they cannot escape, and they will do so in contexts that can lead to widespread inefficiency. For example, in the spring of 2002 a sitting prime minister argued, apparently seriously, that one of the key functions of a Member of Parliament is to help the people of his riding get as large a share of

public munificence as possible. If MPs do take that attitude, it is hard to imagine that public spending and taxation will come to rest at levels that could by any stretch of the imagination be considered optimal.

Mention of taxation raises the other great difficulty with further increases in public expenditure: their cost. Estimates of the marginal cost of public funds are controversial and, as usual in such exercises, depend on the assumptions that are made. But a good bet is that this cost is substantial and has grown. In 1961, three years after *The Affluent Society* appeared, overall government receipts were 27.8 percent of GDP. In 2000 they were 44.3 percent of GDP (Finance Canada 2001, Table 53). A fundamental theorem of public finance is that the efficiency cost of the tax rises with the square of the tax rate. It seems all but certain, therefore, that the marginal cost of taxation is higher now, possibly substantially higher, than it was then. Investments in public activity that were efficient then may well not be efficient now. Canadians who feel they are somehow less selfless than their parents were should not get down on themselves: the social cost of selflessness was lower when their parents were young.

But leave aside this large political question of how big the government should be. Once the allocation problem has been dealt with — once "the Heath problem" has been overcome and we can be reasonably sure that all the different goods on the extensive menu of consumption available in a modern society are being produced in their "right" amounts — then the virtues of productivity improvements, of "more with less," become apparent again, subject to the provisos already stressed about the need not to spend more improving productivity than is available from the productivity improvement. If, for example, Canadians have made clear that they want more health care, and if productivity improvements are available in the health-care sector that cost less than they are worth, then it is hard to see how undertaking them would not be socially beneficial. Whether health care and education are financed publicly in Canada because, as Heath argues, doing so is efficient, or because, as the opinion polls suggest, most people worry that with private finance poor Canadians would receive less of these goods than the rest of us, once it has been decided to finance such things in the public sector, productivity improvements will make more of these services available with less sacrifice in terms of other goods and services. The same is true in the private sector, once its appropriate size has been determined. It is therefore hard to understand how getting more "stuff" for a given effort would be wasteful — even if it is true that more of anything can be harmful if the margin is extended far enough.

SOCIAL POLICY AND PRODUCTIVITY

So, finally, how does social policy come into play in a discussion of productivity? Social policy can be defined in many ways, but for present purposes suppose it comprises public policies in health, education and welfare. Some such policies are probably good for productivity, as the Left has been arguing, often with urgency born of desperation, since the collapse of communism put it on the intellectual and for a time political defensive in the early 1990s. Educated workers may be more productive workers; education is at least publicly financed and in some cases even publicly produced; ergo government can be good for productivity — though it does not follow that the next dollar spent on education will be good for productivity, or anything else for that matter.

The same argument is often made about health care: unhealthy workers may well be unproductive workers, though such a truism is not by itself sufficient to justify increased expenditures on health care.

But if some social policies increase productivity, other social policies probably reduce it, as the Right has argued, with increasing persuasiveness from the middle of the 20th century on as the state has grown, apparently without limit. If you pay people to be unemployed, and pay them year after year, as Canada's unemployment insurance program does, they are more likely to be unemployed and less likely to make investments in themselves. If you pay people to stay in regions of the country where their productivity is low, or grows only slowly, then pursuing such a policy has a cost in reduced productivity. If higher and higher taxes create bigger and bigger "tax wedges" (the difference between what the buyers and the sellers in a transaction receive), then the consequent discouragement to effort and investment may deter productivity improvements that without the tax wedges would have produced benefits greater than costs. If you provide people with all they need in essential goods and services such as education and health care, then the income they derive from their own efforts can be spent only on frivolous things such as tail fins and video games.[4]

EFFICIENT SOCIAL POLICY

The policy strategy described above — to search the economy for market failures that need to be corrected and to undertake the bigger-payoff investments first — is generally the strategy adopted by the contributors to this volume (which is not

315

surprising, since most are economists). Most are concerned, at least implicitly, with using correlation analysis of one kind or another to determine whether the particular social policies they are interested in tend to encourage productivity growth. Once these "drivers" of growth are discovered — be they health care, education, day care, on-the-job training or any other aspect of social policy — it presumably follows that they should be subsidized. To inject Churchillian construction into the jargon of welfare economics: "Give us the triangles and we will finish the job."

As I saw it, my role as a contributor to this volume, one I was happy to play, was to stress just how difficult a job it is to decide what resources to put where. This theme was first developed by Hayek (1945) in his famous essay "The Use of Knowledge in Society." Societies are extremely complex phenomena, and it is very difficult for any agent or set of agents to develop an understanding of their complexity sufficient to allow successful manipulation of the various "policy levers" in such a way as to achieve desired social outcomes. (Indeed, as the quotation marks are meant to indicate, the term is itself a considerable conceit.) A number of difficulties arise, both conceptual and practical.

To begin with, it is not certain that past drivers will be future drivers. Thanks to the work of Vaillancourt, Finnie and others, we have a rough approximation of what the private and (by one definition, at least) the public returns to various Canadian university degrees were in the mid-1990s, by level of education and in some cases even by discipline (Vaillancourt and Bourdeau-Primeau 2002; Finnie 2000). But is anyone really confident that these rates of return will be the same five or 10 years from now, when any new monies

that we decided to devote to education today would start to produce graduates? In a recent note, the Federal Reserve Bank of St. Louis (2001, 1) pointed out that in the latest US recession unemployment rates rose more quickly for highly skilled workers than for less-skilled and unskilled workers — a reversal of the experience of the early 1990s. In some of his writings, Paul Krugman has argued, in a similar vein, that professions like lawyering and doctoring may experience declining demand as new technologies take over routine tasks in their fields. As with mutual funds, so may it be with education: past returns are no guarantee of future profitability. Beyond that, there is the problem that most calculations of the rate of return on education do not even attempt to estimate the size of the externalities that constitute a large part of the potential gain in the minds of those who favour increased public spending on schooling. As a result, anyone who had the job of allocating monies across disciplines — or even across levels of education — in an attempt to maximize the social return would have little more than hunch and anecdote to go on.

A second general difficulty, as already suggested, is government failure. Assume for a moment we are agreed, and we may not be, that social policies should aim at making the greatest possible contribution to productivity. The best way to do this would be to send out battalions of economists to make their best guesstimates of where marginal dollars will pay off most. But of course the age of economist-kings is some way off yet (even if the federal Leader of the Opposition holds a master's degree in the discipline). Other considerations are likely to intrude and, once the "policy process" has acted itself out in full, money may end up very far from where, by economic criteria at least, it would do the most good.

There is also the need for policy-makers to be sure they are not simply duplicating private efforts. Ministers of industry at all levels of Canadian government set great store by the high-tech revolution and in most cases are eager both to be associated with it and to encourage it — sometimes, it seems, the former more than the latter. But does anyone seriously believe that investment in high technology was underfunded in the 1990s?

A further difficulty is that subsidies have to be precise. As suggested above, too much of a good thing can be bad. Externalities can be over-corrected. It is at least conceivable that at some point we will spend too much on education (however heretical that may sound coming from a university professor). Reading some of the final exams and papers submitted in my courses suggests that maybe we already do: many people currently in university pretty clearly should not be there. Or perhaps this anecdotal evidence suggests instead that we need greater investment at the pre-university level.

Finally, it is always important for policy-makers to keep in mind that the funds they are using are expensive, and increasingly so as rates of taxation rise. I do understand that some taxes may now finally be falling — slightly — but the recent declines are not yet enough to establish a trend. Public revenues remain at record ratios of GDP.

WHAT DO WE KNOW?

The greatest difficulty with the "subsidize the drivers" strategy, however, is that

we simply do not know anything very precise about what the drivers are. The correlations that are the stock-in-trade of this kind of analysis simply are not very conclusive. To quote from Richard Harris's paper in this volume (282): "...strong policy conclusions are well ahead of both theory and evidence. Neither provides conclusive support for the proposition that either (a) policies directed at reducing inequality will increase productivity growth, or (b) increased social spending will raise productivity growth." In this inconclusive conclusion he echoes Jonathan Temple's survey in the *Journal of Economic Literature*: "Even the most enthusiastic proponent of cross-country regressions must acknowledge that we are a daunting distance from the ultimate goal, a model with high explanatory power which indicates with precision the relative contributions of different influences" (Temple 1999, 148).

One reason why it is difficult to make strong conclusions on the basis of statistical correlations is that the explanatory variable "social policy" is very hard to pin down. In two recent papers, the OECD's Willem Adema shows how the scale of a country's social policies varies according to its use of different mechanisms for delivering such policies — whether they be direct spending through the public sector, tax expenditures or mandated private expenditures. Thus, for instance, in 1997 gross Canadian public expenditure on social policy was 20.7 percent of GDP at factor cost, compared to just 15.8 percent in the United States. But in the same year, what Adema calls "net total social expenditure," which includes spending, tax expenditures and mandated private expenditures, was 21.8 percent in Canada and fully 23.4 percent in the United States. The two countries' rankings obviously changed dramatically (Adema 2001, Table A2.1).[5]

WHAT DO WE DO?

In his contribution to this volume, Richard Harris observes that "[o]ften in economics, in the absence of decisive evidence for or against a hypothesis, economic theory plays an important role in determining the priors of economists both as social scientists and as policy advisers" (297). Unfortunately, as he also concludes, in the case of the effects of social policy on productivity growth, theory often provides ambiguous predictions. He might have added that ideology will also have a continuing influence on the Canadian policy debate, and ideology, whether of left, right or centre, never provides ambiguous predictions.

In the absence of clear indicators of the likely social return on the next dollar invested in various areas of social policy, what is to be done?

One suggestion is that economists keep correlating. Temple does note a growing view that "regression fatigue" is beginning to set in, "so that hearts sink when yet another dubious growth regression is presented" (1999, 148). But in fact the field is relatively new, the data keep accumulating, computers are becoming ever more powerful, and theoretical work on the determinants of growth continues apace, so it is best for the profession to keep at it, even if the likelihood that clear policy directives will emerge from the effort does seem small. The question of why some countries grow and others don't, which is in a sense the founding question of modern economics, remains compelling even if the answer remains elusive.

And of course, clear directions from economists or not, policy will have to contin-

ue to be made. By all measures, most developed countries have a large chunk of their GDP caught up in one form or another of social policy. Within this very large expenditure envelope, allocation decisions have to be made — and doubtless will continue to be made even if all the growth correlations economists calculate turn out to be statistically insignificant or, for that matter, negative. There are a number of reasons for this: redistribution is important; economic optimality does not always (or perhaps even ever) govern policy; and, try as we might, conservatives will never block all public spending (supposing that is what we wanted to do).

If there will be spending on education, health care and welfare, the policy problem then reduces to where we should increase spending and where we should decrease it. This is probably best done at the margin, in the small, program by program. The fundamental question, as always, is where would you get the biggest payoff, the biggest efficiency bang for the buck, from an extra dollar of spending. Should you provide further tax help for investments in machinery and equipment? Should you boost subsidies to R&D? Should you put more money into higher education? Into high schools? Into health care? Which parts of health care? I'm afraid that on the basis of what I heard at the authors' workshop and have since read in the papers prepared for this volume I don't really see much guidance for beleaguered policy-makers.

We do all have our hunches about where the payoffs would be greatest. In terms of health care, an Ispos-Reid poll released in January found that given a choice between making people more personally responsible for the services they use and cleaning up the mismanagement in the system, 63 percent wanted the system cleaned up, 34 percent said people should be made more personally responsible.[6] That is an interesting tradeoff to read about, but it may not be a policy-relevant tradeoff: cleaning up the mismanagement of the system may not provide savings sufficient to achieve the efficiencies people want. The official political line from most governments seems to be that money is not the problem, that what the system needs is reorganization. Economists, who consider that more money will help most problems of perceived shortages, find this a strange argument, but the "Gorbachev strategy" of reforming the system rather than starting over from scratch seems to be politically saleable. My own view is that we badly need competition within the system. The two places where Canadians feel most abused these days are in hospital waiting rooms and Air Canada departure lounges.

As for education, the question again is: where are the rates of return likely to be highest? Current public policy, particularly at the federal level, seems to put the greatest emphasis on post-secondary education. On the other hand, François Vaillancourt's work seems to suggest the pecuniary returns, both public and private, are greatest at lower levels of education. Those who do worst in this society very likely are not unemployed university graduates. They probably are high-school dropouts who lack basic literacy and numeracy. Of course, it does not follow that the marginal return now would be as high as the average return in the mid-1990s, which is the latest era for which we have estimates. Nor do existing studies have much to say about the size of the externalities from different types of education. As Jeffrey Smith cautions in a recent C.D. Howe Institute book, "While it is handy for

those of us who make our living in the higher education sector to point to the shimmering hope of externalities to justify our funding, the taxpayer would be better served with some hard empirical estimates" (Smith 2002, 278). At the margin, I suspect the financial constraints are more severe for those who wish to borrow in order to complete high school than for those who wish to finance university education. We who have children in the education system, even in Quebec's education system, which was highly praised at the authors' workshop, would also wish to introduce more competition and incentives to good performance.

Regarding welfare, the consensus in the policy establishment seems to support the OECD's preference for active labour market policies. I wonder, though, whether there are not cases in which cash payments are admissible. Since the Clinton reform of welfare, United States policy in effect insists that the mothers of young children go out into the workforce and find gainful employment. The rationale for this must be that work habits are subject to "hysteresis" — that they are self-reinforcing. In this regard, the disappointing long-term effects of the policy measures tried in the Self-Sufficiency Project (SSP) — when subsidies to work were removed participants in the project had essentially the same work patterns as the control group — suggest that the long-term cost of allowing women to take time off to care for their young children may not have permanently debilitating effects on their employability.[7]

That welfare policies can have harmful effects on productivity in other ways is illustrated by the case of Fishery Products International, which in the winter of 2001-02 attempted to rearrange its production methods in Newfoundland so as to provide year-round employment for a substantially smaller number of workers than it currently employs on a part-time basis. Although the total amount paid out in wages would not have changed, and the company's productivity would have increased substantially, fewer people would have been eligible for Employment Insurance premiums. The widespread public opposition to this proposal may have had more to do with the perception that it constituted a double-cross on FPI's part. But whether that is true or not, the company quickly withdrew the proposal, with the effect that its productivity level will remain subject to customary, not accelerated, growth rates. Applying Heathian principles to this case, preserving the status quo may for the time being create greater aggregate happiness in Newfoundland than the firm's proposal would have done, but it is hard to see how what seems bound to be declining competitiveness on this firm's part will help Newfoundland in the long run.

The discussion of this paper at the authors' workshop wound down in an exchange over how much we really know about the effects of various social policies. One or two people better acquainted with the relevant literature than I argued that in fact we know a good deal. I'm less optimistic. It seems to me we have very little idea of the likely payoffs to different types of investment in the area of social policy, which means policy is likely to be determined by politics and by whatever the common sense of the day suggests. That is a sad commentary on economics. I fear it may also lead to sad policy outcomes.

NOTES

1   The contribution by Frank Graves and Richard Jenkins to this volume generally suggests greater familiarity with productivity issues on the part of Canadians, though it does not ask the straightforward question about Canadians' understanding of the concept of productivity in the way that Marzolini did. They, too, conclude that poll results caused the government to recast its productivity agenda as an innovation agenda.

2   Only loosely, however: it does not include transfers in kind.

3   The Statistics Canada chart referred to goes only as far as 1997.

4   The disturbing moral implications of such a situation are described in Acton (1993).

5   Note that the fact that the United States moves from virtually last on the list of OECD countries to first may actually improve the correlation between social policy and productivity, since US growth rates have been so strong in recent years.

6   See Mickleburgh (2002).

7   Conceived and funded by Human Resources Development Canada (HRDC), SSP is a research and demonstration project to test a policy innovation that makes work pay better than welfare. The Self-Sufficiency Project was designed as a social experiment using a rigorous random-assignment research model. In the main SSP study, a group of 5,688 single parents (primarily single mothers) in New Brunswick and the lower mainland of British Columbia who had been on Income Assistance (IA) for at least a year were selected at random from the IA rolls with one-half assigned to the program group which received the SSP supplement while the remainder formed a control group.

REFERENCES

Acton, H.B. 1993. *The Morals of Markets and Related Essays*. Indianapolis: Liberty Fund.

Adema, W. 2001, August. *Net Social Expenditure*, 2nd Ed. Occasional paper #52. Paris: Directorate for Education, Employment, Labour and Social Affairs, Employment, Labour and Social Affairs Committee, OECD.

Federal Reserve Bank of St. Louis. 2001. "A Recession for the Educated?" *National Economic Trends*, December.

Finance Canada. 2001. *Fiscal Reference Tables 2001*. Available: http://www.fin.gc.ca/toce/2001/frt_e.html

Finnie, Ross. 2002. "A Matter of Discipline: Early Career Outcomes of Recent Canadian University Graduates." In *Renovating the Ivory Tower: Canadian Universities and the Knowledge Economy*, ed. David Laidler. Toronto: C.D. Howe Institute.

Galbraith, J.K. 1958. *The Affluent Society*. Boston: Houghton Mifflin Company.

Hayek, F. 1945. "The Use of Knowledge in Society." *American Economic Review* 35(4):519–530.

Heath, J. 2001. *The Efficient Society: Why Canada Is as Close to Utopia as It Gets*. Toronto: Viking.

Hibbert, C. 1992. *The Virgin Queen: Elizabeth I, Genius of the Golden Age*. Reading, MA: Perseus.

Marzolini, M. 1999. "Address to the Summa Forum on Productivity," March 1999. Available: http://www.pollara.ca/new/Fs_lib.html

McKenzie, K.J. 2001. *A Tragedy of the House of Commons: Political Institutions and Fiscal Policy Outcomes from a Canadian Perspective*. Benefactors Lecture. Toronto: C.D. Howe Institute.

Mickleburgh, R. 2002, January 26. "Most Blame Inefficiency, Poll Finds." *The Globe and Mail*: A4.

Rosenberg, N., and L.E. Birdzell, Jr. 1986. *How the West Grew Rich: The Economic Transformation of the Industrial World*. New York: Basic Books.

Smith, J. 2002. "Comments on Chant and Gibson, Finnie, Vaillancourt and Bourdeau-Primeau and Rathje and Emery." In *Renovating the Ivory Tower: Canadian Universities and the Knowledge Economy*. ed. D. Laidler. Toronto: C.D. Howe Institute.

Statistics Canada. 1999. "Family Income After Tax." *The Daily*, July 26.

Temple, J. 1999. "The New Growth Evidence." *Journal of Economic Literature* 37(1): 112-156 (March).

Vaillancourt, F., and S. Bourdeau-Primeau. 2002. "The Returns to University Education in Canada, 1990 and 1995." In *Renovating the Ivory Tower: Canadian Universities and the Knowledge Economy*, ed. David Laidler. Toronto: C.D. Howe Institute.

Notes on Contributors

Keith Banting is Director of the School of Policy Studies at Queen's University and holder of the Stauffer-Dunning Chair in Policy Studies. He earned his B.A.(Hon) from Queen's University and a doctorate from Oxford University. He taught for thirteen years in the Department of Political Science at the University of British Columbia, and has been associated with Queen's since 1986. His research interests focus on public policy in Canada and other western nations. He is the author of *Poverty, Politics and Policy* and *The Welfare State and Canadian Federalism*. In addition, he is an editor and co-author of another ten books dealing with public policy and constitutional issues in Canada and other countries, the most recent of which is *Degrees of Freedom: Canada and the United States in a Changing World*.

Peter Dungan is Adjunct Associate Professor of Economics in the Department of Economics and the Rotman School of Management at the University of Toronto. He is also Director of the Policy and Economic Analysis Program (PEAP) at the University's Institute for Policy Analysis. The PEAP program is centered on the construction and application of macroeconometric models for economic forecasting and policy analysis.

Tony Fisher is an economist in the Economic Studies and Policy Analysis Branch of Finance Canada. He received an M.A. in economics from the University of Victoria. He is currently conducting research on a variety of macroeconomic issues. His research interests are focused primarily on productivity issues, but also include open-economy macroeconomics and economic modeling.

R. Quentin Grafton is a Senior Fellow at the Centre for Resource and Environmental Studies (CRES) at the Australian National University. Prior to joining CRES in 2001, he was the Director of the Institute of the Environment and an Associate Professor in the Department of Economics at the University of Ottawa. He holds a Ph.D in economics from the University of British Columbia and is a former Young Researcher of the Year at the University of Ottawa and a recipient of the Ontario Premier's Research Excellence Award. His main research areas are environmental economics, social capital and institutional economics.

Frank L. Graves is President of Ekos Research Associates Inc., an applied social and economic research firm he founded in 1980. In recent years, Mr. Graves has advised some of Canada's most senior decision-makers. One of Ekos' projects, *Rethinking Government*, a longitudinal research study on the evolving relationship between Canadians and their governments, has yielded fresh insight into the way Canadians view their governments and one another. Mr. Graves lectures and has published widely on program evaluation, research design and related methodological topics. More recently, he has been writing and publishing in the area of public policy, specifically on the impact of Canadians' changing views towards their governments and their country.

Richard G. Harris is Telus Professor of Economics at Simon Fraser University and a Fellow of the Economic Growth Program of the Canadian Institute of Advanced Research (CIAR). His major area of specialization is international economics. He has served as a consultant to a number of Canadian government departments, international organizations and corporations. In addition to a number of technical articles, he has published policy-oriented books and articles on Canada-US free trade, international macroeconomics, economic growth, the Asia-Pacific region, and Canadian public policy.

Joseph Heath holds a Canada Research Chair in Ethics and Political Economy at the University of Montreal, and is Associate Professor in the Department of Philosophy at the University of Toronto. He is the author of *The Efficient Society* and *Communicative Action and Rational Choice*.

Doug Hostland is an economist in the International Department of the Bank of Canada. He received an M.A. in economics from the University of Western Ontario and has worked on a wide range of economic policy issues at the Bank of Canada and the Department of Finance. His main research interests have been monetary and fiscal policy, open-economy macroeconomics, international finance and applied econometrics. He is currently doing research on emerging market issues.

Richard W. Jenkins is a Senior Consultant at EKOS Research Associates. He has published a number of articles on public opinion and electoral behaviour. Before joining EKOS in 2001, Dr. Jenkins was a Postdoctoral Fellow and Assistant Professor in Political Studies at Queen's University where he taught an undergraduate statistics/research method course and a course on elections and public opinion. He holds a Ph.D in political science from the University of British Columbia.

Stephen Knowles is a Senior Lecturer in Economics at the University of Otago, New Zealand. He holds a Ph.D from the University of Otago. His main research interests are in the areas of economic growth and development, especially the effect of human capital, social capital, government intervention and inequality on economic growth.

Nancy Olewiler is Professor of Economics at Simon Fraser University (SFU) and is currently Acting Director of the Public Policy Program at SFU. She holds a B.A. (Hon) from Barnard College, Columbia University, an M.A. from SFU and a Ph.D from the University of British Columbia, all in economics. Prior to coming to SFU in 1990, she taught at Queen's University for 14 years. She teaches undergraduate and graduate courses in environmental and natural resource economics. Her research has focused in recent years on environmental policy and the impact of environmental regulation on the economy. She has published in academic journals and edited books, and she has written two widely used textbooks and numerous reports for government.

P. Dorian Owen is Professor of Economics at the University of Otago, New Zealand. He holds B.Sc. (Hon), M.Sc. and Ph.D degrees from the University of Wales. He has previously taught at the University of Reading (UK) and the University of Canterbury (NZ) and been editor of *New Zealand Economic Papers* (1995-1997). His research interests include empirical modeling of economic growth, applied monetary economics and the economics of sport.

William Scarth is Professor of Economics at McMaster University, where he was award-ed the President's Award for Best Teacher in 1997 and the McMaster Student Union Lifetime Teaching Award in 1999. In addition to publishing many articles in the areas of macroeconomics, labour economics, international trade and public finance, Professor Scarth is the author of several textbooks including *Economics: The Essentials* and *Macroeconomics: An Introduction to Advanced Methods*. In addition to research and teaching (both at McMaster and as a visitor at other universities in Canada, England, Greece, Australia and New Zealand), Professor Scarth has been an active participant in policy debates. He has been an Adjunct Scholar at the C.D. Howe Institute since 1994.

Andrew Sharpe is Executive Director of the Centre for the Study of Living Standards (CSLS), a research organization he founded in 1995. He has held a variety of earlier positions, including Head of Research and Editor, *Quarterly Labour Market and Productivity Review* at the Canadian Labour Market and Productivity Centre and Chief, Business Sector Analysis at the Department of Finance. He is past President of the *Canadian Association for Business Economics*

(CABE) and served as a founding editor of *Canadian Business Economics* from 1992 to 1998. He is the founding editor of the *International Productivity Monitor* and is a member of the OECD Expert Group on Productivity Level Comparisons. He received a Ph.D in economics from McGill University in 1982.

France St-Hilaire is Vice-President, Research at the Institute for Research on Public Policy (IRPP). She joined IRPP as a research director in 1992. She currently oversees the Institute's research agenda and coordinates ongoing projects on economic and social policy. France St-Hilaire is the author of a number of monographs and articles in the areas of public finance, social policy and fiscal federalism. She was also the editor of the Institute's monograph series on City-Regions and co-editor (with Craig Riddell) of *Adapting Public Policy to a Labour Market in Transition*. She holds an M.Sc. in economics from the University of Montreal. Prior to joining IRPP, she worked as a researcher at the University of Toronto's Institute for Policy Analysis and in the Economics Department of the University of Western Ontario.

Janice Gross Stein is Belzberg Professor of Conflict Management and Negotiation in the Department of Political Science at the University of Toronto, and the Director of the Munk Centre for International Studies. She holds the rank of University Professor and is a Fellow of the Royal Society of Canada. Her most recent book, *The Cult of Efficiency* was nominated by the Writers' Trust of Canada for the Shaughnessy-Cohen Prize in Political Writing, by the Canadian Political Science Association for the Donald Smilie Prize, and for the Pearson Readers' Choice Book Award. With David Cameron, Dr. Stein is also the editor of a new collection of essays, *Street Protests and Fantasy Parks*.

325

Arthur Sweetman is an Assistant Professor in the School of Policy Studies at Queen's University. An economist, his focus is on empirical research and he studies issues related to education, health and immigration among others. He received his Ph.D from McMaster University and was previously on faculty in the Economics Department at the University of Victoria in British Columbia.

Emile Tompa is a Scientist at the Institute for Work & Health and holds an adjunct appointment in the Department of Economics at McMaster University. His current research agenda is focused on the consequences of disability policy system design features and other labour market policies and programs for the health of individuals and populations. He also conducts research on labour market experiences and their health and human development consequences, with a particular focus on contingent work. He holds an M.B.A. from the University of British Columbia and a Ph.D in Economics from McMaster University.

Bart van Ark is Professor of Economics at the University of Groningen (the Netherlands). He obtained his Master and Ph.D. degrees in economics at that same university. He is Director of the Groningen Growth and Development Centre, a research group working on long-term economic growth and productivity. He also coordinates the International Comparisons of Output and Productivity (ICOP) project. He has participated in a range of international research projects, including the Productivity Program of the McKinsey Global Institute (1992 and 1993) and the CEPR Program on "Comparative Experience of Economic Growth in Post-war Europe." Presently he consults for (inter)national government agencies, including the Dutch government, the European Commission and the OECD, as well as for private business. He is also associated with the German Institute for Economic Research (DIW) in Berlin as a Research Professor.

William Watson teaches in the Economics Department at McGill University and is a Senior Research Fellow at the Institute for Research on Public Policy (IRPP). From 1998 to 2002 he edited the Institute's magazine, *Policy Options politiques*. His 1998 book, *Globalization and the Meaning of Canadian Life*, was runner-up for the Donner Prize for best Canadian policy book of the year. He writes a weekly column in the *National Post* and in 1996-97 served as Editorial Pages Editor of the *Ottawa Citizen*. In 1989 a story of his in *Saturday Night* won the National Magazine Awards Gold Medal for humour.

AGMV Marquis

MEMBER OF SCABRINI MEDIA

Quebec, Canada
2002